The politics of depression in France
1932–1936

# The politics of
# depression in France
# 1932–1936

JULIAN JACKSON

Lecturer in History, University College, Swansea

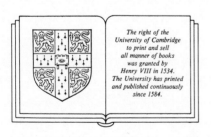

The right of the
University of Cambridge
to print and sell
all manner of books
was granted by
Henry VIII in 1534.
The University has printed
and published continuously
since 1584.

CAMBRIDGE UNIVERSITY PRESS

Cambridge
London   New York   New Rochelle
Melbourne   Sydney

Published by the Press Syndicate of the University of Cambridge
The Pitt Building, Trumpington Street, Cambridge CB2 1RP
32 East 57th Street, New York, NY 10022, USA
10 Stamford Road, Oakleigh, Melbourne 3166, Australia

First published 1985

Printed in Great Britain at the University Press, Cambridge

Library of Congress catalogue card number: 85–4121

*British Library cataloguing in publication data*

Jackson, Julian
The politics of depression in France, 1932–1936.
1. France – History –1914–1940
I. Title
944.081'5   DC389

ISBN 0 521 26559 2

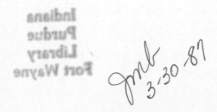

# Contents

The fall of Flandin: 'the force of circumstances'                         99
Laval: *la superdéflation*?                                               105

6  **The programme of the Popular Front**                                 112
   Developments on the left                                               112
   Uncertain beginnings: May to October 1935                             116
   The fall of Laval                                                     126

PART 3: NON-CONFORMISTS OF LEFT AND RIGHT

7  **Plans and planners**                                                 137
   1933: Henri de Man and the origins of planism in France               138
   1934: The defeat of planism                                           145
   1934: Planomania                                                      150
   1935: The defeat of the Plan: the reassertion of tradition            156
   1936: Epilogue to planism                                             163

8  **Devaluation**                                                        167
   Government policy: 1932 to 1936                                        167
   Paul Reynaud: 'My long struggle'                                      180
   'This sort of monetary Dreyfus Affair'                                187
   Alternatives: 'Let us try to cultivate our garden'                    193
   Conclusion                                                            198

   **Epilogue   The politics of rearmament 1936–1939**                   200
   The elections of 1936                                                 200
   The Blum experiment                                                   202
   Liberalism or exchange control?                                       208

   **Conclusion**                                                        212
   *Appendix*                                                            224
   *Notes*                                                               226
   *Bibliography*                                                        282
   *Index*                                                               299

# Acknowledgements

I should like first of all to thank Dr Christopher Andrew of Corpus Christi College, Cambridge, who supervised the Ph.D thesis on which this book is based: not only did he originally suggest that to study reactions to the Depression in France might be a profitable area of research, he provided at all times great encouragement, especially when morale was low. Dr David Stevenson, of the London School of Economics, gave very helpful advice as to how the thesis might be improved for publication without excessively radical surgery. Dr Harold James of Peterhouse, Cambridge, offered helpful observations at a late stage.

M. M. Alfred Sauvy and Jules Moch were kind enough to answer various queries by letter; M. Henri Germain-Martin not only authorized me to consult his father's unpublished memoirs but generously shared with me his recollections of his father and of the period; M. Robert Marjolin kindly granted me an interview. I should also like to thank Mme Paul Reynaud and M. André Lorion of the Société des Amis d'André Tardieu for allowing me to consult the private papers of Paul Reynaud and André Tardieu respectively. I have worked in many libraries and institutions in France and I am grateful to all their staffs for the assistance they have given me. But I would like especially to mention the staffs of the archives of the Ministère des Finances, the archives of the Fondation Nationale des Sciences Politiques and the Bibliothèque de Documentation Internationale Contemporaine at Nanterre who have always been especially friendly and helpful. The various drafts of this manuscript seem to have passed through the hands of innumerable typists; to them all I am grateful, but to none more so than the last, Mrs Joan Cook, who performed heroic labours with an increasingly confusing text.

Finally, I should like to record three more personal debts. First, to Francis Carlin who has put me up at what seems to have been an endless series of Parisian addresses: not only has his hospitality greatly assisted the research on this book (and improved my knowledge of Parisian geography), it also has made all my visits to Paris even more enjoyable than they would otherwise have been. Secondly, Jon Brignell has offered endless practical advice and unstinting friendship: although he may not realise it, I am not sure that this book could have been written without him. Finally, my father made many helpful and detailed comments on part of a very early draft of this book. But my debt to him goes far beyond that, and is indeed deeper than anything I could put into words.

*University College, Swansea*
*May 1984*

# Abbreviations

**Text**

| | |
|---|---|
| C.A.P. | Comité Administratif Permanent |
| C.C.N. | Comité Conféderal National |
| C.G.P.F. | Confédération Générale de la Production Française |
| C.G.T. | Confédération Générale du Travail |
| C.G.T.U. | Confédération Générale du Travail Unitaire |
| C.N.E. | Conseil National Economique |
| C.V.I.A. | Comité de Vigilance des Intellectuels Antifascistes |
| E.C.C.I. | Executive Committee of the Communist International |
| H.E.C. | Ecole des Hautes Etudes Commerciales |
| I.S.O. | Institut Supérieur Ouvrier |
| m | *milliard* (thousand million) |
| mi | million |
| P.C.F. | Parti Communiste Français |
| S.F.I.O. | Section Française de l'Internationale Ouvrière |
| U.S.R. | Union Socialiste Republicaine |
| U.T.S. | Union des Techniciens Socialistes |

**Notes**

| | |
|---|---|
| A.N. | Archives Nationales |
| B.D.I.C. | Bibliothèque de Documentation Internationale Contemporaine |
| C.H.I.M.T. | Cahiers d'histoire de l'Institut Maurice Thorez |
| C.R.C.R. | Congrès du Parti Radical: Compte-rendu sténographique |
| C.R.C.S. | Congrès du Parti Socialiste: Compte-rendu sténographique |
| D.D.F. | Documents diplomatiques français |
| J.O. DOC. Admin. | Journal officiel de la République française: Documents administratifs |
| J.O. Ch. | Journal officiel de la République française, annales de la Chambre des Députés: Débats parlementaires |
| J.O. Doc. C. | . . . : Documents parlementaires |
| J.O. Sen. | Journal officiel de la République française, annales du Senat: Débats parlementaires |

| | |
|---|---|
| J.O. Doc. S. | ... :Documents parlementaires |
| M.A.E. | Ministère des Affaires Etrangères |
| M.F. | Ministère des Finances |
| P.V.C. | *Procès-verbaux* of the Commission des Finances of the Chamber. |
| P.V.S. | *Procès-verbaux* of the Commission des Finances of the Senate. |
| P.R.O. | Public Record Office |
| R.E.P. | *La Revue d'économie politique* |

# Introduction

The 1930s were a sad decade for the French economy: defeated on the battle field in 1940, France had in the previous decade already suffered her 'economic Sedan'.[1] France, the last country to be affected by the Great Depression, was also the last to recover from it. The index of French industrial production, having fallen below 100 (base 1928) in May 1931, was not to reach that level again until June 1939; as for the peak of 1929, this was not reached again until 1950. In Britain, on the other hand, the economy started to recover from August 1932: by 1934, industrial output had attained the levels of 1929; by 1937 it was 24 per cent higher. In Germany, where output had fallen by 42 per cent between 1929 and 1932, the 1929 level was reached in 1935; by 1937 it had been exceeded by 16 per cent. In America also, where recovery was more halting and where unemployment remained high, industrial output which had almost halved between 1929 and 1932, stood in 1937 at only 8 per cent below its peak level of 1929. In France at this time it was 28 per cent below the peak of 1929.[2]

At one time, discussion of French economic history was dominated by the problem of French 'backwardness', of French resistance to economic growth, of the prevalence of a stagnationist 'malthusian' – to adopt the French terminology – mentality.[3] This debate was much influenced by observation of the poor performance of the French economy in the 1930s. More recently economic historians, writing from the perspective of rapid French economic growth in the 1950s and 1960s, have tended to dwell less on the experience of the 1930s,[4] or have pointed out that the decade can also be seen as part of a process of structural transformation of the French economy in which traditional industries such as textiles consummated their decline and others – hydro-electric power, petrol refining, chemicals, pharmaceuticals, rubber, aluminium – continued their expansion in spite of the slump.[5] But even if the picture needs to be slightly modified in this way, the fact remains that France was the only important industrial power in which the 1929 level of production would not be attained again until after the war. The reasons for recovery in each country were varied and remain controversial. In France, recovery until 1936 was prevented by a refusal to devalue the franc and by the deflationary policies of which this decision was a partial cause; and the

1

entirely different policies of the Popular Front after 1936 failed to remedy the situation. The purpose of this study is to examine the course of, and debate over, economic policy in France during these years, and more particularly between 1932 and 1936.

At stake in this debate was ultimately the balance of power in Europe. The decline of the relative economic and financial position of France between 1930 and 1936 had important repercussions on French foreign policy and military power. In the first place, French governments could no longer use economic or financial strength as a weapon of foreign policy. In August 1931, when the gold reserves of the Bank of France were at almost record levels and the French economy was only just being touched by the Depression, the French government's intervention had played a major role in preventing a proposed customs union between Germany and Austria; but in March 1936 the French government had watched helplessly as German troops marched into the Rhineland: one of the factors which prevented the French reacting to this flagrant breach of the Versailles settlement was fear of the effect that such action might have on the franc.[6] In August 1931 the Bank of France had lent the Bank of England £25 million to support the pound; in February 1936 a group of English banks lent the hard-pressed French Treasury £40 million. It is from 1936 – from the reoccupation of the Rhineland – that we can date that dependence of French foreign policy on British foreign policy which has led one historian to talk of London as France's 'English governess':[7] when Edouard Daladier formed his government in April 1938 the British Ambassador in Paris intervened successfully to prevent the appointment of Joseph Paul-Boncour as foreign minister.[8]

Secondly, the decline in French economic strength affected the thinking of the military. French military doctrine between the wars was premised on the probability of a prolonged war in which economic – and demographic – strength would play a determining role.[9] By 1936 French inferiority in both these respects was all too apparent. Another element, then, in the French decision not to provoke the risk of a major war by resisting the invasion of the Rhineland was the erroneous belief, shared by General Gamelin himself, that France no longer had a decisive military lead over Germany in either men or material.[10] The cuts in public spending which the Depression was believed to make necessary had led to a 32 per cent drop in military expenditure between 1931–2 and 1935.[11] Indeed Robert Frankenstein, the historian of French rearmament, has claimed that one can talk of a period of 'disarmament' in these years,[12] while between 1934 and 1936 German arms expenditure more than doubled. And although arms spending in France did start to rise again in 1935, the first steps towards rearmament were faltering and continuously at the mercy of financial constraints.[13] To some extent there was a lack of will as much as of money[14] but General Weygand nonetheless protested vociferously against the cuts.[15] Some politicians, on the other hand, were ready to draw the logical conclusions from the new economic situation: it has been suggested that the 'appeasement' policies of both Laval in 1935 and Bonnet later were a corollary of their belief in a deflationary economic policy; appeasement was all that France could afford.[16] Conversely the new vigour of French foreign policy after the spring of 1939 may have owed something to the marked improvement in the economic and financial position during the previous months.[17] But was it not by then too late to avert a war – and perhaps even to win one?

This is not to argue that the collapse of France in 1940 was an inevitable consequence of the economic stagnation of the 1930s. That defeat was a purely military one and was in no way written in the stars.[18] Yet although one must guard against retrospective reinterpretations of the national mood, the confidence of France's leaders in 1940 was very precarious. J. B. Duroselle has called his book about French foreign policy in the 1930s *La Décadence*. This decadence was made up of many factors: demographic inferiority, fear of social revolution, institutional breakdown and an awareness of relative economic decline.

The attempt to grapple with the Depression also undermined French political stability and faith in Republican institutions. Between 1932 and 1936, out of 11 governments, five fell directly over a question of economic and financial policy, one other would have done so if it had not deliberately chosen to fall on another issue and two others were granted decree powers to redress the economic and financial situation. Although there were other topics of political debate – especially, after 1934, the anti-parliamentary right-wing leagues – it is no exaggeration to say that politics were dominated by the economic problem and its financial repercussions. This study is therefore also in some sense a study of politics between 1932 and 1936.

The interaction between the economy and foreign policy has been noted by historians on many occasions.[19] And yet there has been surprisingly little investigation of the course of economic policy in these transitional years. Alfred Sauvy's pioneering and indispensable four-volume *Histoire économique de la France entre les deux guerres* remains the most detailed study of the evolution of the French economy between the wars. But as its title suggests it is primarily an economic history, and its numerous incursions into discussion of economic policy are marred both by the fact that Sauvy tends to rely mainly on his memories as a very *engagé* participant in the events he describes and by his technocrat's indignation at the folly of politicians – one of the main themes of the work. The relevant volume of Labrousse and Braudel's series, *Histoire économique et sociale de la France*, although it has superseded Sauvy in many respects, has only very general remarks about economic policy.[20] There are of course studies of particular aspects – of public works policies, of Socialist economic policies, of Communist economic policies, of monetary policy and so on[21] – but any overall study which closely

examines economic policy and places it in the context of politics is conspicu-
ously lacking.

The Popular Front period has been somewhat less neglected.[22] But this is
not the primary reason why this book ends in 1936 (except for a brief consideration of the years from 1936 to 1939 in the epilogue). The year 1936 is
an important date for more than historiographical reasons. In the history of
French foreign policy it is of course a crucial date: the invasion of the Rhineland not only removed an important buffer zone and made it effectively
impossible for France to defend her eastern allies, but led to a collapse of
French prestige throughout Europe.[23] But even if, as has been recently argued,
the Rhineland was not quite the diplomatic turning-point that has often been
claimed,[24] there is no doubt that 1936 forms a clear break in economic policy.
This is not only true for the obvious reason that a reflationary Popular Front
government replaced a series of deflationary Radical and conservative
governments. It is also the case that after 1936 the freedom of manoeuvre of
governments had become extremely limited: on taking office in June 1936
Léon Blum was confronted with a semi-revolutionary political situation; his
financial inheritance was catastrophic; devaluation was inevitable; and
financially costly rearmament was unavoidable. Between 1932 and 1936, on
the other hand, governments seem to have been in a relatively privileged
position (although one aim of this study will be to show that there were
important financial constraints on them): France was affected by the slump
relatively late and this gave French politicians the chance to observe the
experience and policies of other countries; in addition, the franc was strong.
The intention is not, however, to stage a new Riom trial with new defendants:
Laval, Doumergue, Germain-Martin and so on. Although Blum did inherit
a difficult situation he undoubtedly made many mistakes in his handling of
it. The problem is to understand, by examining the political situation, the historical memories, the financial constraints and so on, why, between 1932 and
1936, governments with a seemingly considerable freedom of manoeuvre,
pursued economic policies which resulted in economic stagnation (or, at
least, failed to alleviate it); and to consider the alternatives proposed.

It is, of course, impossible to say what would have occurred if different
policies had been pursued. But implicit in what follows is the assumption that
a devaluation, say in 1933, 1934 or 1935, combined with more expansionary
fiscal and monetary policies would, to some extent at least, have improved
the economic situation. Until recently, whatever the controversies which
raged retrospectively about, for example, the 40-hour week, these assumptions would have been accepted by almost all economists and historians.
Today there is perhaps less certainty. While no one would any longer
seriously defend the decision not to devalue until 1936, some writers,
especially on the left, have, by stressing the internal and structural contra-

dictions of the French economy, implicitly minimized the significance of the failure to devalue.[25] And the arguments of those who in the 1930s opposed expansionary fiscal policies – and we should remember that it was not necessary to have read Keynes to be an advocate of increased public spending, even deficit finance – are fashionable once again, especially on the right: what was once stigmatized as the 'Treasury view' is now hallowed as 'crowding out'. But I write as an historian not an economist, and the point can therefore not be argued here, except to make two observations. First, the importance of the refusal to devalue lay less in the inhibiting effect on French exports – this was anyway a period of growing protectionism and declining international trade – than in the depressive effects of the deflationary policy which clinging to gold imposed on the French economy (just as the importance of the British devaluation lay not in its stimulus to exports but in allowing the cheap money policy during the 1930s); and devaluation, when it came, did after all give a strong boost to the economy, even if, for reasons we will consider, this was not sustained. Secondly, with regard to fiscal policy, it is important to remember that the background during the 1930s was one of falling prices not, as during the 1970s, of inflation. In short my aim is a double one: to illuminate the politics of the period by examining the debate over economic policy; and to understand the 'irrational' policies pursued by placing them in the political context.

I have restricted myself almost entirely to the political debate – that is, to the debate between those who made and those who aspired to make policy. If chapter 7 pays a certain attention to trade union planners, this is because their ideas had considerable influence on much of the political left. But although we will more often be inside the Palais Bourbon than outside it, it is important to remember that it did not only take a '6 February' to remind politicians of the realities of the outside world: policy was affected by its perceived social repercussions. In this context a useful – if incomplete – source is provided by the reports of the Prefects and *Commissaires spéciaux* about the state of mind of the population. Even if there was a tendency to tell the government what it wanted to hear, this was one of the major sources available to it in assessing the impact of policy. As for the influence of financial and industrial interests on policy, this is very difficult to determine. The inter-war years in France are the age par excellence of the myth of the 'wall of money', the 'two hundred families'. Jean-Noël Jeanneney's masterly case study of the steel magnate and Regent of the Bank of France, François de Wendel, has shown how despite his immense potential power, even the influence of a man such as de Wendel was very limited.[26] Many further such studies would have to be undertaken before it is possible to arrive at a synthetic view. I have therefore limited myself to examining the views of business as expressed by various newspapers – *Le Temps, La Journée industrielle, Le Bulletin quotidien* and so on – and to considering the declared views of business groups such as the Confédération Générale de la Production Française (C.G.P.F.) or Chambers of Commerce.

The book is divided into three parts. Part 1, having described the historical and institutional background, will examine the first impact of the slump in France and the initial responses to it before 1932. The first two chapters of Part 2 will analyse in detail the course of, and debate over, government policy between 1932 and 1936, laying particular emphasis on the financial constraints under which governments operated, or believed themselves to operate; the third chapter will describe the painful formation of the economic policy of the opposition parties of the Popular Front. Part 3 will examine the two major alternative policy proposals – 'planning' and devaluation – which were adopted neither by governments nor by the Popular Front, and it will examine why this should have been so. Finally, an epilogue will briefly take the story from 1936 to 1939.

PART 1

∾

# The background

# 1 ❧ The context

L'économie politique en est encore à l'âge des magiciens et du grimoire que l'on lisait
solennellement pendant que les choses allaient comme elles pouvaient.

(Alain, *Propos d'économique*, 1934)

The politicians of the Third Republic were unloved by their contemporaries.
And they have fared no better at the hands of historians. J.-B. Duroselle has
recently criticized their *manque de sérieux*: he tells how Pierre-Etienne
Flandin, the premier, and Pierre Laval, his foreign minister, meeting to prepare an important forthcoming visit to London, wasted their time discussing
whether to fly, as Flandin wanted, or to take the ferry.[1] Other less frivolous
concerns could also distract politicians from their national responsibilities:
Edouard Herriot, mayor of Lyon, recounts in his memoirs that he was forced
to leave before the end of a cabinet meeting discussing what measures should
be taken to deal with one of the most serious financial crises of the 1930s, in
order to return to Lyon and preside over the Municipal Council.[2] One is
reminded of Louis XVI's diary entry for 14 July 1789. But such an incident
reminds us that the local responsibilities of a Third Republic politician could
weigh as heavily as his national ones. It was this body of individuals, about
whom neither historians nor contemporaries have found much good to say,
which was to be confronted with the economic crisis of the 1930s. And
although it would be easy to add to the many criticisms already existing, it
would be more useful to examine briefly the historical experience and technical competence with which they approached their task, and the institutional
and political framework within which they were obliged to operate.

## The 1920s: Monetary instability and economic growth

On 21 July 1926 the franc collapsed.[3] At the end of 1925 it had stood at 130
to the pound; on 30 June 1926 at 173.25; on 8 July at 193.50 and on 21 July
it fell precipitously to 240. Families rushed to convert their savings into
goods. Crowds gathered outside the Palais Bourbon; public anger was turned
against supposed foreign speculators: a bus-load of American tourists was
attacked. The government formed by Herriot on the previous day was

9

defeated, and Raymond Poincaré returned to power at the head of a Union Nationale government intended to save the franc.

The monetary crisis of 1926 was only the culmination of the chronic monetary instability which had afflicted France since 1918. The causes of this situation lay in the state's large wartime expenditure. Although the war had been the occasion of a partial reform of the antiquated French tax system, government expenditure had nevertheless been largely financed by borrowing: by a large increase in the floating debt, consisting mainly of newly created *Bons de la Défense Nationale*, by an increase in the long-term debt and by advances from the Bank of France to the Treasury. The result had been an increase of currency in circulation from 6m F. in 1914 to 37.9m F. in December 1920, and a more than threefold increase in prices. This inflation was not reflected in the external value of the franc until 1919 when the British and Americans ended their policy of artificially supporting the exchange rate: by the end of 1919 the franc had fallen from its pre-war parity of 25 F. to the pound to 42 F.; in December 1920 it stood at 59 F.

The hopes of contemporaries that this process could be reversed by deflation and that the franc could be restored to its pre-war parity were dashed by the heavy expenditure on post-war reconstruction which continued to be financed mainly by borrowing: between 1918 and 1924 French national debt rose from 173m F. to 428m F.; by the end of June 1923 the amount of outstanding short-term Treasury paper stood at almost 60m F. As long as it was believed that the 'Germans would pay' the government did not experience any serious difficulty in raising funds; but when, during 1923, a lack of confidence developed in French capacity to exact reparations, the franc came under increasing speculative pressure, and the government found it impossible to issue any long-term loans and had severe difficulty even in renewing the floating debt, a large proportion of which fell due at regular intervals. This 'plebiscite of holders of bills' – or, as the left preferred to call it, the 'wall of money' – was a sword of Damocles suspended over the head of every government. A severe attack on the franc at the beginning of 1924 was halted by a rise in taxation and a loan from Morgan and Company in New York; but the early hesitancy of the left-wing government, elected in May 1924, sparked off a new crisis of confidence. Nemesis was reached in July 1926.

The very presence of Poincaré was enough to redress the situation. Taxation was increased; the major part of the floating debt was taken over by an autonomous Caisse d'Amortissement, funded largely by revenues from the tobacco monopoly: in a year the Caisse had cleared the market of all notes of less than one year's maturity. By the end of 1926 the franc had risen to 124 to the pound; but even this level had a strongly depressive effect on economic activity, and from December onwards the Bank of France intervened on foreign exchange markets to prevent any further appreciation. This *de facto* stabilization passed into law in June 1928, Poincaré having eventually over-come his sentimental objections: the franc returned togold at four fifths of its pre-war parity.

Poincaré's success had been facilitated by the extremely healthy state of the French economy, itself a partial result of the stimulus to exports provided by the weak franc.[4] In the 1920s French industrial production, improving even on the rapid growth of the immediate pre-war years, increased faster than anywhere else in Europe: between 1924 and 1929 it grew by 4.7 per cent per annum, reaching in 1929 a level that would not be regained until 1950. This growth – due especially to the expansion of new industries such as chemicals, petroleum, electricity, motor cars – was accompanied by a process of increas-ing industrial concentration and plant modernization: according to Malinvaud the mechanization of French industry between 1906 and 1931 developed at a faster rate than in England or America, and at a comparable rate to Germany; in the same period the number of small firms (one to five employees) fell by 25 per cent, and the number of very large plants (over 1,000) rose from 215 to 395.

But these developments did not fundamentally transform the nature of the French economy in these years. The structural weaknesses which had slowed French economic growth in the nineteenth century – demographic stag-nation, a large and inefficient agricultural sector, reliance on imported raw materials – had not been overcome. The traditional consumer industries resisted the new trends and such expansion as they experienced in the 1920s was due primarily to the export opportunities opened up by the weakness of the franc: textile production in 1929 had not reached the level of 1913. Agricultural productivity increased only slightly during the 1920s and although the rural exodus accelerated – 950,000 people left the land between 1919 and 1931 – the rural population in 1931 still represented half the total population of the country, and one-third of the workforce. The number of industrial or commercial concerns employing no workers remained high (1½ million in 1931), and in 1931 30 per cent of the industrial workforce was employed in factories with under ten employees.[5] The size of this class of peasants and small businessmen – which formed the bulk of what the French call the *classes moyennes* – gave them great political importance.[6] They were, along with the unemployed, to be the principal victims of the Depression: agricultural purchasing power was to fall by 30 per cent between 1930 and 1935; in the same period industrial and commercial profits fell in real terms by 18 per cent.[7] The *classes moyennes* also included numerous small rentiers (estimated by one study at between 6 and 7 million)[8] who had suffered from, in some cases had been ruined by – and there was in France no general system of retirement pensions at this time – the inflation and devaluation of the 1920s. We shall hear a lot of the *classes moyennes* in the following pages.

The nature of economic and financial debate in the 1920s was conditioned by the developments we have described. Until 1926 discussion revolved around the consequences of, and remedies to, monetary instability;[9] and from 1926 until the end of the decade, around the consequences and nature of economic prosperity and modernization. The Socialists had proposed a wealth tax – capital levy – as a way of resolving the endemic financial chaos.[10] This policy was developed as an alternative to the conservative preference for indirect taxation: in 1920 the Millerand government had introduced a new turnover tax. In between these positions stood the Radicals: with the Socialists they campaigned in 1924 against tax increases imposed by Poincaré earlier in the year; but once in power they showed no enthusiasm for a capital levy. The argument was resolved, largely in favour of indirect taxation, by Poincaré's return to power in 1926. The financial problem was now settled – although a few conservative hard-liners were to resist the Stabilization Law of 1928 – and attention could be focused on the economic situation.

The late 1920s saw an intense debate on the subject of industrial modernization and new managerial techniques (inspired by the writings of F. W. Taylor and the practice of Henry Ford) all subsumed under the label of rationalization. At the end of 1925, the industrialist Edmond Mercier had gathered together progressive industrialists, publicists and others in an organization known as Redressement Français, which aimed to spread the gospel of modernization in France. This neo-capitalism, as it came to be called, was not restricted to industrial circles; the conservative politicians André Tardieu, Flandin and André François-Poncet could all be included among its partisans. The real influence of the movement must not be exaggerated: the Paris Chamber of Commerce was unconvinced about the applicability of such ideas to France; René Duchemin, president of the employers' organization, the C.G.P.F., was suspicious about the whole mystique of modernization.[11] Representatives of small industry were even less enthusiastic.[12] But it is the existence of the debate which is most interesting. It occurred on the left also: in 1927 the non-Communist trade union, the C.G.T., endorsed rationalization, and the question was discussed also by the Socialists. It is no coincidence that 1931 was the year of René Clair's *À Nous la liberté*: the film is an attack on the dehumanizing consequences of mechanization, ending however with a vision of the liberation to which it could one day lead. This ambivalence was at the heart of the debate.

### Politicians and economists

The politicians of this period have been especially criticized for their ignorance of economics.[13] Economics was very definitely a poor relation in the education system. The teaching of economics was almost entirely restricted to law faculties – from 1877, a paper in political economy had been a compulsory part of a law degree – where it held a subordinate position. Professors of economics could not allow their lectures to become too technical knowing that most of their pupils were not going to become economists. The result was that those wanting to follow up their study of economics found themselves ill-equipped to do so.[14] Some economics teaching also took place at certain *grandes écoles* – the Ecole Polytechnique, the Ecole Libre des Sciences Politiques, the Ecole des Hautes Etudes Commerciales (H.E.C). Many of the financial and economic experts of the political parties were products – often the best products – of this system: Germain-Martin taught economics at the Ecole Libre and H.E.C.; Caillaux and Piétri were finance inspectors; Palmade, Bonnet, Auriol, Flandin and Malvy all held at least law degrees. But a few economics lectures dimly remembered from former student days are not likely to have been of much value to those deputies who had not advanced beyond a law degree, and their training would anyway have been largely in financial matters. Those deputies who went beyond this restricted viewpoint – for example, Reynaud (Law Faculty/H.E.C.), Mendès France (Law Faculty/Ecole Libre), Blum (Ecole Normale for one year) – acquired their knowledge either from self-education or *sur le tas*.

More typical were deputies such as Daladier, who admitted his ignorance with shame:

I am very grateful to those teachers who instructed me in the disciplines of Greco-Roman antiquity . . . but perhaps . . . it would have been better for me to be initiated into the mechanisms of credit, into a detailed understanding of these economic forces . . . which have transformed the world with such intensity.[15]

But it is more important to establish the context of economic thought from which the average deputy will have drawn his ideas than to know that in the 1930s the President du Conseil was never, like M. Barre, 'the best economist in France'. It is not obvious that the average deputy of the Third Republic was more ignorant of economic thought than his contemporaries abroad – or if he was, that this mattered very much: Roosevelt's relative success in combatting the Depression was hardly attributable to his economic sophistication[16] and owed more to improvization and determination. Keynes remarked that every practical man is the slave of some defunct man of ideas: to what defunct god did the deputies of the 1930s pay tribute; from what books, what newspaper articles, what vulgarization of economic theory did they draw the neat practical conclusions which contributed to form their political practice?

Again, the picture usually drawn is a bleak one: if the deputies are damned for economic incompetence, the economists are treated no more leniently. They are particularly castigated for ignorance and distrust of Keynes, a distrust said to be based on his reputation of hostility to French interests in *The Economic Consequences of the Peace*.[17] But if ignorance of Keynes is supposed to mean ignorance of the *General Theory*, the accusations are unjust since the book only appeared in January 1936 – a French translation was arranged in 1938 but, owing to the war, it did not appear until 1942. It was reviewed at length in the *Revue d'économie politique* of November 1937 by Etienne Mantoux who confined himself largely to a cautious exposition. And as early as March 1936 favourable comment on the *General theory* had appeared in the C.G.T.'s periodical *L'Atelier pour le plan*.[18] Even if the *General Theory* had no effect on French economic policy before the Liberation, it had just as little on British policy. Of course some of the policy implications of the *General Theory* were already known before 1936 through earlier publications of Keynes such as *The Means to Prosperity* (1933). But only three of Keynes' works had been translated into French by 1936: *The Economic Consequences*, *The Tract on Monetary Reform* and a series of articles collected together as *Réflexions sur le franc*. Professional economists were naturally aware of the existence of his other writings, but they were hardly enthusiastic;[19] to most other commentators his name was synonymous with at best an 'abuse of credit',[20] and at worst, 'monetary fraud'.[21] But there is no reason, although one economist agreed that Keynes' ideas often appeared to French opinion to be 'tainted by prejudice',[22] to attribute this general hostility exclusively – or even most importantly – to memories of *The Economic Consequences*. It is necessary instead to consider the context of French economics in the 1930s.[23]

At the beginning of the 1930s, Albert Thibaudet declared that nineteenth-century *laissez-faire* economics was dead in France,[24] and Keynes wrote, in his Preface to the French edition of the *General Theory*, that the French economics tradition was not dominated by liberalism to the same extent as the English.[25] It is certainly true that the French state had a long history of pragmatic intervention in economic life going back to Colbert:[26] free trade had had a very short life in France, and even Leroy-Beaulieu, the 'high priest' of French liberalism at the end of the nineteenth century,[27] was willing to temper orthodoxy in order to allow protection.[28] But usually the compromises of practice tended to strengthen the purity of theory. The words of Eric Roll, written about the France of Say and Bastiat, could more or less apply to the inter-war years: 'the protectionism of the reaction and, much more so, the Socialism of the revolution were such powerful currents that economic liberalism had at once to be more intransigent and less realistic than in its native country'.[29] In 1933, French-speaking economists met in their annual congress to discuss 'The liberal economy and the managed economy (*économie dirigée*)': one speaker commented that 'it is a great pity that we do not have among us someone who believes in the *économie dirigée*, even if only to tell us what it is'.[30]

Probably the most influential economics teaching texts of the period were the seven volumes of *Cours d'économie politique* by Clément Colson, lecturer at the Ecole Polytechnique, and celebrated for his unbending liberalism by his most distinguished pupil Jacques Rueff.[31] The consensus was not total: as early as 1909 Albert Aftalion had attacked Say's *loi des débouchés* – supply creates its own demand – in his article 'La Realité des surproductions générales'.[32] But the onset of the Depression had if anything served to strengthen the theoretical adherence to liberalism: Charles Rist, editor of the *Revue d'économie politique*, declared to the congress of economists that he had once believed in the death of economic liberalism but 'experience has proved to me that the liberal economy still has a lot of life in it'. The reason for his conversion was partly his belief that a major cause of the Depression had been the attempt of the Federal Reserve Bank artificially to keep up prices by means of open market operations, thereby making the price fall all the more dramatic when it occurred.[33]

The association of ideas is revealing: if the phrase *économie dirigée* meant anything to the French economists of 1933 it meant 'managed currency' (*monnaie dirigée*). And here their opposition was categorical. One feature of French economics in the early 1930s was its liberalism; the other, as can be seen from the writings of Rist, Aftalion, Nogaro (until 1934 a Radical deputy) and Rueff, was a concern with problems of monetary stabilization.[34] Discussing the Federal Reserve Bank policy in 1927, Aftalion commented that, although not theoretically opposed to an active policy of monetary intervention, he was in practice opposed because its advocates always argued for credit expansion: 'we have never seen Cassel admit the need for contraction'.[35]

The reasons for French suspicion of such policies are obvious enough. The Swedish economist Gunnar Myrdal has written that 'Rarely, if ever, has the development of economics by its own force blazed the way to new perspectives. The cue to the continued reorienting of our work has normally come from the sphere of politics'.[36] Thus, if Keynes was writing against a background of chronic unemployment and as part of a debate as to how to overcome it, French economists were overshadowed by the memory of the inflation of the 1920s. The Depression in Britain in a sense represented merely an exaggeration of an already existing problem and thus there were terms already available in which to discuss it. In France the situation had been quite different, and when politicians scorned, for example, Keynes, they were not necessarily only proclaiming ignorance but also reacting to a particular social and historical context: the past was to weigh heavily upon policy making in the 1930s.

Few politicians, of course, will have directly read the works of Rist and others, but their views were faithfully reflected and popularized in the financial columns of Frédéric Jenny in *Le Temps* or *La Revue politique et parlementaire*, in the articles of Lucien Romier (historian and leading propagandist of Redressement Français) in *Le Figaro*, or in the daily articles by C.-J. Gignoux in the employers' journal *La Journée industrielle* of which he was editor. But probably the most widely known economic publicist of the 1930s was Jacques Duboin – 'Duboin que nous aimons bien' in Daladier's words.[37] Duboin was the leading popularizer of the 'theory of abundance', which attributed the crisis to underconsumption arising from the unemployment which had been caused by industrial rationalization: 'for me it is the development of mechanization (*mechanisme*) which is the principal cause of the malfunctioning of the economy'.[38] Although Duboin presented his argument as a celebration of the possibilities opened up by industrial modernization and emphasized the need to expand consumption, such remarks could also be taken as an indictment of the development which they claimed to approve.

## Politics, politicians and institutions

Between May 1932 and May 1936 there were 11 ministries. This political instability derived less from the institutional framework of the Third Republic than from the fragmented nature of the French party system – and particularly from the ambiguous central position occupied by the Radical Party.[39] Moving from left to right along the political spectrum, the importance of party diminished in favour of individuals: the French right was, and indeed still is, temperamentally averse to the whole idea of belonging to a 'party' (hence its penchant for names such as Rassemblement, Union, Alliance). Although, then, there were two nominal major conservative parties, the Alliance Démocratique and the Fédération Républicaine, their members often sat in different groups once elected to the Chamber of Deputies: between 1932 and 1936 the Alliance Démocratique was split into two major groups which often voted differently.

The Alliance and the Fédération were in no sense organized mass parties but rather a series of loosely structured electoral committees, groupings of *notables*; their congresses were merely glorified banquets, occasions for self-congratulation not debate. The division between them was an historical one, deriving from their attitude to the Church–State conflict of the early twentieth century: the Alliance saw itself as the spiritual heir of Waldeck-Rousseau and the Fédération of the religious opposition to him. But if the religious question was no longer predominant in the 1930s, it still served to situate the two organizations politically and geographically: the Fédération was strongest in the old Catholic bastions of France. In practice, on many matters of policy there was little difference between them. The Fédération, led by the Lorrainer Louis Marin, was more stridently nationalist, and more *bienpensant* in tone, than the Alliance. Although it counted among its deputies several representatives of big business – of whom François de Wendel was only the most notorious – it also indulged in a certain anti-capitalist, anti-*laissez-faire* rhetoric. The Alliance, on the other hand, was more openly associated with big business, more 'modern' in tone, and after

Poincaré had withdrawn from politics it was dominated in the late 1920s by Tardieu, who had embraced the rhetoric of 'efficiency' and economic modernization. When the influence of the latter began to wane after 1932 the leading figures in the party were Flandin and Paul Reynaud. But the allegiance and sentimental attachment to a party did not play the major part in the careers of Reynaud, Flandin or Tardieu that it did in those of Léon Blum or Maurice Thorez for whom their party was indeed their life.

On the extreme left of the political spectrum stood the Communist Party (P.C.F.). But by 1932 the combined effects of sectarian policies, government repression and party purges – from which Thorez had emerged as leader by 1931 – had reduced the parliamentary party to a rump of ten deputies and an historically low membership of under 29,000.[40] Although the party's influence both among intellectuals and in certain municipalities, was greater than these figures suggest, its political effectiveness was minimal until 1935. Before this date the Communists' greatest political importance lay perhaps in strengthening the Socialists' resistance to the attractions of power: at no point could they forget that on their left the P.C.F. was always ready to warn the worker that his interests had been betrayed.

By 1924 the Socialist Party (S.F.I.O.) had recovered from the schism of 1920 to become the leading Marxist party of the left. The principal architects of this recovery – Paul Faure and Léon Blum – remained the two dominant figures of the party during the 1930s. Blum, who had come to Socialism via the Dreyfus Affair and the influence of Jaurès, owed his predominance – officially he was president of the parliamentary group – to his enormous intellectual superiority, which he exercised in the cause of synthesis and conciliation, of holding together the *vieille maison* of party unity. Faure, who had come to Socialism via Guesde, owed his position to his control of the Party organization – he was secretary general throughout the inter-war period – and his oratory: Blum appealed to the head, Faure to the heart of the Party members; Blum was respected, Faure loved. The Party's annual congress, which assembled delegates from the local federations, was its sovereign body; executive authority was theoretically in the hands of the Conseil National but this body was too unwieldy to meet regularly and effective power lay usually with the Commission Administrative Permanente (C.A.P.) on which only one third of the members could be parliamentary deputies. On both these bodies members of the federations were represented in proportion to the number of votes obtained by the different motions at the Congress, thereby ensuring representation for all the factions (*tendances*) within the Party.

This complicated structure was only partially successful in containing the divisions between the parliamentary group and the Party, or between the various *tendances*. These conflicts, which to some extent overlapped, centred mainly around the problem of co-operation between the Socialists and the Radicals, even of Socialist participation in Radical governments. This issue

had already surfaced in 1924–5 and in 1929 (when Daladier offered participation which the parliamentary group had accepted only to be disavowed by
the Conseil National): the strains created by the economic depression were to
bring the issue to a head. The conflict between the parliamentary group and
the party partly drew the lines of division between the *tendances*. On the right
was the Vie Socialiste *tendance* which favoured co-operation with the
Radicals, and comprised old participationists such as Pierre Renaudel and
pragmatic opportunists such as Adrien Marquet (Mayor of Bordeaux); its
dominant intellectual figure was the young deputy Marcel Déat, at one time
seen as a possible heir apparent to Blum: but like Oswald Mosley in Britain
his ambition was to outstrip his patience. On the left was the Bataille
Socialiste *tendance*, whose main spokesman was Jean Zyromski, a ceaseless
advocate of mass action and co-operation with the P.C.F. In the conflict over
participation the Bataille Socialiste often found itself aligned with the
upholders of Guesdist orthodoxy – Faure, Séverac and the deputies of the
Nord (Lebas) – who gave the Party much of its political immobility and
ideological sterility. It was in an attempt to conciliate these positions that
Blum had formulated his distinction between the 'exercise' and 'conquest' of
power: the latter was the prelude to the revolution and did not bind the Party
to uphold republican legality; the former would occur when the Party, having
a parliamentary majority, formed a government within the framework of the
existing regime and would accordingly be bound by existing constitutional
practice. Cynics might see this as an apologia in advance for failure in government. But it did not resolve the question of the attitude to adopt to Radical
governments.

If the Socialist Party was bedevilled by conflict with its parliamentarians,
in the Radical Party real power lay with the parliamentarians. Although the
annual Radical congresses could be disputatious affairs, only once did the
Congress exercise effective power when, meeting at Angers in 1928, it condemned Herriot's continued participation in Poincaré's government. Further
*coups d'Angers* were predicted but did not occur. Only rarely did the Party's
Executive Committee impose voting discipline on the parliamentary group,
and it was not unusual to find the Radicals in parliament divided into three
similarly sized groups: those for, those against, and abstainers. This incoherence derived from more than circumstantial factors. At its root lay the
dichotomy between the Radicals' vision of their historical vocation as a party
of the left – the party which had carried out the separation of the Church and
State in 1906 – and their actual economic and financial conservatism. This
meant that the party could form part of very different coalitions, all of which
were mooted between 1932 and 1936: Cartel des Gauches (alliance with the
Socialists); Union Nationale (a government stretching from the Radicals on
the left to the Fédération Républicaine on the right); and Concentration (a

centre–right coalition stretching from the Radicals, even a few independent Socialists, on the left to the Alliance Démocratique on the right). The Cartel majority of 1924 had collapsed in the financial debacle of 1926 when Herriot entered Poincaré's Union Nationale government. After the *coup d'Angers* the Party entered a period of opposition punctuated by abortive attempts to form a cartel (Daladier's offer of participation in 1929) or concentration (Chautemps and Steeg in 1930) majority. During this period of opposition, under the presidency of Daladier, the Party moved back to the left; and it was largely in local alliance with the Socialists that it fought the 1932 elections.

The Radical Party was dominated by the two very different characters of Edouard Herriot and Edouard Daladier: the 'war of the two Edouards' was part of political folklore. Herriot was famed for his huge bulk and gourmandize, his culture and his oratory. All endeared him to the party faithful: the first proved he was one of them, one of the people; the second confirmed their faith in the virtues of an enlightened lay education system; the third charmed them. But like many instinctive orators Herriot tended to rely on inspiration and improvisation. Nor did his famed culture embrace any knowledge of, or interest in, economics or finance. These two factors no doubt contributed to the disastrous performance of his government in 1924–5; and it was he who had presided over the one-day government which collapsed in July 1926. This experience left two abiding scars: a distrust of the Socialists and an obsessive terror of any financial unorthodoxy. Daladier was in most ways the antithesis of Herriot except for his, already noted, equal ignorance of economic matters. His organizational ability contrasted with Herriot's haphazardness, his laconic manner with Herriot's expansiveness. Out of his silence he had cultivated a reputation as a strong man of authority. He was also seen as a man of the left. This was almost as spurious as his supposed strength: it occurred largely because Herriot tended to be of the right. Much influence was also exercised by a small number of extremely conservative Radical senators – such as Marcel Régnier and Henri Roy – of whom the most important was Joseph Caillaux, the imperious president of the Senate Finance Commission, who, after his unorthodox beginnings in politics, had reverted to ancestral conservatism. Although only a minister for four days between 1932 and 1939, Caillaux was nonetheless one of the most powerful politicians of the 1930s: in the words of his faithful collaborator and disciple Emile Roche, he seemed 'to control everything and terrorize ministers'.[41] The Senate Finance Commission saw its role as the preservation of the strictest financial orthodoxy. At times this could be a very useful alibi for a government which shared the same views but could not admit as much: in preparing his financial proposals in March 1933, Lucien Lamoureux, the Budget Minister, first submitted them privately to Caillaux and Roy before revealing them publicly to the Chamber, and some of the amendments later added by the Senate Finance Commission had already been agreed between Lamoureux and Caillaux, but, as Lamoureux put it, it was more politic that the Senate 'seemed to be imposing them on me'.[42]

Many deputies belonged to none of the main political parties described above. Having been elected as members of no particular organization, they joined one of the many other groups which proliferated in the Chamber. There were altogether 16 of these in the parliament elected in 1932. Usually they formed, as it were, the geological sediments of some now-forgotten historical schism. Their main function was to blur the divisions between left and right, and add a further element of political instability.

This instability can be exaggerated: the 11 ministries of these four years saw only seven different ministers of industry and commerce, six ministers of agriculture and six ministers of finance. The Radical Henri Queuille was continuously Minister of Agriculture for over 20 months, the Radical Georges Bonnet continuously Minister of Finance for 12 months and the centrist deputy Louis Germain-Martin Minister of Finance for a total of 22 months. But even continuous ministerial office was no guarantee of effective power: it is necessary briefly to examine the institutional context.

Until Blum set up a ministry of national economy in 1936 there was no ministry responsible for the overall conduct of economic policy.[43] In 1930 Tardieu had set up an under-secretary of state for economic affairs which lasted until 1934, but this was a post without any administrative staff and carrying no political authority. Economic policy was therefore largely the result of bargains between ministries representing the interests of various sectional groups: especially the ministers of agriculture, and of commerce and industry. One writer commented that commercial policy was decided on Wednesday mornings according to the order in which the delegates of different interest groups entered the office of the minister of commerce.[44] At the Quai d'Orsay there was a sub-department (*sous-direction*) concerned with commercial affairs. But most powerful and politically important was the ministry of finance, responsible for assuring that the government was able to meet its expenditure, and highly suspicious of all spending. The Finance Commissions of the Chamber and Senate which discussed all proposed economic and financial legislation – and, most importantly, the budget – also played an important, if largely negative, role: they were powerful enough to emasculate government bills, but too weak to implement an alternative policy. Between 1932 and 1936 the Chamber's Commission, in which left-wing Radicals were by chance disproportionately represented, tended to be to the left of the Chamber. There was also an advisory body on economic policy, the Conseil National Economique (C.N.E.). This was the brainchild of the C.G.T. which had by 1919 abandoned its pre-war anarcho-syndicalism in favour of a reformist platform which included nationalizations and the setting up of an organization to represent the interests of various economic groups. The C.N.E., set up by decree in 1925, but never given legislative status in a vote of parliament, was a partial fulfilment of this idea. It was not a body of professional economists like the Economic Advisory Council recently set up by Ramsay MacDonald in Britain; rather it gathered together representatives from employers, unions and consumers. But although it produced a number of useful reports, for example, on industrial rationalization and unemployment, its influence on policy was minimal.[45]

The finance ministry was dominated by the Inspection des Finances, one of the four great corps which staffed the highest ranks of the administration of France; the inspectors also played an important role in many ministerial advisory cabinets.[46] The inspectors were largely recruited from the *haute bourgeoisie* of Paris; they were young and dynamic: the average age of the members of Flandin's ministry in 1935 was over 57; at the same time Wilfrid Baumgartner, Director of the *Mouvement général des fonds*, the key department of the finance ministry, was 33, and Rueff, his deputy, was 39. The great training ground of the inspectors was the Ecole Libre des Sciences Politiques: almost all of them had spent at least one or two years there in preparation of their exams. Their attitude towards economics was, therefore, in the words of Duroselle, the spirit of the Ecole 'systematized and sanctified':[47] the emphasis was a narrowly financial one; such economic teaching as took place was in the hands of Colson. The system was also self-sustaining: once admitted to the Inspectorate, inspectors often returned to lecture at the Ecole themselves: Rueff and Baumgartner both taught courses there in the 1930s. Their education and background made the inspectors extremely orthodox representatives of the purest economic liberalism, as well as highly competent financial administrators. And this was their most important role.

The short-term needs of the Treasury were met by issuing Treasury Bills (*Bons du Trésor*), the upper limit of which had been fixed in 1926 at 5m F. But this ceiling could be raised by a vote of parliament. These Bills were supposed especially to help the Treasury meet its obligations during the first half of the year before tax revenues had started to come in, the so-called 'low water' (*basses eaux*) period.[48] But, as we shall see, from being a temporary expedient they were to develop between 1932 and 1936, as they had already before 1926, into one of the government's major means of financial survival. This was potentially a very dangerous situation because there was in Paris no highly developed money market on the pattern of London or New York.[49] The money market largely meant the banks, and especially the three largest deposit banks: the Crédit Lyonnais, the Société Générale and the Comptoir d'Escompte. But the banks, partly owing to the prevalence of hoarding in France and partly to the relatively limited use of cheques, were often subject to large withdrawals of deposits, and therefore, anxious to maintain high cash ratios, they were unwilling to take too much government paper without a guarantee of assistance from the Bank of France.[50] The Bank, on the other hand, was reluctant to rediscount government paper: the procedure seemed too close to the infamous advances to the Treasury of the 1920s. Although the government appointed its governor and two vice-governors, the Bank, controlled by 15 regents theoretically elected by the 200 largest shareholders, hung on to its independence tenaciously. It did not see its role as one of controlling fluctuations in credit by means of open market operations: this was viewed as a potentially inflationary interference in the free operation of the gold standard. Besides performing the functions of a central bank, the Bank of France was also a commercial bank maintaining direct contact with the public through its numerous branches. It was therefore in competition with the commercial deposit banks, and this vitiated its relations with them: it was even rumoured that in 1930–1 the Bank had let various banks collapse in order to appropriate their custom.[51] A former governor of the Bank described how the banks, 'mistrustful of the Bank and trying to safeguard their independence', did all in their power to avoid having recourse to the rediscount facilities of the Bank, thereby possibly revealing the names of their clients to it.[52]

Besides the Bank and the Treasury, the money market was also dominated by the Caisse des Dépôts et Consignations. This institution, run by a director appointed by the government, was responsible for the management of a massive body of funds, most importantly those of the public and private savings banks. The Caisse was the largest single holder of government issues. At times it could be an important stabilizing force on the market: the conversion operation of September 1932 was almost guaranteed of success because the Caisse held 17m F. of convertible rentes; it was the largest holder of *Bons de la Défense nationale* and from time to time it helped the government by holding other Treasury paper. But the need to maintain sufficient liquidity to be able to meet important withdrawals from the savings banks limited the extent of this assistance: *in extremis* governments could turn to the Caisse, but without guarantee of success.

# 2 ∾ The inheritance

Il n'y eut peut-être pas dans toute leur adolescence, d'année plus inquiétante que cette année vingt neuf où tout promettait le ronronnement perpétuel.

(Paul Nizan, *La Conspiration*)

On Monday, 7 November 1929, two weeks after the Wall Street Crash of 25 October, André Tardieu presented his Ministerial Declaration to the Chamber of Deputies.[1] Abandoning the vague platitudes traditional on such occasions, he announced a five-year programme of public expenditure financed not by increased taxation or borrowing, but by spending part of the large Treasury surpluses accumulated during the preceding three years of financial prosperity.[2] Later Tardieu was to claim that he had predicted the economic crisis and that his expenditure plan had been intended to forestall it.[3] But there is no evidence for such an assertion. The plan was announced as part of a 'prosperity policy'. It was justified by pointing out that the development of such a programme had been neglected during the years immediately after the war in favour of the reconstruction of the devastated regions; then had followed the financial crisis; only now was it possible to modernize the economic infrastructure of the nation.[4] No mention of an imminent crisis to be prevented. Indeed it would have been surprising if there had been: Tardieu's plan was conceived in a world of prosperity, for a world of prosperity. And even when the crisis did begin to affect France it was not the 'economic blizzard' of which Ramsay MacDonald had spoken in Britain;[5] rather it was a slow paralysis affecting different sectors of the economy with unequal intensity, thereby encouraging illusions that France would not be hit and delaying any reaction from France's political leaders.

## The early effects of the slump in France

The French monthly general index of industrial production reached a maximum of 144 (base 1913) in June 1930 whereas industrial output in America and Germany had declined steeply from June 1929. According to the League of Nations, France was the only country, out of Britain, Germany, America and France, whose level of industrial production was as high in 1930 as in 1929; and in 1931 the decline in French industrial output was only 10 per cent as opposed to falls of 25 per cent and above in the other three countries.[6] But the global estimate of general index of industrial production, weighted in favour of heavy industry and against consumer industries,[7] fails to reflect the different rates at which industries were affected by the Depression. The *Revue d'économie politique* could speak in 1930 of certain industries as 'veterans of the crisis':[8] textiles, the most important export industry, was among the first hit, production declining from July 1928; the leather goods industry (the fourth most important export) was hit early in 1929; the car industry in January 1930; the chemical industry (affected by the fall in textile production) in March 1930.[9] From the autumn of 1930 the decline in output became more general, though the building and rubber industries were hardly affected until 1932. Industrial production in the first quarter of 1932 was 25 per cent down on the first quarter of 1931. But again the global index masked significant differences: the decline was most marked in the export industries – 37 per cent in metal production, 35 per cent in textiles, this last figure largely reflecting an 85 per cent decline in silk production – and least so in those industries dependent on the home market, especially building (down 13 per cent) and coal production (down 15 per cent).[10]

There are various other indications of the persistence of France's relative immunity from the world crisis: the lag in the fall of French prices (although wholesale prices fell by 8.7 per cent in 1929 this was almost entirely due to a fall in the price of imports, and retail prices did not start to fall until December 1930);[11] the unemployment figures which began to increase only in October 1930; and the level of money wages which continued to rise through 1930, and in some industries did not fall until the last quarter of 1931, although the *Revue d'économie politique* estimated that on average they had fallen in 1931 by between three and five per cent.[12]

The explanation for this lag in the impact of the Depression in France is not totally clear. The explanation most commonly given ascribes it to the undervaluation of the franc until September 1931.[13] But we have already noted that the first industries to be affected were the export industries and that industries connected with the home market suffered least, and, in the initial stages, not at all. The balance of trade statistics are revealing on this score: throughout most of the 1920s France had run a small deficit on the balance of Trade. This was not in itself of any importance – before 1913 the French balance of trade had been negative almost every year – since it was compensated for by earnings on invisible exports, and the balance of payments enjoyed large surpluses throughout the period. But in 1929 the trade deficit which had been 4.5m in 1928, jumped to 10m, and in 1930 to almost 13m. In 1931, with a yet larger trade deficit (13.2m F.), there was, for the first time since 1920, a balance of payments deficit (3m F.).[14]

These figures are not merely the reflection of a general contraction in world trade and its inevitable repercussions on French exports. A large part of the deterioration was due to a large decrease in the exports, and an increase in the imports of manufactures: in 1929 cloth exports declined by 1.2m F. and cloth imports increased by 200m F.;[15] from 1928 to 1930 imports of manufactures rose in value from 7.9m F. to 11.2m F., an increase of 24 per cent which, given the fall in prices, represented a 55 per cent increase in volume.[16] If in 1931 there was, compared to 1930, a reduction in the value of imported manufactures, this still represented an increase in volume of 15 per cent compared to 1929; and the fall in exports of manufactures was 8m F. (a 15 per cent fall in volume or a 30 per cent fall in value).[17] Thus not only were French export industries suffering the effects of the world crisis in the loss of markets abroad very early, but French industry also began to suffer from foreign competition in the domestic market over a year before the devaluation of sterling.

It is not enough, therefore, to claim that the French economy was protected until September 1931 by the relative undervaluation of her currency. But the argument has nevertheless considerable validity: first, as Martin Wolfe points out,[18] the large current-account surpluses of 1928 and 1929 contributed to maintaining French income at high levels in 1930 and 1931 owing to multiplier effects which will have taken a year or so to work their way through the economy; secondly, if it is hard to see that French industry still benefited much in 1930 from any undervaluation of the franc, the extremely important receipts from tourism remained at high levels even in 1931, although the number of tourists had dropped by 25 per cent from 2 million to 1½ million.[19] But there was a further reason for the relative prosperity of France until 1931: the existence of a buoyant domestic market owing to a high level of agricultural prices. An exceptionally good harvest in 1929 had led to the hasty imposition of various measures of agricultural protection, which were intensified after a bad harvest in 1930 led to fears of foreign competition. This protection was highly effective until April 1931: wheat prices rose by 25 per cent during 1930 while they fell by 59 per cent on the Winnipeg market.[20]

If most sections of the French economy had been affected by the economic crisis by early 1932, the French monetary position was stronger than it had ever been. Between June 1928 (before Stabilization) and December 1932, the gold reserves of the Bank of France rose from 5.9m F. to 83.2m F.; and by 1932 the Bank of France held about a quarter of the world's gold supply (in 1926 it held eight per cent).[21] This accumulation of gold was not caused, whatever the suspicions of foreign observers,[22] by a deliberate policy of hoarding on the part of the Bank; indeed the Bank seems after 1929 to have tried to prevent it. Certainly most of the influx in 1928 and 1929 was due to the Bank's liquidation of part of the massive foreign exchange reserves acquired during the period of *de facto* stabilization from 1926 to 1928 when it was necessary to prevent the appreciation of the franc: in these two years the Bank sold 13.6m F. of foreign exchange. But in 1930 it had become sensitive to international criticism, and between the beginning of 1930 and the end of 1931 its foreign exchange reserves hardly diminished at all. Only after the devaluation of sterling – when it lost 2.3m F. – did the Bank, following the wishes of parliament, pursue a policy of liquidating its remaining foreign exchange reserves which fell from 20.6m F. in December 1931 to 4.2m F. in December 1932. In 1930 and 1931 it had taken measures to stem the influx of gold: the discount rate was progressively reduced until it reached the historically low level of two per cent in January 1931 and the government effected a number of tax reductions to encourage French investment in foreign securities.[23]

Such measures had little effect on the flow of gold into France: 11.3m F. in 1930; 18.5m F. in 1931. These gold movements were due to the continuing repatriation of French capital which had been sent abroad during the financial crisis of the 1920s, to the purchase of francs by foreigners understandably nervous about financial stability in central Europe (and later Britain and America) and to the attempt by French banks, faced with a minor banking crisis, to increase their liquidity during 1930 and 1931 by repatriating deposits held abroad.[24] As a result of this increase in the gold reserves of the Bank there was a considerable expansion in the number of bank notes in circulation, from an average of 60.7m in 1928 to 83.6m in December 1931; but this increase (38.7 per cent) being less than the increase in gold reserves (122 per cent) the ratio of reserves to liabilities was, at 60 per cent, well above the legal requirement of 35 per cent established by the Stabilization Law of 1928. In 1933 the gold backing of the franc was to reach almost 78 per cent.

By 1932 the financial situation was, on the other hand, less encouraging. The problem of budgetary deficits had, for the first time since 1925, become preoccupying. From 1926 to 1929, as a result of the combination of Poincaré's tax increases and the increasing revenues resulting from economic prosperity, the state's budgets were in surplus and the Treasury had amassed large reserves: in November 1929 Chéron, the Minister of Finance, announced that these stood at 17.5m F. At the same time government expenditure increased from 42m F. in 1926 to 55.7m F. in 1930: even so, in this year tax revenues much exceeded the original estimates, and tax cuts of 6m were carried out. But the budget of 1930–1 showed a deficit, attributable largely to the vote of additional expenditure during the financial year.[25] This deficit was accepted almost with relief[26] because it absorbed some of the Treasury surpluses which encouraged 'profligacy'[27] and could be attributed more to government profligacy than to the effects of the world depression. But it was soon clear that the budget of 1931, in which predicted expenditure was only kept below that of 1930 by an artifice of book-keeping,[28] would show a larger deficit than the preceding one and that this deficit was 'due for a large part to the influence of the crisis':[29] besides various additional credits necessitated by the deepening depression, net tax revenues showed a shortfall of almost 3m F.; and the definitive deficit for 1931 was about 5.5m F. The budget of 1932–3, voted in March 1932 just before the elections, was only theoretically balanced: expenditure was estimated at 41.4m F.[30] but it was clear to everyone that the new parliament would be faced with a difficult budgetary situation. This deficit was seen as all the more worrying because the large Treasury surpluses had been spent[31] or immobilized in loans to foreign governments or banks in financial difficulty. In December 1931 the resources of the Treasury stood at only 2m F. and the budget of 1932 provided for the vote of credits of 75m F. to cover the possible issue of 5m F. of Treasury Bills – though the *rapporteurs* of both the Senate and Chamber Finance Commissions claimed that the sum would be insufficient.[32] Of course, as the *Revue d'économie politique* pointed out, the issue of Treasury Bills to cover a temporary shortfall of revenue during the period of *basses eaux* of the Treasury was perfectly orthodox financial procedure, but it warned against the development of a new permanent floating debt.[33]

Thus the new parliament elected in May 1932 was to face a paradoxical situation: if the economic position of France was still, compared with the rest of the world, 'relatively privileged',[34] the situation was nevertheless serious – with a 20 per cent fall in industrial production since 1928, a deteriorating balance of payments situation and a steep fall, if less pronounced than elsewhere, in wholesale prices. But the financial and monetary situation was quite different: the franc was one of the strongest currencies in the world, France a haven of security for foreign capital, and the reserves of the Bank of France were at unprecedented levels. The only blot on the financial horizon – a severe one, however, in contemporary terms – was the existence, for the third year running, of a budgetary deficit and the likely reappearance of a floating debt. When in May 1932, 2.5m F. of Treasury Bills were issued, it was the first time that this had happened since 1926 – an unpropitious, and also misleading, precedent.

### First reactions to the slump: parliamentary views and government action

The impression is often given that French opinion, mesmerized by the accumulation of gold at the Bank of France, ignored the worsening economic situation – believing France to be largely immune – and viewed the troubles of the rest of the world with ill-disguised *schadenfreude*. It is possible to find numerous instances of such attitudes, for example in Chéron's indignant reply to critics who talked of a danger of monetary inflation: 'one would think we were in a bad situation. Are we being criticized because the Bank of

France has got 43m F. of gold?'.[35] But the views of most economists and politicians were less complacent: the influx of gold was viewed with apprehension as much as relief, and opinion became increasingly preoccupied with the rise in unemployment.

Certainly orthodox economic opinion tended to see the causes of the crisis in the *manque de sagesse* of other countries. For many French economists, we have seen, the distinguishing cause of the Depression of the 1930s had been the policy of the Federal Reserve Bank during the 1920s. Jenny gave a similar diagnosis, attributing the crisis to an 'abuse of credit'[36] and, in his report on the 1932 budget, Lucien Lamoureux, a financially conservative Radical, attacked American attempts at a 'managed currency' and condemned the gold exchange standard which had been adopted by several central banks.[37]

But once it was clear that the fact that France 'has not had gigantic ambitions'[38] was not enough to protect her economy, the primary concern of economic commentators became France's competitive position in the world and the way in which it was threatened by the gold influx. Rist, looking to the end of the Depression in the rest of the world, saw France in a potential position of disadvantage: 'having been for five years one of the cheapest countries in the world we risk today becoming one of the dearest'.[39] Repeatedly the dangers of the large gold stock and the consequent increase in the money supply were deplored by contributors to the *Revue d'économie politique*: the gold influx, whatever its 'psychological benefit' disadvantaged French industry;[40] it hit French exports.[41]

Concern with price levels and the problem of gold was not confined to economic commentators: as early as February 1930 the conservative former Finance Minister, Charles de Lastyrie, while pointing out that the French economic situation was relatively favourable and that the situation of the Bank of France was 'incomparably strong', noted the increasing trade deficits, partly caused, he believed, by the effects of the gold influx on French price levels.[42] A year later the Centrist deputy, de Chappedelaine, called for a gold policy to prevent the influx.[43] And various memoranda among the papers of Daladier sound similar fears: 'let us not be hypnotized by the importance of a gold reserve which is no cause for rejoicing . . . we are losing our markets one by one'.[44] The bemoaning of the accumulation of gold was also partly an oblique way of defusing foreign criticism of the supposed sterilization of gold by the Bank – in the words of Nogaro, France 'excites the envy, the jealousy of the world'[45] – by showing that the gold influx was unfavourable to France. Such admissions did not however imply that France would accept a co-ordinated redistribution of gold: suggestions of this kind were seen as largely British-inspired attempts to lay hands on French gold; the maldistribution was seen as a symptom, not a cause, of the crisis.[46]

Whatever the concern about price levels, there was at first optimism that whether or not the Depression affected France, it was improbable that there would ever be serious unemployment. France was seen as protected both by the existence of 1½ million immigrant workers recruited during the 1920s, who could be encouraged to return home,[47] and, more importantly, by the perfectly balanced nature of the French economy. References to France's happy equilibrium between agriculture and industry were the stock in trade of most speeches or books of the period.[48] Some warned, however, that if measures were not taken to halt the rural exodus 'we will see the future history of our country following the same course as Great Britain'.[49] But perhaps the process could be reversed: a report by the C.N.E. in February 1931 recommended policies to encourage a return to the land as a possible way of combatting unemployment.[50]

It became obvious towards the end of 1930 that France would not completely escape unemployment. The issue of unemployment was first raised in parliament by Blum, in February 1931, in a question to the Labour Minister, Landry, on what the exact number of unemployed workers really was. The question was pertinent because the true figure – as opposed to the figures for those receiving unemployment assistance, the *chômeurs secourus* – was by no means clear. The only precise statistics of the total number of unemployed are those of the censuses of March 1931 and March 1936 which give respectively figures of 452,800 and 820,800: the corresponding figures of *chômeurs secourus* were 50,800 and 465,100. It is noticeable that the ratio of *chômeurs secourus* to the real total of the unemployed increased between 1931 and 1936 from 11.4 per cent to 56.7 per cent: this is explicable by the fact that as the problem became more serious, more unemployment funds were set up or set into motion – there were only 27 in September 1930 but 230 in December 1931 and 900 by December 1935 – and that unemployed workers who might at first have tried to sit out the crisis by falling back on savings were driven to apply for assistance. The most serious contemporary study of unemployment, carried out under the aegis of Charles Rist's Institut de Recherches Economiques et Sociales, suggested, taking account of the evolving relationship between the number of *chômeurs secourus* and the full unemployment figures as revealed by the censuses, that when the former reached their peak of 503,000 in February 1935, the true maximum was slightly over 1 million.[51] But even if the statistics for *chômeurs secourus* are never entirely accurate because communes and departments were not obliged to set up unemployment funds, they are useful in showing the trend of unemployment. More serious in France than unemployment was the practice of short-time working: in November 1931 40 per cent of workers in factories with a workforce of over 100 were employed for under 48 hours a week; by the start of 1935 the average number of weekly hours worked in such factories was 43.7.[52]

In answer to Blum's question, Landry proposed tripling the figure of 49,000 *chômeurs secourus* to arrive at a real estimate of those unemployed, a calculation which at this early stage of the crisis considerably underestimated the truth.[53] That these figures, which seem small compared to Britain or Germany, were considered alarming, is not surprising if it is remembered that in 1929 there had been less than 1,000 *chômeurs secourus*. But still the problem of unemployment was never as acute in France as elsewhere: if the real unemployment maximum was 1 million in February 1935, this represented only 2.6 per cent of the total population; in America the corresponding proportion reached 12.75 per cent, in Germany 9.4 per cent, in Britain 7.6 per cent.[54] But unemployment in France was always highly localized: until 1934 the Seine accounted for over half the total of unemployed – who made up almost 10 per cent of the total active population by the beginning of February 1935 – and ten *départements* were hardly affected at all.[55]

Unemployment was raised again in November 1931 in a series of *interpellations* of the Laval government when the number of *chômeurs secourus* had reached 92,000. In these debates the Socialists fought on the government's territory and did not press their demand for a proper system of unemployment insurance: the argument revolved largely around detailed questions of how to improve the present system of relief. The attitude of conservative spokesmen was strongly hostile to any system of insurance: the French unemployed must not become like the 'English unemployed worker who has perhaps become a little too used to drawing his "dole" in the last 10 years . . . the morphine injection which prevents the patient from suffering'.[56] Such arguments owed much – besides the natural propensity of conservatives to exalt the therapeutic virtues of suffering – to Jacques Rueff's influential articles on the relation between the British dole and the high level of British unemployment: the first article appeared in December 1926 and he had returned to the attack in the *Revue d'économie politique* of March 1931.[57] Conservative deputies advocated a policy of strict control over foreign workers to prevent further entries and expel those who had arrived illegally. But the general impression in the debate was that the crisis had taken the government by surprise and that so far it had done no more than improvise its response.

The accusation was justified. As the effects of the Depression made themselves felt the government reacted by a series of piecemeal measures to deal with particular problems as they arose. Government action was broadly of three sorts. First, a series of decrees throughout 1931 modified, under parliamentary pressure, the rules governing unemployment relief.[58] Secondly, attempts were made to protect French agriculture and industry from foreign competition. During the late 1920s France had negotiated a number of new commercial treaties consolidating customs duties and widely applying most-favoured-nation clauses. The result was that, given also the cumbersome parliamentary procedure involved in raising tariff levels, the government was forced to take action to protect the economy: British devaluation was countered by the imposition of an exchange compensation tax. Most importantly, 1931 saw the institution of import quotas mainly on agricultural goods and in 1932 these were extended to manufactures. This was to become the major weapon in the French armoury of protection, and a serious source of foreign criticism: by 1935 some 3,000 classes of goods were subject to quotas.[59]

Thirdly, the only attempts by governments actually to combat the deepening depression – as well as to palliate its effects – lay in various revivals of Tardieu's ill-fated expenditure programme. Although the original conception of this bill was quite unconnected with the Depression, its progressive reappearances and modifications are a good way of registering the government's evolving realization of the gravity of the crisis. Tardieu's original bill had been opposed by three opposition projects which advocated more extensive programmes to be financed, not as Tardieu's plan, by the Treasury reserves, but by government borrowing.[60] In the face of this opposition, the government in June 1930 modified certain details of its plan and tried to show that, taking into account the expenditure of the local authorities, the total sum involved was 17m F. It proposed the setting up of a consultative comiteee to supervise the expenditure which would be invested differently depending on whether there was unemployment or economic prosperity – both possibilities were envisaged.[61] But in defending the modified bill in the Chamber in July, François-Poncet, the under-secretary of state for economic affairs, while considering that it was improper to talk of a crisis in France, claimed that the situation did not justify 'blind optimism': in these conditions 'a programme of public expenditure to sustain the rate of production for a few years can only have a salutary effect'.[62] Only the first article of this bill had been voted when the government fell in December 1930.

The shortlived Steeg government which followed asked for a first batch of 670 mi F. to be authorized immediately in anticipation of the vote of the full project. De Chappedelaine, the *Rapporteur*, recommended a speedy vote because of the development of the economic crisis,[63] and François-Poncet, now temporarily in opposition, criticized the government's timidity: 'the economic danger seems to worry it less than the financial one. It wants to guard its Treasury'.[64] This measure was passed in March: the conception of a bill of public spending was now linked explicitly to the need to combat the economic crisis. Faced with an increasing level of unemployment, the government of Laval proposed another batch of expenditure from the full programme, and envisaged for the first time the possibility of raising the money by borrowing. This time the motive was quite clear: in preparing the project the government had been 'essentially guided by its preoccupation with unemployment and by a desire to reduce it or prevent its increase'.[65] The bill was conceived strictly as a way of providing immediate employment although the C.N.E. in its December 1931 report on unemployment had pointed out that an important plan of spending might also generally stimulate economic activity. But it was forced to conclude that the present project would only be a 'very partial remedy'.[66] This was also the general opinion of the Chamber: Lamoureux, the *Rapporteur*, showed that of the 3m F. of expenditure proposed, 800mi F. went to pay for spending programmes already agreed in principle and for which it would anyway have been necessary to increase various budget credits – that is, the bill was, to an extent, merely a way of helping to balance the budget.[67] It was passed in December. But, as Daladier put it in a private note in April 1932: 'what is 1.5m a year, what indeed is the 4m a year proposed by the opposition [i.e. in 1930] in the case of a collapse of 60m'.[68]

## A programme for the future: the conservative solution

The programme which Tardieu had announced with such a fanfare in November 1929 in the framework of a 'prosperity policy', although never voted in its entirety, thus became part of a series of improvised responses to a worsening crisis and ended life as a ploy for balancing the budget of 1932. Indeed towards the end of the parliament's life, the question of the budget came to overshadow all others. In spite of the deteriorating economic situation attention was ironically diverted from it as its repercussions on the budget increasingly revived fears of a recurrence of the inflation of the 1920s – in an atmosphere in which people were already worried about a supposedly excessive money supply. We have seen François-Poncet in December 1930 criticizing the government for being more concerned about its financial security than about the economy.[69] But by the beginning of 1932, such remarks would have been almost impossible: the financial problem once again dominated, and although little was yet done about it, the climate of political opinion which was created dictated a course of action for the new parliament which only very determined governments could have avoided. The debate on the budget of 1932 set the theme for the election to follow. Government ministers made no attempt to pretend that the budget was properly balanced.[70] It was, said Flandin, the Finance Minister, a 'transitional budget between the years of budgetary inflation and price rises and the years of price deflation, of budgetary deflation, lower spending'.[71] For another leading conservative, the next parliament would be forced to embark on a policy of 'budgetary deflation, of strenuous, even ferocious, economies'.[72] Judgement varied as to where these economies should fall: for the Socialists, they were to affect military expenditure,[73] and for others it was necessary to reverse the development of *fonctionnairisme* since 1928 and to modify a whole series of social laws voted during the years of 'prodigality'. But the necessity dramatically to cut expenditure was universally admitted: the only alternative seemed to be inflation.[74]

There is a paradox here: as de Lastyrie was attacking various increases in expenditure during the previous four years he was interrupted by a Socialist shouting, 'you have been the majority for the last 4 years'.[75] The decade which had opened in financial chaos had ended with large budget surpluses. It was largely for this reason that the ministries of André Tardieu were able to embark on important projects of social spending. There is much truth in the claim by François Piétri in an adulatory volume on Tardieu, that Tardieu's achievements in social policy were among the most considerable since the beginning of the century.[76] The years 1930, 1931 and 1932 saw the institution of a system of social insurance, of free education for the bottom class of lycées, of family allowances and finally the institution of pensions for war veterans. Tardieu's attitude to these measures is not entirely clear: although he was to declare in June 1930 that the age of *laissez-faire* was over, and to outline, according to one historian,[77] the doctrine of a welfare state, he later claimed that he had been against both social insurance (in the form it was voted) and free education but that these were commitments inherited from Poincaré.[78] Others have seen Tardieu's social policy as an intelligent conservative opportunism.[79] But certainly Tardieu's government liked to present itself as representing the 'modern spirit' and proclaimed the need for the state to intervene in the economy; 'liberalism' was dead.[80]

Whatever his reasons Tardieu was not without criticism from his own supporters, suspicious of any encroachments of the state on private activity. In the debate on the social insurance bill, in February 1930, Loucheur, Tardieu's Labour Minister, was put in the strange position of defending it against the government's own majority.[81] But in April 1930, in spite of the vote by 84 deputies for an alternative scheme proposed by Xavier Vallat, most of the deputies on the right voted for the government bill, although in the elections of 1932 the social insurance legislation was to be one of their major targets. Employers were divided in their attitude: on the whole representatives of large-scale industry were willing to overcome their reservations, but Chambers of Commerce, as spokesmen of small industrialists, opposed until the last moment a measure which imposed on them a considerable financial burden.[82] The historian of French social security has commented on the phenomenon by which this social legislation, after considerable resistance, was eventually passed in semi-unanimity resulting from the sense of an 'obscure necessity to which everyone gives in because a moment comes when it is impossible to do otherwise'.[83] The politics of social reform were the politics of prosperity.

But as the financial crisis became more serious the deputies of the conservative majority were able at last to express apprehensions which they had hitherto suppressed, and the crisis became the pretext for the reversal of government intervention, for a return to the old order of things. As the conservative Chassaigne-Goyon declared in a celebrated speech in 1931: 'for 18 months the approach of elections has made us heap folly on folly, extravagance on extravagance'; the budget of 1930 had been 'transformed into a sort of charity, a budget of weakness and facility . . . the time to draw a halt has arrived'.[84]

Here then was a programme for the future: a return to the virtues of the past. The heritage of the new parliament thus included not only a deteriorating economic and financial situation, but also a recommended course of action as to how to deal with it, a course of action which, given the expectations of public opinion, it would have been difficult to avoid. To resist such pressure, any new majority which might emerge from the elections needed a coherent alternative strategy and the political will to carry it out.

# 3 ∾ Programmes of the left

Pour nous le mal provient non d'une insuffisance de direction volontaire et raisonnée,
mais au contraire, d'un excès d'artificialité dans l'organisation économique du monde
(Edmond Giscard d'Estaing, *Journal des débats*, 8 September 1934)

Aujourd'hui ce qu'il faut ce n'est pas un economisme métaphysique, mais un
economisme pratique

(Léon Blum, 1933)

To conservative economists and politicians, the economic crisis required no
innovatory responses but, on the contrary, a return to 'wisdom', a repudiation of the 'facility' of the 'era of illusions'. The Depression was seen from
this perspective as the pretext for the reversal of years of increasing state intervention, a pretext to modify a social order in which 'the extension of the idea
of the all providing State has made very dangerous progress'.[1] But this programme of a return to traditional virtues was also seen as a remedy for the
economic crisis which was the pretext of its implementation. Far from calling
into question the benefits of the market economy, the Depression only
demonstrated the necessity for it to exist unfettered by any controls: 'liberalism is confirmed by the opposite experience of the last few years' declared *Le
Temps*: 'if the economy is in chaos, it is because freedom has been reversed
and excessive state intervention . . . has thrown everything off course'.[2] The
moral was clear. But what were the alternatives? What were the programmes
of the left?

## The Socialists

The level of economic discussion in the S.F.I.O. was probably marginally
superior to that of other political groups, but Blum was nevertheless very conscious of its shortcomings. One of Jules Moch's very few criticisms of Blum,
whom he revered, was his tendency to overlook flaws of character in anyone
who might be considered as a 'technician'.[3] In 1901 Blum wrote that 'a total
lack of specialists has condemned and will continue to condemn the so-called
"radical" party to a most unfortunate state of powerlessness'; to avoid this
danger the Socialists needed to organize a division of labour within the Party.[4]

35

This practice was adopted, and in the early 1930s various members of the Party had turned themselves into specialists on various subjects: Jules Moch on the railways and transport, Georges Monnet on agriculture, Vincent Auriol on financial problems, Albert Bedouce on public works. From 1934, the economic page of *Le Populaire* was in the hands of the 24-year-old Robert Marjolin (under the pseudonym of Marc Joubert) who was also working for Charles Rist's Institut de Recherches Economiques et Sociales. Recently returned from a year in Roosevelt's America he had embarked on turning himself into an economist and, largely ignoring such French economics as existed, began rapidly to assimilate the works of Keynes and other British economists.[5] Among other professional economists sympathetic to, or members of, the Party were Lucien Laurat, Francis Delaisi and the future deputy, André Philip.

Blum had of course no formal training in economics – 'I would be completely incapable of teaching the subject' – but because 'fate had forced me to reflect upon it',[6] he wrote a lot about economic and financial matters for *Le Populaire* in articles which demanded considerable thought from his readers, and were often consciously didactic. In justifying a detailed consideration of the Belgian devaluation, Blum wrote: 'Why do I insist on this? First of all, because these are matters which it is essential that our party members become used to analysing, understanding and judging'.[7] In spite of these attempts to raise the level of discussion, one often has an impression of astonishing *légèreté* in the consideration of economic problems: René Belin of the C.G.T. describes, in his bitter memoirs, how no serious study had been made of the implications of reducing the working week to 40 hours; the figure was chosen because it had the virtue 'of being round; that it has a good ring to it, that it is easy to turn into a slogan'.[8]

But if one is criticizing Socialist economic policy, perhaps more important than the lack, such as it was, of technical competence was the novelty of the problems posed and the extent to which recent debate in the Party had concerned altogether different questions. Towards the end of the 1920s, a number of Socialists had attacked the malaise of a party plagued by, as one of them put it, the 'paradox of a doctrine without practice combined with a practice without doctrine'.[9] And for most of this group of writers, of these two elements – doctrine and practice – it was usually doctrine which needed to be updated.[10] These writings, if not merely *pièces d'occasion*, were certainly part of the continuous, if intermittent, debate on the desirability of Socialist participation in government – a debate revived by Daladier's offer in October 1929 – and from their revision, explicit or implicit, of Marxist economic theory followed a revision, explicit or implicit, of political strategy. But the two were linked and it is the revision of economic analysis which concerns us here, particularly the reflection upon, to quote Barthélemy Montagnon, 'the haunting example of America'.[11]

In his preface to an exposition of the thought of the Belgian Socialist, Henri de Man, André Philip, who had spent two years in America, considered the relationship between Socialism and industrial rationalization: while insisting that Socialists must distinguish between 'the science of production' and its use by capitalism, he argued that because in rationalized industries labour became a proportionally less important factor of production, class antagonism was reduced and the worker came to be important to the capitalist as a potential consumer.[12] Jules Moch, in his book *Socialisme et rationalisation* (1927), drew similar conclusions: in the United States, where a rational capitalist class practised the policy of paying higher wages, 'there is no longer question of a continuous impoverishment of the masses . . . nor of constant class antagonism (the facts confirm it), nor of industrial crises due to underconsumption (experience confirms it)'.[13] Montagnon was even less cautious: he was dazzled by 'American material well-being'; in America he saw 'a form of capitalist socialism'. Modern capitalism in treating workers as possible consumers, had eliminated even cyclical economic crises.[14] Déat's *Perspectives socialistes* (1930) was, not surprisingly in view of its date, less sanguine about the 'policy of high wages', but nevertheless argued that the increasing cartelization of industry meant that 'crises could be held at bay and a form of international solidarity created'.[15]

It is not the case that such ideas had become the prevailing ones in the Party. Blum, for example, was far from convinced.[16] But even if the revisionist ideas were resisted, it is significant that to the extent that debate over economic policy did occur in the late 1920s, it was often based on a completely erroneous prediction of future events. This perhaps made the Socialists slow to react to the crisis.[17] But by the elections of 1932 the Party had adapted itself to the new situation and formulated its policy to combat the Depression.

According to the Socialist diagnosis, the crisis was not one of overproduction – an absurd idea when people were going hungry – but of an insufficient level of demand in the world economy.[18] In the 1920s, capitalism, having exhausted the possibility of markets abroad – colonization – had turned instead to the home market, creating demand by a policy of high wages and easy credit.[19] The rationalization of capitalism which these developments entailed, and its increasing monopolization and cartelization, meant that the supposed natural laws of liberalism no longer worked: rationalized industries suffered especially badly from any under-utilization of their massive new plant and their overheads were much greater than those of less highly modernized factories.[20] The result, once the crisis struck, was either a sort of 'inverse selection' in which the most modernized and efficient industries suffered most[21] or that these industries used their monopoly power to prevent a fall in prices which, in previous crises, they would have accepted as a means of eliminating less efficient rivals. In either case it was clear the process of natural recovery was prevented.[22] Given that the crisis was one of underconsumption, all Socialist economic proposals were, to quote Blum, 'logically and harmoniously guided by one overriding idea: to use the power of the State to increase the purchasing power of the masses'.[23]

What was the origin of this diagnosis? Underconsumptionist theories are as old as economic crises: the tradition includes Sismondi, Malthus, Rodbertus and Hobson; the 1930s were the heyday of Major Douglas's Social Credit movement in Canada.[24] But whatever the unacknowledged debts, Socialists never referred to such writers. Some historians have mentioned the influence of Roosevelt, but this view needs qualification. First, the Socialist response to the crisis was almost fully worked out by the elections of 1932, but Roosevelt did not become President until January 1933. Secondly, the Socialist analysis of Roosevelt's policies was often highly sceptical – if nevertheless always sympathetic: 'We are not lying in wait for his failure' wrote Blum 'but nor do we want to stake our reputation on his success'.[25] The similarity with certain Socialist proposals was of course often noted[26] but there was no constant Socialist view of Roosevelt's policies simply because these policies changed with such startling rapidity.[27] Thus Socialists tended to criticize the New Deal in terms of an already formulated viewpoint and policy: it might even modify it, but it was not its inspiration. For Socialists, the fundamental difference between their response to the Depression and Roosevelt's was that his actions were the 'result of trial and error and almost a matter of chance' undertaken in desperation and did not derive from a clear conception of the causes of the crisis[28] – that is from an application of 'the methods and proven results of Marxist analysis'.[29]

This is the most important point about the Socialist analysis of the crisis: that it was believed to be derived from the Marxism that was the unifying doctrine of the Party. Certainly few of the leaders or members of the party had knowledge of Marx other than through the expositions of Guesde or Deville (whose exposition did not go beyond Volume I of *Capital*).[30] Certainly if one reads accounts by many of the Socialist leaders of how they became Socialists, Marx hardly figures at all.[31] But this is less significant than the fact that a certain simplified version of Marxism was one of the fundamental assumptions of almost all members of the Party in spite of the reservations of some revisionists. Probably the most influential Socialist analyst of the economic crisis was the Austrian born Marxist economist Lucien Laurat who, after a period as a Communist in Moscow, had come to Paris where he taught at the C.G.T.'s Workers' Institute: Laurat's Marxism was strongly influenced by Luxemburg and Kautsky, and his interpretation of the crisis, published in numerous pamphlets and articles for the Party and the C.G.T., was further simplified and popularized by Socialist politicians such as Spinasse, Moch, Auriol and, of course, Blum.[32]

The economic crisis was, then, inevitable, to quote Blum, in a system which 'by the inevitability of the laws which govern it, subtracts from consumption part of the wealth produced, either to devote it to the modernization of and upkeep of plant or for capitalist profit, and which therefore does not, and cannot, create demand corresponding exactly with the total wealth that it has the capacity to produce'.[33] There were different views as to whether the slump was in fact the final crisis of capitalism: for J.-B. Séverac any such statement was hazardous because in proclaiming an imminent revolution which did not occur at the appointed date, one risked causing disappointment and dis-affection among Socialist supporters;[34] Blum would make 'no prediction', nor would Moch;[35] while for Zyromski, on the left, this was not another cyclical crisis but the final period of capitalism.[36] Such attempts at prophecy were less important than the main issue: 'The cause of the problem? There is only one: the capitalist appropriation of the means of production. The remedy? There is only one: the social appropriation of the means of production'.[37]

But to say that it was impossible, while remaining within the framework of capitalism, to eliminate the causes of the crisis was not a useful programme of action for a party which, despite its ultimately revolutionary aims, was constrained to work within a democratic system; thus the Party was led to promise at least that 'it was possible to offset its effects, to cushion some of its impact, to prepare the conditions conducive to a recovery.'[38] Almost all the measures which comprised the 'purchasing power policy' (*politique du pouvoir d'achat*) were already contained in the comprehensive Socialist pro-gramme of 1927, but at a special congress in January 1932 to prepare a manifesto for the coming election it was agreed to extract from this pro-gramme those measures most applicable to the changed circumstances.[39] At different times different emphasis was placed on different components of the policy, but generally it included first a reduction of the working week to 40 hours at unchanged wages; secondly, unemployment insurance often con-ceived of simply as a humanitarian measure[40] but also put in the context of the economic strategy of stimulating demand;[41] thirdly, agricultural market-ing boards (*offices*) to raise peasant purchasing power; fourthly, tax reform to remove the burden of taxation from indirect taxes; and, finally, a policy of public works conceived of sometimes merely as a means of gaining time before the introduction of more important reforms,[42] and at other times as a measure of economic stimulation.[43]

Some measures carried over from 1927 and before were not at first very successfully integrated into the anti-crisis strategy – and this applies particu-larly to the proposed nationalizations. The nationalization of the insurance companies was, it is true, to pay for unemployment insurance; but Moch, in his propaganda pamphlet of 1932, did not really succeed in explaining how the other nationalizations fitted into the new Socialist policy except to say that the cause of the crisis could only be eliminated by a transformation of the regime, for which the nationalizations were a necessary if not sufficient condition;[44] and the manifesto of 1932 claimed that they would bring the 'beginning of rationality' into an anarchic system of production.[45] Only later were the nationalizations more properly adapted to the Socialist policy to overcome the slump.[46]

The only major new measure to form part of this policy was the 40-hour week.[47] Both Socialist and C.G.T. demands had hitherto been confined to securing a stricter application of the eight-hour day introduced in 1919. But with the development of unemployment throughout the world this came to seem outmoded, and the International Federation of Trades Unions, meeting in 1931, officially adopted the demand for the 40-hour week which became the major theme of C.G.T. propaganda.[48] It has been suggested that it was the C.G.T. which stipulated the figure of 40 hours and that Socialist writers tended not to give an exact figure.[49] But this – although increasingly the case towards 1936 – was not true in 1932 and 1933.[50] The reduction in working hours was not to be accompanied by a parallel reduction in wages: the aim of the measure was to increase aggregate demand[51] not merely to redistribute the limited available jobs among a larger number of workers. But socialists and unionists were not altogether free from such 'malthusian' – as French economists would call them – attempts to restrict production rather than encourage its expansion, and it was generally believed both in the C.G.T. and the S.F.I.O. that production would not again reach the levels of 1929.[52] To objections that the increase in the total wages bill resulting from the application of the 40-hour week would raise costs and drive yet more business into bankruptcy, the Socialists argued exactly the contrary. During the preceding 20 years of rationalization, labour had become an increasingly less important factor of production than fixed capital costs, which of course became proportionally heavier with the decrease in output: unit costs could therefore be most effectively reduced by not reducing wages but by spreading the burden of fixed costs over increased production, that is increasing demand by raising total purchasing power.[53]

The corollary of the Socialist policy in which the primary objective was to stimulate demand, was that to sacrifice everything to attempts to balance the budget was futile because a balanced budget was an 'absurd chimera and unattainable mirage' as long as incomes and profits continued to decline:[54] 'the budget deficit is the effect of the crisis and not its cause'.[55] The argument, then, was not for the deliberate creation of a budget deficit to stimulate the economy – this would have been a heresy in the period – but that a return to balanced budgets was possible only once the crisis had been overcome. The implication – later made more explicit – was that a provisional deficit might be unavoidable. But it is more important to note that the point most constantly stressed was that only Socialist methods could restore a balanced budget – and, as Auriol put it, remembering the 1920s, 'all democracies must avoid the dangers of government borrowing'.[56]

Blum was not sanguine about the chances of putting the Socialist programme into action and was fatalistic about the future course of events. Capitalists would attempt to apply their own self-defeating remedies: 'the crisis will follow the same course as the crises . . . of the nineteenth century. It will no doubt only resolve itself with time'.[57] But rather than await such an outcome, could the Socialists not perhaps find allies with whom to implement their own policies?

## The Communists

The French Communist Party's response to the economic crisis must be considered in the context of Comintern policy, formulated less with regard to the different situations in the countries of the member parties than to the exigencies of Soviet policy. As a result there is an eerie unreality about much Communist propaganda, a feature recognized even by historians particularly sympathetic to the Party.[58] Between 1927 and 1929 the Comintern had effected a complete reversal in its economic prognosis and its political tactics. The new line, introduced in 1928 at the Ninth Plenum of the Comintern Executive Committee (E.C.C.I.) was confirmed at the Tenth Plenum in July 1929. The post-war world had, it was claimed, entered upon the Third Period of development: after periods of world revolution (1919–23) followed by a relative stabilization' of capitalism (1923–8), the world economy had entered a phase characterized as the 'period of the increasing growth of the general crisis of capitalism and of the accelerated accentuation of the fundamental . . . contradictions of capitalism'. The political implications of this view were, first, the adaptation of the previous 'united front' policy to the policy of the 'united front from below', that is the adoption of 'class against class' tactics which treated social democratic parties as 'social fascists'; secondly, the necessity to be alive to the danger that the crumbling capitalist economies would attempt to overcome the crisis by an imperialist war against the Soviet Union; and thirdly, a belief in the increasing radicalization of the masses.[59] The beginning of the world economic crisis confirmed this new line: the crisis was leading to 'the further expansion of the revolutionary surge', revealed, 'even in those countries where the number of industrial strikes has diminished', by the 'sharper character of strikes themselves'; and the task of the Communist Parties was to liberate the masses from the influence of 'reformist traitors', by means of strikes and mass demonstrations.[60]

It is wrong, however, to see the Comintern analysis as applied completely inflexibly without any appreciation of the different situations of different countries. At the presidium of the E.C.C.I. in February 1930, Manuilski, the

Latin Secretary, had stressed the unequal nature of the development of the crisis and had put France in a fourth category of countries which were as yet only at the 'stage of pre-crisis'; and just over a year later, at the Eleventh Plenum in April 1931, he again insisted on the 'varied picture' of the developing revolutionary movement, and criticized certain parties for 'blind enthusiasm' in applying the directives of the Comintern without taking sufficient account of the specific characteristics of different countries.[61]

Such criticisms remind us that, although the action of the P.C.F. cannot be viewed separately from Comintern policy, it is also necessary to observe how it interpreted and applied that policy. One historian has shown, for example, how for two years the P.C.F.'s analysis of the probable consequences of an eventual stabilization of the franc was consistently at odds with the views of the Comintern.[62] That a Communist Party lacking experienced analysts, whose young leadership had spent much of the period up to 1932 in hiding or in jail, should have been prone to crudity in its analysis is not surprising. And between 1930 and 1932, the Party was to be constantly singled out by the Comintern for its faulty interpretations, for its incapacity fully to exploit the revolutionary possibilities opened up by the crisis – more specifically, for its sectarianism, its underestimation of the revolutionary potential of 'limited demands' (*revendications partielles*) by the proletariat.

These criticisms, first levelled at the French leadership when it was summoned to Moscow in May 1930, prompted self-criticism by Thorez and others at the Central Committee meeting of July 1930 and led to his declaration of the need for a 'decisive turning-point' (*tournant décisif*).[63] But the *tournant* proved not to be decisive enough: party membership and readership of *L'Humanité* continued to fall and the Party was held up for renewed criticism at the Eleventh Plenum of the International in April 1931.[64] Again there followed a bout of self-criticism by the leadership[65] which culminated on this occasion in the exposure of the so-called 'Barbé-Célor Group', and Thorez' definite emergence at the head of the Party. The details of this murky political struggle are somewhat obscure, but whatever the real reasons for the disgrace of the 'Group', one of the main pretexts was its supposed reluctance to accept the necessity for the 'struggle on two fronts' – that is, the realization that the dogma of a 'leftist' exaggeration of the revolutionary possibilities thrown up by the crisis was as serious as an 'opportunist' underestimation, leading as it did to sectarian policies which cut the Party off from the masses.[66]

Whatever the truth about this affair it does testify to the disarray which the Depression seems to have caused in the ranks of the Party. There were differences of appreciation as to the intensity and revolutionary potential of the crisis: some, such as Gitton, were criticized for an over-schematic analysis which assumed it to be the final crisis of capitalism;[67] others conversely were attacked as 'opportunists who do not believe in the possibility of continuing the struggle during an economic crisis'.[68] The *Cahiers du bolchévisme* opened a series of articles in February 1931 under the general heading of 'A Study of the Crisis' in which the editorial board occasionally added disclaimers or notes of rectification.[69] Although exactly how much of this was genuine debate is uncertain, it is clear that the Party's first responses to the crisis were far from monolithic.

Having made these reservations, it is nevertheless possible to summarize the main features of an official line. From the beginning it was emphasized that France was closely integrated into the world economy and that French immunity from the crisis was only provisional.[70] Thus throughout 1930 the *Cahiers du bolchévisme* closely monitored the slow impact of the crisis on different sections of French industry,[71] and whatever the crudities of some of the analysis, Wolikow seems correct in writing that having announced the imminence of the Depression a year before its effects began to be felt, the French Communists were the first party to react and draw attention to it.[72] Discussion was at first carried out in the terms set out by Manuilski in February 1930 but by the autumn of 1930 it was being asked whether the description 'pre-crisis' was not outdated and whether France was not entering a 'slow but visible phase of regression'.[73]

Once it was clear that the French economy was moving fully into depression, discussion revolved around two questions: first, the reasons for the delayed impact of the crisis; secondly, its nature and probable future course. The delayed impact of the Depression could be attributed to numerous factors: the stability of the French banking system; the undervaluation of the franc;[74] the delayed renewal of industrial plant after the war owing to the monetary uncertainties of the 1920s.[75] But these causes of delay, far from guaranteeing a continued relative immunity, could become factors which prolonged and deepened the crisis in France: the strength of the domestic agricultural market depended precariously on a relatively bad harvest in 1931, and the system of agricultural protection, combined with the gold influx, meant that French costs and retail prices were rising while world prices fell rapidly.[76]

But what was the nature of this crisis? Was it merely an exceptionally severe cyclical crisis or was it the final crisis of capitalism? To answer this it was necessary to study the relationship between the general crisis of the capitalist system and the economic crisis: to what extent would the latter accentuate the former? The crisis was certainly of an unprecedented intensity but it was not certain how long it would last: 'one cannot *a priori* dismiss the prospect of a bourgeois solution to the crisis'.[77] But this would only be a 'temporary solution'[78] because the crisis occurred not in the 'ascendant phase of capitalism' but as part of the general crisis of decadent capitalism which had begun during the First World War.[79] Several factors, however, made this capitalist solution (as opposed to a revolutionary solution) more difficult than in the past: the existence of chronic unemployment;[80] the combination of severe industrial and agricultural crises which reacted upon and exacerbated each other;[81] the fact that whereas in the past a cyclical economic crisis had been resolved through the disappearance of the inefficient industries this was no longer the case because cartelized industries and monopoly capital prevented the process of adaptation;[82] and, finally, the subversive effects of the edifying example of the construction of a Socialist society in the Soviet Union.[83]

The point of this emphasis on the possibility of a temporary capitalist solution to the crisis was to prevent a mechanistic interpretation which saw the role of the Party as merely the 'impassive spectator of a drama unfolding before it';[84] the Party had to play the 'decisive role of the subjective factor which is alone able to transform objective tendencies into the elements of a revolutionary crisis'.[85] Because it was claimed that the attack on living standards which was the capitalist solution to the crisis would lead to a recrudescence of revolutionary activity[86] – as was prescribed by the doctrine of the Third Period – any signs that such radicalization was not happening had to be attributed to the failures of the Party: hence the criticisms of the P.C.F. by the Comintern noted earlier. The Communist tactics were to propose a series of 'limited demands' to bring immediate short-term relief to the working class.[87] These measures included the 40-hour week and seven-hour day at unchanged wages; a system of unemployment relief entirely at the expense of the state and employees; an increase in the rates of unemployment relief to at least 20 F. a day; and equal pay for men and women. The details of these measures varied but this was because they were to be formulated entirely according to the preoccupations of the moment: 'no demand, however insignificant, can be ignored by the Party'.[88] There was no analogy with the Socialist policy because, according to the Communist argument, the struggle for improved wages would indeed worsen the crisis of capitalism.[89] Thus the programme of limited demands was not an 'economist' or a 'reformist' programme but only a point of departure leading the Party from secondary battles to the final struggle.[90]

To what extent was this tactic successful? Communist historians tend to contrast the periods before and after the *tournant*: before it the Party is seen as increasingly sectarian and isolated from the masses; after it they talk, to quote a recent study, of 'a leadership more organically linked to the mass of workers'.[91] But although the motives behind this argument are obvious enough – Thorez was at the head of the new leadership – very little evidence is ever given to support it.[92] The electorate of the Party reached an historical low in 1932 and the membership in 1933. Although these are not the only criteria of influence most other indicators give a similar impression. The tactics of the Third Period had advocated political mass strikes as a means of radicalizing workers. But as the Depression began to bite and the fear of unemployment grew, it obviously became increasingly difficult to organize strikes of any kind, even at a time when employers were imposing wage cuts on their workforce. Although the Communist trade union, the C.G.T.U., attempted to resist any such cuts by means of strikes while the Socialist C.G.T. tended to resign itself to negotiations to limit their extent,[93] this tactic met with little success either in radicalizing the workers or stemming the fall in wages: in January 1932, for instance, a meeting of a regional Communist committee at Lille concluded that indiscriminate strike calls would meet with certain failure and decided to call strikes only in factories where the C.G.T.U. was particularly strong.[94] In these circumstances, the Communists, under instruction from the Comintern, turned their attention to another potential source of revolutionary activity: the unemployed. The aim was to rally the unemployed around a number of slogans and organize them into committees which would keep up a barrage of demonstrations, meetings and general political activity in the street. Already in March and August 1930 the P.C.F. had, on the orders of the Comintern, organized demonstrations against unemployment to coincide with those occurring in other countries, but, given that unemployment was at this time almost non-existent in France, these demonstrations were doomed to failure.[95] A similar *journée* in February 1931 was also a complete fiasco.[96] In April 1931 a Communist writer could conclude that the P.C.F. had organized only 'an infinitesimal number of unemployed',[97] and in August the Party was again criticized by the Comintern on this score.[98]

After the *tournant*, and once unemployment started to rise, the picture does not seem to have changed a great deal: throughout France the activities of the P.C.F. and the C.G.T.U. were closely, even hysterically, monitored by the Prefects, and the overwhelming impression which emerges from their reports is that Communist attempts to organize the unemployed were almost uniformly unsuccessful.[99] In the Paris region, where most of the unemployed were concentrated and the P.C.F.'s support was most important – the Seine and Seine-et-Oise accounted for 31 per cent of Communist votes in 1932 – the Party's influence among the unemployed was more considerable: by the end of 1931 there were 85 Communist organized unemployment committees frequented by some 12,000 unemployed (out of a total of 74,000) and loosely grouped together by a central body known as the Regional Union of Committees of the Unemployed; there was also a paper *Le Cri des Chômeurs*; and in spite of police repression various demonstrations were organized. This success was enough to worry the C.G.T. which was stimulated to step up its own propaganda among the unemployed, although this did not stop several C.G.T. members themselves joining the Communist committees. But the success of Communist propaganda was constantly vitiated by its sectarianism: membership of the committees was supposed to be quite independent of membership of the Party but incidents such as one in which 20 unemployed Algerians were forbidden membership of a committee until they joined the

Party[100] were not uncommon, and there were constant battles between the local committees and the Regional Union which tried to enforce the discipline of the Party. The result was that at the beginning of 1932 Communist influence among the unemployed of the Paris region was, if anything, declining.[101] In St Denis, on the other hand, where the Communist municipality distributed part of its unemployment relief through the local committee of unemployed, the position of the committee was stronger – there was considerable incentive to join – and in December 1932 it organized a Hunger March in which 5,000 people participated. But, as elsewhere, tensions existed on the committee between Party and non-Party members.[102] One of the most spectacular events organized by the Communists was the Hunger March between Lille and Paris in November and December 1933: although only a small number actually marched the full distance because of a police ban, several thousand attended the demonstration which terminated the march at St Denis. Given the official pressure exerted against such action – at Amiens, for example, the unemployment office announced that any worker participating in the march would no longer receive benefit – such successes were not insignificant.[103] But they were isolated and fell short of both the claims and aspirations of the Party. The Communist leader Jacques Duclos himself admitted to the Latin Secretariat of Comintern in 1936 that the Communist committees of unemployed had remained largely 'sectarian'.[104]

The astuteness of much of the Communist economic analysis contrasts, then, with the wishful thinking of the political implications drawn. Certainly the problem of a 'discordance between the development of the economic crisis and the action of the masses on one hand and the establishment of our influence on the other'[105] was readily admitted, but this was always attributed to the failures of the Party. Only rarely are we allowed glimpses of a suspicion that this 'mass movement' was largely illusory. And the official line continued to affirm the increasing revolutionary agitation of the masses and the necessity for the Communists to exploit it, at the same time denouncing the activities of the 'social-fascists'. The consequences of this strategy were well summed up by Thorez when, noting that in 1928 *L'Oeuvre* had written 'the Communists have placed themselves outside the Republic', he commented, 'it was our aim'.[106] And until a revision of this line, it was clear that the P.C.F. would not form part of any common effort of the parties of the left to restore economic prosperity.

## The Radicals

Edouard Daladier's *cri de coeur* regretting his ignorance of economic questions might serve as a motto of his party as a whole. The spirit of the Radical Party was, and remained, thoroughly 'political'. This is not to say that the Party was more lacking in competent technicians than its rivals: on the contrary, it contained a large number of highly competent specialists, though these were, it is true, specialists in financial rather than economic matters. But economic questions did not arouse much interest in the Party. The high spot of every Radical congress was the political debate. As Picard, a delegate from the Seine, noted with disappointment: 'when one talks here about political questions the hall is full . . . and when one comes to economic issues the number of delegates interested is more restricted'.[107] But this is perhaps true of all party congresses: the Socialists tended to be much more enthused by the questions of participation or the 'conquest of power' than strictly economic issues. More significant of the highly political nature of the Radical sensibility are the very terms in which economic issues were discussed. Albert Bayet in his resolutely modern book *Le Radicalisme* (1932), intended as a populariz-ation of the ideas of the so-called Young Turks, called for an 'Economic 1789' to free the state, which was 'in thrall to the privileged classes', from the power of industrial cartels and financial speculators who had formed a 'state above the State'.[108] And in the repeated Radical demands for an *économie dirigée* it was always this political justification which predominated: it was necessary, said Jacques Kayser, to impose 'the supremacy of political power over the powers obtained by the economic oligarchy'.[109] Such examples could be multiplied: they show clearly that the Radical conversion to an *économie dirigée* owed less to an understanding of the modern economy than to a simple substitution of *congrégations économiques* for the old enemy the *congrégations religieuses*.

Besides their highly 'political' orientation, there is a second problem dis-cussing the attitudes of the Radicals to the crisis: there was no 'Radical' attitude in the sense that there was a Communist or Socialist one. There were almost as many Radical analyses of the crisis as there were Radicals. To take the national Radical press, the views of *La Lumière* (Georges Boris, Bayet, etc.) were nearer those of *Le Populaire* than those of *L'Ere nouvelle* (Albert Milhaud) which would usually have agreed on economic matters with *Le Temps*, while *L'Oeuvre* (the editor was the Radical deputy Jean Piot and many Radicals contributed occasional articles) and *La République* (the paper which, under the editorship of Emile Roche popularized the ideas of the Young Radicals, but later became increasingly conservative in content) stood in between. This lack of unified outlook did not shock Radicals because the predominant doctrine of Radicalism was to be undoctrinaire, and also because Radicalism was 'science inspiring politics' and policy was supposed to be judged only in the light of reason and experience.[110] The result was often a bewildering eclecticism: the Congress of 1933 voted a motion calling for more budgetary cuts and the re-establishment of the gold standard at the same time as agreeing to study 'with attention the development of the American experiment'; a year later Daladier was given a long ovation for his speech which contained tentative approval of the experiment in the Austrian village of Woergl, which, following the ideas of Gessell, had introduced a 'melting currency' that lost 12 per cent of its value every year.

It is not possible, therefore, to do more than briefly mention the most widely shared Radical views on the crisis and then to examine the remedies proposed at the Congress of 1931. Numerous different explanations were given of the causes of the Depression, varying from an excessive expansion of credit during the 1920s[111] to the 'errors of modern large-scale capitalism'[112] or the accumulation and sterilization of gold by the Bank of France.[113] But two explanations stand out as most commonly offered: first, the excessive industrialization of the post-war world. If there was a Radical economist it might be Jacques Duboin who, besides frequent articles in *L'Oeuvre*, was mentioned with approval on various occasions at Radical congresses,[114] and at many other times his ideas, shared by Caillaux, were expressed even if his name was not mentioned.[115] Secondly, the crisis was most commonly attributed to the 'economic anarchy . . . of the present system', the fact that 'the old liberal economy is bankrupt'.[116]

The corollary of this view was the necessity for an *économie dirigée* or *contrôlée*, which had by 1934 become one of the most popular themes of Radical rhetoric thanks particularly to the influence of the Young Turks – Kayser, Henri Clerc, Pierre Cot, Bayet, Bertrand de Jouvenel, André Sauger, later Mendès France – who, like the revisionists of the S.F.I.O., had in the late 1920s, and especially during the period of opposition from 1928–32, embarked upon a process of political re-evaluation.[117] There were in fact political sympathies and similarities of analysis between them and the Socialist revisionists,[118] and one of the political implications of the Socialist revisionist analysis was, of course, the possibility of co-operation with certain sections of the Radical Party.[119] De Jouvenel's *L'Economie dirigée* (1928), the most considerable work produced by the Young Radicals, expressed many ideas common to the Socialist revisionists.[120] He analysed the growing concentration of economic power in the hands of a small number of financiers and industrialists more influential than democratically elected governments, acting in their own particular interest and against the public interest. The second part of his book was intended to show how it was possible to reach a synthesis between the stimulus provided by private initiative and the more rational organization provided by state direction, to enable the citizen to 'play a public role which conforms to the general interest, and to play it with the enthusiasm which only comes from personal interest'.[121] De Jouvenel proposed a regenerated, controlled liberalism: a return to small-scale factories producing highly specialized components for standardized industries. This part of the argument is not very convincing, but it was at least an attempt to give the notion of the *économie dirigée* some content. Usually, it must be said, it had very little, and Kayser seems right in saying that it was a slogan which would have horrified most party members had they under-stood its possible implications or seen any likelihood of its applications.[122]

The demand for the *économie dirigée* was first officially adopted at the Radical Congress of 1931 which demanded 'the nation's control over its economy'.[123] This congress, in a special debate on the economic crisis, also called for a rational organization of credit, the development of the Empire, tax relief to help exporters, the control of monopolies and possibly a shorter working week – but only as part of an international agreement. Except for the declaration on the working week, this was all vague enough to be possibly compatible with elements of the Socialist programme, and indeed much of the political confusion of the next two years was to stem from the ambiguity of the Radical economic policies which could mean very different things to left-wing Radicals such as Kayser, de Jouvenel and Bayet and conservative Radicals such as Caillaux, Régnier or Georges Bonnet.

But there was a further element of ambiguity: in 1934 the conservative Radical, Georges Potut, agreed that the Radicals had an important pro-gramme of economic proposals but, he said, these were reforms that could be implemented only when 'having completed the task of restoring our finances, we have some elbow room' – not before.[124] If, then, the Radical rhetoric was different from that of conservatives – the *économie dirigée* as opposed to the restoration of the liberal economy – this did not immediately make any necessary difference, because for the Radicals, as for the conservatives, the immediate priority was the restoration of financial stability. This preoccu-pation, this fear of a recurrence of the inflation of the 1920s, was an especially important memory for the Radicals: it was a Radical government which had presided over, and fallen as a result of, the collapse of the franc, and the onus was on the Party to show those who claimed that Radical governments were synonymous with inflation, that this was not the case.[125] Over and over again, speakers at congresses invoked the precedent of 1924–6[126] – and even if there were admissions that there were differences between the situations of 1924 and 1932, 'in practice they are the same'.[127] And this, from the point of view of political majorities, was all that mattered.

# PART 2

# The course of policy: government and opposition 1932–1936

# 4 ∾ From *Le 8 Mai* to *Le 6 Février*: the misunderstanding

The elections of 8 May 1932 resulted in the greatest parliamentary success for the left since the war: in 1924, the victorious cartel had been dependent for its majority on the votes of the centre–left Gauche Radicale; in 1932, the combined forces of the Radicals (157 deputies), the S.F.I.O. (129) and various independent Socialists, commanded a comfortable majority, although a majority was also theoretically available between the Radicals and the right (259). The results were greeted enthusiastically by Radicals favourable to collaboration with the Socialists: 'the task now,' wrote the political correspondent of *La Lumière*, 'is to build the bridge which will allow Radicals and Socialists to join together: they are entrenched on the two opposite banks of a river which is not wide'.[1] But on what was this bridge to be constructed? To insist, as did the same writer, that any 'misunderstanding' between the two parties would be resolved if the new premier implemented 'the policy of *le 8 Mai*'[2] begged more questions than it answered. The history of the next 18 months was to demonstrate that the river was indeed wide – at least as far as economic policy was concerned. But in retrospect it was clear that the 'misunderstanding' could at least be traced back to the election result which was supposed to resolve it.

## The elections of 1932

Elections do not often allow one to draw very useful conclusions about future policy but they do offer a privileged opportunity to situate a particular issue among the various preoccupations of politicians and their electorate. And the picture which emerges from the elections of 1932 is that if the presence of the economic crisis was present in most people's minds, it was by no means considered as the most important issue.

At the special Socialist Congress of January 1932 intended to draw up a Socialist strategy for the imminent elections, the economic crisis figured no more prominently than the question of international peace (disarmament was to be debated at the forthcoming Geneva Conference).[3] At the opposite end of the spectrum of the 'left', the declaration issued for the elections by the Radical senators – the Gauche Démocratique – concentrated exclusively on

53

foreign policy and the budgetary deficit, blamed on the mismanagement of the right.[4] Most deputies, in their own election manifestos, made some reference to the crisis or its effects: it was a 'crisis without precedent';[5] 'a crisis such as has never been seen before'.[6] But such remarks were usually dosed with optimism or complacency: France was, after all, 'less affected' than elsewhere[7] and the crisis which had hit France late – owing to 'the basic virtues of the French race . . . order, method',[8] to her resistance to an 'exaggerated development of industry'[9] – would cause 'less damage and disappear sooner'.[10] In short: 'France is at present the most morally, materially and financially healthy country in the world'.[11] Such comments playing down the severity of the crisis tended to come from conservative candidates who had an interest in defending the record of the previous parliament; but over a quarter (28 per cent) of Radical deputies did not mention the crisis at all, or, if they did, only in insignificant terms.[12] And even in a *département* like the Seine-et-Oise – one of the three *départements* suffering from the highest rate of unemployment in 1932 – the picture is barely different: of 15 deputies elected one did not mention the crisis, and four made it the central feature of their programme;[13] the remaining 11 all referred to it – especially unemployment – but only as one of a variety of other matters given equal or greater importance; two conservatives both noted – even in this *département* – that France was less affected than elsewhere (which was true);[14] and Dalimier, a Radical, could even claim that the crisis was diminishing (which was not).

Far more than by the economic crisis, the election was dominated by the budgetary deficit, sometimes seen, it is true, as a consequence of the crisis,[15] but usually considered separately. More than half the manifestos demanded a return to balanced budgets by cutting public expenditure. The alternative was a return to the 'terrible years' of 1924–6.[16] Conservatives tended less to defend their own record than to predict worse if the left came to power; and although there were some complacent references to the vast gold reserves of the Bank of France,[17] it was usually noted that this was a dangerous 'façade of wealth'.[18] In short: 'No, 8 May 1932 will not be another 11 May 1924'.[19]

The theme of the deficit and its inflationary dangers was no less important in opposition propaganda, which, rejecting the 'blackmail of bankruptcy',[20] directed its main attack at the financial mismanagement of the outgoing parliament. These attacks on the waste of the Treasury reserves accumulated by Poincaré are particularly found in the Radical manifestos, but in fact formed – with the issue of peace – the burden of the whole opposition campaign.[21]

If the election campaign showed that 1924 and 1926 were dates much more emotively present than the reality of 1932, it provided no clear answers as to the composition of the future majority – Cartel, Concentration, or Union Nationale. Tardieu, Blum and Herriot – and, to a lesser extent, Reynaud and Flandin – dominated the national campaign, sparring around each other but avoiding commitments: if Reynaud played the card of financial catastrophe in the event of a left-wing victory, and anchored himself firmly on the right,[22] Tardieu extended a cautious hand to the Radicals, but, meeting little response, he hardened his tone at the end of the campaign.[23] Herriot was even more cautious: he ruled out only an alliance with the right (i.e. Fédération Républicaine), who were separated from the Radicals by 'the whole divide of *laïcité*'[24] and a repetition of a ministry on the lines of 1924;[25] this left, theoretically at least, the possibility of Concentration or Socialist participation. Herriot's view was, in brief, that 'no one has the right at present to mortgage the decisions of universal suffrage'.[26] Left-wing Radicals warned against the danger of coming to power without sufficient preparation, thereby becoming susceptible to the influence of the government bureaucracy.[27] But there was no preparation; there were no consultations between the parties of the left. In effect, Herriot's strategy was that advocated by Jean Piot – at all costs to prevent 'premature quarrels from compromising the victory of the left.'[28]

Only Blum seriously considered the political possibilities for the future, and related them to policy. He envisaged four possibilities: that the Socialists might win an overall majority and thus form a government (this, would have been the 'exercise', not the 'conquest of power'); or that the Socialists, forming an indispensable part of a left-wing majority but without having an absolute majority, would be faced with the choices of participating in government with the Radicals, supporting a Radical government (as in 1924), or merely giving such a government the benefit of the doubt (*prejugé favorable*).[29] While not openly declaring a preference among these three latter options, he suggested that agreement on a minimum programme of three points should be the precondition of any possible future participation in government: an immediate and appreciable reduction in military spending, a national system of unemployment insurance and the nationalization of the railways and insurance companies.[30]

When the Socialist Congress met in May – after the elections but before the formation of a government – only the first of Blum's four possibilities was obviously not applicable. But of the other three, support in the conditions of 1924 was almost universally unpopular –'all the disadvantages of participation without the advantages'[31] – and participation was the question which most absorbed the Congress. The popular pressure for participation seemed irresistible to many delegates;[32] even Blum, who was not enthusiastic, admitted that it could not be dismissed lightly.[33] One indication of the current mood was that very few delegates actually openly declared themselves against participation[34] and preferred instead to impose conditions which made it almost impossible.[35] Thus, rather than fitting neatly into pro- and anti-participationists, the opinions of the delegates ranged over a whole spectrum of possible conditions varying in severity according to their real views as to the desirability of participation. But even the most ardent participationists demanded a minimum of Socialist policies combined with measures to deal with the crisis: the 40-hour week, unemployment insurance, no cuts in the salaries of government employees and so on.[36]

The result of the negotiations to reach a conclusion acceptable to the Congress was a nine-point programme – the so called *Cahiers d'Hughyens*, named after the hall in which the Congress met. In spite of Blum's later attempts to show that the *Cahiers* formed a coherent plan to combat the economic crisis,[37] it is clear, as he admitted at the end of the Congress, that they were the unsatisfactory result of an attempt to combine all views and therefore somewhat too exigent.[38] A delegation from the Congress was to present the *Cahiers* to the Executive Committee of the Radical Party. Few can have believed that they were likely to be accepted as they stood, although Renaudel, on behalf of the participationists, established that the delegation would have negotiating powers and was not merely presenting an ultimatum.[39] But there was to be no negotiation: the *Cahiers* were presented to the Executive Committee on the evening of 31 May, and after five hours of discussion it issued its rejection of them in a communiqué, drafted by Herriot.

Why the failure to achieve a Socialist and Radical government? The Executive Committee's answer to the Socialist proposals made no mention of two of them (a political amnesty, and the setting up of wheat and fertilizer boards), accepted pious wishes about foreign policy and the control of banks, and was cautious about the action to take against unemployment; but it totally rejected any commitment to reduce defence expenditure to the level of 1928 within two years, to exclude the salaries of *fonctionnaires* from any budget cuts, to nationalize insurance companies and railways, to prohibit private arms manufacture and to institute the 40-hour week – except on an international scale.[40]

But more important than the precise details of the Radical communiqué, was, in the words of Blum, a 'fundamental difference of tone', a failure even to allude to the 'wish of the country as expressed in the course of the electoral battle'.[41] This difference of tone is striking: even the conditions posed by the most participationist Socialists[42] were far from anything acceptable to the Radical leadership; the consequences of the lack of any attempt to work out a common programme of the left to fight the crisis was that the two parties barely knew each other at all. Herriot's answer to the *Cahiers d'Hughyens* may have owed something to the influence of Caillaux,[43] but it is clear that his mind was made up against Socialist participation before the Socialist proposals had even been formulated – when the British Ambassador asked on 25 May for the name of the future finance minister, Herriot was already able to give him the name of the highly orthodox Germain-Martin[44] – though the proposals were exigent enough to make his task fairly easy.[45] Of the reasons for Herriot's attitude, one predominated, which he put to the Finance Commission in July when trying to salvage his first financial bill: he found 'a strange coincidence between what could happen today and what happened in 1924 . . . and which I do not at any price want my ministers or myself to see again in 1932'. According to Herriot, in 1932 his government faced three major issues – inter-allied war debts and reparations, disarmament and the financial problem.[46] The economic crisis took a second place.

The enthusiasm of 8 May did not, then, last for long: neither Herriot nor Blum had wanted Socialist participation in government, but, recognizing the desire for it, both had worked to place the responsibility for failure to reach it on to each other.[47] But if Socialist participationists and cartellist Radicals were bitter at what they saw as sabotage by their leaders, in fact little sabotage was needed: the river was indeed unbridgeable.

## Herriot's third government: a pattern for the future

Herriot proceeded to form a cabinet made up largely of conservative Radicals and totally excluding any left-wingers. If his aim was to build a Concentration majority, he failed because on the vote of the ministerial declaration his government received a cartel majority, the centre–right either abstaining or voting against. But the composition of the government was hardly likely to produce a policy which would satisfy this majority, especially given that the Radical parliamentary group had fallen into the hands of the left, excluded as they were from power.[48] On economic policy in particular a clash was inevitable. In the two key posts of budget minister and finance minister, Herriot, after consultation with Caillaux, had chosen respectively the very conservative Radical Maurice Palmade and the centrist deputy Louis Germain-Martin whose financial orthodoxy was impeccable: he had already held the same post in the conservative government of Tardieu in 1931. Germain-Martin saw himself as a financial technician – he lectured in economics at the Law Faculty and the Ecole Libre – rather than a politician; his outlook was a narrowly financial one and his view of the financial crisis which faced the new government was that of the right: France was paying for the prodigal expenditure of the 1920s; severe economies were necessary.[49] Although Germain-Martin and Herriot had hardly known each other before 1932 they shared a common friend in the ubiquitous banker Horace Finaly – school friend of Proust and model for Bloch – with whom Herriot had forged close links after the debacle of 1926 in order to improve his contacts in financial circles.[50]

After the announcement of the formation of his ministry, Herriot received a letter from the conservative financial commentator and editor of the *Journal des finances*, Gaston Jèze. Congratulating Herriot on the choices of Germain-Martin and the 'very reliable' Palmade, Jèze wrote: 'this time you have chosen collaborators of worth . . . this time you have reassured the opinion of capitalists, which is not to be neglected. It is a force which broke you six years ago and which would break you again like glass'; the two essential tasks for the future were to work out an agreement with Germany, and restore a balanced budget by means of 'severe economies'.[51] Jèze's confidence was not to be belied, and the debate over Herriot's first financial bill was to contain in miniature most of the elements of the political conflict of the next 18 months.

Germain-Martin's original proposals, rumoured to contain a reduction in the salaries of *fonctionnaires*, caused an outcry in the left-wing press.[52] The attack was not exclusively on the deflationary effects of such measures on demand but also on their social implications, to show that they were intended to encourage a further general fall in wages.[53] Whether or not such fears were believed, the campaign was intended to undermine government and conservative attempts to drive a wedge between the *fonctionnaires* and private sector workers: '*fonctionnaires*, workers and peasants must stick together'.[54] The reasons for this campaign were simple enough. Money wages had, we have seen, begun to fall in 1930, and between 1930 and 1935 the average hourly money wage in those industries for which figures are available fell by some 5 per cent. Given a 20 per cent fall in retail prices in the same period this of course implied a 15 per cent rise in real average hourly wages. But besides the fact that the fall in money wages varied from sector to sector – miners were badly hit, for example – this calculation does not take account of the important level of short-time working. One historian has estimated the total fall in workers' real income – taking account of short-time working and unemployment – between 1930 and 1935 at 15 per cent.[55] This figure obviously masks dramatic falls in real income for some and increases for others. But almost all will have suffered falls in money wages, and this, as Sauvy stresses, is what people actually noticed.[56]

In these circumstances the *fonctionnaires* appeared as a privileged class. And the left's campaign was not entirely successful. During the coming months the protests of the *fonctionnaires* against salary cuts do not seem, if the reports of the Prefects and *Commissaires spéciaux* are to be believed, to have attracted very general support. In March 1933 the *Commissaire spécial* of Dunkirk observed that the debates on the cuts 'have met with indifference from manual wage earners . . . who, hit by unemployment and with their wages recently lowered, are generally less well paid than State employees'.[57]

There is in fact no evidence, although there were a few isolated calls for 'general deflation',[58] that the government's measures were conceived on any more than the narrowest financial grounds. The bill which finally emerged, abandoning any reduction of *fonctionnaires'* salaries, was intended, by a mixture of economies – over half of which were to come from cuts in military expenditure – and tax increases, to reduce the deficit of the current financial year by 1m F., and that of 1933 (when the measures would apply to the whole financial year), by 4.4m F.; without such action, it was estimated that the deficit of 1933 would be around 7m F.[59] On 4 June the government had inherited an unenviable situation:[60] a Treasury with only 70m F. of available funds, the authorization to issue a further 1m of Treasury Bills (of the possible 5m F. limit, 1m F. had been issued in April, and a further 3m in May) and the prospect of 2m F. of expenditure during the course of June. If the immediate situation was tided over by the issue of 3.4m F. of bonds, the aim of the bill was to alleviate the pressure on the Treasury, and avoid any need to increase the authorized limit of 5m F. on Treasury Bills until the financial situation could be further relieved by a conversion operation in the autumn.[61]

The perspective was, then, rigorously financial, and although Palmade talked of the possibility of implementing a spending programme as soon as possible in order to compensate for the contractionary effects of cutting back military expenditure,[62] such promises were vague, and probably merely intended to make the measures more palatable;[63] they show, however, that the government's bill was indeed admitted to have possibly adverse economic effects. But for a harassed finance minister the immediate problem was financial. As Delbos remarked at the Radical Congress later in the year, Herriot's destiny seemed to be to form 'ministries of financial reckoning'.[64] Although it was to be a feature of the next four years that governments were distracted from the underlying economic situation by recurrent short-term financial crises, that is not to say that these crises were imaginary. By being talked about they could become real: even those such as Georges Boris, economic commentator and editor of the left Radical weekly *La Lumière*, who called in vain for action to combat the slump, and saw nothing dramatic about an increase of 30m F. or so in the national debt, agreed that expectations had been created which made some attempt to appease opinion necessary; otherwise borrowing would become very difficult and expensive.[65]

The government's financial measures were severely amended by the combined forces of the Socialists and most of the Radicals on the Finance Commission. Most of the economies except those on defence expenditure were detached by the Commission, and after the first session of discussion, Lamoureux, the *Rapporteur*, could declare that despite his best efforts the bill was 'already totally transformed'.[66] Herriot was later on to claim that the government had not been able properly to watch over its majority because of the absence of its leading ministers either at Geneva or at the Reparations Conference at Lausanne, and he characterized the Chamber as 'highly undisciplined . . . electorally motivated'.[67] But the difference between the government's position and that of the Socialists and left-wing Radicals – who urged the government not to assume the financial chaos inherited from the previous government, but to tell the nation the truth, which, far from causing a wave of pessimism, would make it possible to tide over the immediate situation by borrowing[68] – stemmed from more than bad management by the government.

Herriot was forced to accept most of the modifications of the Finance Commission but he posed a question of confidence over its proposal, inspired by Blum, to raise 120mi F. by suppressing manoeuvres for the army reserves in 1932 – economies on the army being the only ones acceptable to the left. The resulting vote caused a split in the government majority: the Socialists and a few Radicals voted against or abstained, and the bill passed by dint of the support of Flandin and the Républicains de Gauche and the abstention of Reynaud and the Centre Républicain. These divisions in the right had no relation to divergences on economic or financial policy: like de Lastyrie of the Fédération Républicaine who voted against, Flandin argued the need to complete the task of restoring sound finances, and Reynaud brandished the 'terrible threat' of 'monetary inflation'.[69] The divergences were purely tactical: in spite of the intention of the centre–right deputies of the Alliance Démocratique to form a unified parliamentary group after the election,[70] they had split into two groups on the vote of the Ministerial Declaration – Reynaud, Tardieu and others (Centre Républicain) voting against and Flandin, Piétri and others (Républicains de Gauche) abstaining in an early attempt to build bridges towards a concentration majority. If on that occasion Tardieu's belligerence had wrecked Flandin's attempts to woo the Radicals,[71] throughout the next four years the attempt was repeated with varying degrees of success.

Some members of the Senate Finance Commission attempted to reverse the work of the Chamber. But in spite of the attitude of such conservative senators as François de St Maur – 'I care very little about the existence of the Cabinet' – and such influential Radicals as Caillaux, Roy and Milan, who attacked the bill as insufficient, it was accepted without amendment under the influence of those Radical senators who did not at this stage want a ministerial crisis. Germain-Martin reassured the senators that once the negotiations at Lausanne and Geneva were concluded the government would, in the autumn, risk such a crisis over further financial measures in the budget.[72] The government had, then, obtained only half the resources it demanded – at the cost of a crisis in its majority. But the rupture was not definitive, and the ambiguity over the nature of the government's majority was to continue for 18 months before it was really clear that, in Blum's words, 'the link was broken'.[73] And indeed the cartel majority was quickly reconstituted later in July on a vote to increase the authorized limit on the issue of Treasury Bills by 2m F. – a measure partly necessitated by the amendments to the government's proposals.[74]

The skirmishes of the summer had only postponed a resolution of the financial problem. The shortfall of tax revenues over the original estimates had in September 1932 reached 21.3 per cent – greater than for any preceding month of the financial year – and the government's estimate of the likely deficit for 1933 was raised from 7m F. to 12m F., which, taking account of the savings already made by the financial measures of July, and the successful conversion of part of the debt in September, left a deficit of 8m.[75] The Cabinet was divided on how tough its measures could be,[76] and most deputies predicted the government's imminent fall on this issue,[77] but it refused to reveal the definitive budget proposals until after the Radical Congress in early September.

The debates of this congress give a slightly distorted picture of the economic policies of the Radicals: it was the occasion for the expression of the accumulated resentments from the left of the Party at the composition and policies of Herriot's government, and some of those who might have defended Herriot's government did not do so for reasons of frustrated ambition or personal antagonism.[78] The result was to leave the field almost totally to the left – to Kayser, Bergery, Martinaud-Deplat, Mendès-France and others. But although it was clear that what was being attacked – an obsession with balancing the budget,[79] the 'anti-democratic character' of any policy of cutting the salaries of *fonctionnaires*[80] – it was less clear what exactly was the alternative being proposed, other than a fairly traditional set of 'republican' demands: action against certain monopolies, the repression of tax fraud, public works.[81] Although these left-wing Radicals were on many points close to the Socialists, they rarely mentioned the main Socialist measures against the Depression – notably the 40-hour week. In spite of these strong attacks, the Congress was a personal and oratorical triumph for Herriot. But it solved nothing: the final motion called for a restoration of sound finances by expenditure cuts which did not reduce demand, and for an *économie dirigée* as a solution to the crisis,[82] and the government pressed on with its budget rather as if the Congress had not happened.

The budget proposals, revealed after the Congress, were much what they had been rumoured to be in October: the predicted deficit of 8m F. was to be covered by increased taxation and by action against tax fraud (2.5m F.), by reducing expenditure on *fonctionnaires* and on pensions by 1.3m F. and by transferring certain expenditure (1.5m F.) to a special public spending programme (*outillage national*). Obviously this transfer of expenditure was merely an accounting measure, which, although balancing the budget as newly defined, required government borrowing. But the bill of *outillage national*, although avowedly budgetary in intention, also contained 3.4m F. of supposedly new 'exceptional' expenditure intended to stimulate economic activity.[83] In spite of the very limited nature of this expenditure it met with reserved disapproval from Escalier, head of the *Mouvement général des fonds*, who opposed any increase in borrowing.[84] The bill met with little enthusiasm. Lamoureux, who anyway opposed any such spending programmes, showed in his report that the government at several points had overestimated the level of exceptional 'expenditure' in order to give the project a more 'economic' and less budgetary appearance than it in fact had.[85]

The Socialists and some Radicals on the Finance Commission criticized the government's timidity: to Germain-Martin's reminders about the difficulty of raising loans at reasonable rates of interest, Bedouce replied that a well-conceived large-scale plan of expenditure responding to perceived local needs would easily attract funds.[86] But on the government's insistence that its bill was only limited in intent, and should not be confused with a more important programme planned for the future, the Socialists agreed not to press a bill of their own.[87] Meanwhile the Senate Finance Commission saw the whole operation as a ploy to cover the budget deficit, and directly counter to the government's supposed pursuit of budgetary deflation.[88]

In this case at least the senators need not have worried: the government was brought down before detailed discussion of the bill could begin. Herriot was ostensibly defeated on 15 December over the question of whether to pay the next instalment of the war debt owed to America, but there were few illusions that if he had not fallen honourably on the debt, he would have fallen dishonourably on the budget. His passing was not bemoaned: his third and last government had been as ineffective as his first. Although the left-wing Radical opposition had, whilst not sparing him personally, invented a picture of him as someone who had been swallowed up by the bureaucrats of the Rue de Rivoli, by the '*camarilla* of experts', by the 'experts of right-wing governments, the Rueffs, the Rists',[89] there is no doubt that Herriot was a very willing victim. And the lack of many *experts de gauche* in the Radical Party made no difference to him: with his eyes firmly fixed on 1924, it was precisely the 'experts of the left' that he most distrusted. Herriot had already once been broken like glass – and it was not going to happen again.

The Socialist policy of 'support by fits and starts', as Renaudel disparagingly called it[90] – the attempt to obtain as much satisfaction as possible without actually voting against the government unless pushed too far – had not achieved very much either: a bill to oblige departments to create an unemployment fund and, if necessary, to oblige communes to adhere to it,[91] had not even been discussed by the Chamber's Commission when the government fell, and was a long way from the system of national insurance against unemployment which the Socialists demanded. The most conspicuous Socialist 'victory' was the government's acceptance, after some manoeuvring, of a motion proposing the creation of a wheat board.[92] But this government promise – and it was only a promise – was not much to show after six and a half months.

If little action had been taken to alleviate the economic situation during the Herriot ministry, there had nonetheless been signs of economic revival towards the end of the year: the index of wholesale industrial prices reached a minimum in June, and although fluctuating slightly for the rest of the year, showed in December only a 5 per cent decline over the whole year (as opposed to 18 per cent in 1931); and the index of industrial production (base 1928), after falling to 77 in July 1932, rose steadily through the rest of the year to stand at 84 in January 1933.[93] This general improvement in the economic situation was also reflected in the figures for *chômeurs secourus*, which after reaching 317,000 in March declined steadily and stood at 277,000 in December. The signs of recovery were enough for Rist to write that although having suffered from the crisis last, the French economy was recovering at the same time as the rest of the world.[94] The only exception to this picture was agriculture: the price of wheat and other cereals, which had hitherto been largely protected from the Depression, dropped dramatically from 126 F. a quintal (100 kg) in August to 109 F. in December; between April 1932 and April 1933 it had fallen by 40 per cent. This price collapse showed that however effective government measures to keep up French prices by protecting the French market against cheap foreign grain might be as long as domestic production was below the needs of the home market, they were without effect as soon as there was a domestic surplus – which was the case in 1932, when the harvest of 90 quintals (as opposed to 71.8 quintals in 1931) was excellent. The agricultural crisis was to prove an increasingly dangerous legacy for the governments which followed.

### 1933: 'At last Daladier arrived . . . ' (B. de Jouvenel)

At the end of 1932 the question of wheat prices was a minor matter compared with finding a solution to the financial crisis – a solution which the fall of Herriot had only postponed. But the shortlived Paul-Boncour government which followed was incapable of carrying out this task. Indeed it proved almost impossible to find a candidate to take on the sacrificial role of finance minister: Rist was offered the job but refused to enter the fray. In the end. Paul-Boncour, who, as a former Socialist and now member of one of the independent Socialist groups, enjoyed a left-wing reputation and aroused certain expectations on the left,[95] was forced to fall back on the slightly ridiculous figure of the Radical Senator Henri Chéron, formerly Tardieu's Finance Minister, who, in Paul-Boncour's words, administered public finance 'like a good father runs his household'.[96]

The government, basing its proposals on the report of a committee of experts presided over by the vice-governor of the Bank of France, took the suicidal course of presenting a bill to eliminate immediately the entire deficit, now estimated to be 10m F., a figure which represented almost one-fifth of total budget expenditure for 1932.[97] The government's argument was that even without the economic crisis there would have been a severe budgetary crisis owing to the social expenditure of the early 1930s, and that therefore even if the slight economic revival were to gather momentum, a policy of retrenchment would still be necessary.[98] Such action could not be delayed because at the beginning of 1933 the available funds of the Treasury stood at

only 750mi F. – with the prospect of paying out funds not only to cover its
normal expenditure but also the large budget deficit. But because of the lack
of confidence in the economic and financial situation, the government could
not rely on the possibility of raising important sums in the capital markets
and was forced instead to rely on being able to issue more Treasury Bills.

This raised an old fear – that of the reappearance of a large floating debt.
The authorized limit for the issue of Treasury Bills had, since July 1932, been
increased in various stages from 5m F. to 10.6m F., and the amount of these
bills actually in circulation had risen from 1m F. in December 1931 to almost
10m F. at the end of December 1932.[99] To tide the immediate situation over
until further financial measures could be voted, Paul-Boncour's government
received parliamentary authority to raise the ceiling by another 5m F. In
theory this therefore left a further balance of some 5.5m F. of bills to be
issued: but it was feared that the moment was near when the banks might be
unwilling to take any more government paper.

There was nothing in the government's diagnosis that would not have been
accepted by the most conservative commentators: indeed Jenny gave an
identical analysis of the situation just before the publication of the bill, but he
made the additional point that while 15m F. of Treasury Bills was not perhaps
much in comparison with the level of the floating debt in Britain (the equivalent of 83m F.), the situations were not really comparable, because besides
the fact that the Paris money market was not as well developed as the London
one, in France any increase in the floating debt 'risks provoking psychological
reactions . . . which can be explained by the memory of the years 1925 and
1926'.[100] Chéron reminded the Chamber of the 'terrifying' situation in 1926
when the floating debt of 48m F. had meant that every month 7m F. to 8m F.
of bills came up for renewal: 'one was at the mercy of the slightest lack of confidence'.[101] Thus in 1933 policy makers were not only haunted by a general
memory of 1926 but also by their perception of the effect that this memory
might have on the public: in this way, governments were trapped in a vicious
circle of collective memory and fear – paralysed except to propose a series of
narrowly conceived financial measures designed to propitiate the demons
that they feared, and that they feared that the public feared.

In response to Chéron's financial bill the Socialists presented a detailed bill
of their own which, besides certain immediate measures to balance the
budget, proposed a six-year programme of 30m F. of capital expenditure to
be administered by a specially constituted fund (*Caisse des Travaux*). These
proposals involved a large increase in government expenditure, but this was
not seen merely as a *pis aller* and derived from a totally different conception
of what the budget should be: current expenditure was distinguished from
spending on capital investment which, the Socialists argued, should not be
included in the annual budget.[102] But although there were enough disaffected
left-wing Radicals who were concerned enough by the government's

abandonment of any extra-budgetary public spending programme to join with the Socialists in destroying the government's bill, they would not on the other hand go as far as fully to support the Socialist bill.[103] And there were limits to how conciliatory the Socialists could afford to be: there was talk of reaching a compromise over the issue of *fonctionnaires*' salaries which the government proposed to cut; but after receiving a delegation led by Léon Jouhaux, head of the C.G.T., and Charles Laurent of the *fonctionnaires*' union, the Socialists felt unable to go any further towards meeting the government's position.[104] André Delmas describes in his memoirs how his union, the Syndicat des Instituteurs, kept the Socialists under constant pressure to protect the interests of its members.[105]

The result was deadlock. The debate in the Chamber took place against a background of street demonstrations against the proposed cuts, and the discussion was more imbued with a spirit of moralism than any sense of economic realities: the financial problem was 'a simple question of will'.[106] Paul-Boncour chose to fall on the tax increases proposed in his original bill: he was defeated by the united right, the Socialists and a few Radicals and centrists. The government, lasting barely over a month, had served little purpose except, as Larmour remarks, 'to contribute to the disaffection of the French people from their parliament':[107] the air was thick with rumours of Union Nationale: the name of Gaston Doumergue was mentioned;[108] and the tone of much of the right-wing press became increasingly anti-parliamentary in tone.

It was probably for this reason – combined with the belief that he came from the extreme left of the Radicals – that when the new President de Conseil designate, Daladier, made an offer of participation to the Socialists, the Socialist deputies, in spite of Blum's personal opposition,[109] not only accepted but asked him for no more than a promise to adhere to the spirit of the *Cahiers d'Hughyens*.[110] This acceptance seems to have been neither expected nor desired, and if Daladier, whatever his original intention, was tempted by it to try to form a government containing Socialists, the influence of Herriot, Roy, Lamoureux and others was enough to prevent such an outcome.[111]

In spite of this inauspicious start, Daladier was greeted with muted hope by left-wing Radicals and even Socialists, thanks to his left-wing reputation: de Jouvenel wrote that it was possible that one day in the future historians would write of 31 January 1933: 'At last Daladier arrived . . . !'[112] But in February 1933 Daladier's government had inherited a situation which severely restricted its room for manoeuvre. First, the pessimistic pronouncements of Chéron and others had created an atmosphere of public expectation and disorder that made some kind of immediate financial measures almost unavoidable: on the day of the formation of the government there were demonstrations throughout France by *fonctionnaires* protesting against cuts in their pay – they staged a one-day strike on 20 February – and by shopkeepers, small traders and others demanding budget cuts and opposing any increase in taxes. Such demonstrations were inspired by a number of right-wing pressure groups which had mushroomed during the crisis (or been invigorated by it). Of these, the two most vociferous were the National Tax-payers Federation (Fédération Nationale des Contribuables), run by an ex-auditor Louis Large, and the Comité de Salut Economique, headed by Pierre Nicolle, who resurfaced after the war as a defender of *Algérie française*. During the coming months these and other organizations kept up a well organized campaign of leaflets, posters, public meetings, demonstrations and pressure on individual deputies: the Comité assembled some 17,000 at a meeting in the Salle Wagram in January and organized a day of shop closures in February; on 19 March the Federation held meetings in 46 cities. The real movers behind these organizations were often hidden: the Federation had at one point been financed by the perfume manufacturer Coty and also had links with Action française (it was to participate in the events of 6 February); both organizations worked together with the agricultural demagogues Dorgères and Fleurent Agricole.[113]

Secondly – and linked to the disorder inasmuch as it made borrowing more difficult – the state of the Treasury was disastrous: on 31 January available funds were almost exhausted; on 3 February, the day of the Ministerial Declaration, the Treasury account was in deficit by about 350mi F., and Bonnet, the new finance minister, after appealing to 80 different banks for funds, was forced to contract a loan in Holland.[114] The government was also able to raise 1.8m from a post office loan but, given that the expenditure of the Treasury was estimated to be some 6m until the end of June, the financial situation remained highly precarious and Bonnet later recalled that during February 'we were at one time living from day to day'.[115] Although the ceiling on Treasury Bills stood at 15m F. the prevailing political and financial uncertainty, combined with the slight economic recovery, had resulted in a tightening of the money markets[116] and it had been impossible to issue more than a total of 1m further bills in January and February.

Bonnet therefore turned to the Bank of France, asking it to clarify its position on the rediscount of Treasury Bills: after a cagey initial response, Moret, the Governor, eventually accepted, on 23 February, the principle of the rediscount of government paper providing that the government was not by this means attempting to obtain indirect loans from the Bank; but he insisted that the banks also present commercial paper for rediscount.[117] This affair caused a little excitement on the left,[118] but Bonnet, playing down any possible political repercussions, claimed that the conflict was not so much between the state and the Bank as between the Bank and the banks: it did not want to hold only government paper; they were reluctant to present commercial paper to a possible rival.[119] Because the Bank's statement did not distinguish between the different types of paper held, it is impossible to know exactly what assistance it did give after Moret's statement, but although Bonnet later claimed that this had been considerable, he told the Senate Finance Committee on 9 March that the Bank was holding only 300mi F. of Treasury Bills.[120] During March and April it proved impossible to renew even those bills already issued and the number in circulation dropped by almost 700mi F. And in April therefore the government was forced to appeal to the London money market and open a six-month credit with a group of British banks. But such assistance did little more than tide the Treasury over its difficulties in renewing Treasury Bills, and until the end of May the remaining balance of 4m F. remained unused.

To alleviate the financial situation the government proposed to act in three stages: first, a *douzième provisoire* (one monthly provisional appropriation) containing measures to reduce the likely deficit for 1933 at once; secondly the vote of the budget to further reduce the deficit slightly; and, thirdly, a bill of extra-budgetary public spending to which Lamoureux, the new Budget Minister, claimed to have obtained an assurance from the Senate that it would drop its hostility once the first two stages of the government plan had been voted. The government did not intend in these two financial bills to balance the budget: the deficit was to be reduced but not eliminated. Various reasons were given for this change in policy: first, although the general atmosphere of public disorder required some action to be taken, measures which were too harsh 'would cause uproar in the country' whether from *fonctionnaires*, war veterans or groups defending the interests of tax-payers;[121] secondly, the continuing slight signs of economic recovery justified a limited optimism about future tax revenues; thirdly, the government attacked any 'fetishism about a balanced budget': 'when the interest of the economy so requires . . . it is perhaps not unreasonable not to insist upon a mathematically balanced budget.'[122] This concession to the left was probably merely an attempt to draw the maximum propaganda advantage from a political situation which made any other course impossible.[123] The intention was to reduce the potential deficit for 1933 by 5.5m F.: 2.4m F. of economies and 2.6m F. of fiscal measures.

On the politically sensitive issue of the *fonctionnaires*, the government proposed, in Article 83, a progressive levy on the salaries of all those earning above 20,000 F. Lamoureux had already squared most of his proposals with Auriol and Blum,[124] and the Chamber's Finance Commission accepted them without too many objections. But on an amendment by the Socialist Ernest Lafont, it turned Article 83 into a special crisis tax on all incomes which had not undergone a decline of over ten per cent between 1930 and 1932. The attitude of the Socialists is interesting: although they were theoretically against any measures of deflation on economic grounds, Lafont's amendment was no less deflationary in its effects on demand than the original government version; and anyway the sums involved were tiny in comparison with a budget of about 50m F. But while the Socialists were able to modify their position on general economic policy, compromise was less easy on measures which hit the *fonctionnaires* 'only because they are *fonctionnaires*'.[125] Not only were the Socialists, as we have already seen, under considerable pressure from the C.G.T. and the *fonctionnaires*' union, but waiting on the left were the Communists ready to welcome all those who felt that the Socialists had betrayed their interests.[126]

The Chamber eventually accepted a slightly modified version of the Commission's amendment. But this solution was quite unacceptable to the Senate which proposed a text even tougher than the government's original bill, and after the bill had commuted several times between the two assemblies, a compromise was reached in which the Chamber accepted an article hitting all *fonctionnaires* earning over 15,000 F.[127] On the vote of this article the Socialists split: 104 in favour, 20 against, with four abstentions. The adoption of the rest of the *douzième provisoire* was comparatively easy. The Senate Finance Commission introduced a number of supplementary economies affecting war veterans (barely touched in the government's bill) which it refused to withdraw in spite of Lamoureux's assurances that the representatives of the veterans had agreed to accept reductions in their pensions in the budget itself, but that they insisted on being the last to be touched – and that, anyway, it would be impossible to find 20 votes for such measures in the Chamber, where defence of the rights of veterans was a popular pastime among deputies of all groups. But on this matter the Commission was disavowed by the rest of the Senate among whom there also existed a strong pressure group in favour of the veterans,[128] and the bill which was eventually passed at the end of February contained measures to reduce the deficit by 4.6m F. (about 1m less than the government had originally wanted), of which only 1.4m consisted of economies.

The debate on the budget itself provided for an almost exact repetition of these events, and only after shuttling numerous times between the two assemblies was it eventually passed – five months late – at the end of May.[129] The vote of any financial bill was in the circumstances of 1933 a considerable achievement, but neither of these bills was anything other than irrelevant to the economic situation: more significant was the fact that on 19 April America left the gold standard and that a world economic conference was about to meet in London. Perhaps the most important – both for the French urban landscape and as a minor feature of French social history, where it was to play such an important role in the daily life of the *petit peuple* of the novels of Queneau – and certainly the most permanent feature of the budget of 1933 was the institution of a state lottery. All else was soon forgotten.

On 1 July 1933 Bonnet could tell the Chamber's Finance Commission that the state of the Treasury was at last satisfactory.[130] The financial action of the Daladier government – and even more its firm defence of the gold standard at the London conference in July[131] – had had the intended effect of restoring confidence and making it possible to borrow. In March the government had obtained authorization to issue 10m F. of long- or medium-term bonds, and the success of this loan, of which 5.2m F. was issued in April and another 3.2m F. in July, secured the Treasury sufficient resources until the end of the year. From the end of June it became possible during the summer to issue 2m F. of new Treasury Bills and lower the rate of interest on them. The Bills seem to have been taken up largely by hot money coming into France from abroad out of fear about the monetary situation elsewhere, whereas the bonds were, according to Bonnet, taken up by French capital which had so far been hoarded.[132]

But, if the financial policy of the government was successful in the short term, the removal of the financial pressures which had restricted the possibilities of action when it first took office, did not lead it to implement any more general measures of economic stimulation at a time when the slight economic revival which had started in mid-1932 was coming to an end. The programme of public spending which had been promised in February was quietly buried in spite of protests from the Chamber's Finance Commission.[133] There was, however, action to try to remedy the continuing wheat crisis. A wheat bill passed in January and various other measures implemented since[134] had been insufficient to halt the decline in wheat prices: from 108 F. a quintal in January, the price quoted in Paris had fallen in June 1933 to 96 F. compared with 169 F. in June 1932; but during the debates on this situation much lower regional prices of as little as 75 F., were quoted.[135] There were increasingly violent protest meetings in the countryside – most notably the occupation of the Prefecture at Chartres by angry wheat farmers – and with the prospect of the 5.5m quintals held over from the harvest of 1932 (under the provision of the previous bill) swelling a harvest for 1933 that was predicted by many to be exceptionally promising, the government proposed a bill which was largely a codification of various different *ad hoc* measures hitherto applied to the wheat market over the previous four years.[136]

But in the Chamber the government came under irresistible pressure, especially from Socialists and Radicals, to introduce into the bill a minimum grain price which the Minister of Agriculture Queuille, in spite of considerable reluctance, was obliged to accept. This 'veritably revolutionary measure', in the words of one conservative,[137] was in fact much less important than at first seemed the case since it did not oblige the state to buy up all unsold wheat at the minimum price. The provision for a minimum price was merely tacked on to the original bill without increasing the financial resources it made available, and Queuille disclosed that, for financial reasons, the government would never agree to become a buyer.[138] Thus the government was relying on no more than the 'discipline' of the wheat farmers: if unable to find a buyer at once, they were not to be tempted to sell immediately at a lower price but must delay their sales, using the facilities provided by the government bill. If the harvest of 1933 turned out to be very good, Queuille recognized that these facilities would be inadequate,[139] and Lamoureux admitted in the privacy of the Senate Finance Commission that the minimum price would indeed be largely fictitious.[140]

The discussion over this bill brought out clearly the difficulty of consistently applying the conservatives' economic policy: as Monnet pointed out, the adoption of the minimum price was first an abandonment of the free market in favour of economic intervention, and secondly, since the increase in wheat prices would probably also result in a slight increase in bread prices, it showed that the government would need to abandon any hopes of pushing down wages further.[141] Of course, this was a useful political point to make. But conservatives drew similar conclusions: the bill would, said Caillaux, encourage 'unsustainable expenditure with disastrous consequences' – the collapse of public finances and, ultimately, an 'unavoidable inflation . . . the ruin of the *classes moyennes*'.[142] Nevertheless, in spite of these forebodings no senator actually voted against the introduction of a minimum price. In the Chamber, also, the minimum price bill met with little opposition, though it is noticeable that very few conservatives spoke in the debate at all (not wanting to approve, they dared not oppose). The conservative press could afford more detachment: the *Journal des débats* accused the Chamber of instituting Socialism.[143] But for most deputies and senators ideological purity was tempered by electoral pressure.

The timid economic policy of Daladier's government seems, then, to have been curiously at odds with the reputation that he had acquired as a strong man of the left, the man who had offered participation to the Socialists in 1929, the patron and hope of the Young Turks. There is, however, some evidence that he had long before been meditating a move to the right: in a letter to Daladier, the economist Henry Michel, with whom Daladier seems to have had some correspondence, drew his attention to two articles by Jenny – 'on which a statesman ought to mediate' – which, he said, attacked the ideas of the 'generous but badly grounded team at *La République* (Boris, de Jouvenel, Henri Clerc, etc.) [who] have taken on board the ideas' of economists such as Keynes, Cassel and d'Abernon.[144] And Blum feared that Daladier would try to divide the Socialists by attracting the participationists to himself in order to form a government of left Concentration.[145]

The truth about Daladier's intentions is highly obscure; probably they were imperfectly formulated. But there is also evidence that his instincts remained on the 'left'. In various scattered notes for his never completed or published memoirs, Daladier, in discussing his policy of budget cuts, remarked that: 'I had doubts about the efficacy of this remedy. After all, was not the budget deficit essentially the consequence of the economic crisis. Was it not, I said privately to various senators, the shadow cast by the crisis'. As for the French declaration of faith in the gold standard at the London conference, Daladier merely took the advice of 'M. Rist whose competence was universally acknowledged' and who advised gradually continuing the work of restoring budgetary stability – since the state of the economy had not deteriorated in recent months – while at the same time watching the development of the pound and the dollar.[146] Of course, memoirs are no more disinterested if unpublished than if published, and there is little evidence that these 'doubts' really existed (or that Daladier was not reading his 1935 self into 1933). But on the other hand, being untranslated into action, these misgivings do not show Daladier attempting to portray himself in a particularly favourable light, and the picture which emerges is very plausible: a man who had been saying that he was of the 'left' long enough to believe it, but who, being on his own admission ignorant of economic matters, had no alternative policy with which to confront his advisers. Daladier, then – a much better candidate than Herriot for the Young Radical theory of someone who had been captured by conservative financial experts – having no other particular idea of what to do or, if he had one, being too frightened to do it, did what he was told – and waited.

### The end of the cartel

But it was not possible to wait for ever. On both the right and the left action was expected, and soon it would be necessary to choose what this action should be. During the summer of 1933 the two conditions which had created the political respite responsible for the survival of the Daladier government, were brought to an end: first, the Socialists held a congress to resolve the issue of whether or not to continue supporting a government of whose economic policy they disapproved; and, secondly, the failure of the London Economic Conference gave urgency to demands for an immediate end to the budget deficit.

The Socialist congress of July 1933 was the culmination of a series of conflicts between the Socialist Party as a whole and the parliamentary Group – a conflict reopened by the Group's acceptance of participation in Daladier's government. This had led the Conseil National to condemn the majority of the Group and stipulate that it could not take such decisions in future without consulting it first; but the majority of the Group appealed over the head of the Conseil National to a special Party congress and, meanwhile, voted Article 83 of Daladier's first financial bill. The special Congress of Avignon, meeting at Easter 1933, passed a complicated motion which forbade the group to allow itself to become an integral part of the government majority, and, if its votes were needed to support the government, forbade it to approve any measures conflicting with the Socialist or *à la rigueur* the theoretical Radical programme.[147] Although this motion allowed the Group some latitude, it was a severe condemnation of the past attitude of its majority which decided regardless to vote the second reading of the budget and, in spite of a further warning by the C.A.P., persisted in this attitude until the budget was passed.[148] Although there were certain institutional reasons for this disagreement between the Group and the Party,[149] underlying the conflict was the recurrent problem of a party 'which wants to destroy the capitalist system but at the same time lives within that system'[150] – a problem now exacerbated by the effects of the slump, which heightened the immediate responsibilities incurred by living 'within the system' and yet also seemed to increase the prospects of its imminent destruction.

The contrast between the enthusiasm of the Congress of May 1932 and this Congress meeting just over a year later, could hardly have been greater: delegates expressed acute disillusion with the 'utter failure of the Radical governments';[151] there were complaints about the allegedly low quality of *Le Populaire* (except if one was interested in the Comtesse de Noailles!),[152] and, finally, there was the spectre of 'fascism' which had since January 1933 become a problem which could not be ignored.[153] But the July Congress was not a conflict between those responsibly aware of the dangers of fascism and therefore advocating a cautious parliamentary attitude and those too short-sighted to see the possible dangers of causing parliamentary chaos: the majority of the Group did not have a monopoly of anti-fascist awareness. Everyone was conscious of the possibility of 'a fascist adventure',[154] but the question at issue was how most effectively to combat it: as Auriol put it, fascism could certainly arise from 'the transience of ministries, the over-rapid succession of cabinets', resulting from intransigent Socialist opposition, but also from popular disillusion resulting from Socialist complicity, in which case 'we will go down with the others'.[155] On the related question of how to combat the slump, the divergences were – except for rather atypical speeches by Marquet, Montagnon and Déat[156] – tactical rather than doctrinal. Whether they attacked or supported the attitude of the Group, most Socialists in mid-1933 shared broadly similar views about economic policy; the dispute revolved about the political application of that policy.

At one level the debate was merely about whether or not the Group had, in voting the budget, remained faithful to the line defined at Avignon. But it soon widened into an examination of the activity of the Party since May 1932 in fighting the crisis, and increasingly called into question the equivocal tactical line laid down at Avignon – whether, as in the cases of Déat and Renaudel, to demand closer collaboration with the government or, as in those of Faure and Lebas, to demand total opposition. Déat tried to show that the policy of 'continuous pressure' had achieved results: defence expenditure had been reduced by 2m; a minimum wheat price had been introduced.[157] But this achievement seemed paltry even to those like Moch who defended the centrist compromise motion: the Socialists, he said, had not obtained the long-promised bill of *outillage national*, and such tiny reforms as had been implemented could easily have been obtained if the Party had been outside the majority.[158] The advocates of renewed parliamentary opposition accused the Group of appearing before the Socialist electorate with 'empty hands'; but it was not obvious in what sense their strategy was one of 'full hands' – unless of course it was argued that the revolution was near. Perhaps it was: capitalism, said Lebas, was undergoing its most severe crisis ever; rather than offer minor social reforms it was necessary for Socialists to proclaim that 'the rot is so deep, so widely spread, that the only remedy consists in a great social revolution'.[159] But Faure, who took the same view, warned that 'we have never said that we would make the Revolution during the Daladier parliament'.[160]

The Congress ended in a predictable defeat for the defenders of the Group.[161] In the immediate term this Congress solved nothing: the Group was condemned and it was made clear that any repetition of the indiscipline would meet with sanctions. But no new directives for action were given and the policy of Avignon remained the official line – although without much enthusiasm. Only Blum (and Auriol) had supported it with any conviction, rejecting the antithesis of total collaboration or total opposition; but on the whole the Congress had been a *dialogue de sourds* between, as one exchange put it very pithily, 'reformists without reforms' and 'revolutionaries without revolution'. The implications of the Congress for Daladier were also unclear: Renaudel, knowing that he would have a majority against him, threatened that the Party would soon be forced to expel certain members.[162] But the question was, how many: if the majority of the Group remained faithful to its earlier policy, then Daladier could be assured of continued support from a large number of Socialist deputies.[163] But it was probable that a lot of them would not go so far: Marius Moutet, a supporter of the actions of the Group, appealed to Renaudel not to make an issue over whether or not the Congress eventually condemned it with 'blame' or 'regrets'.[164] Just how many rebels there might be would depend partly on Daladier, on whether he could offer enough to attract a substantial number of deputies into rebellion.

If, then, one of the consequences of the Socialist Congress was to put pressure on Daladier to formulate an economic policy likely to attract the parliamentary Socialists, other forces were operating to push him into the opposite direction. In the first place, in conservative circles, the Daladier budget with its deficit of about 3.5m F. was not acceptable.[165] The Alliance Démocratique, the Fédération Républicaine and the small progressive Catholic Parti Démocrate Populaire[166] all called for more budget cuts, for the Radicals to choose between the Socialists and the *modérés*. This was of course the most effective way of driving a wedge between the Radicals and the Socialists. But it is also the case that many conservative deputies in particular could not ignore the campaign of the Taxpayers Federation and the Comité de Salut Economique. Although owing partly to internal disputes and partly to a calmer political situation – the budget had now been voted – their campaigns had lost some momentum, they remained vociferous: the Comité assembled some 30,000 people at a meeting in Paris in May. Reynaud's papers contain notes of a visit from Nicolle in June as well as hundreds of copies of the Comité's tracts sent in by his constituents.[167] It was no coincidence therefore that a few weeks later he publicly called on the government to eliminate the remaining deficit immediately.

There was a second reason for the intensified pressure on Daladier to grasp the nettle of the budget: the collapse of the London World Economic Conference on 3 July and the refusal of the British government to subscribe to a declaration calling for the stabilization of currencies. In the spring Boris had written to a correspondent in England that there was 'a growing feeling here against the orthodox theories of the Bank of France and the high officials of the Treasury. Several ministers, among the most important, are in favour of anti-deflationism'.[168] But after July the atmosphere had completely changed. The immediate results of the conference and the psychological effects of the declaration of fidelity to the gold standard by France and other countries, were very favourable to France: Baumgartner of the *Mouvement général des fonds* estimated that foreign funds had taken up some 2m F. of Treasury Bills between June and August; but he warned that this influx of money was highly precarious: once the pound and dollar were stabilized this hot money would, if French finances had not in the meantime been restored, be liable to leave France, followed perhaps by a flight of French capital as well. And he warned Bonnet in ever more insistent tones that for this reason the balancing of the budget must not be delayed.[169]

The theme was taken up by the conservative press. The collapse of the London conference implied, wrote Jenny, that for France 'the financial problem is again going to move to the forefront of our preoccupations'.[170] The right had never had great expectations of the conference anyway: *La Nation* – official organ of the Fédération Républicaine – saw a plot to extort from France part of her 80m F. of gold.[171] The respite to French finances was, then, a temporary one built on unstable foundations: France must take advantage of it to act at once and restore a definitively healthy financial situation. In the words of *La Nation*: 'the salvation of our currency lies not in London but Paris'.[172]

A hardening of the tone of opinion in favour of financial orthodoxy can also be detected at the Radical Congress of October 1933. The Congress was a better-managed affair than the previous year: the financial debate was dominated by conservatives and effectiveness of the left-wing opposition was reduced by Bergery's departure from the Party.[173] That is not to say that the economic and financial debates revealed no opposition to the official line of continuing budgetary cuts: of the 16 speeches in the economic debate, nine were extremely hostile to this policy and two (Mendès France and Clerc) were fairly critical. De Jouvenel launched a blistering attack on deflation;[174] other delegates proposed that the government implement a programme of public spending, act against tax fraud, institute administrative reform and control the power of monopolies.[175] But these dissenting voices were not very representative: more than half of them came from the Paris region and their speeches met with a stormy reception: when one delegate announced that he was a *fonctionnaire*, there was uproar and heckling.[176]

The official speeches of Caillaux, Régnier and Potut, which were all very well received, restricted themselves to the financial problem. Potut condemned the Socialist arguments against deflation which would, he said, have been valid if the state had been able to create demand: 'but the State budget has a significantly more limited role . . . it does not create purchasing power, it is limited to distributing the existing purchasing power'. The enemy was inflation and the pernicious ideas of Anglo-Saxon economists on the need to expand credit.[177] The Congress proceeded to pass a highly orthodox motion – demanding further economies and the re-establishment of the gold standard – and moved on to the political debate which resulted in a vote affirming, with supreme incoherence, continued support for a cartel majority. Whatever conclusions could be drawn from the Congress, one was certain: the economic policy it seemed to demand was diametrically opposed to that which was necessary even to retain the allegiance of all but the most participationist Socialists.

The revelation of the government's financial proposals had been postponed until after the Radical Congress. But their slow preparation had proceeded throughout the summer, and Lamoureux's account of this process supports the picture of Daladier as pusillanimous and hesitant: during the preparation of the budget he was 'suspicious, cunning . . . profoundly irresolute', changing his mood 'according to passing incidents and visits which he received'; the budget became 'a sort of veil of Penelope; . . . every morning Daladier undid what we had done together the day before'. But Lamoureux had an ally in Caillaux, who telephoned Daladier, from time to time, to threaten him into submission with the prospect of a defeat in the Senate.[178]

The proposals which resulted from these negotiations were nevertheless one of the few attempts of the period to present a combined programme of financial and economic recovery: largely this was a result of the attempt to conciliate the Socialists; partly also of the improved short-term financial situation which freed the government from too narrow a concentration on the state of the Treasury. After the success of the two bond issues of April and July, the available funds of the Treasury – short of any unexpected difficulty in renewing the 13.5m F. of Treasury Bills in circulation[179] – were sufficient to cover expenditure until the end of the year. The Treasury was faced in 1934 with the prospect of total expenditure of 20m F. – of which some 8m F. consisted of the redemption of the outstanding balance of the 1924 'Clementel' ten-year bond issue. But, providing that there was no budgetary deficit to add to these calls on the Treasury, Bonnet was optimistic about covering this expenditure and also envisaged the consolidation of 5m F. of Treasury Bills, believing that the existing ceiling of 15m F. represented more than the money markets could absorb.[180] The deficit for 1934 was estimated at 6m F. even after projected expenditure for the budget of 1934 had been kept at the levels of 1933, although taking account of expenditure inevitably incurred by the progressive implementation of social legislation voted in the early 1930s it should have risen by 3m.

The government proposed to eliminate the deficit in two stages – by 5.4m F. in a special financial recovery bill and by another 600mi F. in the budget itself – but it was categorical that the policy of balancing the budget was separate from attempts to revive the economy: the financial bill was therefore to be linked to an economic programme in order to avoid the dangers of 'narrow accounting measure . . . which risks bleeding the patient to death'.[181] The centre piece of this economic programme was a spending programme of 13.5m F. to be spread over four years, and explicitly intended to stimulate the domestic market.[182] The vote on this programme would follow the passing of financial measures, if only because without them it would not be possible to raise the necessary funds: such a programme in February would, said Bonnet, have meant inflation.[183] And it was these financial measures which were to prove the sticking point on the left: their most important feature was a six per cent levy, rising progressively, on most payments made by the state to individuals (*fonctionnaires*, war veterans and so on) – to provide 1.3m F. of the necessary 6m F. – and on all other incomes which had not fallen by more than ten per cent since 1930.[184] Even if it was true, then, that 'this plan is not one of massive deflation . . . that it restricts itself to intensifying the economies already made',[185] for the Socialists that was sin enough. And the pattern of the previous winter resumed again – with a rapid decline in the government's authority.

Daladier's measures had contained enough concessions to the Socialists to exclude any support from the right or centre, and he appealed firmly to the left; but, although he was prepared slightly to modify the proposed reductions in the salaries of *fonctionnaires*, even this was insufficient for Blum who would go no further down the path of concessions.[186] The debate ended in bitter acrimony between Blum and Daladier, Daladier at the last moment attempting to rally the right against Blum.[187] The spirit of 8 May seemed far away. Daladier was defeated by the combined votes of the right, centre–right (including Flandin's Républicains de Gauche) and Socialists: in the end only 28 Socialists, led by Renaudel, defied the Party to vote with the government.

Although Bonnet had been sanguine about the financial situation in the early autumn, in the last two months of 1933, after the fall of Daladier, politics were once more dominated by a financial crisis and a situation was once more created in which governments, lacking room for manoeuvre, had to fulfil the expectations their predecessors had aroused. On 17 November Bonnet's account of the state of the Treasury was less optimistic than in October: available funds (2.4m F.) remained sufficient until February 1934 providing that there was no problem in renewing Treasury Bills, but the number of Bills in circulation had fallen to 12.4m F. on 13 November.[188] At the end of November and December, 7m F. of Bills were due to come up for renewal, and if 5m F. of this was in the hands of the major French banks who would probably hold on to them without hesitation, the rest was held by foreigners and was feared to be at the mercy of the slightest lack of confidence in French finances.[189] Faced with this prospect, the Treasury announced the immediate issue of the 1.5m F. outstanding on the 10m F. bond issue authorized in March. This new issue was quickly taken up. But since the middle of October gold had started to trickle out of the Bank of France: in six weeks the Bank lost 6.5m F. of gold. Although this provided no immediate danger to the franc, it badly hit the money markets on which the government was so reliant: although some of the gold withdrawals were made in exchange for hoarded notes, purchases of gold and foreign exchange also resulted in withdrawals of bank deposits; and the banks were forced, in order to preserve liquidity, to offload some government paper. A further 1.4m F. Treasury Bills were traded in during October. The Socialists attempted to place the financial problem on the political terrain of the lack of co-operation from the Bank (and the banks): they proposed that the banks be obliged to hold one-tenth of their deposits in short-term government paper.[190] But for most other observers the moral was different: an immediate vote of financial measures was essential to restore confidence.

Daladier was replaced by Albert Sarraut who formed a government which, although containing two Républicains de Gauche, was not admitted to be based on a new majority; indeed, it was unclear what majority it would receive. His financial proposals aimed to eliminate the deficit in two stages, of which the first was to procure 3m F., mostly by a series of administrative cuts.[191] Although the bill demanded less from the *fonctionnaires* than Daladier had done, even those, such as Renaudel, who had voted for Daladier, attacked it because Sarraut's government was vague about any commitment to a programme of public spending.[192] The bill was, therefore, completely transformed by the Commission,[193] largely through the influence of some Radicals and the dissident Socialists. Sarraut accepted most of these modifications and although he in fact obtained a Concentration majority against an amendment of Denais's (Fédération Républicaine) which rejected totally the new article concerning the *fonctionnaires*, in going only half-way to meet an amendment by the dissident Socialist Gounin, which exempted *fonctionnaires* earning below 12,000 F. (the government and the Commission's figure was 10,000 F.), he managed in the end to lose both the votes of the dissident Socialists (in the eyes of whom he was being unnecessarily intransigent) and half the Républicains de Gauche (in the eyes of whom the government's last-minute bargaining had made it ridiculous). And he fell exactly one month after Daladier.

The Socialists had proposed a counter-plan as ambitious as that of January; but this was overwhelmingly rejected (a few Radicals, and the dissident Socialists, abstained) and had indeed been little more than a piece of theatre to allow *Le Populaire* to announce after the fall of Sarraut's government that 'we demand power'.[194] But power had never been farther away. The Chautemps government which followed Sarraut's managed to pass a bill which, in its final form, theoretically reduced the deficit by 4.5m F. On the issue of *fonctionnaires*' salaries the government accepted the amendment of Gounin, which Sarraut had refused: this involved a total saving of 275mi! The measure was supported by much of the right and centre–right (but Reynaud and much of the Centre Républicain continued to vote against), and of course the Radicals and dissident Socialists, now a separate group, known as Neo-Socialists, voted in favour. The Socialists, who would be, in Auriol's phrase, 'neither dupes [of a process of bringing the parliamentary system into disrepute], nor accomplices [of a cut in salaries]', left the Chamber.[195] In Blum's words: 'Concentration has been achieved . . . Daladier wanted it . . . Sarraut prepared it . . . Chautemps consummated it'.[196] The Senate Finance Commission was also sensitive to the dangers of a new ministerial crisis: Régnier proposed that the government bill be amended to hit all *fonctionnaires*; but the Commission, while accepting Régnier's amendment, agreed that Caillaux would not defend it in the Senate if the government made the issue a question of confidence,[197] thus making no more, as *Le Temps* put it, than a 'platonic' objection.[198]

The passing of the bill had solved very little: a cartel majority no longer seemed plausible but it was not clear if any alternative was more so. Although Flandin had continued his policy of wooing the Radicals for a Concentration majority,[199] Chautemps' bill had been passed by default – it seemed to be the last chance for the parliamentary system to prove it could function – not because the Radicals had clearly embraced the majority which their financial conservatism seemed to imply. On the composition of that majority, however, depended the future course of economic policy – an issue that became all the more pressing in the second half of 1933 as the economic situation again began to deteriorate, owing to the devaluation of the dollar in the spring. The index of industrial production (base 1928) fell from 91 in July to 87 in December; wholesale prices began to fall again at the same time, and the number of *chômeurs secourus*, which had resumed its rise in October, stood at 313,000 in December, a figure which, while not a record for the crisis, was higher than the corresponding figure for December 1932. The balance of trade remained, as during 1932, about 10m F. in deficit: whilst 1932 had seen a dramatic contraction of foreign trade – the value of imports falling by 29 per cent and exports by 35.5 per cent over 1931 – in 1933 it had remained largely stagnant, the value of imports falling by 4.6 per cent and exports by 6.5 per cent over 1932. In terms of volume however this represented an increase of 61 per cent over 1932: the price of exported manufactures had fallen by 20 per cent, but French costs had not fallen in proportion.[200] One solution to this problem was further deflation, the other was of course devaluation. And, although as yet devaluation had few public advocates,[201] it is not insignificant that in November 1933 Baumgartner should have written a note denouncing a tendency in 'certain circles' to see devaluation as a solution – a devaluation which he saw as 'bankruptcy' and liable to lead to the 'total ruin' of the country's finances and economy.[202]

The renewed fall in economic activity, although somewhat underestimated by contemporaries[203] and overshadowed in the autumn by the financial crisis, added to the prevailing gloom about the political impasse at the end of 1933. But this situation was spectacularly transformed by the Stavisky affair. Stavisky was a minor swindler who had been protected from prosecution by the complicity of various Radical deputies. This standard politico-financial scandal, fuelled by Stavisky's mysterious 'suicide' in January, was dramatized out of all proportions by a right-wing press which found in it an ideal means of discrediting the Radicals. Chautemps, having failed to take the affair sufficiently seriously, was forced into resignation. On 6 February 1934, the day on which the Daladier government which followed was to meet the Chamber, a mass demonstration of extra-parliamentary right-wing Leagues and ex-servicemen's organizations, stormed the barricades of the Pont de la Concorde: 15 people were killed. Whether this was as the right claimed, an unprovoked government aggression against patriots or as the left claimed, an attempted fascist coup, it resulted the next morning in the resignation of the second Daladier government. And ex-President Doumergue was brought out of rural retirement to restore order.

The formation of a new majority less than two years after a left-wing one had been elected had not yet acquired the familiarity of tradition; but nor did it cause great surprise. What did cause surprise – and made 6 February so traumatic an event – was that this should occur in the worst Paris street violence since 1871.[204] On 8 February 1934 Doumergue formed a government of Union Nationale from Marin to Herriot (and indeed Marquet). The conservatives now had power: all that remained was to see how they would use it.

# 5 ❧ Varieties of deflation 1934–1936

Notre devoir était de maintenir le crédit de l'Etat par une gestion économique et financière qui nous valait la confiance des épargnants dans la monnaie.

(Louis Germain-Martin, *Le Problème de la dévaluation du franc en 1934*)

After 6 February 1934, discussion of economic policy, as opposed to a narrow concentration on government finances, occupied a more central position than during the previous two years. There were three reasons for this. First, it was generally agreed, especially on the left, that the underlying cause of the violence lay in the economic crisis.[1] Secondly, in solving the political problem of the previous 18 months, the events of February freed space for the discussion of economic policy. There could be no question among the Socialists about their attitude to Doumergue's government, and so it was now possible to discuss policy rather than, as in 1932 and 1933, merely political tactics.[2] On the right the financial issue had been largely presented as a problem of political bad faith, as a consequence of the Radical Party's failure to accept its responsibilities. But once the right was again in power and the government had been granted the authority to issue decree laws, the political aspect of the budgetary question was largely resolved, and attention was directed towards the economy. For the Radicals, however, tactical political questions continued for a while to dominate.[3] This was not only a sign of the congenitally 'political' nature of the Radical sensibility, it also reflected the fact that for the Radicals 6 February had solved nothing. Certainly Herriot and colleagues were now in the government; but this 'capitulation' only increased the opposition of the Young Radicals: 28 Radicals abstained on the vote of the Ministerial Declaration and 13 voted against (24 abstained) the grant of decree powers. And even for its Radical supporters Doumergue's government was not a definitive solution but only a 'government of truce'.

Thirdly, the events of 6 February coincided with – indeed accelerated – the gold exports which had begun at the end of 1933: the Bank of France lost 2.6m F. of gold in the first two weeks of February. This underlined the fact that France's strong monetary position was due to very special circumstances and did not reflect an underlying healthy economy; to ensure the continued strength of the franc it was urgently necessary to reduce the trade deficit.[4] The threat to the franc was of course not immediate, and Daladier's later claim that he had resigned because to have continued in power he would have been forced to impose an embargo on gold exports[5] was a retrospective attempt to give respectability to his weakness, and is not mentioned as a factor by other participants.[6] It is wrong however to see 6 February as a total break. The existence of a budgetary deficit remained a hypnotizing issue and continued often to be discussed in moral terms independently of the economic situation: it needed, said Doumergue, another victory of the Marne to reassert France's economic strength.[7] The analogy was more apt than intended: the Marne marked the beginning of four years unremitting warfare.

### Doumergue's deflation: continuity or change?

On leaving a Cabinet meeting on 24 February 1934, Doumergue's Finance Minister, Germain-Martin, who had lost none of his orthodoxy since serving under Herriot in 1932,[8] remarked to the latter that 'we have returned to the bad old days of 1925. Yesterday morning I had a million in the Treasury and I needed 300 millions for the evening'.[9] Whatever the ultimate consequences of 6 February for the discussion of economic policy, the government's immediate problem was once again the 'rock of Sisyphus'[10] of an almost empty Treasury: at the end of 1933 Bonnet had been granted the authorization to issue 10m F. of bonds, partly to enable the government to consolidate part of the floating debt on which the ceiling was to be progressively reduced to 10m F. by September 1934;[11] in January he had issued 4.1m F. but by 10 February the Treasury had only 102mi F. left (with another 300mi F. of the January loan to be collected).[12] The expenditure of the Treasury, estimated at 2m F. for February, had been put under exceptional strain owing both to a continued shortfall in tax revenues, and to the impossibility of renewing Treasury Bills – of which 1.2m were traded in during January – a result partly of the political crisis but also of a tightening of the money market caused by the resumed gold exports.[13] Germain-Martin produced a chart for the Chamber Finance Commission indicating a close correlation between the gold losses and the level of Bills in circulation:[14] these stood at almost 10.5m F. at the end of 1933 but had fallen to 8.3m F. by the middle of March 1934.

At the beginning of March, Germain-Martin summoned the representatives of the three largest banks to the Rue de Rivoli and appealed to them to take exceptionally an extra 1.5m F. Treasury Bills. But given that their deposits had fallen considerably since the beginning of the year and that they had nonetheless kept their holdings of Bills constant, they were reluctant to help any further without assurances about rediscount from the Bank of France. As in 1933 the Bank would make no firm commitments, and in these circumstances the three banks would agree only to accept a certain unspecified number of extra Bills: on 13 March they took an extra 200mi F., only the Société Générale making use of the rediscount facility. Germain-Martin, whose bitterness against the banks emerges from his memoirs, was saved by the intervention of his friend André Mayer of Lazards who negotiated a loan for the Treasury on the Dutch market through Fritz Mannheimer of the Mendelssohn bank of Amsterdam.[15] This was sufficient to tide the government over until the vote of a financial bill would permit an appeal to the capital markets.

This, then, was Germain-Martin's inheritance: at one point he had feared that the Treasury would have to suspend payments.[16] The first priority of the government was to restore confidence by voting the budget of 1934 – which parliament had not even started to discuss – as quickly as possible. Lamoureux's original expenditure estimates had been further reduced by the succeeding three ministries, and the remaining deficit supposedly eliminated by the financial measures introduced by Chautemps' government. It was clear that in reality this budget would be in deficit; the government, in order to act quickly, preferred to accept it as it stood, demanding at the same time powers to implement any additional savings by decree law. The budget was quickly passed and the government, armed with these new powers, was freer than any government since 1932 – indeed 1926 – to pursue the policy of its own choosing.

The aim of this policy was to be – and in this it differed from that of its predecessors – a general deflation affecting prices as well as government expenditure. As Germain-Martin wrote: 'the worries which financial difficulties have caused our leaders distracted their attention from the grave problem of the disparity between domestic and foreign prices'; now it was clear that 'deflation is first necessary for the State, but also for private business if we want to return to price elasticity'.[17] This deflation was to consist in acting upon the two factors which kept up French costs: high interest rates and high taxation. The former would be reduced by the disappearance of the deficit and the latter by economies and tax reform.[18]

The first stage of this policy comprised the economy decrees issued in April 1934: the first batch implemented economies of 2.7m F. – of which 360mi F. consisted of a reduction of between 5 per cent and 10 per cent on the salaries of *fonctionnaires* – and the second saved another 1m F. by imposing a 3 per cent reduction on the pensions of the war veterans who had so far managed to secure exception from any economy measures. But although the immediate purpose of these measures was to eliminate a deficit estimated at 6m F. they were set in the context of the wider policy of contributing to a reduction in prices and wages.[19] The decrees were followed up by a tax reform bill which was presented by the government as the 'logical economic counterpart of its policy of budgetary deflation': reductions in direct taxation, totalling about 2.1m F., were intended both to encourage new investment and reduce industrial costs, although a corresponding increase in indirect taxation hardly assisted the policy of price reduction.[20]

These measures were at first greeted favourably by most of the right: this was a government which seemed prepared to take unpopular measures – washed down by the saccharine of Doumergue's radio homilies – in order to balance the budget, something which all conservatives had demanded, and had announced its intention of pursuing a programme of general deflation – something which an increasing number were coming to see as the only alternative to a devaluation. There were reservations: Blaisot of the Fédération Républicaine, for example, found that the government had not gone far enough in the direction of 'brutal economies'.[21] But it had at least 'embarked resolutely down the right path' and providing that these early measures were seen as merely a beginning to be supplemented by others they could command provisional assent.[22]

The key to the government's survival lay, however, in the attitude of the Radicals. For the Young Radicals, 6 February had at least had the saving grace of underlining the redundancy of the Radical policies – indeed de Jouvenel, like Bergery, had by now left the Party in disgust – and of indicating, as Kayser wrote, the necessity to 'define clearly our programme of reforms, to revise completely our forms of action'.[23] To this end they drew up a 'plan of reform of the economy and the State'.[24] The Plan pronounced the crisis to be a consequence of an 'outmoded economic regime' in which competition no longer acted as a regulator of the market and a few monopolies held consumers, and most small producers, in thrall; the solution was to 'institute the control of the collectivity' over banks and basic industries in order to guarantee the functioning of liberalism in the rest of the economy. But because these structural reforms would not have immediate consequences, various provisional measures were proposed: public works, a revision of leases and mortgages and so on. Although the leadership of the Party was unable to ignore demands for the convocation of a special Congress to purge those Radicals directly involved in the Stavisky Affair, it was able to prevent this Congress from having any further implications for party policy by taking as the basis of the economic debate not the Young Radicals' Plan but an alternative plan drawn up by Emile Roche.[25]

Roche's proposals eschewed attempts to construct 'a sort of ideal city', and, without offering any diagnosis of the crisis, set out concrete and limited reforms to alleviate unemployment, control prices, extend credit facilities and reduce agricultural costs; and they also declared support for budgetary and price deflation. The innocuous mixture was washed down by obligatory references to the *économie dirigée*. Roche's timid 'Plan' provoked little enthusiasm at the Congress,[26] but was nevertheless accepted in preference to support for the Young Radicals.[27]

What, then, can be concluded about the evolution of Radical economic policy? First, the economic debate was of only secondary importance. Real interest was focused on the political debate which followed, and which in spite of left-wing protests, ratified Radical participation in the government. The corollary of this participation was acceptance of government economic policy. Participation was accepted because there was no alternative. Short of accepting an undiluted right-wing government there were, Herriot argued, three possibilities: dissolution – which no one wanted; a Cartel government – which experience had shown to be unworkable; or participation.[28] Doumergue, then, was the only safeguard against 'the leap into the unknown'.[29] Any government of the left seemed further away than ever: the Young Radical Plan consisted of little more than an unhappy mixture of generalities, based largely on the precrisis ideas of de Jouvenel and a few piecemeal reforms hardly more adventurous than those proposed by Roche: it was the left-wing Radical rhetoric of 1929 dressed up in a sauce of 1934 and could hardly serve as a prescription for future action or as a basis for alliance with the Socialists.

But the ratification of government policy did not mean that there was much enthusiasm for it: certainly, the decrees did not provoke in the Party the protests which they raised among the Socialists; and, although one of the most powerful onslaughts on the tax bill came from Mendès France, only 22 Radicals voted against it. Even so doubts were expressed by Clerc, Jacquier and others about the implications of carrying out thorough deflation: did the weak state of the French economy, asked Clerc, make further deflation possible without measures of unacceptable brutality?[30] But until there was an alternative there was little to do but sit out the experiment. This was the great problem for the Radicals: if the truce was to be broken and deflation abandoned, it would be 'to put what in its place, to carry out what policy?'[31] Even Daladier, who had no reason to support the government which had supplanted him, as yet dared only express minor reservations: he called for loyalty to the 'truce' as the only practicable government. On economic policy he was agnostic: 'an experiment is being undertaken . . . we must not cut the ground from under the government's feet, as was done to us'.[32] This could be treated as a statement of reserved acquiescence, even scepticism; it was hardly a rallying call for alternative action.

Outright opposition to deflation was therefore restricted to the Communists and Socialists. The arrival of Doumergue's government allowed the Socialists to oppose deflation without any of the constraints which had existed since May 1932.[33] Vigorous but distinct campaigns were waged against the decrees by the Communists, and the Socialists in semi-collaboration with the C.G.T.: *Le Populaire* for several days headed its economic page 'Against the decrees' and published articles against the decrees by trade union leaders; meetings of protests and one-hour strikes were called by various public service unions. On 12 February the left had successfully mounted a general strike and demonstrations to protest against the fall of Daladier. These had been an undoubted success but they were an essentially *republican* protest.[34]

The action against the deflation decrees in April seems to have been considerably less successful, according to the weekly reports of the Prefects: in Paris the call by the public services union for a one-hour strike at the post office and for meetings of protest by other *fonctionnaires* on 16 April was observed only very sporadically; in the Seine-Inférieure only 12 per cent of *fonctionnaires* obeyed these instructions, and the demonstrations were an 'undeniable failure'; the Prefect of the Haut-Rhin wrote that the *fonctionnaires* 'seem generally to realize how unfavourably the public views their demands'.[35] The traditional May Day action, to which the Communists especially had given particular importance as a day of protest against the decrees,[36] was even less successful.[37] Nor do such reports seem to have been wishful thinking: the same impression emerges both from *Le Populaire* which felt obliged to explain away events, and from the self-criticism of the *Cahiers du bolchévisme*.[38]

There were good reasons to explain why the decrees should have been so easily imposed: effective action was hindered by disputes between the C.G.T. and the Communist C.G.T.U. and between the S.F.I.O. and the P.C.F.; government propaganda pointing out that the cost of living had fallen more than the salary cuts may have had some effect, if only in causing the *fonctionnaires* to doubt whether they would receive popular support; individual public servants may have been afraid to strike against a government likely to take action against them.[39] Thus the relative ease with which the decrees were swallowed does not of course imply that, among the *fonctionnaires* at least, they were popular, only that, given the disorganization of the left, deflation had not reached the limits of political and social tolerance. It also suggests that unified action by the left against the government would result more easily from the reflexes of republican solidarity than from an opposition to an economic policy which affected the population in different ways. History and tradition were more effective ralliers than economic self-interest, *liberté* a more powerful symbol than '*pain*'. The Communists, especially, tried to demonstrate that the two were linked: 'the anti-fascist struggle' wrote Duclos, 'is also the action of the masses against the decree-laws, expression of the fascisation of the regime'.[40] But in spite of such warnings it is hard to disagree with the relieved complacency of Herriot that in the end the decrees had 'provoked fewer incidents than we feared'.[41]

Deflation may however have been all that more easily accepted because it was not carried out with the full thoroughness of the government's intentions. This is noticeable in government policy towards agricultural prices; towards government expenditure; and towards public works.

The effectiveness of the minimum wheat price had been undermined by a harvest even larger in 1933 – 92 quintals – than the already substantial one of 1932. The price of wheat, therefore, continued to fall: the unofficial price varied regionally but was estimated by the government to be on average 80–5 F. This did not mean that the law had been a total failure: French agricultural prices remained above world levels and thus even those, like the Senate's Agricultural Commission, keen for a return to a free market, agreed that the abolition of the regulatory legislation would lead to a 'catastrophic collapse in prices'.[42] The government therefore introduced first, a bill designed to improve the working of the minimum price legislation, and secondly, in July, a law carrying it over for another year.[43] As Germain-Martin pointed out, the need to keep up agricultural prices was one of the most important factors working against deflation particularly since whatever the real price at which grain was being sold, the price of bread was fixed according to the official grain price.[44]

But this was a highly sensitive area: the Radical Congress had made its acceptance of deflation conditional on an exemption of agricultural prices and in so doing the Radical delegates were only responding to the same pressures which the government heard directly through the report of its Prefects. While the Prefects had reported a muted reaction to the decrees, they were less sanguine about the situation in the countryside. From all over the country there were reports of the increasing militancy of the peasantry: 'their state of mind makes one fear a grave danger for the country' commented one Prefect, 'the discontent of the peasantry grows and grows'; another noted that the peasants of his *département* were secretly buying *L'Humanité*; from Brittany came reports about the growing influence of the peasant demagogue leader Dorgerès.[45] No government could afford to ignore such warnings.

On government spending also it proved necessary to compromise. Already in January, Bonnet had written to Chautemps to complain that the spending plans of the war ministries threatened the government's budgetary policies.[46] But it was not until June that the government demanded authorization to raise an extra 3.1m for military expenditure over the next three years. Although the actual expenditure involved for 1934 itself was insignificant – indeed 1934 saw the low point of French military expenditure – this was a harbinger for the future.[47] And the left was able to reap considerable propaganda advantages from this breach in the deflation policy.[48]

All governments since 1932 had promised to offset the depressive effects of deflation by instituting a public works programme; ironically Doumergue's avowedly deflationist administration was to be the only government successfully to do so. Although Germain-Martin had replied to criticisms that the cuts in the budget of 1934 were so severe as to endanger even the continuance of building projects already started by promising to embark on an extra-budgetary spending programme as soon as a healthy financial situation was restored,[49] if he had been left to his own devices nothing would have happened. The doctrine of the finance ministry officials on this issue was clearly set out in a note by Boisanger of the *Mouvement général des fonds*: 'my department has always been energetically opposed to the adoption of plans of *outillage national*'; they were merely a new version of old extra-ordinary budgets and 'contrary to the present policy of adjusting expenditure to the available resources'.[50] That any action was taken was partly due to parliamentary pressure, but even more to Marquet's presence in the Cabinet as Minister of Labour: already involved twice in well-publicized disputes with Germain-Martin over the public expenditure cuts,[51] Marquet was very much a hostage in the government, under pressure from his own party to prove the validity of the Neo-Socialist attitude to participation in government. But he also embodied the government's only claim to be more widely based than a traditional Union Nationale: the possibility of his resignation[52] was therefore sufficient to cow the recalcitrant members of the Cabinet into submission; and a programme of public works was presented to the Chamber in July.

The so-called Marquet Plan was formulated in two stages. A decree law of 15 May blocked 75 per cent of the resources of the Assurances Sociales until 1940 in a fund (*Fonds Commun*) – estimated at about 9m F. to 10m F. – to be managed by the Caisse des Dépôts and put at the disposal of communes, departments and various other bodies; a second decree set up a public works committee to work out a programme of expenditure in which the criterion of priority was to be the local density of unemployment. The bill which Marquet presented in July stipulated that the state was to participate in this programme by earmarking 2.9m F. from the *Fonds Commun* and using it to subsidize expenditure undertaken by local authorities; this sum was not to be paid in one block: rather the state would, by means of annuities, service that proportion of loans made by local authorities which corresponded to its own contribution of 2.9m F. Thus the government, in effect borrowing from the *Fonds* through the intermediary of the local authorities, would contribute to the programme without needing to increase its expenditure in the short term.[53] Marquet stressed that the plan must not be judged as the programme of *outillage national* promised by Germain-Martin but merely as a limited attempt to provide works in areas most hit by unemployment, and to create the 'mystique of a struggle against unemployment'.[54] On the left comparisons were drawn with Daladier's abortive spending programme of October 1933 which made Marquet's 9m F. expenditure over five or six years – of which only 2.9m F. by the state – seem even more insignificant. And Daladier's plan had been conceived before the budget cuts carried out at the beginning of 1934.

The public works committee started its deliberations during the summer and the finance ministry was successfully able to impose its views that only profitable expenditure should be undertaken.[55] By the end of the year, works amounting to 1.8m F. had been approved and the first *chantier* opened in early October. By February 1935, 22,000 workers were being directly employed as a result of the plan, and a maximum of 61,800 by the autumn of 1935:[56] but, given a total of almost 490,000 *chômeurs secourus* – and a real total of about 1 million – in February 1935, this was a fairly modest achievement.

The irony is, however, that under Doumergue's administration anything was done at all: it illustrates again that whatever the moral authority it enjoyed as a barrage against political violence, and whatever political power it wielded through the decree powers, it was no less susceptible than preceding Radical governments to political pressure to mitigate the effects of deflation. The main difference between Doumergue and his predecessors was that whereas they cut budget expenditure and denied that this was deflation because it was politic to do so, he cut expenditure and called it deflation because it was politic to do so. But, except that the decree powers made it possible for the economies to be distributed differently than before, the content of policy was barely different.

### Deflation by constitutional reform

The results of the policy were hardly different either. Charles Rist's introduction to the *Revue d'économie politique*'s survey of the French economy in 1934 was more unreservedly pessimistic than in any of the previous four years. The index of industrial output had fallen steadily: it stood at 87 in January and 78 in December; this represented an average of 82 for the whole year, a drop of eight per cent on the average for 1933. The number of *chômeurs secourus* had risen from almost 233,000 in October 1933 to 344,000 a year later. The trade deficit for 1934 had fallen to 5.2m F.: but far from representing any increase in exports – which indeed declined by 35 per cent over 1933 – this was due to a fall of 19 per cent in imports of industrial raw materials and food, an indication of the depressed state of activity in France; and the fall in the value of the exports of manufactures concealed an increase of 13.5 per cent in their volume, an increase caused partly by price reductions which, since they were not covered by equivalent reductions in costs, increased the squeeze on profits.[57]

The government's defence rested, therefore, on the improved financial situation. By September it had been possible to repay the Dutch loan and issue two long-term loans which raised sufficient funds to cover the maturing of the 1924 Clementel bonds in October and to reduce the level of Treasury Bills in circulation to 10m F. – in accordance with the law fixing the ceiling on them at 10m F. by September – still leaving the Treasury, according to Germain-Martin, with a 'considerable margin of safety'.[58] But even this financial success was precarious: given the level of forthcoming expenditure – includ-

ing the new military spending and also the likely budget deficit for 1934 –
Jacquier, the new *Rapporteur* of the budget, predicted that the government
might soon be forced again to raise the ceiling on the issue of Treasury Bills.[59]
Once more all came back to the budget deficit: owing largely to a continued
shortfall on tax revenues it was clear that in spite of the decrees there would
be a deficit in 1934. Expenditure planned for the budget of 1935, when the
decrees would apply for a whole year, was to be kept at the level of 1934
(47m F.) which, given that previously voted social legislation would have
automatically increased expenditure by 1m F., imposed a further tightening
of expenditure. But no more sacrifices were demanded from individuals: 'we
have, we believe, taken this budget deflation to its extreme limits'.[60] Although
the planned budget of 1935 was intended to be notionally in surplus,
Germain-Martin admitted that it would not be certain of being balanced
without a slight increase in economic activity, also claiming that the likelihood of such a recovery was not helped by the contradictions of a policy
which, although supposed to be deflationary, nevertheless supported agricultural prices for political reasons.[61]

But perhaps there was a way out of these contradictions: 'we expect',
announced the proposed budget for 1935, 'that future budgets will be
backed by an economic recovery, helped by a profound reform of the state'.[62]
In the autumn of 1934, constitutional reform came increasingly to be seen by
conservatives as a precondition of economic prosperity, and it is in this context that the constitutional reform proposals of 1934 must be discussed.[63]
Ideas of constitutional reform were hardly novel, but the theme had been
vigorously revived in 1933 by Tardieu, who published his proposals in
*L'Heure de la décision* in January 1934. Tardieu's reforms were designed to
strengthen the executive: they included enabling the executive to dissolve the
legislature without consulting the Senate; withdrawing from deputies the
right to initiate expenditure; refusing *fonctionnaires* the right to strike; and
allowing the premier to appeal to the country by means of referenda.[64] But
although the campaign for revision came to be associated primarily with
Tardieu, it was generally accepted in 1934 that all was not right with the
Republic's political system. The comparative ease with which the granting of
decree powers was accepted for only the second time in the history of the
Republic was itself tacit admission of the breakdown of parliamentary
government. The same admission was explicitly made when in March the
Chamber set up a Commission for Reform of the State: in the Commission's
vote on the crucial issue of dissolution without consultation of the Senate,
only three out of 40 present voted against.[65]

But when Doumergue presented his own constitutional proposals in the
autumn, his initiative was quite independent of that of the Chamber and
formed part of a specific campaign by conservative opinion and business
pressure groups. The conservative response to the first months of

Doumergue's government had been reserved. The economy decrees were approved, but only as a temporary expedient to precede a constitutional reform 'indispensable for a durable financial recovery'.[66] What was meant by constitutional reform varied, but it usually included part or all of the reforms. advocated by Tardieu, now a member of the government. At the same time as these ideas met with increasing favour in right-wing circles, the conservative press continued to develop its campaign of anti-parliamentarianism. The Finance Commission's legitimate attempt to examine seriously the tax reform bill was violently condemned: in the words of the *Journal des débats* 'the decadent parliamentary regime is setting the seal on its decline'.[67]

It was against this background that Doumergue announced his intention to institute constitutional reform. His original tentative proposals were eventually reduced to four in a half-hearted attempt to reach a compromise with the Radicals: the creation of an organized Présidence du Conseil; allowing the executive to dissolve the Chamber without the consultation of the Senate, providing one year had elapsed since an election; tighter definition of the status and rights of *fonctionnaires*; and a limitation of the right of deputies to initiate expenditure.[68] In the controversy over these proposals the deeper motivation of the revisionist campaign, already discernible earlier in the year, became clear. *Le Temps* wrote: 'The policy of reducing public expenditure must not . . . succumb to the attacks of demagogy . . . the reform of the state affects everything else'.[69] The same argument was put by Gignoux in *La Journée industrielle*, Romier in *Le Figaro*, Guérin in *La Nation*.[70]

However generally, then, the need for some kind of political reform might be accepted on the left, the idea became politically unacceptable once it had been explicitly taken up as a means of implementing a particular economic policy. The Communists made the link most clearly: 'the bourgeois is unable by traditional methods to persuade the workers and peasants to commit suicide in the name of its sacred financial doctrine'.[71] Blum's series of articles on the proposed reforms tended to present their importance more narrowly as an operation of 'personal power' backed by the threat of fascist riots: Doumergue was MacMahon.[72] But these articles, written before the Radical Congress in October, were designed primarily for a Radical audience, and Blum also insisted on the importance of the proposals relating to *fonctionnaires* as a step towards the suppression of trade union freedoms.[73]

But Doumergue had not, anyway, counted on support from the Socialists or Communists, and his announcement of reforms had been accompanied by vitriolic attacks on the unity pact formed between the two parties in July. The fate of the reforms depended on the attitude of the Radicals, and it was the resignation of Herriot and his colleagues over Doumergue's refusal substantially to modify his proposals which brought the government down. The Radicals were attacked by the right for the hypocrisy of attacking reforms which were no more far reaching than those to which members of the Party had in principle already agreed on the Commission for the Reform of the State.[74] According to Lamoureux, the Radicals' overthrow of Doumergue was the result of a plot by Herriot, who had developed a hatred of Doumergue.[75] Certainly Herriot was, as far as this was possible from within the Cabinet, one of the leaders of the Radical opposition to Doumergue's proposals. But the reasons for his opposition were more complex than Lamoureux allowed. He had never felt happy in the government – 'Union Nationale is a trap for Republicans of good faith'[76] – and an intemperate public attack on the Radicals by Tardieu in July came as a last straw; also, he may well have been genuinely worried by Doumergue's ambitions, his 'strange eulogy of MacMahon'.[77]

But more interesting than Herriot's personal attitude are the reasons why the Radical Party as a whole turned against Doumergue during the summer of 1934. To some extent Doumergue's success in restoring political order – which his presence alone had been sufficient to do – made him no longer indispensable.[78] And the Radicals, becoming braver, were concerned at the lack of any government legislation to control the activities of the extra-parliamentary Leagues whose strength seemed to be growing during the year. Tardieu's attack – a traumatic example of the perfidy of the right – was another cause of disaffection. And finally the Radical senators resented Doumergue's attempt to restrict their influence.[79] All these factors contributed to the erosion of Doumergue's position. But what is most striking about the Radical Congress of October 1934 is how relatively little attention was devoted to Doumergue's constitutional reforms, the pretext for his downfall: even in the debate on constitutional reform, two out of the eight speakers did not mention the issue at all and spoke instead of the deteriorating economic situation, of the inadequacy of the Marquet Plan;[80] and it is striking that Daladier, who used this congress to make his political *rentrée*, directed his attack on the government's economic record and paid little attention to constitutional reform.[81] By all accounts – that of the press, that of Herriot, that of Daladier himself – Daladier's speech was the greatest success of the Congress.[82] This view that the state of the economy was a more important source of Radical alienation from Doumergue than constitutional reform also emerges from the Radical press: *L'Oeuvre*, for instance, which had given Doumergue cautious support, now wanted to see 'the slightest business recovery, the slightest fall in unemployment'.[83]

But what should replace the government? What alternative economic policy should be pursued? Here the answers of the Radicals were less clear. The most striking feature of Daladier's sensational speech was its lack of any real content: it was a carefully prepared meditation on the errors of the past but contained little helpful about the future. He told the Congress: 'I have been to night school, I have reflected in silence. I have allowed all kinds of experiments to be tried out'. But what had he learnt? – that 'orthodoxy is

bankrupt', that it was necessary to stimulate demand by a programme of public spending, that 'the methods of 1926 . . . are powerless' during a depression,
that it was necessary to be open-minded about experiments taking place
abroad, such as the 'melting currency' of the village of Woergl in Austria.
Daladier invented, or revived, a slogan which was to have great success – 'the
200 families'; he earned the adulation of the Congress and the obloquy of the
right who pretended not to notice that he had specifically ruled out the
methods of Woergl for France;[84] and, finally, he earned a large postbag which
even included a letter from Irving Fisher.[85] The attraction of his attack on the
government lay precisely in its vagueness. But if Doumergue was to be
removed an alternative had to be found. From the left of the Party, Bayet
warned that it would be fatal for the Radicals to resume power without an
immediately applicable programme, but was noncommital as to what this
should be except that it must include an 'economic 1789';[86] Daladier at
Nantes had on the other hand proclaimed 'the Death of 1789'.[87]

   The political solution was in fact to come from a different wing of the
Party. In July Emile Roche had invented the notion of 'the third party' to be
based on a programme common to all parties from Flandin to Renaudel via
Herriot.[88] An enormous amount of ink was spilled over this idea which was,
in effect, Concentration under a new name; but its implication for policy was
clearly set out by Roche in a letter to his mentor Caillaux: 'to pursue deflation
in every area'.[89] At the end of August a meeting took place between Roche
and Baréty, of the Alliance Démocratique, representing Flandin; Herriot,
who had been gently courted by Flandin since February, gave his approval.[90]
As the government moved towards its death agony Flandin came out into the
open: in a speech at Arras he neatly disassociated himself from the government of which he was a member, and made himself available for an alliance
with the Radicals. This sealed the fate of Doumergue and made Roche's idea
a political possibility. On 10 November Flandin formed the next government.

   The Radicals, then, had turned against Doumergue partly because of the
failure of his government to bring about economic recovery; they opted for a
new government which seemed at the time as if it would continue the same
economic policy; and they took as a pretext for his downfall, constitutional
proposals which were partly designed to allow that economic policy to be
effectively applied.

### 'The Flandin experiment': the end of deflation?

No government between 1932 and 1936 more openly linked its fate to overcoming the economic crisis than did Flandin's.[91] The contrast with
Doumergue could hardly have been greater: Doumergue, the oldest premier
of the parliament, was brought back from retirement for the largely negative
role of restoring order, after which he became dispensable; Flandin, at 45 the

youngest premier and the first to occupy the Hotel Matignon, had a reputation as a specialist in economic matters,[92] as a man of energy and action and also of conciliation towards the Radicals. He immediately set up an 'interministerial economic committee' which met weekly,[93] and a second committee, under the chairmanship of Herriot, to examine solutions to unemployment;[94] and he asked Germain-Martin, who remained Finance Minister, to draw up an economic recovery plan.[95] In a series of speeches inside and outside parliament – later published together with a justificatory preface[96] – Flandin presented the actions of his government as a coherent programme of economic recovery. The expectations aroused were considerable – the failure all the more dramatic.

The origins of Flandin's economic policy – and of its contradictions – are to be found in the political constraints which affected its formulation. A cartoon by Sennep put the situation most succinctly: the extremely tall Flandin is pictured as a flamingo standing on his right leg and asking 'On the right or on the left'. Although the political composition of Flandin's Cabinet was in fact similar to that of Doumergue's it was greeted with enthusiasm by Radicals of the left and right, and with relief by the Socialists.[97] This relief was not only felt because Flandin's victory was Doumergue's defeat – a fact which Flandin emphasized in his Ministerial Declaration by postponing constitutional reform indefinitely – but also because he seemed to put the economic crisis at the centre of his preoccupations. For this reason left-wing Radicals such as Kayser and Cot were willing to give him the benefit of the doubt,[98] and no Radical voted against the Ministerial Declaration. But if the left welcomed Flandin as the replacement of Doumergue, it was precisely this which won him the distrust of the right: for de Kérillis he was the 'traitor of Arras'; Tardieu refused to serve in his Cabinet 'born of treason'.[99] And even when he was not personally attacked, his abandonment of constitutional reform was deplored.[100] The antagonism of the right could not be expressed openly in parliament; but the moment that Flandin ran up against any difficulties, it was clear that he was unlikely to receive much assistance from his natural political supporters. As one commentator put it, Flandin had the 'favourable consideration of the left and . . . the forced support of the right'.[101] His task in economic policy was to retain the latter while consolidating the former.

Flandin's economic policy was based on the assumption that deflation was 'almost completed': this applied both to reductions in public spending and to the fall in prices. Without unacceptable cuts in defence expenditure, it was 'an illusion to believe that expenditure could be much further reduced'.[102] From an arch deflationist of 1933 this was a considerable admission. But it did not imply a conversion to devaluation: the reduction in French prices was also over, because world gold prices were, it was claimed, rising to the level of French prices. While awaiting this imminent realignment of prices, it was necessary to prepare the conditions of economic revival within France itself.

This involved two elements. First, in conjunction with the Bank of France, the government would pursue a more liberal credit policy: by keeping out of the capital markets it would allow a fall in interest rates which, besides provoking 'the last possible deflation of French prices', would encourage new invest-ment. Secondly, Flandin proposed a progressive return to economic liberalism, an abandonment of attempts to control the economy: only by eliminating the distorting effects of government intervention in the economy would it be possible to adapt production to demand. But this return to liberalism could not happen overnight: it might be necessary to introduce 'the reign of counter intervention', to intervene in the economy in order defini-tively to remove the distortions caused by previous intervention so that the newly functioning free market should start from a solid foundation.[103]

It is easy to see the part that this proposal played in Flandin's attempts to resolve the political problem: the rhetoric of liberalism was a bone thrown to appease the right;[104] the abandonment of budgetary deflation was partly a corollary of the abandonment of constitutional reform, and, like it, endeared Flandin to the left;[105] from the abandonment of budgetary deflation stemmed the new credit policy, which, whatever else it may have been, was a way of tiding the Treasury over difficult months to come: since October 1934, Ministry of Finance officials had been predicting that it would be necessary again to raise the ceiling on Treasury Bills;[106] finally, the claim that the gap between French and world prices was narrowing fast did no harm, and had the beneficial political effect of giving comfort to those who were against devaluation. But it was precisely this claim – the assumption on which his policy was based – which doomed Flandin to failure. In the words of *The Economist*: 'to the outside observer it would seem that deflation had com-pleted its first stage of rendering production unprofitable at present costs but not in succeeding in reducing the cost of living and so enabling costs to be lowered'[107] – a point which was made forcefully by Reynaud.[108] Neither Flandin nor Germain-Martin attempted to provide any real evidence to support their argument for a middle way between devaluation and deflation, and even more astonishingly, apart from some isolated commentators,[109] no one questioned the flawed assumption of the policy.[110] But the truth was, according to Sauvy, that in February 1935 French prices were 22 per cent above English prices.[110] In short, Flandin's claim was in his own words, a 'speculation'.[112]

The budget enshrined the government's view that further budgetary deflation was impossible. It was the same budget that had been prepared by Germain-Martin under Doumergue: projected expenditure had only been kept at the level of 1934 by revising downwards the expenditure demands of most departments. But this still left a small planned deficit of 600mi F.,[113] which Germain-Martin admitted would be nearer 2m F. or 3m F. if economic recovery did not take place.[114] Although the budget was passed quickly there were strong reservations among conservatives about the government's claim that economies could be pushed no further.[115] For the moment Flandin had to be supported; but few conservatives would have disagreed with the political commentator of the *Revue politique et parlementaire* that 'the question of deflation . . . will come to the fore and through the force of circumstances'.[116] Until it should, Flandin, with the budget voted, was free to implement the two stages of his programme of economic recovery.

The centrepiece of Flandin's much vaunted liberalism was the abandonment of the minimum grain price and the return to a free market in grain. This was to apply within France only: there was no question of ending the protection of the French market from foreign grain. And because the market was still burdened with the large surpluses of 1933 and 1934, the government proposed to take in hand the 20 to 23 quintals of grain which it estimated that the market could not absorb: the total cost of this measure of 'counter-intervention', necessary to prevent price freedom leading to an immediate and catastrophic fall in prices, was estimated to be 1.5m F., to be covered by borrowing.[117] Whatever the government's long-term objective, the immediate aim of the bill was clear: to end the anomaly by which the price of bread was kept artificially high by a fictitious minimum price for wheat; this was the 'Christmas gift' that Flandin promised to the hungry unemployed.[118] But in fact it seems likely, as the Socialists claimed, that the government expected the price of grain to stabilize well below the old minimum price, thus in effect shifting more of the burden of deflation on to the agricultural population.[119] Although Flandin's bill met with little enthusiasm – especially from many conservative senators from rural areas – the failure of the minimum price legislation meant that there were few passionate defenders of the status quo.[120] The most accurate judgement on the new bill was that of the Socialists, who pointed out that it solved nothing: the future price of grain would depend on the weather; another large harvest would merely leave the government with large unsaleable stocks on its hands.[121]

The second component of Flandin's return to economic liberalism was a project of industrial reorganization to make industrial cartels enforceable by law. It was an act of considerable political legerdemain to present this piece of interventionism as a manifestation of economic liberalism: the government argument was that years of piecemeal intervention had distorted the free market, and, once again, preliminary counter-intervention was necessary to ensure 'the necessary adjustment between production and consumption . . . and prepare the return of liberty'.[122] The origin of the bill was a proposal by the C.G.P.F. for compulsory organization under government control of the badly hit silk industry.[123] But the government extended this idea to include any industry in which a large enough majority of producers demanded intervention. These cartels were only to be provisional: they were to lapse with the end of the crisis. And Marchandeau, Minister of Trade and Industry, was insistent that his bill represented the most liberal option available.[124]

Although the bill was easily passed when the government made its adoption a question of confidence, it was almost universally unpopular. On the right and left it was condemned for often largely similar reasons: its aims were criticized as being entirely restrictive – 'a veritable economic malthusianism'[125] – and its most likely effect was predicted to be an increase in industrial prices while agricultural prices were continuing to fall. But conservatives were also suspicious of the wider implications of the bill: 'Is M. Flandin leading us to *étatisme* under the banner of liberty?' asked *La Nation*.[126] In spite of its origins the new law was greeted largely with hostility in business circles as well: there was no co-ordinated response and differences of opinion existed,[127] but it was officially condemned by the C.G.P.F. in March, and by the Paris Chamber of Commerce in June.[128] The vagueness of the bill makes one wonder if it merited the opprobrium heaped upon it; but whether the fears of its critics were justifiable is a purely speculative question, because, after Flandin's fall, it was quietly buried by the Senate and died an unlamented death.

Whatever the long-term effect of Flandin's attempts to prepare the conditions of economic recovery, it was clear that in the short term it was the second element of his economic programme – the credit policy – which had the greater importance. The immediate preoccupation behind this policy was to meet the needs of the Treasury during 1935 which, providing the level of Treasury Bills did not fall for any reason, were estimated at between 14m F. and 18m F. including the deficit of the railway companies; of this figure about 10m would be required during the first two quarters.[129] This estimated borrowing requirement was lower than that of 1934 (19m F. excluding the railway deficit) when there had been large maturities of bonds; but it was large enough to cause problems. For the expenditure arising from the wheat bill and from the increase in military spending – besides the extra expenditure approved in June 1934 a further extra 800mi F. had been approved in January 1935[130] – the government intended to appeal to the Caisse des Dépôts; but the help that the Caisse could provide was limited. There were 9.4m F. of Treasury Bills in circulation at the end of 1934, and if the government was to pursue its policy of avoiding direct intervention in the capital markets, as Germain-Martin claimed it intended to do for at least the first three months of the year,[131] it would clearly be necessary to increase by 5m F. the ceiling on Treasury Bills, which had stood at 10m F. since September 1934. But since it had been found in 1933 and 1934 that the money market could not easily absorb more than about 8m of Treasury Bills – any figure above this having proved to expose the Treasury to the risk of sudden and massive demands for reimbursement[132] – the government intended on this occasion to secure a definite agreement from the Bank of Finance to redis-count a number of Bills held by the banks, if this should prove necessary.[133] Germain-Martin told the Senate Finance Commission with some bitterness – and only slight exaggeration – how in March 1934 he had turned to the Bank for help and the Bank 'refused to make any promises whatever'.[134] But in January 1935 Flandin replaced Moret, the Governor, by Jean Tannery, pre-viously director of the Caisse des Dépôts, who was considered less likely to be under the thumb of the Regents.[135]

The government's strategy was to present its plan, on the one hand, as innocuous and altogether normal in its financial aspects, and, on the other, as far reaching in its economic effects: innocuous because there would be no innovation in the relations between the Bank and the government (no infringement of the Bank's independent right to examine all paper presented), because the amounts discounted would never be very large,[136] and because, since the law raising the ceiling on the issue of Bills stipulated that the govern-ment would consolidate the 5m F. before the end of the year, the rediscount would only be short term and therefore not inflationary; far reaching because it was the high level of long-term interest rates, caused by the competition between government and industry in the capital markets, which was seen as the main obstacle to recovery. Finally, the new policy would, it was hoped, be the first step towards setting up a more active money market in Paris.[137]

The debate over Flandin's cheap money policy – strictly speaking the vote was only over the decision to raise the ceiling on Treasury Bills – showed again the ambiguous nature of his political position: while the Socialists were almost alone in voting against, the right and centre which accepted the policy with the greatest scepticism, voted almost unanimously in favour; the left, if not enthusiastic, was less hostile, and, when Flandin seemed to be meeting resistance from the Bank, positively rallied to his support. Just as the govern-ment had minimized or maximized the import of its policy depending on the audience which needed to be persuaded, so criticism tended either to show that the hopes invested in it were wildly exaggerated or that its risks were dangerously underestimated. For the Socialists, many Radicals and much of the moderate right, behind the rhetoric lay a simple measure of budgetary management, the only way of dealing with another inevitable budget deficit.[138] And, even if genuine, the government's wider claims were doubly unconvincing: first, they assumed that reducing the rate of interest was the key to economic revival whereas the stimulation of demand was more important;[139] secondly, even if the reduction in interest rates was important, it was far from certain that the policy would achieve it: on the government's own arithmetic the combined aid of the Caisse and the newly authorized Bills would be far from sufficient to cover its needs during 1935, and it would almost certainly be forced to intervene in the capital markets well before the end of the year.[140]

For the financially orthodox but not unsympathetic Jenny, Flandin's policy was therefore only a way of gaining time – time which should be spent in introducing further budgetary cuts.[141] This latter conclusion would have been welcomed by those conservatives who, taking their lead from François de Wendel – arguing from his at the same time powerful and exposed position as both a Regent of the Bank and a Senator of the Fédération Républicaine – attempted to play up the inflationary implications of the government's proposals.[142] Thus whatever differences of opinion existed among conservatives about Flandin's credit policy – whether it was considered a reasonable respite or an unacceptable postponement of the inevitable – the conclusion drawn was the same: sooner or later it would be necessary to continue the task of reducing government expenditure.[143]

It was not even clear that the respite gained would be very long: the Chamber and Senate had been easily conquered; the resistance of the Bank was more tenacious.[144] When Tannery asked the Bank's Council, in February, to authorize the rediscount of 1m new Treasury Bills in accordance with the government's policy, the Regents, prompted by de Wendel and de Rothschild, resisted his demand, in spite of Flandin's thinly veiled attack in the Chamber on 'certain oligarchies who dare not fight out in the open'.[145] On 16 February a compromise, suggested by de Wendel, was reached: the Bank would introduce a new item on its balance sheet, headed 'Up to 30-day loans on three-month or two-year Treasury Bills'; the rate of interest would be considerably below the rate of loans on securities – at that time 4½ per cent – but slightly above the discount rate, so as to inflict a slight penalty on would-be speculators; finally, an unofficial ceiling of approximately 2.5m F. would be imposed on the number of Bills which the Bank would be willing to hold.[146]

Although Germain-Martin, putting on a brave face, told the Chamber's Finance Commission that the Bank 'has accepted . . . unanimously the government's views on this matter',[147] this was not the view of Flandin, who told the British Treasury official Sir Frederick Leith-Ross in March that 'he was not going to put up with this obstruction' and would, if by May there had not been some progress in carrying out his programme, consider reforming the statutes of the Bank – whatever the political risk.[148] As Jeanneney points out, the government's defeat lay less in the limits and restrictions put on the Bank's acceptance of Treasury Bills than in the inhibiting effects of the publicity involved in the new procedure agreed on by the Bank: the Bank's balance sheet did not distinguish between the rediscount of commercial and government paper, and in this way the government had hoped that the Bank could if necessary quietly rediscount large quantities of Treasury Bills without alarming the public; but, by creating the new rubric of 30-day advances, the Bank ensured that the amount of government paper in its possession would be absolutely public, and that for fear of causing a financial panic the government would only appeal for the Bank's help very sparingly.[149] The

Regents' strategy worked well: up to the middle of May the amount of Treasury Bills held by the Bank – appearing under the new rubric – did not rise above 150mi. An altogether insignificant figure: the Bank had won.

Flandin was later to blame the Regents for sabotaging his economic policy. But even with the active support of the Bank it is hard to see that it had much chance of success. Besides the already noted flaw in its fundamental assumption, the policy was incoherent and contradictory. First, Flandin, who had proclaimed the end of the *économie dirigée*, was led – in his industrial reorganization bill and his wheat bill – further down the road of state regulation and expenditure. The 'apostle of liberty' was in fact its betrayer. Secondly, as was pointed out by his more lucid critics, the tendency of many of Flandin's policies – the domestic expansion of credit, the industrial reorganization bill – would have been, if successful, to push up French prices; whereas the aims of the policy, although eschewing further deflation, was to allow world prices to rise to French levels. In short, to quote Boris: 'Credit expansion and gold block discipline are incompatible. Consider this and draw the conclusion'.[150] The conclusions drawn might differ: but a choice had to be made.

### The fall of Flandin: 'the force of circumstances'

By the early months of 1935 the image of a government that had at last seemed prepared to act energetically against the crisis was much tarnished; but the contrast between the expectation aroused by Flandin in November 1934 and his fall five months later in the most serious financial crisis since 1926 remains striking. Out of the circumstances of Flandin's fall the left was to forge a powerful political myth, which, in giving substance to Daladier's revival of the slogan of the '200 families' was to contribute to the rise of the Popular Front and importantly to influence the content of its programme. According to the myth, de Wendel, the villain of the piece, having persuaded the Regents of the Bank to sabotage Flandin's credit policy, outlined a massive programme of deflation at the April Congress of the Fédération Républicaine in Nice; then, when the franc came under pressure in May, de Wendel and the Regents of the Bank delayed taking any defensive action in order to push the government into adopting de Wendel's plan of deflation; and only when, on 23 May, Germain-Martin asked the Cabinet for decree powers to implement further economies, did the Bank move to protect the franc by raising its discount rate.[151]

The truth was more complicated: even before the financial crisis of May, Flandin's political position was increasingly precarious. The crisis shook a government whose strength was already severely eroded by the failure of its economic policy. The economic policy had failed in two ways: it showed neither any signs of bringing about an economic recovery nor did it succeed in holding together the government's fragile majority.

In the spring of 1935 France had reached the deepest point of the Depression. The index of industrial production had by April fallen to 76 – the minimum previously reached in July 1932. No sectors of industry were untouched. The situation in agriculture was no less disastrous. The immediate result of Flandin's wheat bill had been another fall in wheat prices: at the end of December the true market price of wheat was estimated to be on average 80 F. a quintal; after the imposition of the new legislation, prices of as low as 65 F. were reported in places. The real purchasing power of the peasantry had, according to Sauvy, fallen by 30 per cent since 1931.[152] The government could only claim one success: after reaching a peak in mid-February the numbers of *chômeurs secourus* had started to fall at the end of the month, reaching 403,000 in June; although this was partly a seasonal decline, it was strikingly more important than the fall of 50,000 in the similar period of 1934. But even this trend was less encouraging than it seemed: rather than indicating any real improvement in the economic situation, it was due probably largely to the combination of a tightening up of government measures against immigrant workers; to the effects of the Marquet Plan which, according to Germain-Martin, was employing 31,000 workers by April;[153] and possibly to the increase in military expenditure which led one commentator to talk of a 'conjuncture of armaments'.[154]

Flandin's economic policy was no more successful in consolidating his parliamentary majority. He continued to enjoy a certain goodwill from much of the left, partly because most conceivable alternatives seemed worse, and partly because of his conflict with the Bank: his attack on the Bank in a speech at Lyons, where he declared that 'this country has not conquered her liberty over the centuries only to chain herself to the chariot of Money The King',[155] led *La Lumière* to report that he had spoken like 'an authentic man of the left'.[156] But if Flandin could count on the sympathy of the left, this did not give him votes: he could not be voted for because he was of the right. For parliamentary support it was necessary to look to the bulk of the Radicals and the right. But Radical enthusiasm for Flandin had diminished considerably by January 1935: the fall in wheat prices confronted rural deputies with the growing militancy of their electorate; Flandin's effigy was burnt in the countryside[157] and in April Dorgères almost won a by-election in the Radical stronghold of Blois.[158]

In January the Radical group met to consider whether it should demand the reimposition of the minimum price.[159] Although the government managed to hold off any such initiative, Radical discontent expressed itself when 47 Radicals voted against it in a debate in early February over a possible revision of Doumergue's deflation decrees.[160] This Radical mutiny which gave the government its lowest majority so far (318–262) led to rumours of a reconstitution of the Cartel majority.[161] And although the dissident Radicals had intended only to give the government a scare, although a week later Flandin's vigorous, if indirect, attack on the Bank won back all but one of the Radical votes, the honeymoon of 1934 was definitely over.

The right saw no reason to modify its attitude of quiet hostility: Flandin's rhetoric about economic liberalism was seen for the sham that it was; his attacks on the Bank were seen as almost subversive.[162] The fall in the price of wheat had affected not only the Radical electorate: one member of the Fédération Républicaine told of being 'plagued by complaining letters' from his rural constituents,[163] and another, Jacques Bardoux, wrote to Tardieu that the agricultural situation was driving his constituents into the arms of the Parti Agraire and the Socialists.[164] And most importantly, Flandin was attacked for his continued refusal to contemplate further cuts in government expenditure. The abandonment of budgetary deflation had, we have seen, never been accepted by any sections of the right, and during the early months of 1935 the campaign for further cuts gathered in intensity, especially as rumours spread that the Treasury was in some difficulty: de Wendel's notorious speech at Nice was part of this campaign, but it was neither the first nor the last statement of its kind.[165] The hostility of the right was not openly expressed in votes against the government; but once 'the force of circumstances' had brought Flandin up against the necessity to change his policy, it would be possible to exact revenge. This occurred in May when a financial crisis allowed him to measure the decline of his political support.

Two distinct, although related, factors brought about the financial crisis of May: first the critical state of the Treasury, and, secondly – both partially caused by and helping to exacerbate this situation – a run on the franc. Owing to the stagnant economic situation, tax revenues continued to fall well below original estimates: for the first quarter these shortfalls were almost 800mi F. at the same time as the Treasury had to pay out increased sums on defence and – as a result of Flandin's wheat bill – on the wheat market, which accounted for 21 per cent of the Treasury's expenditure in the first quarter.[166] The opposition of the Bank had prevented the government from following its policy of intervening only in the money markets and although the circulation of Treasury Bills rose by 1.8m in February and March, the Treasury used the new borrowing facilities granted in January to issue 3.3m or long- and medium-term bonds; it also obtained assistance from the Caisse des Dépôts. This was enough, it was hoped, to tide the government over until the beginning of May.[167]

Germain-Martin put on a brave face to the Chamber's Finance Commission at the start of April,[168] but the situation was in fact very precarious. As early as 5 March, following the advice of Baumgartner, he had written to Flandin warning that the fall in tax revenues since September 1934 and the increase in government expenditure on defence and unemployment necessi-

tated further severe cuts in spending.[169] But Flandin's speech at Lyons on
10 March which explicitly rejected further economies shows that this view
was not yet held by the government as a whole.[170] And two weeks later
Flandin told Leith-Ross that further deflation was impossible since it would
only further reduce government revenues; the only way to get the budget right
was by a little reflation or inflation. The latter commented: 'all this was a
rather familiar theme to me, but was very different from what M. Baumgartner and M. Tannery had told me'.[171]

At the end of March and beginning of April there was a certain tension on
the markets: 500mi of Treasury Bills were cashed in by secondary banks in
the first week of April. Although this minor crisis passed over fairly
quickly,[172] it provided Baumgartner with ammunition to reiterate his demand
for further economies – 'whether on economic or social spending programmes' – especially if defence expenditure was to go on rising.[173] On
30 April Germain-Martin sounded the alarm to the Senate Finance Commission: without further government action he predicted a deficit of 6m F. for
1935 and 7m F. for 1936; the choice was between 'the suspension of payments, ... devaluation' or further financial measures.[174] And by the beginning
of May he was privately converted to the need for further decree powers.[175]
This obviously represented a total repudiation of Flandin's policy of avoiding
further deflation. But Germain-Martin had probably never been entirely convinced by the policy anyway and had been waiting for an opportunity to
resume the deflation which he had all along considered both inevitable and
desirable: as early as January – before the successful resistance of the Bank to
the government's rediscount policy – he had told the Senate Finance Commission of his belief that further budget cuts would be necessary if devaluation was to be avoided; but added that for the moment he was powerless in
the matter.[176]

Flandin's own views remained uncertain: throughout the first three weeks
of May there were rumours of violent differences of opinion between Flandin
and his finance minister over whether – and when – to introduce new
measures of deflation.[177] It was the sudden run on the franc in the second half
of the month – the most serious since 1926 – which finally overcame
Flandin's reluctance. Although the importance of the Bank's gold losses only
started to cause public concern from about 20 May, the speculation had
started on a large scale at least a week earlier, and its causes went further back
still. At the beginning of the year a new fall in sterling had taken place; this
made Flandin's policy of awaiting an alignment of French and world prices
without further deflation (or a devaluation) even more unlikely than it had
already been.[178] But its immediate consequence was to force a devaluation of
the Belga at the end of March, isolating the gold block even more. These
developments, occurring at much the same time as the victory of the left –
especially the Communists – at the municipal elections of 12 May, combined

to produce a double wave of speculation against the franc. First, between 1 May and 17 May the Bank lost almost 1m F. of gold; from 17 May this trickle became a flood: between 18 May and 26 May it lost 5.8m F. Secondly, from 24 May onwards, in addition to this largely foreign speculation, originating in London, New York and Brussels, there was a financial panic within France itself: the Bank was presented with bundles of banknotes of denominations as small as 5 F. or 10 F. as individuals gathered together all their hoarded money in an attempt to find the 215,000 F. necessary to obtain an ingot of gold.[179] On 25 May (Saturday morning) the bank lost 549mi F.; on 27 May 1.2m F.; on 28 May 1.2m F.; on 29 May 940mi F.[180] Jeanneney has found no evidence for left-wing allegations that the Bank allowed – or even encouraged – this situation to develop in order to pressurize the government into taking deflationary action: the bank rate was raised from 2.5 per cent to 3 per cent on 23 May, to 4 per cent on 25 May and to 6 per cent on 28 May.[181]

The result of the gold losses was to overcome the last resistance of Flandin or other members of the government to the necessity for further cuts in government expenditure. Although the franc was in no immediate direct danger given the Bank's enormous reserves, the gold losses had an immediate impact on the circulation of Treasury Bills.[182] On 23 May Germain-Martin was forced to ask the Bank to agree to rediscount 1m F. of Bills falling due at the end of the month; in exchange he promised to demand decree powers or institute important budgetary cuts.[183] In the Cabinet he threatened to resign if such a bill was not presented to the Chamber by 27 May:[184] the 'Flandin experiment' was over.

The government's bill demanding decree powers to save the franc and promote economic revival was more far-reaching in its scope and in the period of its application than either Poincaré's in 1926 or Doumergue's in 1934.[185] The government's exact intentions were obscure, probably even to itself,[186] and it was only clear that the powers would be used to impose new budget cuts. But no energetic protestations could save the government now: the Chamber's Finance Commission rejected the bill, largely because of a revolt by several Radicals, but made it clear that this was not a vote for devaluation; similarly, in the Chamber, Reynaud and Déat, who made powerful speeches in favour of devaluation, stressed that they did not favour a devaluation imposed during a financial panic but rather *à froid*. The government was defeated not in order to bring about devaluation but because there was no confidence in its ability to prevent it. During the course of the final debate Germain-Martin handed in his resignation and Flandin announced that he would take over the Ministry of Finance himself. But in spite of a certain degree of personal sympathy for Flandin who was recovering from a severe car accident, Flandin's government was defeated on the morning of 31 May by 353 votes to 202 votes. The government was brought down by the combination of the opposition of the left, a revolt of over two-thirds of the Radicals and of large numbers of the deputies of the right and centre where almost all groups split down the middle.

The true explanation of Flandin's fall was, then, different from the legend constructed by the left: although it does not seem that the Bank of France provoked, or at least failed to prevent, a run on the franc in order to bring pressure on the government to implement deflation – and Germain-Martin, for one, needed no conversion – by sabotaging Flandin's credit policy it had considerably accentuated the problems of the Treasury, and probably made further spending cuts almost inevitable. Here at least the left was justified in giving the Bank a central role. Flandin's defeat in the Chamber came about not because of what he proposed but because it was he who proposed it: as Marin said 'he has no luck . . . the only time he acted courageously, with authority, he is brought down'.[187] The financial crisis of May was a pretext for conservatives and Radicals to express the accumulated resentments of five months.

In the prolonged ministerial crisis which followed the fall of Flandin the Bank's influence seemed more prominent than ever. On 31 May, Bouisson, the President of the Chamber, formed another Union Nationale government with Caillaux as Finance Minister. Tannery made his attitude to, and expectations of, the new government clear, when, writing to Caillaux on 3 June to enclose reports from the local branches of the Bank which showed slight signs of economic recovery, he commented that this was an improvement 'which a modification of the political situation such as has just occurred and a rapid restoration of public finances could significantly reinforce'.[188] But after only five days the government was narrowly defeated in its demand for wide decree powers necessary to save the franc. The defeat was caused largely by the Radicals' fear of the extreme deflationist tendencies of Caillaux, and by an unskilful parliamentary performance by Bouisson:[189] 65 Radicals voted against the government. Laval tried to form a government acceptable to the Radicals by intimating that he would only demand very limited decree powers: but after a meeting with Tannery, Baumgartner and others, he told Herriot that after all more extensive powers would be necessary. The next attempt to form a government – by the respected centre–right deputy Piétri – met a similar fate: he too proposed decree powers limited to the repression of speculation, but was warned by representatives of the Bank that the assistance which it had been giving the Treasury since the end of May would cease if the government showed any weakness about deflation. Meanwhile negotiations were proceeding between the Radicals and Socialists about the possibility of reconstituting the Cartel majority – but once again the gap between the parties was too wide. Thus when Laval made his second attempt to form a government, with a formula on decree powers acceptable to the Bank, the Radicals had no alternative but to accept. Laval was supported by them not with enthusiasm – only seven voted against but 72 abstained – but because there had to be a government. As Chautemps told the Radical Group 'we are on 5 February. A solution must be found'.[190]

## Laval: *la supérdeflation*?

When he came to power in June 1935 Laval did not have a reputation as an extreme advocate of deflation,[191] and indeed his close links with Raymond Patenôtre, a fervent supporter of devaluation, might even have raised suspicions to the contrary. His main ambition was to shine on the world stage, as he had already in 1931. On financial and economic matters, of which he admitted his ignorance,[192] he was partly prisoner of his own self-created image of the wily-down-to-earth peasant: 'It is better to get 9 F. in sound money than 10 F. in adulterated money – a common-sensical truth which the most humble people have understood'.[193] But Laval, like his old patron Briand, was essentially an improviser who would do what the situation required. And in June 1935 there was no doubt what he had been designated to do: to save the franc.

The decree powers granted to Laval's government were more narrow in their aim than those which had been refused to Flandin and Bouisson; but they were unspecific – and therefore potentially limitless – as to the means to achieve that aim: to avoid devaluation. To carry out this mission Laval and his extremely conservative Radical finance minister, Régnier, were assisted by Gignoux, Raoul Dautry, director of the state railways and Rueff, at this time assistant director of the *Mouvement général des fonds*. But the latitude permitted to this brains trust – or, as the Communists described it, this 'brain of trusts'[194] – was limited: Rueff was, so he later claimed, by this time in favour of devaluation; his function however was merely to advise how it might be avoided.[195] But the scope of the decrees was in fact to be much greater than merely the prevention of devaluation; and the hopes invested in Laval were greater still: he was the saviour who would carry out the economic programme for which conservatives had called in vain during the last four years.

Although 549 decree laws were issued by Laval's government, most of them appeared in three main batches: on 16 July the government issued 29 decrees largely involving expenditure cuts; on 8 August another 41 (86 during the whole month) concerned economic recovery; and on 31 October – the date of the expiry of decree powers – a 'veritable avalanche' of 400 decrees which had very little to do with the defence of the franc.[196] The range of the decrees was enormous, and defies any simple classification: the decrees of 31 October, far from introducing further economies, actually resulted in the creation of over 3,000 new government jobs, causing a net increase of 60mi F. in government expenditure;[197] some decrees were merely minor administrative measures which had been lying untended on some civil servant's desk; others merely adapted or extended legislation which had been adopted in the last few years or even months; yet others took up legislation which had been proposed many years before but had been blocked by the Chamber. The *Revue d'économie politique*'s expert on commercial law claimed that as a result of the decrees 'in a few months 30 years of legislative work has been achieved'.[198]

But if the decrees were heterogeneous, and often insignificant when taken individually, government spokesmen attempted to show that they did form a coherent whole, and, following these commentators, one can group them into broad categories.[199] First came a series of strictly financial measures, the centrepiece of which comprised a 10 per cent reduction in all expenditure by the government, the local authorities, the colonies and the state concessions (notably the railways). This reduction, which included the interest on rentes, spared no aspect of public expenditure except the payment of unemployment and various other social allowances.[200] These and various other cuts were intended to save a total of 9.8m F., of which 6m F. would come from central government expenditure.[201] In addition, another 1.1 m F. was to be saved by various tax increases. To make these measures more palatable, gas, coal and electricity prices, non-commercial rents and mortgage payments were to be reduced by ten per cent, and non-convertibility clauses in private and public contracts were abolished. These financial decrees were followed by a whole series of measures to revive economic activity: intervention in the wheat, wine and sugar markets in order to push up agricultural prices;[202] a speeding up of the Marquet Plan accompanied by various measures of intervention in the labour market intended to reduce unemployment;[203] and finally, numerous decrees relating to industrial reorganization, trade liberalization and improved protection for investors, designed to stimulate investment, encourage international trade and restore profits.[204]

The Laval decrees were attacked on the left as the culmination of the policies which had been pursued intermittently for the last four years: throughout July, *L'Humanité* denounced daily the 'poverty decree laws', 'the famine decrees', 'the wreckers of the franc';[205] Blum talked of a 'policy of superdeflation'.[206] For some opponents of deflation the very severity of this new deflation gave it certain hidden virtues, since, in Kayser's words, the unpopularity of deflation would 'rid us definitively of deflation'.[207] The truth was, however, less simple than this: budgetary deflation was combined with 'malthusian' measures to hold up prices; the budget deficit was supposedly reduced but borrowing for public works was speeded up; trade liberalization was announced, but at the same time as 23 minor industrial quotas were abolished, some agricultural quotas were made even more restrictive. What is more, government spokesmen such as Gignoux actually denied that the aim of the policy was deflationist: the prospect of further price falls would, he argued, only further diminish economic activity. This is not to say that the question of prices no longer caused concern; but now that the disparity of French and world wholesale prices was considered to have been largely over-come, the obsession during 1935 became the disparity between French wholesale and retail prices – a disparity which had elsewhere been cured by devaluation. But direct action that could be taken on costs was limited, and the long-awaited reduction in taxation had to await a definitive improvement in the financial situation. This left one other important way in which costs could be reduced: by a lowering of the interest rate. Laval's economic policy was, said Gignoux, 'incontestably centred around a fall in interest rates'.[208] This was what the government meant by claiming that 'we have never intended to carry out a deflation policy . . . in the proper sense of the term' – that is a restriction of credit: on the contrary, the economies were to allow the pursuit of a more liberal credit policy carried out with the aid of the Bank.[209] As the ever-perspicacious Boris pointed out, this was exactly the policy that Flandin had proposed in January.[210]

But there was a difference between the cases of Flandin and Laval: the attitude of the Bank of France. Already the Bank had promised on 23 May to help Flandin's government with the maturities of 31 May once the govern-ment had agreed to modify its budgetary policies; thus at the end of the month the three major banks agreed to take a further 1m F. of Bills which were immediately rediscounted by the Bank.[211] Régnier, who revealed this to the Chamber's Finance Commission, pointed out that it meant that there had not been a monetary deflation corresponding to that which would otherwise nor-mally have occurred as a result of the gold losses.[212] But was this merely a temporary aid or did it herald a new policy? On 15 July Tannery met Régnier and reconfirmed the Bank's co-operation; and with the Treasury continuing to find itself in financial difficulties – owing to continued shortfalls and increased expenditure on unemployment, wheat and defence – the Bank rediscounted further amounts of Bills and was by September holding some 2.1m F.[213] On 15 August a declaration by Tannery stated the Bank's position publicly: 'the Bank of France will do all in its power to ensure that the credit mechanism operates with the maximum efficiency'. *Le Temps'* gloss on this statement was that the Bank believed that the 'technical conditions' for a policy of credit expansion now existed.[214] But although the government and its apologists might put a brave face on the need to have recourse to the Bank, presenting it to some extent as part of the economic strategy, by the officials of the Ministry of Finance the policy was never seen in this light: it was an undesirable slide towards inflation necessitated by the precarious situation of the Treasury; there was no alternative.[215]

The precariousness of the government's financial achievement was shown in the preparation of the 1936 budget.[216] Government revenue in 1936 was estimated to be 30m F. Even taking account of the savings made by the decrees – now put at 5.1m F.[217] – this meant that the budget could only be technically balanced by transferring 2.6m F. of supposedly exceptional expenditure to a special fund (*fonds d'armement d'outillage et d'avances pour travaux*) to be covered by borrowing. In effect this was an extraordinary budget totalling 6.3m F., which was intended to group together all non-recurrent government expenditure: 5.3m F. of defence spending – including not only that approved in July 1934 and January 1935 but also further spending decided upon in July 1935 – and the rest largely taken up by the Marquet Plan. But the *fonds* was not as scrupulously drawn up as the government had claimed: it did not contain by any means all expenditure which would need to be covered by borrowing, and the expenditure transferred from the budget was not strictly non-recurrent; thus the balancing of the 1936 budget was achieved, despite the decrees, by an artifice of book-keeping: in this way the military spending contained in the budget itself was actually kept below that of the previous year.[218] The Senate Finance Commission's *rapporteur* estimated that the government would need to borrow 10m F. during 1936, excluding the railway deficit and any possible deficit on the budget.

This ought not to have been an excessive sum to hope to raise on the financial markets. But the immediate situation was nonetheless worrying: a threat in the autumn that the Chamber's Finance Commission would amend the decrees[219] had led to a renewal of gold exports in October and November, and although the crisis was less severe than in May – the Bank lost 6m F. of gold – once again it had been necessary to raise the Bank's discount rate in stages to 6 per cent after it had been reduced to 3 per cent in August. From September to November 720 mi F. of Treasury Bills were traded in. A 2m F. loan, using a previous authorization to borrow for defence expenditure, was issued in December; and this was expected to tide the Treasury over until February. But what then? The loan had been subscribed only very slowly after the Treasury had considerably extended the period during which it could be taken up. Further large appeals to the financial markets therefore seemed out of the question; and further cuts in expenditure were considered by Régnier to be economically desirable but politically impossible.[220] The circulation of Treasury Bills had reached – indeed had technically breached[221] – the legal limit, and the Chamber refused to raise the limit by allowing the *fonds d'armement* to be financed by short-term loans, as the government had hoped. Baumgartner was even led to consider the possibility of renewing the practice of open and direct advances from the Bank; but this also was politically unacceptable. The only other possibility seemed to be a foreign loan. Whatever solution was adopted, Baumgartner concluded in January that from the end of the month 'the Treasury will be faced with difficulties almost equal to those of the previous years and in what are undoubtedly less favourable conditions'.[222]

Conservative opinion was, however, remarkably indulgent about this situation. It was left to Auriol to denounce the government's secret advances from the Bank.[223] But however much conservatives might gloss over the truth of the financial situation – seeing Laval as the last card against devaluation – the government was to come under increasing criticism from many sectors of conservative opinion. That is not to say that at any point it lost the votes of conservative spokesmen: the attempt to modify the decrees, led to an outcry in the conservative press,[224] and the congresses of the Alliance Démocratique and the Démocrates Populaires in the autumn expressed measured confidence in the work of Laval's government.[225] But although it was easy enthusiastically to defend Laval from the attacks of the left, there was increasing scepticism about the success and consequences of his economic policy.

In a debate on Laval's economic policy at the end of November a conservative deputy noted that although the government had successfully saved the franc, there was no sign of economic recovery: he attributed this to the uncertainty of the political and international situation (the Abyssinian crisis and the influence of the Popular Front).[226] Throughout the autumn of 1935 this became the theme of official propaganda.[227] This implicit belief in the failure of Laval's economic policy is all the more surprising because in the last months of 1935 there were signs of economic recovery. The index of industrial production which had been more or less stagnant throughout 1935, falling to 93 in August, began to rise in September and ended the year at 96. Two features characterized this recovery. First, it affected consumer industries more significantly than capital goods industries. Secondly, it was based on the domestic market: the trade deficit in 1935 was, at 5.4m F., slightly larger than that of 1934; more important than this slight deterioration was the continued contraction in the total value of foreign trade: the value of exports had fallen by 13 per cent since 1934 and the value of imports by 16.7 per cent.[228] This economic revival seems therefore to have been due to a variety of entirely internal factors: to a rebuilding of stocks; to the government's liberal credit policy; to the increase in armaments expenditure, one involuntary cause of the liberal credit policy; and to an increase in agricultural prices: after three exceptionally good harvests that of 1935 was much less substantial (75.8m quintals), and from August 1935 wheat prices began to rise from the exceptionally low level of 69 F. reached in July, to reach 78 F. at the end of the year.[229]

Although the government did attempt to obtain some propaganda advantage from this slight recovery[230] most of the government's supporters remained as sceptical as the opposition. This scepticism is not easily explicable on the part of the right, which, one would have thought, would have grasped at any straw to defend the government's record. Various reasons can be suggested. Unemployment started its seasonal rise in September, and in spite of the upturn in production in December it was, as it had been every year since the beginning of the crisis, higher than in the December of the previous year (439,800 as opposed to 419,000).[231] Secondly, the very existence of the economic recovery threatened another of the government's major objectives, indeed its primary one: the reduction of prices.[232] In July the index of wholesale prices began to rise, largely because of the rise in agricultural prices; and retail prices soon followed suit in August. As both the *rapporteurs* of the budget observed, this rise in prices put at risk all attempts to restore France's international competitiveness.[233] Was the franc, then, again to be put under threat – as a result, paradoxically, of an economic recovery?

The possibility that even the 549 decrees of 1936 had not been enough to save the franc was bound to be disturbing to those for whom many of the decrees already issued were dangerous in their social implications and in the political precedents that they provided. The problem is simply stated. One of the most important and consistently held of conservative objectives had been the reduction of state interference in economic life; the government itself declared, in the budget, that it was necessary to free the economy from an 'artificial web of controls'.[234] But whatever the government might claim – 'it is not our ambition to police the French economy by decrees' – the decrees represented probably the most extensive intervention in economic life ever hitherto undertaken by a French peacetime government, and also an unprecedented repudiation of the state's financial obligations to rentiers. The left was quick to seize on the point: Blum saw 'precious precedents that we will remember and some day use'.[235] But from the right criticism mounted on all sides: Denais accused the government of having 'seriously undermined the cause which you claim to defend';[236] the publicist Joseph Barthélemy denounced the 'legislative fervour' which had afflicted it;[237] a report presented to the C.G.P.F. criticized the interventionism of many of the decrees;[238] and in November the President of the General Assembly of French Chambers of Commerce declared that 'we are moving towards an *économie dirigée*'. This did not mean that he had lost confidence in Laval, but his confidence was largely a negative one: the Popular Front offered only the alternative of 'integral communism', of the 'absolute domination of the state in all areas'.[239]

Laval's government confronted conservatives more clearly than ever before with the possibility of a contradiction between two of their most tenaciously held beliefs: economic liberalism and resistance to devaluation. But if deflation meant ever more *étatisme*, if the alternative to devaluation was the progressive abandonment of liberalism, then were the dangers of devaluation perhaps not preferable? It was this question which many conservatives were increasingly led to ask themselves in the winter of 1935.[240] Of course there was no question of public advocacy of devaluation on the eve of an election, any more than there was any possibility of deserting Laval. If the financial and economic achievements, as well as the wider social implications of Laval's policies left little enthusiastically to defend, the right nevertheless found its cohesion in reaction to the increasingly vocal opposition of the Popular Front. Whether that opposition could itself find the necessary cohesion to topple Laval and fight the elections united on a common programme of economic recovery, was a question that, at the end of 1935, remained without answer.

# 6 ❧ The programme of the Popular Front

Lorsque le Tiers-Etat et les prolétaires sont unis ils font 1789, ils font 1793, ils font 1848, ils font le 4 septembre. Lorsqu'ils sont divisés on fait contre eux Thermidor, Brumaire, le 2 décembre.

(Edouard Daladier at the Radical Congress of 1935)

The origins and rise of the Popular Front have been described many times: the Amsterdam–Pleyel movement, inspired by Barbusse and Rolland, and Bergery's Front commun in 1933, can be seen as abortive attempts to create a unified movement of the left; but it was the events of 6 February and the continued activities of the Leagues which made such a movement seem urgent and possible.[1] Less well-known than this story is the formation of the Popular Front's programme, particularly of its economic and financial proposals.[2] It would of course be absurdly restrictive to reduce the history of the Popular Front to a somewhat arid account of the negotiations which preceded the appearance of its programme. Much more than this it was above all an immense popular celebration punctuated by increasingly massive demonstrations and meetings, the Jemappes and Valmy of a new revolutionary epic occurring on the battlefields of republican Paris: 'If we are equal to our destiny' declared *La Lumière* '14 July 1935 will stand in the history of humanity alongside 14 July 1789'.[3] But the largely secret negotiations to produce a programme of government for the left were not irrelevant to the spectacular public expressions of republican solidarity: it was precisely the lack of such a programme which had fated the left in 1932. The search for a common programme was an attempt to guarantee that the unity of opposition could also be the unity of government, that republican symbolism could be accompanied by agreement on practical policies to overcome a crisis which seemed to threaten the very existence of the Republic.

## Developments on the left

A common programme of the left had been demanded by left-wing Radicals and others long before the name of Popular Front had even been conceived, long before the crowds had stormed the barriers of the Place de la Concorde, and these events only gave renewed force to such demands.[4] But it was the protracted ministerial crisis of May 1935 which gave a real impetus to what had hitherto been largely a vague aspiration: it was clear that the government of Laval which had emerged from this crisis only existed because the left had been unable to agree on any alternative, and given that this government born of lassitude seemed likely to fall immediately after the summer recess,[5] it was all the more urgent that the left be ready to assume power. But in the past, differences of economic and financial policy between the Socialists and the Radicals, not to mention the Communists, had always made such a programme impossible. Had there been any evolution in the economic policies of these three parties to make an agreement more likely?

The economic diagnosis and policies of the Socialists had remained largely consistent since 1932. Laval's supposed deflation, like that of his predecessors, was attacked for its social inequity,[6] and its economic futility.[7] The Socialists claimed to provide an alternative to both devaluation and deflation: although the state might be 'incapable of creating purchasing power it can nevertheless *provoke* its creation';[8] for another Socialist writer 'only the state can create wealth'.[9] The confusion of vocabulary is not important: the theoretical underpinning which Keynes was to provide for such views had not yet been published, although it is noticeable that the name of Keynes was not mentioned by Socialists in spite of the publication of *The Means to Prosperity* in 1933.

There had however been, since 1934, an attempt by some Socialists to improve the quality of the Party's economic analysis. This occurred in three ways. First, by a reflection on the experience of other countries: foreign examples provided Socialists with empirical support for their policies, and partly compensated for the lack of theoretical support. Foreign experience could be brought in both to demonstrate the consequences of deflation – 'National Socialism owes a lot to M. Brüning'[10] – and, more importantly, to show how the Socialists' policies could work in practice: here the cases of America and, less often, Sweden,[11] were most significant. Socialist writers followed the course of the New Deal particularly closely: Robert Marjolin's *Les Expériences Roosevelt* appeared in 1934; and André Philip's *La Crise et l'économie dirigée* (1935) was largely devoted to events in America. Certainly it was recognized that there were great differences between America and France and certainly the limitations of the New Deal were constantly stressed; but in observing Roosevelt's policies it was nonetheless necessary to 'draw the lessons that they hold for our own country'.[12]

Secondly, the Socialist congress of 1934 had instructed the Party's propaganda organizations to draw up detailed studies of particular aspects of policy. But when, at the Congress of 1935, André Blumel reported on what had so far been achieved, he had to admit that the instructions had only been very partially carried out: André Philip, and an anonymous collaborator, were working on the 'unworked areas' of the nationalization of credit;[13] Moch had promised to undertake an examination of the electricity industry, but this would take time; it had proved a 'technical impossibility' to draw up industrial codes on the reduction of the working week, but Marjolin had been deputed to follow studies on this subject being made by the C.G.T.; it had not yet been possible to find anyone to make a study of agriculture. The problem, Blumel concluded, was that very little detailed study of these subjects had been done in the past, and the Party lacked economic and financial experts.[14]

As early as the spring of 1932, Moch, in an attempt to remedy this situation, had grouped together the few Socialist members of the famous Centre Polytechnicien d'Etudes Economiques – better known as 'X Crise' – which had from 1931 assembled *polytechniciens* and ex-*polytechniciens* to discuss the economic crisis and ways of overcoming it.[15] Then, in 1934, he was instrumental in setting up the Union des Techniciens Socialistes (U.T.S.), which itself was to include many *polytechniciens*:[16] at the Congress of 1935 he proposed that the C.A.P. examine the possibility of officially integrating the U.T.S., or some similar body of experts into the Party hierarchy.[17] But, although Blum was sympathetic to such initiatives, Moch claims that the Party hierarchy was more hostile.[18] These attempts to endow the Party with a group of expert advisers had not had time to have much effect on policy before 1936, although it was from the U.T.S. that Moch was to recruit his team of advisers in Blum's government after the victory of the Popular Front. But there was a new note of caution in one of the most important Socialist policies: the reduction of the working week. Whereas in its 1932 manifesto the Party had called for a 40-hour week, in 1936 it called only for a reduction in the working week, without mentioning a figure, and Moch suggested that it should vary according to the sector involved.[19]

Thirdly, in a series of articles in the summer of 1935, Blum examined the question of the nationalization of credit and of certain sectors of industry. Nationalizations had been proposed by the Party in 1932, but it had never been clear exactly what role they played in the Party's specific strategy to fight the crisis. Blum admitted that he had not been very sure of himself, and he attempted to resolve the question by 'more careful reflection'.[20] Having examined exactly what was meant by the notion of nationalization, and shown that it would almost certainly improve the conditions of the workers and free the state from the pressures of a venal press, of anti-parliamentary Leagues financed by business and, in general, of an industrial and financial oligarchy exercising its influence in the very corridors of the Chamber,[21] Blum claimed that nationalizations could contribute in three ways to overcoming the crisis. First, only if the state had direct control over a certain number of large industries could it enforce the implementation of the reduced working week and of collective wage bargaining; and this example would be sufficient to affect private industry without the need for legal controls.[22]

Secondly, the nationalizations would enable the government to alleviate the disparity btween costs and prices: the nationalization of electricity would, for instance, allow the government to reduce electricity prices and significantly alleviate costs – and this of course applied equally to coal, steel, transport and so on. Thirdly, the nationalization of credit would enable the government to control and stimulate different sectors of the economy.[23] By 1935, then, nationalizations had come to play a considerably more important part in Socialist policy than hitherto, although there was by no means a consensus about exactly which sectors it was necessary to nationalize.[24] This was, however, hardly a development likely to facilitate agreement with the Radicals – or even the Communists.

Two points are important in the evolution of the Communist analysis of, and response to, the crisis. First, although the P.C.F.'s attack on the effect of the Laval decrees – and on deflation in general – was no different from that of the Socialists,[25] it had from the very beginning formulated its economic proposals less for their efficacy in alleviating the crisis than for their efficacy as political slogans: the emphasis was on economic demands intended to mobilize the masses. One of the most important developments which, it is said, made the Popular Front possible, was the new conciliatory attitude of the Communist Party after June 1934. Obviously this is true in spite of the Party's claim that it was the Socialists who had prevented unity before 1934;[26] but inasmuch as the Party's response to the crisis had always consisted in the formulation of slogans, it is also true that the Party's evolution towards the Popular Front strategy did not involve a fundamental transformation of its attitude. What changed was the content of the demands: the evolution was from one kind of slogan to another.

Secondly, the most distinctive feature of the Communist analysis of the crisis was its stress on the differential effects of the Depression on various sectors of the economy: whereas it was certainly the case that many industries, particularly consumer industries, had suffered disastrously, others had, it was argued, succeeded in protecting their interests, whether by organizing into cartels and driving smaller producers out of business, by using the state to encourage the movement towards industrial concentration[27] or by relying on state orders for armaments.[28] In short, there was an industrial sector which had succeeded in holding up prices and driving its competitors out of business[29] while the rest of the economy was devastated by the crisis.[30] This analysis was not carried out in great depth; on the other hand, it was not mere demagogy: in an important article in the *Revue d'économie politique* which succeeded in arousing the wrath of the *Bulletin quotidien*,[31] the eminently bourgeois statistician Jean Dessirier showed how the profits and dividends of the large semi-public services and of certain cartellized industries had either risen, or at least fallen less precipitously than those in the rest of the economy.[32] The practical conclusions which the Communists drew from their analysis – 'let the rich pay' – were however somewhat different from those of Dessirier whose article was a disguised plea for devaluation.

It is difficult to generalize about the attitude of the Radical Party: indeed the Party was, in 1935, more deeply divided over economic policy than it had ever been before. Certainly there had been a progressive disillusion with the policies followed by governments since 1932, and the refusal of 72 Radicals to support Laval was in part a reluctance to undergo yet another bout of deflation. But no more than in 1932, 1933 or 1934 was there a clear, alternative Radical policy. Two points should be noted in this context. First, many of the most articulate original critics of deflation, or those who had at least become increasingly sceptical – such as Henri Clerc, Bertrand de Jouvenel, Gaston Bergery, or the economist Bertrand Nogaro – had, often through disgust or frustration, left the Party by the end of 1934; none had been more articulate than Georges Boris whose articles were certainly influential on the left of the Party, but he was too independent a spirit and his advocacy of devaluation too unpopular, for his ideas to be adopted by all but a very few in the Party. Thus the leadership of the Radicals opposed to deflation passed to Daladier[33] whose self-professed ignorance in such matters has already been mentioned.

Secondly, the brunt of the left-wing Radicals' attack on government economic policy remained primarily *political*: Pierre Cot claimed that one of the main Radical contributions to the Popular Front would be a Jacobin tradition which believed in a strong state and in the struggle against 'the 200 families which control our economy, and hold the state in their power'.[34] The point was perhaps best made in a speech to the 1935 Radical Congress by a delegate who was discussing nationalizations and the notion of the *économie dirigée*: 'it is in the name of the political liberation of the state, and not for economic considerations, that we are forced to meet the economic feudalities on the battleground that they have chosen; in the name of Richelieu . . . the name of the French Revolution; the experiment of a managed economy that we are obliged to undertake from political necessity cannot produce immediate economic results'.[35] The preoccupation of even those Radicals who attacked deflation with largely political questions, and the loss of many articulate critics of deflation, meant that, for lack of a specifically Radical economic policy, the Radicals' contribution to the formation of the Popular Front programme was to consist largely in drawing the limits to what was acceptable in the proposals of the Communists and Socialists: the role was important, but it was a negative one.

## Uncertain beginnings: May to October 1935

It would be wrong, however, to see the Popular Front programme as emerging merely from the discussions of the Communists, Socialists and

Radicals. The negotiation of the programme was a long and complicated process involving numerous organizations and individuals. It was the result of the coalescence of four distinct, although often simultaneous and related, attempts to produce a programme of the left which would also be a programme to fight the crisis, or a programme to fight the crisis which could also be a programme of the left. These four attempts consisted of negotiations between the Socialists and Communists; various proposals of a whole series of extra-parliamentary groups; negotiations outside parliament between ten organizations, including the three main parties of the left; and, finally, negotiations between the Radicals, Socialists, Communists and various independent Socialists in parliament.

The 'Unity Pact' signed between the P.C.F. and the S.F.I.O. on 27 July 1934 had above all been made possible by the new Communist tactic, defined by Thorez at the Party's conference in June as 'At any price, we want unity of action'. The aims of the pact were extremely limited – to end the parties' public attacks on each other – and provided for the setting up of a joint co-ordinating committee to organize demonstrations against a variety of targets such as the Leagues or fascism in Germany; but including also the deflationary decree laws of Doumergue. At a meeting of the co-ordinating committee on 9 November, the Communists, attempting to extend the narrow bases of this agreement, proposed a common programme of action to the Socialists; and at the Conseil National of 27 November the Socialists produced a set of counter proposals of their own. But there was total disagreement, which was to characterize all future negotiations, over whether the programme should be purely a set of demands as the Communists wanted – their proposals were divided into sections entitled 'For the workers, the railwaymen and the *fonctionnaires*', 'For the unemployed', 'For tenants' and so on – or whether it should attempt to introduce structural economic reforms, such as the nationalization of credit. The Socialists were shocked by the timidity of the Communist proposals – 'not a single socialist measure' – which excluded any nationalizations, and even the setting up of agricultural marketing boards. A compromise text was proposed by Zyromski, but rejected by the P.C.F. which broke off the negotiations in January 1935.[36]

The Communist argument was both doctrinal and tactical. First, the Socialists, indiscriminately using the terms socialization and nationalization, were accused of believing that nationalizations could fundamentally alter the nature of the regime; nationalizations within the framework of capitalism in fact strengthened the power of the bourgeoisie: to believe the contrary assumed that the state was above class whereas it was in fact in the hands of monopoly and finance capital.[37] Secondly, by insisting on nationalizations, the Socialists made it difficult to transform unity of action into a wider antifascist movement: in November 1934 Thorez had proclaimed the need for 'the Popular Front of liberty, work and peace'. Even if this did not at this time necessarily imply an alliance with the Radical Party, it did mean that 'the race [between Fascism and the left] has begun for the conquest of the *classes moyennes*'.[38] As a result many Communist demands had to be abandoned because, as one Communist put it in September 1934, 'to hope to carry out an alliance with the *classes moyennes* using all the slogans of the Communist Party is equal to not wanting to carry out that alliance at all'.[39] The same obviously applied to many Socialist *mots d'ordre* as well. Thus, as Blum himself observed, the negotiations between the two parties were broken off because the Socialists wanted only a programme common to the two parties while the Communists wanted to avoid any measure which might prevent a wider coalition 'beyond the limits of our two parties'.[40]

The failure of these negotiations did not jeopardize the unity pact which continued in spite of the reservations of many leading Socialists. The Conseil National of 3 March voted to continue it, and to try and find a platform of policies common to the two parties.[41] But little was done about this, and the Socialist Congress in June 1935 was uninterested in the problem. Certainly there was a vigorous debate over whether unity of action had, as Zyromski, Bracke and others strongly denied, any responsibility for a further fall in Party membership during 1934;[42] certainly Moch, Paz, Auriol and one or two party workers spoke of the need for a programme or a plan of immediate action which would serve to unite not only Socialists and Communists but all of the left;[43] but most of the speeches concerned entirely different questions: should the Socialist Federations arm themselves to deal with the possibility of fascist aggression?[44] When and how exactly would the final Socialist seizure of power occur?[45]

In spite of the indifference of the congress, in the summer of 1935 Zyromski reported in *Le Populaire* that negotiations between Communists and Socialists were proceeding more smoothly[46] and on 23 September a 'Platform of Joint Action of the Socialist and Communist Parties' was published.[47] There were two main reasons why agreement was possible where it had not been before. First, the Laval decree laws had brought the two parties closer together in common opposition to government policy. Secondly, Blum's reflections on the question of nationalizations in the summer of 1935 had intended not only to show their practical usefulness as a weapon against the crisis, but also to overcome the objections of the Communists. Responding to Communist criticisms, Blum drew a distinction between 'socializations' and 'nationalizations': the former could not occur until after the Socialist revolution, and consisted simply of the expropriation of the owners of the means of production, carrying with it no compensation;[48] nationalization, on the other hand, which could be undertaken within the framework of capitalism, did carry with it compensation and could therefore be imposed by a government that was not necessarily Socialist.[49] In short: 'Nationalization is to socialization what the exercise of power is to the conquest of power'.[50] This analysis was not without effect: once the P.C.F. had received satisfaction on the question of nationalization, it was able to accept the Platform[51] which, besides containing various standard left-wing measures to stimulate demand, also called – under the heading 'The Protection of Liberty' – for the liberation of the state from the yoke of the financial powers by nationalizing the Bank of France and important monopolies, although it was specified that this was not equivalent to a beginning of Socialism and could occur with the capitalist system. This was a verbal concession to the Communists; but one so vague as to commit no one to anything. On their side the Socialists conceded that the public works would be partially financed by a tax on large fortunes – in line with the Communist demand to 'make the rich pay'. Blum stressed that this important document, as he called it, was not intended to undermine the negotiations for a programme which were at this time proceeding with the Radicals and other groups.[52] But the opposite would have been nearer the truth: agreement between the two parties had anyway lost most of its interest because the most important negotiations were those now taking place between the Radicals, P.C.F., S.F.I.O. and other groups assembled in the Comité du Rassemblement Populaire, and in these negotiations the Communists' second – tactical – objection to nationalization retained its importance. Thus, there was a third – perhaps primordial – reason why agreement was possible between the two parties in September 1935: developments had rendered the Platform largely irrelevant. Interest was now directed altogether elsewhere.[53]

To study the origins of the Comité du Rassemblement Populaire it is necessary to go back to the events of 6 February 1934: if one conclusion that could be drawn from them was that the possibility of fascism was a reality in France, another was that the traditional parties of the left had some responsibility for allowing this situation to develop. The result was a whole series of initiatives by extra-parliamentary – and hitherto largely extra-political – organizations proposing their own plans of action to fight fascism and, in most cases, *a fortiori* the economic crisis.[54] Of such initiatives, two were particularly important: the formation of Comité de Vigilance des Intellectuels Antifascistes (C.V.I.A.) and the drawing up of a Plan by the C.G.T. The C.V.I.A. had been set up in March as a result of an initiative of an auditor at the Cour des Comptes, F. Walter (known as Pierre Gerôme), sympathetic to the P.C.F., who became the Comité's Secretary. Presided over by three famous, and politically different, intellectual figures – the philosopher Alain, the physicist Langevin and the ethnologist Rivet – the Comité's aim was declared to be the defence of political freedom, which implied the necessity to 'free the state from the yoke of capital'.[55] At more or less the same time the C.G.T. decided to draw up a Plan to combat the crisis which it published in October 1934.[56]

It was in the course of 1935 that these two extra-parliamentary initiatives became linked to the traditional parties of the left, whose failure they had been to some extent intended to remedy: in June 1935 the C.V.I.A. invited a number of organizations to set up a committee to prepare a republican and anti-fascist demonstration on 14 July, at which the left would pledge itself to remain united in the fight against fascism; among these organizations was the Radical Party, which agreed, with reservations, to participate in the committee and the demonstration which it was preparing.[57] The demonstration was an undoubted triumph. But two participants – the trade unionist André Delmas and the writer Jules Guéhenno – wondered what would follow: 'will our leaders be able to turn this powerful force to the full possible advantage? Or will it finish in a terrible disappointment'.[58] It was to avoid this that the Comité du Rassemblement Populaire which had been originally set up to prepare the demonstration of 14 July did not dissolve itself afterwards, but decided to continue to meet in order to draw up a programme which would make it possible in practice for the left to 'be faithful to its vow' of 14 July.[59] At the same time, in June, as the C.V.I.A. had proposed the idea of gathering the left in a demonstration of republican unity, the C.G.T. had taken the parallel step of sending a letter to various organizations of the left inviting them to a meeting to approve, after if necessary modifying, the C.G.T. Plan as the basis of a uniting of the forces of the left.[60] This meeting, which took place on 3 August, gathered together representatives of 19 organizations, and set up four commissions to examine the Plan in detail and propose a definitive version for the end of the month.[61] Once the commissions had reported back, a second meeting in September unanimously accepted their modifications to the Plan – certain reserves being expressed by the Radicals and Communists – and it was decided to present the Plan to the Comité du Rassemblement Populaire.[62]

The Comité du Rassemblement Populaire consisted of the representatives of ten organizations: four political parties: the S.F.I.O., the P.C.F., the Radicals and the intergroup of three small groups of independent Socialists, including the Neo-Socialists; two unions: the C.G.T. and the C.G.T.U.; and four non-parliamentary and non-syndical organizations: the C.V.I.A., the Mouvement Amsterdam–Pleyel, an organization of war veterans and the Ligue des Droits de l'Homme, whose President, Victor Basch, presided over the Comité largely by virtue of his age.[63] The Comité was not without precedents to guide it in its negotiations to produce a programme: in the municipal elections of May Paul Rivet had been elected as the first ever Popular Front candidate – in the 5th *arrondissement* of Paris – when the other parties of the left stood down for him at the second ballot; and at a meeting held to celebrate this victory on 28 June Daladier appeared publicly with Blum and Thorez, to announce what was in effect a Radical programme for a Popular Front, including the 40-hour week, public works and the nationalization of credit.[64] The result of this meeting was a 'minimum programme' of the Popular Front of the 5th arrondissement, grouping 38 organizations.[65] But this programme – a list of aims rather than policies – had no official status and was purely a local initiative: Daladier had contributed in a purely private capacity; and Paul Faure described it as 'a pallid electoral programme of the end of the last century'.[66]

The deliberations of the Comité took place in private, and no communiqués were issued. Progress was slow because the delegates, particularly the Communists, had to refer back constantly to their parties.[67] Although it cannot be known precisely what questions caused most difficulty during the summer and early autumn of 1935, it was the financing of an eventual programme which caused the most public controversy at this time. The problem was stated by Bayet, who supported most of the measures likely to be included in the programme – an end to deflation, public works and so on – but claimed that it was not enough to hope that these measures could be financed by ordinary loans: perhaps it would be possible to issue special 'Economic Defence Bonds'. Whatever method was adopted, he demanded that experts on the left agreed on 'some means – orthodox or not – of ensuring that the government can, for a year, pay its way at the end of the month and finance public works'.[68] And from the other wing of the Radical Party Lamoureux asked a similar question: how could the budget be balanced if the deflation decrees were repealed?[69] The Communists' answer was to publish in August a detailed financial programme whose main feature was a capital levy.[70] Walter, to whom Delmas attributed an important part in the final appearance of the programme,[71] published an article in *Europe* which accepted the principle of financing it largely by increased taxation. At all costs he wanted to avoid inflation: 'all theories claiming that a balanced budget is outmoded are pure fantasy'; if this advice was not followed the left would once again give a weapon to the opposition which would triumph for a third time.[72]

Blum's solution was very different: explicitly taking up Lamoureux's challenge, he declared that a government of the left would repeal the decrees, and, until its policies, by stimulating an economic revival, had improved the financial situation, it would meet its obligations in the same way as Laval – by the rediscount of Treasury Bills by the Bank of France; and if the Bank should refuse this facility to a government of the left, 'the government would simply not meet its payments', and appeal to the patience of the *fonctionnaires* until opposition had been overcome.[73] But Blum preferred to avoid arguments about the financing of a future programme: 'A balanced budget? No one is capable of guaranteeing it in present circumstances'.[74] Obviously this was hardly likely to reassure the fainthearted; and even the highly sympathetic *La Lumiére* was critical of a solution which had no chance of being accepted by most of the delegates to the Comité du Rassemblement Populaire.[75] But perhaps this whole argument was proceeding too fast: to ask

how to finance the abrogation of the decrees and other measures implied that
there was at least consensus that this was the ultimate aim. Was this not going
far ahead of the wishes of the Radical Party as a whole and the Radical parliamentary group in particular? After all the demonstrations of 14 July had
taken place *before* the issue of the first Laval decrees.[76]

The attempt by the parties of the left in parliament to negotiate a programme had preceded the formation of the Comité du Rassemblement
Populaire, and went back to the ministerial crisis at the end of May.[77]
Immediately after the fall of Flandin the Communists had proposed a meeting
between all parties of the left: on this occasion, which took place on 31 May,
Ramette and Thorez declared themselves ready to support a government as
far to the right as Bonnevay of the Républicains de Gauche, provided that it
was prepared to act against the leagues, 'tax the rich' and defend the franc.
Many Radicals were tempted by these Communist advances, but, after the
interventions of the conservatives Malvy and Potut, the Radical Group voted
unanimously – minus 14 abstentions – to support the Bouisson government,
while the Socialist Group voted not to, in spite of some dissenters.

After the fall of Bouisson, occurred a more sustained attempt on 5 June to
negotiate an agreement, once again at the instigation of the P.C.F. Thorez was
again infinitely accommodating, and in reply to Auriol he intimated that the
Communists would even vote for the budget.[78] Herriot declared that he
supported a left-wing government in theory, but the moment was not pro-
pitious: 'we are in the position of an industrialist who wants to shake off the
yoke of his creditor but remains in his power until he has paid off his debt'.
This time the left-wing Radicals were less prepared to capitulate: Daladier
and Mendès France claimed that the immediate problem was to ensure the
rediscounting of Treasury Bills by the Bank; but the conservative Radicals
attempted to shift responsibility from the Bank to the Socialists: what
policies, Guernut asked, did the Socialists propose for a government of the
left. As usual the role of the Radicals was merely to respond to the proposals
of others. Blum envisaged two possibilities: either a government to carry out
nationalizations, public works, set up agricultural Boards and so on; or a
'sequestration government' whose main task, although carrying out certain
immediate measures and obliging the Bank to rediscount Bills so that the
government could survive, would be to prepare elections to be held by pro-
portional representation.[79] But even this, during a financial crisis, was too
much for the Radicals, and although a sub-committee of the newly reconstituted joint committee of representatives of the left (the Délégation des
Gauches) was set up to consider the proposals on 6 June, the Radical Group
was at the same time coming round to the inevitability of Laval: at the
Group's meeting on the afternoon of 6 June, Herriot asked if anyone was prepared to form a government of the left; Daladier pointedly left the room; the

Group mandated its bureau to act as it thought best, and in the evening Laval formed his government with Radical participation.

There were various accounts of the reasons for the failure to form a government of the left. For Herriot 'the Radicals are frightened of the Socialists who are frightened of the Communists. Once again fear determines everything'.[80] Blum blamed the duplicity of the Radicals, negotiating with Laval at the same time as with the left.[81] *Le Temps* was probably nearer the truth in commenting that the ploy of the Radicals and Socialists consisted in shifting responsibility on to each others' shoulders.[82] There was indeed much bluff in the Socialist attitude: in private Blum told Herriot on 11 July that he was worried about the possibility of the premature formation of a left-wing government.[83] But the failure of the negotiations was a beginning not an end: first, the Délégation des Gauches had been reconstituted, and it continued to meet after the end of the session. At the end of July, it was agreed that the recent ministerial crisis had shown the need for a programme of the left, and it was decided that the sub-committee set up on 6 June to consider the Socialist proposals should be reactivated to produce a programme as soon as possible.[84]

Secondly, Blum drew positive conclusions from the prolonged ministerial crisis in spite of his supposed bitterness about the Radicals' 'treachery'. Not all Socialists took the same view: the crisis was hardly mentioned at the Socialist congress which almost immediately followed it, except by Rivière, an old participationist, who claimed that Socialist doctrinal intransigence had played into the hands of the Radical leaders;[85] and Faure and Lebas expressed public distrust of the Radicals, recalling the bad old days of minis-terialism.[86]. But Blum's analysis was quite different. First, he noted the sig-nificant fact that during the ministerial crisis the P.C.F. had for the first time 'boldly taken its place in the debates of the democratic parties', that indeed the Radicals had found agreement easier with the Communists than the Socialists.[87] Secondly, he developed his idea of a 'sequestration government' into the notion of defensive, preventive 'occupation of power': Socialists might be forced to join a Popular Front government before the conditions hitherto laid down for their acceptance of office – whether the 'conquest' or the 'exercise' – had been fulfilled, in order to act as a bulwark against fascism.[88] But thirdly, he argued that to be effective such a government could not be passive: it had to eliminate the causes of fascism by acting against the economic crisis.

Therefore, instead of concluding that the Radicals' views on economic policy were unacceptable and that an alliance like the Popular Front was dangerous to the integrity of the Socialist Party, Blum, perhaps feeling that the impetus for such an alliance was irresistible, attempted preemptively to stake out its acceptable limits – limits beyond which the occupation of power would indeed become 'ministerialism'. Laval's decrees had, he pointed out, hit rentiers, war veterans and *fonctionnaires* – 'these *classes moyennes* whose support has always and everywhere determined the victory of fascism' – and therefore the 'primary duty' of the Popular Front must be a commitment to reverse deflation.[89] With fake naivety he claimed that it was merely necessary to 'cross the t's': the Popular Front's first act – 'it goes without saying. But it is still better to have said it' – would be to abrogate the decrees.[90] And for Blum the significance of the ministerial crisis had been to show that a sizeable proportion of the Radical Party no longer accepted deflation: Daladier now talked as the Socialists had talked when he was in government.[91] But Blum's conditions were far from universally accepted: not only were many Radicals – Herriot, Lamoureux, Potut, Roche[92] – favourable to deflation and primarily worried by financial collapse, the Communists themselves even seemed ultimately prepared to compromise on this point. Certainly they attacked the decrees with more ferocity than anyone else, but Duclos warned the opponents of the Popular Front that even if agreement could not be reached on this point, this should not affect the solidity of the Popular Front: 'even if the basis of agreement is narrow, it must be maintained because the fascist threat has not been removed'.[93] This attitude was welcomed by Kayser, who, as a Radical opposed to the decrees, nevertheless preferred, if necessary, an alliance on some basis to no alliance at all.[94]

If then it was not even certain whether the Popular Front was against the deflation decrees, questions about how to finance the programme of a government which had abrogated them were largely academic; though not entirely; it was partly because they could not believe in the financial soundness of the alternatives that many Radicals continued to cling to the decrees. The question became increasingly pressing for the deputies of the left-wing groups as the new parliamentary session approached, because in many eyes a vote for the budget would be at least a temporary implicit ratification of the decrees. But what alternative was there? In September the Délégation des Gauches met at least weekly. The sub-committee continued to work unenthusiastically on a programme: it was rumoured to be having difficulties in agreeing on financial and economic policies, and in mid-September it heard a report from four representatives of the Comité du Rassemblement Populaire which was said to be on the point of completing its programme, and agreed to collaborate further with this body in the future; in effect this meant that it had more or less given up the attempt to create a programme of its own and decided to see what the Comité, whose representative Walter it heard again on 18 September, could do. Suggestions that the representatives of the left on the Finance Commission should refuse to discuss the budget until the decrees had been separately voted on were rejected by the Délégation because to cause a political crisis seemed futile before the left had created its programme.[95]

It was therefore potentially a significant event when on 2 October Walter presented the sub-committee with the draft of a programme which had supposedly received the support in principle of the Comité du Rassemblement Populaire.[96] In fact it seems unlikely that this proposed programme, which was leaked to the press, can have emanated from the Comité as a whole – being far removed from the conceptions of the Socialists – and it seems more likely to have been a personal draft of Walter's to be submitted for consideration by the Comité since it followed very closely the spirit of his article in *Europe* mentioned above: although containing the standard set of measures to stimulate demand, it attacked inflation – accepting, however, that the Treasury's immediate needs would have to be met by help from the Bank – and left out any mention of nationalizations.[97]

Whatever the status of this document it was discussed by the Délégation des Gauches whose members gave their theoretical support and agreed that the draft would be submitted to their respective parties as soon as possible, so that the parliamentary groups could 'draw the immediate necessary measures' – that is the fall of Laval.[98] And a few days later the Radical Group considered the draft favourably and agreed to present it to the Party's financial commission for possible discussion at the imminent Party Congress.[99] As for the Chamber's Finance Commission it too decided to adjourn its decision about whether or not to discuss the budget before the decrees until 29 October – the end of the Radical Congress.[100] Not for the first time all eyes were fixed on the Radicals. But not for the first time the results of the Congresses did little to clarify the situation. The Leagues were the dominant theme of the Congress and, if there was no repetition of the *coup d'Angers*, the final motion enjoined the Radical ministers to make their participation in government conditional upon firm action against them. The Congress also declared its support for the Popular Front. But what this meant in terms of economic policy seems quite unclear: the draft programme approved by the Group seemed to have been forgotten; the only new contribution to the debate on economic policy was the demand for the 'rectification' of the worst injustices caused by the decrees, and this motion was obviously invented to paper over deep divergences of policy while at the same time paying lip service to the evident unpopularity of the decrees among much of the Party rank and file, an unpopularity which clearly emerged in the debate on war veterans.[101] In the words of Jean Zay, then, all Radicals insisted on these rectifications 'however deeply they might debate *the principle* of the deflation decrees'.[102] Opponents and supporters[103] of deflation could at least unite on this point. Interest was aroused by the conservative Potut's report on financial policy which not only accepted the probability of a limited budget deficit but actually seemed to see possible benefits in the idea: 'Our ambition is to transform this deficit imposed by the crisis into a deficit which will bring economic recovery'.[104]

Blum tried to show that such a statement from a conservative indicated that Radical economic policy had moved in the direction of that of the Socialists;[105] while *Le Temps* claimed that Potut had not denied that an expansionary economic policy was conditional on a restoration of financial stability, and that therefore his report could be approved by supporters of the government,[106] a view which Potut himself confirmed. The attempts of Blum and *Le Temps* to annex Potut's remarks are somehow perfectly symbolic of the struggle for the soul of the Radical Party; but perhaps even more significant – and symbolic of the kind of Party that the Radicals were – is the fact that the remarks passed largely unnoticed by the Radicals themselves. Only Campinchi seriously attempted at the Congress to consider the implications of the Popular Front of which he was a supporter: the Radicals should not, he said, be frightened that the Popular Front represented some lurch to the left because on the contrary 'the Communists are now much more radical than we will ever be Communist'; but an important question remained: was there 'a fundamental incompatibility between the franc and democracy, between a left-wing policy and the financial prosperity of the country'?[107] Campinchi did not satisfactorily answer his own question; but no one else had asked it at all.

## The fall of Laval

Although the Radical Congress seemed to have contributed in no way to the negotiation of the economic programme of a government of the left, the situation had been considerably clarified since the summer. At one point it had seemed so inextricably complicated – discussions between the Socialists and Communists alone, between the C.G.T. and other organizations, between the members of the Comité du Rassemblement Populaire, and those of the Délégation des Gauches – that Moch had proposed that the programme should be drawn up by a committee of seven individuals, representing the main organizations of the left.[108] But by October it was clear that the Socialist–Communist platform was redundant, that the C.G.T. had decided to submit its Plan to the Comité du Rassemblement Populaire and that the Délégation des Gauches had more or less abandoned any attempt to produce a programme itself and decided instead to await the result of the deliberations of the Comité. Thus it was the Comité which was now recognized to have the exclusive responsibility for negotiating a programme.

The political survival of Laval depended directly on his majority in parliament; but whether the left in parliament could unite to overthrow him, partly depended on whether there was a viable alternative, that is whether the opposition had its own programme. Thus there was a loose relationship between Laval's survival and the discussions of the Comité. The relationship was loose because there were many different conditions under which Laval might be brought down. The unpleasant truth that the threat of imminent power might not be enough to produce a viable programme made the solution of a Popular Front government increasingly less desirable: it continued to be advocated by Déat and Paul-Boncour,[109] and, publicly at least, by the Socialists,[110] although Blum's private opinions fluctuated.[111] But the difficulties that such a government might meet without prior agreement on its aims and policies, inclined many on the left to prefer not to bring Laval down at all.[112] It was to resolve this problem that the idea emerged of a transitional government, merely to prepare the elections: the Communists had in effect advocated a transitional Radical, or even more conservative, government during the ministerial crisis of June, and they continued to support this idea on the grounds that anything was preferable to Laval.[113] After the Radical Congress, Zay envisaged three possibilities: that Laval would continue in power; that there would be a Popular Front government before the elections; that there would be a transitional government not necessarily headed by a Radical. He inclined towards this latter option.[114] By mid-November, Herriot himself was coming round to the same view.[115] But what would the nature of the government be? The Communists wanted it to be Radical,[116] and the Socialists were ready to support such a government;[117] but the Radicals did not want to be pushed into government alone,[118] and Herriot made it clear on several occasions that he would not head a Radical government of transition.[119] Various other possibilities were mentioned such as a transitional government headed by Piétri;[120] or even a transitional senatorial government.[121]

These hypotheses assumed of course that Laval would, could or should be brought down. There were three issues over which this might occur: the decrees; foreign policy; or government policy towards the Leagues.[122] Even before the start of the new session – which Laval had delayed as long as possible – it seemed as though the government might suffer defeat over the decrees. The Radical Congress had led Blum to modify his earlier optimism about building the Popular Front principally around opposition to deflation: 'once the quarrel is no longer about the principle of the decrees but their extent . . . it lends itself to all kinds of compromise and even someone less adroit than M. Laval would be able to extricate himself'.[123] But when the Délégation des Gauches, while abandoning, as a result of the Radical Congress, any ideas that it might have had of demanding the abrogation of all the decrees, decided at least to amend them, the situation became very tense: at two sessions on 29 and 30 October, and in spite of a warning from Laval, the representatives of the left on the Finance Commission proceeded to modify the decrees affecting small rentiers and small *fonctionnaires*; according to Régnier the net effect of these amendments would have been to cause a budget deficit of 1.5m F.[124] The activities of the Commission led to a violent campaign by the conservative press and a renewed run on the franc; the

Radicals on the Commission were suddenly frightened by the consequences of their actions, and following an intervention by Herriot,[125] they mostly supported compromise proposals which, as Blum wrote,[126] effectively destroyed the original amendments: the total effect of the new proposals was to reduce the savings made by the decrees by 156mi F.

The reasons for the capitulation of the Radicals are simple enough: what was the alternative to Laval and to the decrees? In an atmosphere of renewed financial panic (Herriot, ever susceptible to gentle blackmail, tells how, at a Party meeting, Régnier passed him a note showing that, owing to the political crisis, some 400mi F. of gold had been expatriated during the course of the day[127]), during which Herriot had made it clear that he would refuse the succession to Laval, and where there was as yet no alternative economic and financial programme, even those Radicals sympathetic to the Popular Front were reluctant to act. As Kayser wrote, although a passionate supporter of the Popular Front, he did not want it to 'throw itself into some adventure which could result in its collapse'.[128] Blum pretended to be shocked by this new example of Radical pusillanimity,[129] but it after all only confirmed the analysis he had made after the Radical Congress, and had the benefit of making the Radicals seem responsible for avoiding a ministerial crisis which the Socialists may well not have wanted even if they could not have said so. The situation was best summed up by the Neo-Socialist Varenne at the Délégation des Gauches: 'It would be unfortunate if our opponents could accuse us of shipwrecking the franc'.[130] This narrowly averted crisis largely guaranteed the government's survival in any debate on financial policy. Thus, in spite of a further flurry of discussion as to how to bring Laval down after the occurrence of violent incidents at Limoges believed to have been caused by the Croix de Feu,[131] in the debate which finally took place in the Chamber on financial and economic policy, 63 Radicals voted for Laval, 73 voted against and 14 abstained.[132] To the astonishment of the political world Laval managed also to survive the debates on the Leagues and on foreign policy:[133] the government which had hardly been expected to last the summer had assured its survival into 1936. This extraordinary success was due partly to the support of Herriot; but important also was the continuing absence of any alternative policy if Laval was indeed to be replaced by a Popular Front coalition.

The Comité du Rassemblement Populaire was meanwhile continuing its laborious discussions. Although these negotiations were private, the testimony of three participants – Belin, Kayser and Delmas – gives some indication of their nature. Belin and Delmas describe the Communists as siding continuously with the Radicals against the Socialists;[134] Kayser's account is slightly different: the Radicals, he claims, could usually rely on the support of the Communists when differences arose with the Socialists, but not necessarily on the Socialists when differences arose with the Communists.[135] These differences were partly about the purpose and status of the programme being negotiated: here Radicals and Socialists united against the Communists in wanting to limit its political significance, and Kayser's position – that it should be 'neither an electoral programme, nor a programme of government, nor even a simple programme' but merely a declaration noting points of agreement – was accepted by the Comité in mid-November; this removed the possibility of single Popular Front candidatures at the elections.[136] But on the issue of economic and financial policy, the Radical representatives, who had to be very cautious because of the divergences on view within the Party[137] were more likely to find the Communists siding with them against the Socialists.

There were three important areas of disagreement: the financing of the programme; devaluation; and nationalization. Most of the various attempts by the left to formulate an economic policy had, we have seen, contained a certain number of measures in common which were intended to stimulate demand and reverse deflation: public works, a shorter working week, a wheat board; but Kayser complained that the Comité's technical experts had said nothing about how to finance such proposals.[138] This was the question which had already been raised during the summer. The Communist solution was of course to 'make the rich pay': this was presented by them as a traditional republican demand which had long been advocated by the Socialists and by Radicals like Jammy-Schmidt;[139] and indeed the tireless Communist campaign against the '200 families' was partly designed to appeal to the republican instincts of the Radicals. Blum was sceptical as to the resources that could be expected from the Communist tax proposals, and he saw them as deflationary in their effects.[140] And the C.G.T. engaged in angry public controversy with the Communists over this question: the formula 'make the rich pay' was, in its view, merely a piece of propaganda.[141] Where indeed were the 'rich'? 'They are no longer individuals, they are companies. Property is no longer individual, it is collective and anonymous'.[142] In short, it was certainly desirable to improve the tax system, but the fundamental problem was elsewhere – to stimulate demand and thereby restore prosperity.[143] But for the Communists, behind these arguments lurked another less openly expressed argument: resignation to the necessity for devaluation.[144]

There was certainly truth in this accusation; but as a result of the Communist refusal even to consider the possibility of devaluation the question could barely be discussed by the Comité. Therefore at Christmas 1935 Basch assembled representatives of the non-communist organizations to discuss devaluation: according to Belin's account, he and Auriol declared themselves in favour; and Delbos, for the Radicals, claimed that he was not competent to judge; the result was inconclusive.[145] But if the C.G.T. was, as the Communists accused, quite ready to accept the need for devaluation, it believed that much more important was a profound transformation of the economy by a series of judiciously selected nationalizations;[146] and the Socialist position, if not identical, was similar: Blum, hoping that his articles of August 1935 had overcome Communist scruples, suggested that Zyromski propose to the Comité that the level of compensation of shareholders of nationalized industries should be calculated in inverse proportion to their wealth or to the number of shares held.[147] The Radicals, however, were reluctant to accept the nationalization of any more than the arms industries – and this for entirely political reasons – and so even if Blum had to some extent overcome the doctrinal objections of the Communists, their tactical objection remained: nothing must be done to cause any obstacle to the unity of the left.

At the beginning of 1936, events moved with sudden rapidity: the programme of the Comité du Rassemblement Populaire was published on 10 January; on 15 January the Radical Party Bureau, rebutting accusations in the conservative press that the Radical representatives on the Comité had acted without any authority, declared that it had approved the programme;[148] and on 19 January the Executive Committee of the Party confirmed this approval. This same meeting of the Committee elected Daladier to the presidency of the Party, which Herriot had resigned a month earlier, and it also declared its hostility to Radical participation in the government, insisting on the imposition of voting discipline by the Radical Group; two days later Herriot and the other Radical ministers resigned from the government, and Laval's charmed existence was finally over.

In fact these events were not directly related: the denouement of Laval's government was obscure, but it seems that Herriot's decision to resign, prefigured by his resignation from the presidency of the Party in December, had been taken before the meeting of the Executive Committee which merely provided the pretext;[149] and it was not connected – nor as far as one can see was the decision of the Executive Committee – with the publication of the programme of the Comité du Rassemblement Populaire. This is not as surprising as it might seem: the Sarraut government which replaced Laval's, although the first government headed by a Radical since February 1934, was not a Popular Front government but rather a transitional government of the type that had been mooted at various times during the autumn. And indeed the publication of the programme had not really solved any of the problems which had made the left reluctant to embark on a premature Popular Front government. It contained a predictable series of measures to stimulate demand: a shorter working week (no figure specified) without any reduction in wages; a national unemployment fund; a programme of public works (no figure specified); a wheat marketing board; the immediate repeal of the most inequitable decrees followed eventually by the repeal of the rest. Of the three questions which had been at issue during the autumn, devaluation was not mentioned although the possibility of exchange control was envisaged; the nationalization of only the arms industries was proposed, under the rubric of the 'defence of peace', and the Bank of France was to be more tightly controlled by the government, although outright nationalization was rejected; and, finally, the programme envisaged raising revenue by tax measures to hit large fortunes, but few details were given.[150]

The programme was much nearer to the Communists' ideas, that is a list of demands, than to the more doctrinally pure programme which the Socialists had proposed since November 1934 or the plan of structural economic reform proposed by the C.G.T. Certainly the preamble gave some comfort to the Socialists – 'the urgent demands . . . will have to be followed up by more far reaching measures' – but it was more or less openly disavowed by the Communists.[151] In no sense was the programme a detailed blueprint for government, and Kayser made it quite clear why: 'if there is nothing on the nature of the immediate revenues to cover the immediate expenditure resulting from the application of the planned reforms, this is because, for the moment, each party has its own specific solutions'; but he warned that agreement must go further or disaster would lie ahead.[152] But the programme does not perhaps merit all the criticisms of 'moderation' which have been levelled against it: in accepting a reduction in the working week – which as Rolland, the *rapporteur* on social policy, admitted at the Congress of 1935, was a subject that continued to divide the Party[153] – a wheat board and a national unemployment fund, the Radicals were accepting policies which committed them to a total reversal of those they had pursued or supported since 1932. To the extent that the economic proposals were somewhat unadventurous this was because the Popular Front was more than anything else a traditional union of republican defence. It was not Laval's economic policy which had pushed the Radicals, or the Communists, into the Popular Front: that policy was hardly popular, as the protests at the 1935 Congress had shown, but to many Radicals the alternatives continued to seem worse. Even Kayser could write in December 1935 that it was not impossible to be 'both an unyielding supporter of economies and an intransigent republican'.[154] Indeed we have seen that the Radicals were if anything less critical of government economic policy in the autumn of 1935 than in the autumn of the previous year, and this in spite of the movement of protest sparked off by the Laval decrees.

But this is less surprising than at first seems the case: it is possible to overestimate the unpopularity of the decrees. Certainly the agitation against them was of a much more spectacular nature than against the Doumergue decrees in 1934: on the first pay day after the promulgation of the decrees there were riots at the naval bases of Brest and Toulon, in which one demonstrator died; meetings of protest took place throughout the course of July and August, and although they had mostly died down by the early autumn,[155] in some places they continued intermittently until the end of the year. It was also the case that the very extensive nature of the decrees brought together a much wider coalition of opposition to them than in the previous year: many Prefects observed in their reports that *fonctionnaires* had been joined in their protests by landlords who opposed the cuts in rents and even by small shopkeepers – 'they no longer attack the *fonctionnaires* as they did previously' commented the *Commissaire Spécial* of Pau – worried about the effect that further deflation would have on business.[156]

But having said this, the decrees caused less opposition than is often supposed. There were perhaps two explanations for this. First, as we have seen, the decrees cutting salaries were accompanied by measures which reduced prices, and although retail prices did in fact begin to rise towards the end of the year, the importance of the decrees on prices in terms of propaganda was nonetheless important and once again possibly succeeded in driving a wedge between public and private sector workers: to quote one Prefect, 'the measures taken to reduce the cost of living . . . seem to me to have greatly contributed to the lowering of tension among wage earners'.[157] Alain Corbin's retrospective study of public opinion in the Haute-Vienne concludes that at least in this primarily agricultural *département* opposition to the decrees was not among the primary reasons for opposition to Laval, and he also shows that over half of those giving reasons for their satisfaction over the decrees gave price reductions as their main reason.[158] Secondly, and more importantly, the rise in agricultural prices – quite independent of any action taken by Laval – had by the autumn contributed significantly to relieving the situation in the countryside which had so preoccupied governments since 1933. Noting the decline in political tension since the summer, one Prefect attributed it 'for a large part to the rise in wheat prices';[159] the Prefect of Belfort noted that a petition organized by the peasant protest movement in his *département* had been a complete failure.[160] This relative peace in the countryside was noted again and again.[161] The rise in agricultural prices – occurring shortly after the issue of the decrees – was to remove the greatest threat to social order since the beginning of the Depression in France.

It would, of course, be absurd to deny the existence of any link between the economic crisis and the successes of the Popular Front; in that case the popular explosion of strikes in June 1936 would be inexplicable. It has often been noted that many workers had experienced a rise in real income since 1930. But besides the fact that it was the nominal wage level of which people were most conscious, it is also the case that every cut in money wages represents an exercise of arbitrary power against the workforce and the revolt of 1936 was as much about this as about levels of pay: many employers exploited the Depression to intensify factory discipline, stamp out trade-union activity and increase productivity by means of 'rationalization'. But Laval's decrees, on the other hand, did not directly affect workers in the private sector except in reducing certain prices and rents (unless it was believed, as the Communists and Socialists had tried to show since 1932, that cuts in public sector pay were a signal for cuts in wages). Once again, therefore, economic policy did not necessarily provide the most effective cement of opposition. The great demonstrations of 14 July occurred, we have noted, before the decrees were issued. Various Prefects observed that demonstrations of the Popular Front in the summer of 1935 attracted much larger attendance than those protesting against the decrees; and the Prefect of the Côtes du Nord drew the following conclusion: 'the struggle against fascism is the leitmotive of these meetings much more than the decree laws, for it is a theme on which the three parties, Radical-Socialist, Socialist and Communist can agree'.[162] The Popular Front was, before it was anything else, a great republican protest. It is ironic that the demonstration of 14 July 1935 should have taken place on the day of the death of Alfred Dreyfus: on the day of the death of the symbol of one great republican *rassemblement* of the past, the bases of another were being laid. And it is fitting that Victor Basch, who had been President of the Ligue des Droits de l'Homme during the Dreyfus Affair, should have lived to preside over the Comité du Rassemblement Populaire. After four years of economic stagnation, political upheaval and erosion of the authority of parliament, the Popular Front seemed to offer the prospect of a republican revival in the widest sense of the term. In short, it was *la Grande Espérance*.

But there is another side to this picture. For many of those who had enthusiastically supported the idea of a union of the left, the programme of the Popular Front represented a bitter disappointment. To the C.G.T., and to many members of the S.F.I.O., the Popular Front had seemed the opportunity to implement a profound transformation of the structure of the economy – by the 'Plan'. The programme of the Popular Front, wrote Delmas later, 'provided no serious and effective solution as regards economic and social organization';[163] there was nothing, said René Belin, which the C.G.T. could not accept in the programme, but it was quite inadequate as it stood.[164] Like those conservatives suspicious of much of the unorthodox interventionism of the Laval government but willing to support it – reluctantly – as an alternative to devaluation and as a bulwark against 'revolution', many supporters of the Popular Front found themselves reluctantly led to defend a programme which disappointed their hopes but which offered a bulwark against 'fascism'. It is, therefore, to these two 'unorthodox' solutions of devaluation and the Plan that we must now turn.

# PART 3

# Non-conformists of left and right

# 7 ᔐ Plans and planners

Les plans sont le monument rationnel et lyrique dressé au sein des contingences.

(Le Corbusier, *La Ville radieuse*, 1933)

In 1932 Lucien Laurat summed up his vision of the world crisis: 'in front of the very eyes of the hungry masses who produced them, coffee is thrown into the sea, wheat is burnt, cotton destroyed'.[1] There was nothing unusual in this choice of example: for writers both inside and outside France the destroyed coffee of Brazil had become an *image d'Epinal* of the futility and waste of economic crisis.[2] But out of this irrational world of economic chaos developed a search for order and rationality, for organization and control. And it was this search which lay at the root of the flowering of 'plans' in France – and not only in France[3] – during the 1930s. We must not exaggerate the novelty or importance of a word: the idea of 'plans' had already enjoyed a certain vogue during the 1920s as a reaction against that previous example of anarchy and human folly, the First World War. Given a certain currency by Rathenau and the advocates of *Planwirtschaft*, the word had been later popularized by the First Soviet Plan. Two examples demonstrate that by the beginning of the 1930s, the idea was well established in France: first, the series of books, predating the crisis, published by Georges Valois under the general heading *Crises and Plans*; secondly, the review *Plans*, appearing between January 1931 and 1933 and including Lagardelle and Le Corbusier on its editorial boards.[4] Before the economic crises affected France, then, the notion of a 'plan' was quite familiar in certain circles. And the coming of the crisis could only confirm the importance of the idea and transform it from a preoccupation of various minor groups on the fringes of politics,[5] to one of the central questions of political debate. But although it must be seen in this general context, the movement known as 'planism' which developed in France during 1934 was more than just a vague yearning for an end to the present chaos; its specific origins are to be found outside the borders of France in the writing and action of the Belgian Socialist, Henri de Man.[6] (To avoid scattering the text with italics, I have coined the neologisms 'planist' and 'planism' from the French *planiste* and *planisme*.)

## 1933: Henri de Man and the origins of planism in France

'The new Socialism will be as different from that of the Communist Manifesto as the Socialism of Marx was from that of the Utopian Socialists.'[7] With these words Henri de Man announced planism in the autumn of 1933. Born into a bourgeois Flemish family at Anvers in 1885, and educated at the University of Leipzig, de Man had been an active Socialist since 1902. Already a significant figure in the Belgian Socialist Party before 1914, he had spent extended periods abroad: in America (1919–21), Switzerland (1925–9) and, finally, Germany where he held a chair in Social Psychology at Frankfurt from 1929 to 1933. Able to write with equal fluency in Flemish, German, French and English, de Man was an extremely impressive intellectual figure who not only wrote on a wide variety of subjects – social psychology, industrial sociology, history – but also had considerable practical experience of the Belgian labour movement, having between 1911 and 1914 been the first head of the Centrale d'Education Ouvrière in Brussels.[8] Although his post-war reputation has suffered from his collaboration with the Nazis, in the inter-war years he was one of the most controversial figures of European Socialism especially after the German publication in 1926 of his revisionist book, translated into English as *The Psychology of Socialism*.[9]

The title of the slightly modified French translation of this work, *Au delà du Marxisme* (1927), is revealing: de Man's revisionism was explicitly intended to go beyond Bernstein's in that it attacked the philosophical foundations of Marxism.[10] Situating Marx relativistically as a product of eighteenth-century rationalism, nineteenth-century materialism and classical economics,[11] de Man attacked the principles of economic hedonism, rationalism and determinism which he saw as the bases of Marxism.[12] Declaring, with Spengler, that the twentieth century was the 'century of psychology', he proposed instead a psychological interpretation of the origins and nature of Socialist belief – Freud appears many times in his pages and one of his key notions was that of the 'social inferiority complex' – which emphasized its ethical foundations, especially in Christianity.[13]

The attack was not only on Marxism as an inadequate tool of social analysis but also as a tool of political action: 'My doubts as to the validity of Marxist doctrine arose from my disappointment at seeing the lack of radicalism of the Marxist working-class movement'.[14] The Marxist emphasis on the class struggle had paradoxically resulted in the cultural embourgeoisification of the proletariat, and, as it increasingly found its material needs gratified by capitalism, in its integration into the capitalist regime, with a resulting atrophy and bureaucratization of the Socialist movement. De Man attempted, therefore, to displace the centre of Socialist doctrine: 'Just as the economic category of the method of production was the pivot of the old doctrine [i.e. Marxism], so man himself, as a spiritual individuality, will be found at the centre of the new'.[15] Socialism ought to be less concerned with the transfer of property than with restoring a sense of joy in work,[16] with ending the alienation of the worker from his social and economic environment.[17] This did not mean that the idea of the class struggle was abandoned, but that it needed to be reinvigorated: 'Let us found the class struggle on socialism instead of founding socialism on the class struggle'.[18] In short, although de Man's highly theoretical book contained little specific advice on what form the new Socialism should take – he did propose that the trade union movement should concentrate less on demands for higher wages and more on questions of workers' control and industrial democracy[19] – the aim of his theoretical critique was highly practical: 'A theory which descries the fundamental motive of Socialism in the moral judgement inspired by the community sentiment, *understands* more than a theory which can see no deeper than the struggle of interests on the surface of things; and the former theory is more vivifying than the latter'.[20]

Between 1926 and 1933 the situation had obviously changed. But de Man retained a fundamental continuity of objective: to reinvigorate Socialism, to replace passivity with action. If *The Psychology of Socialism* had been intended to provide a theoretical justification for voluntarism,[21] it was planism which provided the *content* of a 'voluntarist politics'.[22] The Plan, then, would be the practical action implied in 1926, and adapted to the new conditions of 1933: the economic crisis and the success of fascism in Germany. Of course these conditions were linked: 'it is not by anti-fascism that one fights fascism, it is by combatting the crisis itself'.[23] The shortest definition of planism was, therefore, 'anti-crisis Socialism'.[24]

These were not entirely original sentiments, but de Man accompanied them with an analysis of the origins of fascism which led him to propose a new form of anti-fascist political action. Fascism was a 'reactionary movement which exploits revolutionary feelings'[25] and the problem of anti-fascism was to orient these feelings in a different direction. There were several stages to the argument. Modern capitalism had not resulted, as Marx predicted it would, in the disappearance of the *classes moyennes*, but on the contrary in their reappearance in a new form: the independent artisan and peasant classes had been replaced by a new class of clerks and government employees; this new class created by an 'upwards leakage' from the proletariat, had been matched during the crisis by another new class created by a 'downward leakage' – the unemployed. But, although the *classes moyennes* were not proletarianized as individuals, their objective class situation had drawn them collectively nearer to that of wage earners in that they had become increasingly dependent on the power of monopoly capitalism (peasants had become dependent on trusts which controlled the production of fertilizers, shopkeepers had become the employees of vast multiple chain stores); this precarious class situation, however, only strengthened their resolve, as individuals, to resist proletarianization.[26] Thus it was possible – and indeed necessary if fascism was to be avoided – to unite the *classes moyennes* and the proletariat in a common struggle against monopoly capitalism, taking account, however, of their different class interests.

At one time it might have been possible to centre this struggle around the exaction of greater material gains from a reluctant capitalist class; but this was no longer conceivable now that capitalism had entered a 'stage of regression and decadence'. The revitalized reformism which had been one of the possible practical conclusions implied in *The Psychology of Socialism*[27] was no longer feasible either economically, since the capitalist economy was no longer expanding, or politically, since unemployment undermined the workers' capacity to resist their employers.[28] Rather than attempt to obtain larger slices of a rapidly diminishing cake by 'redistributional reforms' (*réformes de répartition*), it was instead necessary to increase the size of the cake itself by 'structural reforms'. But this did not mean Socialism. The economic crisis was driving capitalism into a vicious circle of protection and economic nationalism: an international Socialist revolution had, therefore, never been less imminent. From this analysis three inferences could be drawn: first, solutions to the crisis must be sought in the framework of the national economy; secondly, it was necessary to embark on profound structural reforms of the economy which would eliminate the causes of the economic crisis; thirdly, such reforms had to be acceptable to the majority: that is, not only must they not alienate the *classes moyennes* but, on the contrary, win their support.

These three conclusions formed the premises of the Plan drawn up by a special *Bureau d'études* set up by the Parti Ouvrier Belge (P.O.B.) and presided over by de Man who had left Germany specially for this purpose in 1933.[29] The Plan envisaged a mixed economy between capitalism and Socialism, which would also be a necessary stage on the road to Socialism. The structural reforms included the nationalization of credit and of certain basic industries: large sectors of the economy would not be nationalized but state ownership and control of credit and of these basic industries – transport, energy, and so on – would both free the rest of the economy from subservience to monopoly capital, thus attracting the support of the *classes moyennes*, and allow the state to exercise a general surveillance over the private sector, directing its activities according to a plan (a plan within the Plan, as it were) to be drawn up every four years. With these means at its disposal the state could implement an expansionary economic policy to increase demand and stimulate the economic revival that capitalism was incapable of providing.[30] The Plan was not only a blueprint for a future mixed economy; it was also banner – an instrument of propaganda – under which to rally the forces of anti-capitalism. All allies were welcome: the only condition was acceptance of the Plan. Thus the Plan was the means to its own end. And the first step towards this end was taken at Christmas of 1933 when, helped considerably by the support of the unions, the Plan was adopted by the Congress of the P.O.B. of which de Man became vice-president.

The Belgian *Plan du Travail* at once aroused enormous interest on the left in France. In the words of the Socialist George Soulès, part of the attraction of planism, of which he became an ardent supporter, lay in its 'intelligent newness, the last hope of breaking up the frozen structures of the old Socialist Party'.[31] Indeed, after the stale works of party piety by such figures as Paul Faure, Jean Lebas or J.-B. Séverac, content to repeat well-known Marxist verities,[32] de Man's densely argued prose must have come as a revelation. 'At last a few ideas' exclaimed Robert Lacoste of the *fonctionnaires*' union.[33] The S.F.I.O. lacked a first-rate theoretical thinker: Blum saw his role not as a theoretician but as a subtle interpreter of the Party to itself.[34] He directed his enormous intelligence not so much to speculation as to justifying and theorizing practical positions already adopted.[35]

But by the end of 1933 Socialist parliamentary action had, as we have seen, reached a deadlock: the abstention over Chautemps' financial bill in December had temporarily relieved them of the dilemma of being 'dupes' or 'accomplices' but it hardly offered a way forward; nor had the Neo-Socialists solved their own problems by splitting from the S.F.I.O.: having voted against Sarraut's government, after failing to persuade him to soften his financial proposals, they had voted for Chautemps for no other reason than to avoid a ministerial crisis, and without even the assurance that after the vote of the financial bill the government would turn its attention to the economy, which had been the *raison d'être* for their support of Daladier three months earlier. In this situation of impasse de Man offered positive action (volontarism) against the crisis: on the one hand, this was more than a passive wait for the revolution; on the other, it was more than the reformist semi-collaboration in budgetary deflation to which the Socialists and, ultimately, the Neo-Socialists, had been condemned between 1932 and 1934. At the end of 1933 there were three political groups of the left most willing to accept this new challenge: the Neo-Socialists (Parti Socialiste de France); and two groups within the S.F.I.O.: Révolution Constructive and Combat Marxiste.

The Neo-Socialists were by no means an ideologically united group: what had initially divided many Socialists from the Party was, we have seen, the purely tactical question of the extent to which it was justifiable to support governments of the left which pursued conservative economic policies; and to the end Renaudel insisted that the quarrel was tactical and not doctrinal, similar to that between his old mentor Jean Jaurès and Jules Guesde.[36] But having said this it is true that many Neo-Socialist leaders were searching for a doctrinal alternative to Socialism. The roots of this search ante-dated the economic crisis. In 1928 Montagnon's revisionist *Grandeurs et servitudes socialistes* attacked a rather crude version of Marxist economic determinism,

and demonstrated that Marx's predictions about the increasing proletarianization of the population had been belied by the growth of a new stratum of
*classes moyennes*: the moral of this analysis was that effective political action
must rest on a wider base than the proletariat alone; in this view violent
revolution was replaced by a gradual reorganization of society on syndical
lines. Déat's more substantial and influential work *Perspectives socialistes*
(1930) also called for a coalescence of all the 'anti-capitalist forces (which)
spill widely beyond the working classes',[37] and attempted to divert the objectives of Socialist action from the question of property relations to the issue of
control: 'What counts now is *not the ownership of property* but the control
of power'.[38] Both books were the result of a variety of influences: the de Man
of the 1920s, the participatory Socialism of Albert Thomas during the First
World War (Montagnon had headed the Cabinet from 1914 to 1918), the
pre-war writings of Sembat and the reformist policies advocated by the
C.G.T. immediately after the war.[39] Both books were partly explicit doctrinal
justifications for a policy of parliamentary collaboration, even governmental
participation, with at least some of the Radicals.[40]

The political and economic crisis of the 1930s only seemed to Déat,
Montagnon and others to reinforce the necessity for such a policy, and led to
a development of the earlier analysis. This occurred most spectacularly at the
Congress of Paris in famous speeches by Montagnon, Marquet and Déat,
republished in October 1933, with a preface and commentary by Max
Bonnafous, as *Néo-Socialisme? Ordre, autorité, nation*, a title which took up
the trinity of themes which had so 'horrified' Blum. The speeches were very
different – they were not prepared in collaboration[41] – but they contained
three important themes in common. First, the priority of Socialists must be to
fight fascism: this could be done only by winning over the *classes moyennes*
– 'ferments of revolution' who were terrified of being proletarianized – and
conquering unemployment. But, secondly, it was necessary to recognize that,
temporarily at least, action against the crisis had to be applied within
national boundaries and that to be effective it was necessary to have a strong
state able to control the economy: with this power at its disposal the state
should, claimed Montagnon, direct the economy according to the 'mystique
of a plan in the style of the Five Year Plan'.[42] Thirdly, Socialists must act in
the present by building on the examples of, and learning from the mistakes of,
the social and economic experiments being conducted in Italy, Germany,
Russia and Roosevelt's America; only at cost to their survival would
Socialists ignore these new forms of social organization midway between
pure capitalism and pure Socialism.

This interest in 'intermediary regimes', considered very unhealthy by
Blum, became one of the most distinctive features of Neo-Socialism.[43] But
although the Neo-Socialists might have some idea of the principles on which
such a regime might be built in France,[44] its precise form was extremely

vague. To cite examples as different as Italian Fascism, Soviet Communism and the New Deal hardly provided clarification or analytical rigour. For the Neo-Socialists, then, the publication of the Belgian *Plan du Travail* seemed to give specific policy content to what had been only a vague aspiration, and the fact that it had been adopted by another Socialist Party seemed retrospectively to have vindicated their opposition to the S.F.I.O.: the Plan, wrote Déat, was 'born under the star of Neo-Socialism'.[45] The Neo-Socialists had been among the first observers in France to draw attention to de Man's articles on planism;[46] and the publication of the Plan itself was hailed as a major event: it was 'one of those intermediary forms of which Léon Blum is so terrified and for which he wants Socialism to take no responsibility'.[47] Now it was necessary to draw up such a plan for France.[48]

The similarities between their own ideas and those of de Man enabled the Neo-Socialists to overlook the main difference: the Belgian Plan did certainly define the maximum limits of Socialist action during the economic crisis, but it also defined the minimum acceptable limits; while the logic of the Neo-Socialists' position impelled them towards collaboration with the Radicals, the Plan set the conditions of collaboration far higher than anything the Radicals would be likely to accept. Whether recognizing this fact, or embarrassed by the patronage of these dissident Socialists, de Man confided the publication in France of the Plan, and his commentaries on it, to a group within the S.F.I.O. itself: Révolution Constructive.[49] This was originally a group of 11 young Socialist intellectuals – including such later well-known figures as Claude Lévi-Strauss, Robert Marjolin and Georges Lefranc[50] – who had collectively published a book, *Révolution constructive*, after the elections of 1932. Although directly concerned with those questions of the appropriate forms of political action which had been raised by Déat, the book was not part of the argument about the relevance of Marxism to contemporary Socialism; rather it was a meditation on the failures and betrayals, as the authors saw it, of Socialism in power in Germany, Britain, Sweden and Russia, resulting in the conclusion that to hold *political* power was not a guarantee of success. Political action should be displaced from the parliamentary political arena to direct involvement with unions and co-operatives: 'a decree is not enough to transform the organization of production and exchange'.[51] With its stress on the importance of Socialist participation in trade union action, *Révolution constructive* was already very close to many of the preoccupations of de Man's *Psychology of Socialism*.[52]

During 1933 the group had not sympathized totally with any of the *tendances* of the S.F.I.O.;[53] but an attempt in December 1933 to convey their concern to Blum was unsuccessful.[54] And when the Party a few days later issued its manifesto 'We claim power', in an open letter to Paul Faure Révolution Constructive condemned the mixture of verbal extremism and parliamentary opportunism which had characterized Socialist action since

May 1932.[55] The reflection of Révolution Constructive was therefore less on the economic nature of the crisis and economic solutions to it than on the forms of Socialist action most appropriate to it. In particular the crisis heightened the dangers of becoming too closely associated with a regime which seemed to be in decline: 'Let us take care not to be implicated in its collapse'.[56] But the conclusion to which this reflection led – that the Party should define a few specific, practical and immediately realizable objectives: the nationalization of banks, insurance companies and war industries – made them, as Lefranc says, 'psychologically prepared' for the planism of Henri de Man; and in December 1933 they published the Plan, and his commentaries on it, as their first *Cahier*.

If the Neo-Socialists had come to planism by means of parliamentary reformism, and Révolution Constructive precisely by reaction against it, Combat Marxiste, the third group of French Socialist planists, of which Lucien Laurat was a leading member, had arrived at the same conclusions by a more theoretical route – as a result of its discussions since 1928 on the problem of the economic transition from capitalism to Socialism. Laurat had started from very different premises to de Man's: far from searching *au delà du marxisme* he believed, on the contrary, that 'capitalism conforms strictly to the predictions of Karl Marx',[57] and criticized the inadequate grounding in Marxism of most French economists.[58] But since Marx's economic work was largely critical and since the economic crisis marked a further decomposition of capitalism, it was necessary to have 'a more concrete idea of *the first stages* of the transformation. We envisage a *mixed economy* in which a large sector will remain in the hands of capital'.[59] Laurat had been in Russia between 1923 and 1927 and it was the experience of N.E.P. which provided his model for the transition to Socialism: Russian experience between 1919 and 1920 had taught that 'in the economic field, a *tabula rasa* policy can lead to the most terrible upheavals'.[60] In short: 'we want to do without the experience of War communism'.[61]

At the end of 1933 Révolution Constructive and Combat Marxiste drew up a common motion, based on planist principles, for submission to the congresses of the Socialist federations preparing for the National Congress of the Party in February 1934: it proposed that the Party draw up both a programme of immediate action and a plan. This programme, the aim of which was to unite the *classes moyennes* and the proletariat, would include the 40-hour week, public works, fiscal reform and so on. Such measures were not in themselves new; but the motion added that the Party must emphasize that 'those redistributional reforms are no longer possible without a structural revolution through the plan'. The Party should set up a special commission to work out the details of such a plan; and, once this had been done, acceptance of the plan would mark the limits of co-operation with other political groups, whether in government or opposition.[62] The struggle for the future of the Party was now on.

## 1934: The defeat of planism

The success of this motion was, in the words of Georges Soulès, 'prodigious'. His own federation, the Drôme, voted for it,[63] as did those of the Pyrenées-Orientales and the Manche; there were intense debates even in the traditionally Guesdist Nord; and the important Seine Federation voted on 28 January 1934 for a compromise motion, drafted largely by Georges Lefranc, which expressed many planist ideas.[64] The success of the planists was helped by the at least partial conversion to their ideas of important figures from different wings of the Party: Jacques Grumbach and Zyromski (both from Bataille Socialiste), Jules Moch (very close to Blum), André Philip (the expositor in France of de Man's *The Psychology of Socialism*) and Maurice Paz. The Congress, planned for 10 February, was postponed after the events of 6 February, but the Conseil National instructed the Party to prepare for the Congress, which was now to be held in May, a 'plan displaying two aspects: an instrument of mass propaganda ... and an immediate programme of action for the Party in power'.[65]

The Party was, however, by no means won over to planism. *Le Populaire*, to the irritation of the Socialist planists,[66] had given only very limited space to the Belgian Plan and Blum had written a series of far from enthusiastic articles under the general title of *Au delà du réformisme* (insidiously reminding his readers of de Man's revisionist tendencies).[67] Blum's articles had a double purpose. First, to prevent the Neo-Socialists draping themselves in the respectability of a policy adopted by a sister party, he showed that the Plan had performed the same service for the P.O.B. as the *Cahiers d'Hughyens* for the S.F.I.O. in 1932: it provided a minimum condition for participation in government; the Plan was therefore as far from reformism of the kind proposed by the Neo-Socialists as it was possible to be.[68] Seen in this light there was nothing very new about the Plan either: in stressing the primordial importance of the nationalization of credit, de Man was merely making a tactical modification by choosing to highlight one part of the Socialist programme for propaganda purposes, rather as the French Socialists had done with the capital levy during the 1920s.[69]

But, secondly, having tried to defuse the importance of the Plan, Blum proceeded to criticize it in two ways. First, at this stage ignoring that the Plan included the nationalization of more than just credit, he questioned whether this measure would, in France, have either the economic importance or the mobilizing force that it had in Belgium.[70] Secondly, he noted the danger that the mixed economy proposed by de Man might become permanent: the Plan did not envisage the 'progressive diminution . . . of the market sector . . . rather it helps to preserve it, to consolidate it, at the same time as adapting it'; but once in power the Socialists could not restrict themselves in this way: 'Socialism must obey its destiny'.[71] Thus, having claimed that the Plan was not the reformism of the Neo-Socialists, Blum, in rather contradictory fashion, accused it of reformism nonetheless. The battlelines were drawn: in the months leading up to the Congress the planists of the S.F.I.O., in the columns of the monthly journal *Combat marxiste*, in the *Cahiers* published by Révolution Constructive and in the 'Tribune' column of *Le Populaire*, were forced not only to argue their own ideas but also to refute the implicit charge of reformism.

The defence of planism was mounted by expounding both its economic and its political implications. Economically, planism did not, it was argued, propose a renovation of capitalism '*à la Bernstein*';[72] indeed a plan would not be applicable within the structures of capitalism[73] because it represented a complete break with the present regime: 'One aim: halt the economic crisis. One means: break with capitalism and break with it today'.[74] But at the same time as being such an important economic transformation, the plan did, unlike the full Socialist programme, envisage the possibility of action in the present: it must be '*practical, immediate* and *realizable* in today's con-ditions'.[75] What would make the nationalizations of the plan different from state capitalism – different, that is, from nationalizations which had taken place within the structure of capitalism – was partly the more democratic way in which the nationalized industries would be run[76] and, even more, their quantitative importance: 'a series of collectivizations affecting vital industries and services . . . and carried out under the control of workers' organizations must be considered as a socialization, because it would change the very struc-ture of the economy. Quantity is transformed into quality'.[77] The plan was, therefore, the first stage on the road to total socialism.[78]

Economically, then, the plan stood half-way between the complete Socialist programme and a merely electoral programme of immediate action within the present economic structures. This implied, politically, that it rejected the polarities of revolution and reform, or Blum's 'relaxing idea' of either the conquest of power for integral socialism or the exercise of power for parliamentary reformism.[79] The importance of the changes represented by the plan would make the capture of power essential: 'as long as the property owners are the dominant class, nationalization will still be capitalism'.[80] There was a danger that this argument could become circular: the extensiveness of the nationalizations was evidence that the capture of power was necessary, and therefore also the guarantee that it had taken place.[81] By definition, the plan was the capture of power.[82]Thus, although the alliance with the *classes moyennes* was an essential part of the strategy of planism – indeed the key to the plan's realization[83] – this was 'quite different from a liaison with what in France is considered as their political equivalent: the Radical Party'.[84] Indeed planism solved the vexed question of how far it was justifiable to collaborate in parliament with other parties: they either accepted or rejected the plan.[85]

The plan, then, would not be drawn up as a platform for parliamentary elections: 'We no longer believe in the possibility of electoral enthusiasm after 1926 and 1934'.[86] This attitude shaded into one of open anti-parliamentarianism, as in the controversial declaration to the Party Congress in May by Jean Itard of Révolution Constructive: 'Parliamentarianism is dead. When I say parliamentarianism, I don't mean democracy. Democracy which in the nineteenth century was concretized in the parliamentary system has today gone beyond parliamentarianism, which has no more to offer';[87] and another planist spoke of the 'disrepute into which the parliamentary regime has *quite rightly* fallen'.[88] But having, if not rejected, certainly relegated parliamentary action to a secondary role, the planists were imprecise as to what form of political action they intended to employ to capture power. While the planists were strongly critical of the Party hierarchy's belief that it was un-Marxist, impossible and indeed unnecessarily restrictive, to plan in advance what the Socialists would do in power, they were open to the same reproach in their consideration of the political question: 'it is during the course of the struggle that the practical means will emerge'.[89] But whatever the form of this action, the Plan would play a primary role in reinvigorating the anti-fascist struggle and giving it a positive content. In short: 'we will realize the Plan by taking power, but we will take power by the Plan'.[90]

It was this formal aspect of the Plan as a mobilizing force rather than the content of its policy for overcoming the economic crisis, which dominated the debates of the Socialist congress at Toulouse in May 1934.[91] The reason for this was simple enough: in May 1934 there was no plan, and therefore discussion necessarily revolved around the question of principle. The Belgian Plan was obviously not applicable in all its details to the different circumstances of France; de Man himself wrote that 'the Plan is not for export',[92] although planism was. But by May 1934 the Party had, in spite of the resolution of the Conseil National, done nothing towards drawing up a plan of its own. As a contribution to discussion, Révolution Constructive had, in its second and third *Cahiers*, published two foreign plans and its fourth *Cahier* had outlined the 'Elements of a French Plan', based heavily on the Belgian Plan but containing more consideration of political reform. The plan to receive most publicity before the Congress was one produced under the aegis of the C.G.T., but it had been criticized even by the planists themselves as a reformist travesty of their ideas.[93]

Not only had the leadership of the Party made no attempt to draft a plan, the report drawn up for the Congress by Paul Faure had described the whole idea as an 'absurd chimera'.[94] And, following up this attack, at the Congress leading figures of the Party – Séverac, Faure, Lebas and Lévy[95] – all expressed their hostility to planism; and Blum attacked the idea that the crisis made redistributive reforms impossible: 'the American example proves that the crisis can have the opposite effect . . . The disarray of capitalism can lead it to redistributional reforms even bolder than those we are demanding'.[96] But although repeating his earlier criticisms, it was precisely in his partial acceptance of planism that Blum delivered the most effective *coup de grâce*: once again he reduced the plan to a purely tactical change, merely a question of 'imaginative and effective presentation which can raise the party member's enthusiasm to its highest pitch'.[97] And the final motion drawn up by the committee responsible for drafting a synthesis, on which various planist sympathizers sat, effectively rallied to Blum's conception in calling for a 'plan to be spread by brochures, tracts and lectures'. It did advocate the socialization of credit, insurance and important monopolies, a reduced working week, the setting up of agricultural marketing boards and the implementation of public works, but these measures were not articulated by any clear overall conception, as they would have been by the planists; and the motion finished by adding that once in power the Party would not allow itself to be restricted by any plan or programme.[98] Although most planists did vote for the motion,[99] it was clearly recognized by them as a defeat.[100]

There were several reasons for this failure. First, in spite of the planists' attempts to clarify their position and to show in simple language how the idea of the plan differed from that of previous programmes – it must be a 'section extracted from Socialist doctrine suitable to the events of the moment', a 'coherent whole'[101] – the debates at Toulouse were at times extremely confused, revealing that many delegates had little idea what planism involved. One delegate wondered what the arguments were about: 'The Plan will say what we said before, in a form better adapted to modern psychology ';[102] another refused to make any 'subtle distinction' between a plan and a programme.[103] The whole argument was difficult to take entirely seriously: 'I have no plan, I am anti-planist, but I am not planetary' proclaimed one delegate to laughter.[104] Secondly, some of the more prominent sympathizers with planism had a somewhat different view of it from the more 'orthodox' planists of Révolution Constructive or Combat Marxiste, and this meant that once it had served their purposes they could be more easily won back to support the Party hierarchy; this was particularly the case of Zyromski and other members of Bataille Socialiste. Zyromski had written several articles in defence of planism,[105] and he was obviously an important recruit to the cause;[106] but for him planism was a means of steering the Party away from parliamentary reformism to the struggle for the seizure of power which he believed the crisis made inevitable: far from placing emphasis on the *classes moyennes*, on the contrary, he believed that the experience of the previous two years had highlighted the need for an 'autonomous class policy'.[107] In short, the content of the plan was less important than its function as an instrument of propaganda for the Socialist accession to power; and for Zyromski, therefore, the Congress of Toulouse was a success.[108] Thirdly, the fact that the 'plan' which had received the most attention before the Congress was that of the C.G.T., which, we have seen, had been disavowed by the planists themselves, encouraged fears that planism was a new reformism. At a meeting of the Congress of the Seine Federation at the end of April to vote on a new motion for the new deferred Congress, there were shouts of 'down with Jouhaux' and attacks on the C.G.T. by Faure and others.[109]Fourthly, although the events of 6 February were in a sense dramatic confirmation of the planist claim that fascism was an imminent danger, ironically they also undermined the appearance of planism by making its anti-parliamentarianism highly suspect. Although Révolution Constructive might emphasize that its attacks on parliament were not attacks on democracy – indeed the contrary – after 6 February it was questionable whether defenders of democracy would best serve their cause in making this distinction; there was, in Rivière's words, a danger of supplying 'grist to the fascist mill'.[110]

But perhaps the most fundamental cause of the defeat of planism in the S.F.I.O. lay in the fact that only five months after the defection of some 30 deputies – and only 14 years after the Congress of Tours – the *vieille maison* was once again threatened with an internal dissent which, what is more, seemed to share many characteristics with that of the Neo-Socialists. Any questioning of the simple Marxist – or Guesdist – principles which held the Party together stimulated the old reflexes of Party solidarity. Of course Laurat was a much more sophisticated Marxist than Lebas or Faure, but a few functional truths simply understood are often less adaptable than a doctrine meditated upon and profoundly understood. And the economic crisis seemed after all the most striking possible confirmation of these simple truths. Indeed Lebas, attacking Déat's *Perspectives socialistes* in 1931, had made the telling polemical point that it was precisely those, like Déat, who had announced the death of Marxism during – and partly through observation of – the prosperity of the 1920s, who were still preaching revisionism even though the crisis had revealed the hollowness of their optimism.[111]

When Marquet and Déat had challenged the Party in 1933, Blum, while admitting that fascism was a danger, had warned against trying to fight it by using its own weapons: 'one does not fight fascism by becoming infected by it'.[112] Blum saw three signs of this tendency in the future Neo-Socialists: first, in their emphasis on attracting classes outside the proletariat and transforming 'Socialism, a class party, into a party of *declassés*';[113] secondly, in their emphasis on restricting action within the boundaries of the nation;[114] thirdly, in the approval of 'intermediary regimes': although there might well be intermediary regimes between pure socialism and pure capitalism, and although at least one of these regimes, that of Roosevelt, could even be viewed sympathetically, the Socialists must at all costs avoid becoming involved with them, even if this meant undergoing temporary unpopularity; the task was to 'maintain socialist doctrine in its integrity, in its purity'[115] – especially at a moment when the crisis seemed such striking witness to its validity.[116]

Now obviously the assimilation of the Neo-Socialists and the Fascists – however prescient it may have been – was largely polemical in intention, and furthermore the Neo-Socialists were not the same as the Socialist planists. But de Man did emphasize the importance of the *classes moyennes*, the need to act on a strictly national basis, and he explicitly advocated an intermediary regime for which the Socialists should accept full political responsibility. Besides these disconcerting similarities with a doctrine which the Socialists had recently fought so strenuously to eliminate from their ranks, there were two aspects of planism in particular which affronted their traditional 'Marxism'. First, the planists did not view the transformation of property relations as the main criterion of radical change: in the words of one planist, the Plan 'separates . . . the idea of property from that of power'.[117] Nationalization would only affect certain sectors of the economy, and would therefore involve compensation rather than outright expropriation; but the planists claimed that because this change nevertheless gave the state a completely new power over the economy, it could be described as radical, structural transformation. Not, however, in the eyes of Blum.[118] Secondly, the prospect, implicit in planism,[119] of a peaceful and gradual transition to Socialism, while theoretically acceptable, undermined an important psychological prop of Socialist belief: the almost eschatological idea of the revolution as a total rupture with the present, as a leap into an unknowable future. To quote Séverac: 'How can the changing reality of a struggle for which nothing in the past offers us useable experience . . . be contained in advance within certain formulae, however flexible they might be'.[120] Paul Faure put the point in its most lapidary form: 'A Plan? Socialism'.[121]

## 1934: planomania

The rejection of planism at Toulouse was far from signalling the end of the movement. The year 1934 was *par excellence* the year of 'planomania', or 'planophiles', and also of 'planophobes'. The point is most easily made merely by listing some of the so-called 'plans' drawn up in this year.[122]

| | |
|---|---|
| Foreign Plans published in France: | Belgian Plan |
| (all published by Révolution | British Plan (Socialist League) |
| Constructive) | Polish Plan (Victor Alter)[123] |
| Radical Plans: | Emile Roche Plan (May 1934) |
| | Young Radical Plan (May 1934)[124] |
| | Committee of Vigilance Plan (May 1934)[125] |

Socialist Plans:                            *Eléments    d'un    Plan    français*
                                            (Révolution Constructive's Plan)
Others:                                  Plan of 214 Deputies (April 1934)[126]
                                            *Nouvel age* Plan of Georges Valois (June 1934)[127]
                                            9 July Plan[128]
                                            Plan of the War Veterans (officially the Programme Civique de la Confédération Générale des Anciens Combattants – but it was rapidly known as their Plan) (March 1934)
                                            *La République des Combattants* (the Plan of the Union Federale des Combattants) (September 1934)
                                            Plan of the Etats Généraux du Travail (April 1934)
                                            C.G.T. Plan (September 1934)[129]

To this far from exhaustive list might be added the Plan français (December 1935) drawn up by the Comité du Plan, presided over by Déat.[130] The content and precision of the 'plans' varied so considerably as to defy any detailed comparative analysis. More important than their detailed content is the state of mind to which this sudden vogue testifies: they all proclaimed the need for some degree of control over the economy. However vague their content, all the 'plans' expressed a revolt against the helplessness of the political parties confronted with economic stagnation, social disorder and the threat of political collapse. And here of course the crucial date was – once again – 6 February 1934.

The *journée* of 6 February had to some extent undermined the positions of the planists within the S.F.I.O.; it nevertheless contributed enormously to the general spread of planist ideas throughout the country. The events of 6 February had highlighted the bankruptcy of political parties; but they had also ended the political impasse which existed between 1932 and 1934. After 6 February there was at last a government that could govern; but there was also a political void. There were two ways in which this void could be filled: either by a reinvigoration of the action of the discredited political parties – hence the largely unsuccessful campaigns of the Young Radicals at the Congress of Clermont or that of the planists at the Congress of Toulouse – or by the intrusion into the political arena of extra-parliamentary forces whose protest was given a content and a coherence by planism and the mystique of the plan. 'Political majorities', commented Déat, 'are now unmade . . . in the Place de la Concorde'.[131]

The first organization implicitly to accept this challenge was the C.G.T.: on 20 February, Robert Lacoste, of the *fonctionnaires'* union told the governing committee (C.C.N.) of the C.G.T. that 'it is towards the C.G.T. that all those who have lost confidence in political parties are looking';[132] and it was decided to set up a *Bureau d'études* (as the P.O.B. had done) which would draw up a Plan. The C.G.T.'s attitude towards political parties, including the Socialists, was, of course, somewhat ambivalent. Syndicalist memories died hard,[133] and Jouhaux's personal relations with Blum were far from warm: the idea of initiating a new political movement which Blum and the Socialists might have to follow cannot have displeased him and might have contributed to Blum's hostility to planism.[134] But the C.G.T.'s early sympathy for planism can be explained by other causes also: besides the fact that the trade unions in Belgium had played an important part in drawing up the Plan of the P.O.B., there were many similarities between the content of this plan and the C.G.T.'s proposals in 1919, which had also influenced the reformism of Montagnon and Déat. Among the first leaders of the C.G.T. to draw attention to the Belgian Plan and its significance for France were Charles Laurent and Robert Lacoste (editor of the influential *Tribune des Fonctionnaires*);[135] Léon Jouhaux and René Belin, his heir apparent, were quick to follow.[136] When at its meeting of 20 February the C.C.N. not only proposed the setting up of a *Bureau d'études* but also gave a summary indication of what the plan should contain – nationalization of credit and control of banks and key industries[137] – the planists of the S.F.I.O. were guardedly optimistic – 'the working class has a Plan'[138] – at the seeming conversion of an organization which had, since the beginning of the crisis, been exclusively concerned to obtain, in planist terminology, 'redistributional reforms'. But the Plan (not actually called such) which emerged from the so-called 'Etats Généraux du Travail' convened by the C.G.T. in April, which was the C.G.T. Plan in existence at the time of the Congress of Toulouse, caused, we have seen, widespread criticism for its timidity – it contained no mention of nationalizations – and for betraying hopes aroused by the earlier declarations of the C.G.T.: 'this is a step backwards', in the words of one planist.[139] In spite of these disappointments, various Socialist planists, such as Laurat and Lefranc, increasingly pessimistic about the prospects of influencing the Socialist Party,[140] became members of the C.G.T.'s *Bureau d'études*, the aim of which was to produce a definitive C.G.T. Plan, where they were joined by many other unionists and economists, including Francis Delaisi and Jean Duret, both lecturers at the C.G.T.'s workers' education institute (I.S.O.), the economist François Simiand, Achille Dauphin-Meunier, an employee of the Paribas bank and a specialist on banking questions, as well as Laurat, Lacoste and Lefranc.[141]

   In March 1934 another extra-parliamentary organization had also announced that it would 'intervene in public life to ensure the predominance of the general interest'. It was with these words that the National Council of the Confédération Nationale des Anciens Combattants – a body which had since 1927 loosely united the innumerable different war veterans' associations – adopted its *Programme Civique*.[142] The objectives of this programme were vague – it proclaimed the bankruptcy of liberalism, and the need for a reform of the state and a reorganization of the credit system – but its real significance lay in the fact that the Confédération had decided to take such an initiative at all.[143] Like the C.G.T., the organizations of war veterans showed a certain distrust of politicians – in this case perhaps the residual suspicion of the man at the front for the *embusqué* in Paris – and like the C.G.T. they were led to claim for themselves a political role partly by the need to defend their sectional interests. The transition in both cases was from that of a simple pressure group to that of a constructive political force, or, in planist terminology, from 'redistributional' to 'structural reforms'.[144] Simultaneously with embarking on its campaign for planism, the C.G.T. was attacking the Doumergue decree laws. Similarly the Confédération Nationale had, at the same time as it adopted its *Programme Civique*, condemned 'blind and systematic deflation'; but neither this, nor the fact that Georges Rivollet, Secretary of the Confédération, had become Doumergue's Minister of Pensions, prevented the government from announcing the need to cut the war veterans' pensions, which had so far managed to escape government spending cuts.

After meeting Doumergue in April the National Council of the Confédération held an exceptional meeting and agreed to accept a cut of 3 per cent from 1 July providing that by this date the government had begun to implement the reforms proposed by the veterans in the previous month; the Confédération announced that it would meet again on 8 July to consider whether the government had indeed fulfilled these conditions; if not it would consider what action to take next.[145] With extraordinary confidence – or presumption – the veterans seemed to be negotiating on equal terms with the government; and although Doumergue ignored their conditions and instituted the economies immediately, 8 July loomed as a moment of potential conflict: not only had the veterans announced their entry into politics, they had fixed a date as well.

The action of the C.G.T. and the Confédération was greeted with enthusiasm by much of the left. The comparison between the two organizations might seem strained, except that it was made by almost all contemporaries: in this association of 'the war and post-war generations'[146] all seemed suddenly possible. Belin himself noted, with reservations, certain similarities of attitude between the ideas of the veterans and the C.G.T.,[147] and representatives of the former were invited to the Etats Généraux du Travail; Neo-Socialists such as Paul Marion and Barthélemy Montagnon[148] welcomed these new forces into French politics, and the second Congress of the Neo-Socialists in May 1934 proclaimed its hope that the Party, 'within the framework drawn by the C.G.T. and the war veterans, will be able to gather together all the working people and sound elements [*éléments populaires et sains*] of the Nation';[149] Paul-Boncour also saw a striking similarity between the ideas of these two important forces which, he believed, should be integrated into the economic and political life of the nation,[150] and a year later, when the C.G.T. Plan had become a reality, he claimed that the plans of the two organizations 'resemble each other like brothers'.[151]

But the most vocal prophet of this new development in political life was undoubtedly the prolific Déat: the veterans, he wrote in March, 'have come forward while the political parties are in disarray';[152] but it was necessary for them to join up with the C.G.T. and other organizations which had drawn up plans: 'it will not be difficult to bring the various texts together . . . they all tend towards a managed economy, they are all hostile to deflation'.[153] Déat heralded 8 July – the date not only of the next meeting of the Confédération Nationale of the veterans but also of the next National Council of the Neo-Socialists when the question of Marquet's participation in the government would be debated – as the 'great turning-point' (*grande relève*) of French politics when the increasingly hapless government of Doumergue would be swept away by the new political and social forces.[154] Even when this sup-posedly dramatic day passed without incident – the veterans narrowly voting not to insist on Rivollet's resignation from a government which they nevertheless broadly condemned and the Neo-Socialists doing the same with regard to Marquet – Déat's enthusiasm for a gathering together of all forces between the traditional right and left was undiminished.[155]

It is clear, therefore, that during 1934 the notion of the plan underwent a considerable evolution. The idea had become increasingly nebulous. For de Man the limits of the *rassemblement* had been defined by the plan; now the limits of the plan were being increasingly defined by who could be brought into the *rassemblement*. Voluntarism was in danger of becoming merely a vague heroism, planism a political version of the fraternity of the trenches. Déat claimed that by comparing the ideas of the veterans, the C.G.T., the Neo-Socialists and others, a solution would emerge by 'spontaneous gener-ation'.[156] Another Neo-Socialist wrote that 'being planist is what defines us . . . as did our belief in the existence of intermediary regimes . . . Being planist means wanting to gather the maximum number of people of goodwill against the crisis'.[157]

It was perhaps fitting therefore that the most widely discussed plan of 1934, and that which was both a consecration of this imprecision and an indi-cation of the total flux into which 6 February had thrown French politics, should have been drawn up under the aegis of Jules Romains, author of *Les Hommes de bonne volonté*: this was the Plan of 9 July (so called because it was published after the 'great reckoning' of 8 July).[158] It claimed to have been drawn up by individuals, acting on their own account, drawn from groups ranging from the S.F.I.O. and the Neo-Socialists to the Croix de Feu. Among the 19 signatories were Paul Marion, Alfred Fabre-Luce (editor of *Europe nouvelle*) and Jean Coutrot (a progressive industrialist and leading figure of

X *Crise* who had a finger in most proto-technocratic plans to reorganize the French economy in these years); among those who participated in its drafting but remained anonymous because of their official responsibilities were the Finance Inspectors Gilbert Devaux and Dominique Leca. Interest was expressed by figures as diverse as Caillaux and Montagnon and participants at the first public meeting of the 9 July Group in October included Henri Clerc, Jacques Kayser and, of course, Déat.[159] At this meeting Kayser declared that the Plan was less important for its content than for the state of mind which it represented; and indeed little more than vague pre-Pétainist pieties could have been expected to emerge from such a heterogeneous pedigree: the plan exalted the notion of 'service', condemned liberal capitalism, advocated a reform of the state and outlined a vaguely corporatist organization of the economy. This *'bouillabaisse* Plan' was condemned by some planists faithful to the ideas of de Man: Lacoste defended himself from having played any part in its drafting;[160] Marjolin, who had participated in the early discussions of the 9 July Group but then left and refused to allow his name to be attached to it, warned against 'empty alliances which have no other common basis than a desire to organize the economy . . . Be careful of chimeras and universal harmonies'.[161] In short, to adapt Péguy's famous phrase, having begun as *politique* the Plan had turned into *mystique*.

This distortion of the idea of the plan may seem to have little to do with the planism of de Man, Révolution Constructive or Combat Marxiste, but these developments brought into the open an important tension contained in de Man's original conception. Although he had insisted that his Plan was not for export, planism, on the other hand, provided criteria for the drafting of different plans for different countries. These criteria could be summed up in the formula that the Plan combined 'what is necessary to end the crisis [with] what can be done with the present majority, a social not a political majority'.[162] The same point was put slightly differently by Déat when he declared that there was a coincidence between the 'technical organization of the Plan and the psychological conditions of its realization'.[163] But was this always true? And if there should be a conflict between these two aspects of planism, which should prevail? Marjolin's criticism of 'universal harmonies' implied that economic coherence was being sacrificed in favour of the vagueness necessary for widespread political support. The increasing vagueness of planism during 1934 was, therefore, certainly a deviation from the original concept but it was to some extent inherent in the potential contradiction which existed between the plan conceived as an end, that is as the blueprint of an intermediary regime, and as means, that is as an instrument of propaganda for the capture of power. Towards the end of 1934 this contradiction might have threatened to destroy the political credibility of the planist movement, had it not been for the publication by the C.G.T. in September 1934 of its *Plan de rénovation économique*.

**1935: The defeat of the Plan: the reassertion of tradition**

In February 1935, Jacques Branger, among the signatories of the 9 July Plan, remarked that 'we always discuss planism but never actual plans'.[164] This observation was largely accurate, and the phenomenon was due to the fact that the plans which existed were either too vague to be treated as a serious basis for future action or were not backed by any influential organizations. But after the appearance of the C.G.T. Plan this was no longer true: the result of the deliberations of the *Bureau d'études* was a fairly detailed plan which was close to de Man's ideas; and most advocates of planism, even if not entirely satisfied, quickly rallied to it. During the next 18 months the content of this Plan was developed and clarified in a series of lectures given under the auspices of the I.S.O. in the C.G.T. daily *Le Peuple* and in *L'Atelier pour le plan*, a monthly journal set up by the C.G.T. in May 1935. This process of clarification, exposition and propaganda was undertaken especially by Laurat, Lefranc, Ludovic Zoretti (Secretary of the C.G.T.'s Fédération de l'Enseignement), Lacoste, Delaisi and Duret – all lecturers in the I.S.O. – as well as Samana, an actuary at the Cour des Comptes (under the pseudonym Jacques Dupiol), Dauphin-Meunier and Belin (of whom all but Belin had been members of the *Bureau d'études*). Although a slightly modified version of the Plan was published in September 1935 – the *Plan de rénovation économique et sociale* – for formal adoption by the C.G.T. Congress, it did not fundamentally alter the broad lines of the Plan which had already been in existence for a year.[165]

   Jean Duret made clear the dual nature of the Plan: it was a 'plan of combat against the crisis and at the same time . . . a plan of profound transformation of the existing economic system'.[166] There was no contradiction between these short-term and long-term objectives. The planist analysis of the nature of the economic crisis was similar to that of the S.F.I.O.: the crisis was the result of a 'divergence between increased production and consumption which is constricted by the mechanism of capitalist profit';[167] it followed that it could only be resolved by a transformation of the structure of the economy. The Plan was above all directed, in the short term, against a deflation affecting both industrial workers and the peasantry.[168] The immediate remedies to deflation were of course those which had been proposed by the C.G.T. (and the S.F.I.O.) since 1932: first, the 40-hour week, the financial consequences of which would be borne by establishing financial solidarity between prosperous and weak industries of different sectors;[169] secondly, both to provide jobs and to stimulate recovery, a public works programme costing between 5m F. and 7m F. a year over four or five years, and becoming less extensive once recovery was underway;[170] thirdly, for agriculture the Plan proposed a whole series of piecemeal measures, including an extension of agricultural credit, the downward revision of debts and leases and so on. But whereas the

40-hour week and public works had been the basis of C.G.T. policy between 1932 and 1934, it was now argued that they could have no lasting effect unless more fundamental reforms were undertaken: 'to draw up a plan against the crisis without mentioning the need for nationalizations is to build on sand'.[171]

The question of nationalization was central because it was necessary to exercise an effective control (*direction*) over the economy; this control would be exercised to 'develop consumption in order fully to use, and extend, productive capacity'.[172] First, therefore, the state must entirely control the distribution of credit by nationalizing the banks. This was the era, it was argued, of financial capitalism, characterized by the dependence of the industrial sector on a small number of banks (the concentration of the banking sector having driven most small local banks out of business) which exercised their power according to no rational system, and, consequently, with disastrous results.[173] The Bank of France would also be nationalized, but since it was dangerous to alienate small shareholders and expensive to buy them out, and since anyway the essential feature of modern capitalism was the separation of ownership and control, the simplest solution would be to change the Bank's statutes in order to allow the state to nominate all the Regents.[174]

Secondly, the state must nationalize the 'key industries' defined as that group of industries '*as restricted as possible in number*, on which all other economic activity is closely dependent'.[175] The decision to nationalize did not, then, simply depend on whether an industry was sufficiently concentrated to permit nationalization but rather on its strategic position in the economy: the sectors to nationalize included, therefore, transport, energy and important raw materials. The 1935 version of the Plan included the nationalization of arms industries. These were hardly 'key industries', and their inclusion was obviously for propaganda purposes: the Plan as means rather than end.[176] As for the administration of the nationalized industries, the C.G.T. explicitly took up again, and adapted, the ideas which it had formulated after the war: to avoid the dangers of bureaucracy resulting from a situation of simple state control, these industries would be run by tripartite committees representing the interests of producers, consumers and the state, and in each industrial sector these committees would be grouped together into co-ordinating councils with responsibility for the whole group.

The main reason why the number of nationalized industries had to be as restricted as possible was simply put by Jouhaux: 'among small traders, among artisans, above all among the peasantry, *there are forces which we must rally to us*'.[177] But although large sectors of the economy would not be nationalized, this free sector would nonetheless be controlled: if the nationalization of credit and industry provided the means of this control, its objectives would be set by a Higher Economic Council – a considerably modified version of the C.N.E. crowning the hierarchy of tripartite councils and co-ordinating councils – which would draw up a 'plan of national economic development', although parliament would retain its legislative power intact; the aim of the first such plan would be of course to end unemployment and stimulate demand. The ideas contained in the C.G.T. Plan were not by any means entirely new, but they were, as Amoyal points out,[178] transformed by being put in the new context of a policy of economic growth. To quote Laurat himself: the Plan took up many ideas of the C.G.T. dating back to 1919 and 'adapted them to the situation created by the crisis' in order to end 'the chronic stagnation and the unemployment which is tending to become permanent'.[179]

From September 1934 the activities of almost all the different advocates of planism could now converge in favour of the C.G.T. Plan: within the S.F.I.O. both the planists of Révolution Constructive[180] and Combat Marxiste[181] some of whose members had after all helped to draw up the Plan – the planist sympathizers in Bataille Socialiste[182] and various individual sympathizers such as Paz,[183] all rallied to the Plan with varying degrees of enthusiasm. At the end of 1934 the Neo-Socialists who had tended to welcome every plan that was produced, emphasized the need for '*a* Plan and no longer just plans',[184] and the Party set up various commissions to prepare for its forthcoming congress in January a single Plan based on the C.G.T. Plan, the Belgian Plan and the Plan published by one of the two biggest war veterans' associations in September.[185] This Plan was not however ready in time (and indeed never appeared) and so the Congress rallied to the C.G.T. Plan with slight reservations.[186] This was profoundly embarrassing to those who considered themselves orthodox planists – 'the worst possible thing has happened to the Plan'[187] – and Révolution Constructive attempted to show how the Neo-Socialists' position (and in particular that of their most articulate member Déat) diverged from de Man's[188] (though it was surely good planist doctrine to welcome all those who sincerely accepted the Plan). Belin himself could not but express slight reservations about this politically somewhat compromising support: the Plan was not a 'raft abandoned to the waves, subjected to the caprices of all comers'.[189] Although there were obvious political reasons for distancing oneself from the Neo-Socialists, Déat's interpretation of planism was certainly different from the C.G.T. and Socialist planists. This difference was encapsulated in their respective attitudes towards the New Deal: for Déat planism was above all a 'revolutionary pragmatism' of which the New Deal was the supreme example;[190] the C.G.T., on the other hand, while not questioning Roosevelt's good faith, claimed that the results of his policies showed the 'limits of the managed economy within the framework of capitalism . . . that a real and effective control of the economy is impossible without the nationalization of the key industries and of credit'.[191]

In spite of their attempts to drive a wedge between the Neo-Socialists and the C.G.T. Plan, the planists of the S.F.I.O. were not without criticism of the C.G.T. Plan, especially in its first version. These reservations were of two kinds. First, that the Plan did not devote sufficient attention to agriculture.[192] The observation seems not unfounded[193] since the Plan relegated agriculture to a final section beginning with the unpromising statement that the C.G.T. 'does not want to forget agriculture'. This relative neglect of the peasantry is surprising given that the *raison d'être* of planism was to attract the widest possible alliance. It perhaps reflects the origins of planism in Belgium, where the peasantry was hardly the force that it was in France.[194] But the C.G.T. leaders seem to have been aware of this shortcoming,[195] and the 1935 version of the Plan did slightly extend the number of measures devoted to agriculture, by including the creation of various agricultural marketing boards; and agriculture was given a somewhat larger place in C.G.T. propaganda.

The second, and more important, planist criticism of the C.G.T., was of its failure even to broach the issue of how its Plan would be implemented, and for exposing itself to accusations of reformism because it had not made it clear that structural reforms could only follow a 'profound political trans-formation involving the coming to power of the working masses'.[196] Combat Marxiste argued that it would be the role of the S.F.I.O. to give this economic plan the politically indispensable complement ignored by the C.G.T.[197] The C.G.T. had in fact deliberately left out this political aspect in line with tra-ditional syndicalist practice.[198] And there were varying opinions within the organization as to the means of implementation. Belin claimed that the choice was between Lenin and Jaurès, between insurrection and the Plan, even if he had little faith in the present parliament to carry it out; on the other hand he preferred the word 'coalition' to *rassemblement* in order not to frighten off the political parties.[199] By others in the C.G.T. such an attitude was seen as restrictively legalistic.[200] And taking an intermediate position, Zoretti declared that it would be for parliament to implement the Plan under the pressure of a broad *rassemblement* of public opinion, and if parliament was not up to the task then syndical and other forces would have to act by them-selves.[201] But how? We have already seen that although the Plan was supposed to be the means to its own realization the problem of its implemen-tation was a weak point in the doctrine of planism. But once the C.G.T. had actually produced a largely acceptable Plan this was no longer a hypothetical problem; on the contrary, it now became an urgent problem of political action.

In the atmosphere of 1934, when the war veterans could believe that they had the power to topple governments, when the P.C.F. and the S.F.I.O. were, at least until July, locked in mutual hostility, and Déat could write, with a mixture of plausibility and wishful thinking, that 'the links are broken between the narrow doctrinaires of the S.F.I.O. and the masses',[202] it did for a moment seem that planism might be able to fill the political void on the left, that the C.G.T. – or some other organization – might implement its Plan by circumventing the traditional politics of parties. But the Popular Front came to restore tradition. Already at the end of 1934 Combat Marxiste was worried that the planists might be 'overtaken by events and submerged by positions imposed on us from outside',[203] and this danger obviously increased as the Popular Front became a more serious political movement. We have already examined the course of events during the next month: in June 1935 the C.G.T. had submitted its Plan directly to a whole range of political groups on the left; by October, when the definitive version of the Plan was ready, the main hope for its future lay in its adoption by the Comité du Rassemblement Populaire; but this did not occur, and the programme published by the Comité in January 1936 was a severe blow to the planists.

It remains to examine the reasons why the Comité should have rejected the Plan and the principles on which it was based. The hostility of the Socialists was not among these reasons: indeed the Socialists were among the supporters of the Plan on the Comité. At first sight, given the outcome of the Congress of Toulouse, this seems surprising. But the apparent change in the Socialist attitude went back to the end of 1934: in rejecting the Communist proposals for a common programme in January 1935 the Socialists had employed to some extent the language and arguments of planism (the need for 'an overall programme', for 'structural reforms'); and this development was noted by the planists: 'if this is a conversion, we note it'.[204] At the Socialist Congress of Mulhouse in June 1935, planism was, in contrast to the previous year, hardly mentioned (except by Moch and Paz) but the Congress unanimously voted a motion proposed by Auriol declaring that the Party would draw up a programme of immediate action based on the C.G.T. Plan,[205] and the Plan was explicitly supported by such Guesdist figures as Lebas[206] and Séverac[207] – both anti-planists at Toulouse. Combat Marxiste hailed the Congress as a victory for planist ideas.[208]

Furthermore this seeming conversion occurred at a time when de Man's own influence among Socialists in France was to some extent declining: in December 1934 he had given a lecture at the Sorbonne (under the somewhat compromising chairmanship of Jules Romains) in which he had outlined the 14 planist theses first delivered to the first Congress of the Plan held at Pontigny in September;[209] the content of these theses – and especially their readiness to accept a form of corporatism – was the occasion of a cooling of relations between Vandervelde and de Man;[210] and although the lecture at the Sorbonne was published by Révolution Constructive as its eighth (and last) *Cahier*, Lefranc was not without criticism of de Man's views on corporatism.[211] Hitherto the French anti-planist Socialists had refrained from direct criticism of de Man in person; but after the lecture at the Sorbonne, Lebas for one had no inhibition about doing so.[212] And disillusionment was only increased by de Man's entry into the far from planist coalition government of Van Zeeland, formed after the Belgian financial crisis of March 1935. The 14th thesis of Pontigny had put the formula 'nothing but the plan, the whole plan' as the condition of a Socialist participation in government. De Man seemed to have betrayed his own principles.

It was, however, at this moment that the Socialists chose to rally to the C.G.T. Plan. There were perhaps three reasons for this. First, the fall of Flandin had suddenly made the nationalization of the Bank of France a central political issue: no longer could it be claimed that the nationalization of credit did not have the political resonance in France that it had in Belgium. Secondly, at Toulouse, as we have seen, what had been discussed was planism rather than a plan, and this had led to suspicions about what a plan might contain, suspicions heightened by the existence of the plan published by the Etats Généraux du Travail. But the C.G.T. Plan was, it turned out, much more radical than such fears might have suggested, and therefore it could be accepted even by those who did not subscribe to the ideas of planism.[213] Thirdly, anti-planists who had once considered that any possible plan represented timid reformism now found themselves presented, by the Communists and others, with proposals much less far reaching than those contained in the C.G.T. Plan: thus, ironically, for Séverac, Faure, Lebas and others the Plan became a way of preserving the integrity of Socialism so that it did not disappear 'in a Popular Front conducive to all kinds of manoeuvres in which Socialism would pay the cost'.[214] In short, the Socialists had become advocates of the Plan; but they had not thereby become planists.[215]

Why, then, backed by the C.G.T. and the Socialists, was the Plan nevertheless rejected by the Popular Front? Important of course was the opposition of the Communists who, both from Moscow and in France, had attacked de Man's Plan and then the C.G.T. Plan as a utopian attempt to control the economy within the structure of capitalism, thereby in fact reinforcing the power of the bourgeois state.[216] But the opposition of the Communists of course only became conclusive because it joined that of the Radicals. This was the ultimate irony of planism: that the movement which had above all emphasized the necessity, and its ability, to win over the *classes moyennes* should have failed to be translated into reality precisely because it had frightened the party, which was considered to represent the interests of that class. Certainly, rallying the *classes moyennes* meant more than a simple liaison with the Radical Party. But once the Popular Front had reasserted tradition – had rehabilitated the party – what else could it mean?

The dilemma of the relation between planism and party politics is perfectly illustrated by the case of Déat. His first enthusiasm was for the *grand relève* of 8 July: once the government had fallen a planist majority could be formed.[217] In the winter of 1934–5 he invested some hope in the Ligue d'Action Civique, an organization of Republican defence founded by Paul-Boncour, Renaudel and others: but although it received the support of numerous Republican luminaries and even gave formal approval to the C.G.T. Plan, the Ligue, not anyway an effective political force, intended to restrict itself purely to the defence of political liberties, especially since many of its adherents were in fact hostile to the Plan.[218] Déat's next project was the Comité du Plan which would group together individuals and organizations accepting the broad lines of the C.G.T. Plan: the aims of the Comité would be both to complete the Plan where it was lacking and to mount a propaganda campaign for it; the main result of these efforts was the *Plan français* (in whose drafting Clerc and Coutrot had played a part) which was published in December 1935, and bore little relation to the C.G.T. Plan.[219] Finally, concurrently with this enterprise, Déat worked to have the C.G.T. Plan accepted in parliament: in January 1935 the Neo-Socialists and the two other groups of independent Socialists – the Party Socialiste Français and the Parti Républicain Socialiste – signed a declaration accepting the Plan,[220] and this agreement culminated in a rather unenthusiastic fusion of the three parties in the autumn into the Union Socialiste Républicaine (U.S.R.).

The reasons for the oscillations of Déat's attitude are clear enough: by leaving the Socialists he had cut himself off from a political base. This problem became all the more acute as the Neo-Socialists failed to develop into a mass party. The controversy over Marquet's participation in government had quickly undermined their credibility;[221] voting discipline was poor; in 1935 Renaudel died disillusioned with the direction which the Party was taking and Compère-Morel rejoined the Socialists; Lafont was expelled for joining Bouisson's ephemeral government (there would be no new *Cas Marquet*); Montagnon made embarrassingly sympathetic remarks about fascism;[222] Marion moved on to the more robust politics of Doriot's Parti Populaire Français; and after the fusion with the two other socialist groups, Marquet and his Girondin associated seceded to form their own Party, the Parti Neo-Socialiste de France.[223] Déat's dilemma was nowhere better analysed than by Révolution Constructive: he was condemned to a position of eternal *attentisme*, forced to wait for 'popular movements to develop outside his influence in order to canalize or exploit them'.[224] But this criticism could up to a point have been turned against its authors. Of course the planists of Révolution Constructive and Combat Marxiste had hoped that the Socialist Party could be the instrument for the realization of the Plan, which would itself extend the appeal of the Party. The Plan would save the Party; the Party would save the Plan. And Duret of the C.G.T. saw the Plan as a potentially new Sorelian myth which would play the same mobilizing force as the myth of the general strike before the war.[225] But even among trade union members, outside the restricted circle of the leaders, the Plan does not seem to have generated this kind of enthusiasm: Lefranc told the Congress of the Fédération des Fonctionnaires in November 1934 that 'it is undeniable that the

C.G.T. Plan has not aroused among the masses the response for which we had hoped'.[226]

Ultimately the myths of the Popular Front proved to be more powerful than those of the Plan: planists appealed for an attack on the 'system', and the Popular Front, especially the Communists, revived the traditional Republican attack – the language, *mutatis mutandis*, of 1792, or 1871 – on individuals – 'the 200 families', 'let the rich pay', *le petit* against *le gros*.[227] The use of this vocabulary was not among the least of the signs of the Jacobinization – the Radicalization – of the P.C.F. in 1935. It disproved Déat's far from disinterested prediction that any union of the left which included the Communists 'will necessarily result in cutting the S.F.I.O. off from democracy, from the *classes moyennes*, and from the nation'.[228] The success of the Communists' slogans – their emphasis on the demands of different groups – also invalidated at least half of the planist critique of the action of the political parties in 1934: that they no longer provided directives for action capable of mobilizing the masses. In 1935 a member of Révolution Constructive had written: 'It is not by offering a few ineffective palliatives, redistributional reforms which are today impossible to obtain, moratoria, special payments to those hit by the crisis, etc. . . . that we will win over the mass of small traders, artisans and peasants'.[229] When such predictions were proved wrong the planists felt betrayed. But their failure was at least partly the failure of their doctrine, of its claim to provide the only means of reinvigorating the politics of the left. The situation in 1934 had perhaps in one respect a certain similarity with that ten years later: in 1944 – as in 1934 – all had for a moment seemed possible, but once again hopes for political change were dashed. The moral (understood in 1934 by the Communists) was that although the parliamentary democracy of parties may not perhaps be the necessary or most perfect expression of democracy, the hold of political parties is deeply entrenched, and only in brief and exceptional moments does it seem possible to replace or circumvent them. One of those moments was 1934; the planists attempted to seize their opportunity; and then the Popular Front reasserted tradition.

## 1936: Epilogue to planism

Although planism continued to be important in C.G.T. circles up to 1939, the planists had largely lost any political influence after 1936. But it would be wrong to claim that they were totally without influence in their own time. The intellectual stimulus they provided certainly provoked the Socialists to think harder about economic policy: when Blum began to write about the question of nationalizations in 1935 he admitted that before the publication of the Belgian Plan his views had been vague, and it was this event which forced him into considering the question more deeply.[230] And the studies undertaken by the C.G.T. planists – of the banking system, of the nationalizations, etc. – were of a much higher quality than the analyses of the C.G.T. and the Socialists before 1934. All plans, including that of the C.G.T. had, we have seen, contained some reference to the need to exercise greater control over the economy: it was therefore not altogether a coincidence that in March 1936 parliament voted a bill to give more importance to the C.N.E. However, the extent of the reform, which for the first time gave it official legislative status, was very limited; hardly surprising in a bill which was unanimously passed by the Chamber (with 16 abstentions) and had only 16 opponents even in the Senate.[231] This timid measure had no direct link with planism: it had first been proposed by the short-lived government of Paul-Boncour in January 1933, realizing an ambition that Paul-Boncour had harboured since his youth;[232] nevertheless the crisis gave an old idea new relevance, and the *rapporteur*, the Neo-Socialist Ramadier, put the reform in the context of the proposals of the Etats Généraux in April 1934 and the war veterans a month earlier.

   Planism has been interpreted in various ways. The ambiguity stems partly from the fact that, in its period of greatest popularity in France, it meant very different things to different people. The craze for it has been likened by one historian to the vogue for *autogestion* in the early 1970s.[233] Thus interpretations depend partly on which planists one chooses to discuss. Zeev Sternhell has seen the planism of Henri de Man, and of his French followers, as one of the forms which fascism took in France, or, at least, as part of the process of the infiltration of a fascist sensibility into France during the 1930s. Planism, he argues, laid the bases of a national, authoritarian, anti-Marxist, anti-parliamentary 'socialism' which attempted to stand above class, and to appeal to all classes.[234] This view has some plausibility. Much of the planist rhetoric – the emphasis on heroic action at all cost, on gathering together the 'healthy elements' of the nation, the 'men of goodwill' – has a decidedly 'fascist' resonance. Many of the planists, including de Man himself, were to tread the path of fascism or collaboration: this was true not only of Neo-Socialists such as Déat, Marion, Montagnon, Lafaye, but also of others such as Desphelippon, Albertini, Zoretti, Soulès; Belin was to end up as Vichyssois. Furthermore Sternhell also shows that there is no need to argue for a radical rupture in, say, Déat's thought between 1935 and 1940, that the Déat of the Rassemblement National du Peuple is already quite visible in the planist Déat of five years earlier. But this argument can be taken too far. First, there were many factors – anti-Communism, pacifism and so on – which could account for transition from left to right in the 1930s. Secondly, most planists – Moch, Philip, Jouhaux, Laurat, Vallon, Marjolin, Lacoste, etc. – did not after all become fascists, and did not thereby renounce their belief in planism. Thirdly, nor was planism, at least in its French incarnation, necessarily anti-Marxist, as the examples of Laurat and Duret show. Fourthly, the emphasis on the *classes moyennes* was in the mid-1930s a necessary part of any anti-fascist policy and was shared by the P.C.F. at this time; planism was indeed conceived as a specifically anti-fascist strategy – the U.S.R. formed part in 1936 of the Popular Front electoral condition – and even if there was, as Blum pointed out, a danger of borrowing so much from fascism as to become indistinguishable from it, this had surely not happened to the planists in 1936. That planism was one possible – even common – route on an intellectual itinerary from socialism to fascism is not the same as assimilating it to fascism, any more than, say, syndicalism can be assimilated to fascism.

By others planism has been seen as a precursor of *planification*, as one of the roots of the post-war emphasis on modernization, economic growth and state planning.[235] Once again there was a continuity of personnel: Robert Marjolin played a major role in the origins of the first post-war French Plan. The technocratic element of French post-war economic management can certainly be traced back to planism. De Man had been importantly influenced by the American idea of the business manager (rather than owner) who was motivated by efficiency rather than personal profit: this 'efficiency', harnessed to a public not private cause, could provide the basis for a rationally directed economy.[236] And, one might add, a very technocratic one. Laurat wrote of the need for a more scientific, Marxist, training for those who were to run the Socialist economy of the future.[237] Of course the level of sophistication of the planists' economic analysis was much inferior to that of the post-war planners and they lacked any tools of macro-economic analysis, but the spirit of the enterprise was not so different.

Planism can also be seen, however much many planists would have resented the imputation, as a version of Socialist reformism. This perhaps is what it represents in the intellectual development of André Philip, Jules Moch, or, in Britain, Hugh Gaitskell. And it is noticeable that, in the C.G.T., it was taken up particularly by the white-collar *fonctionnaires*' unions. The socialism of François Mitterand's Socialist Party, at least as defined by Maurice Duverger, has certain similarities with the planist socialism of the 1930s, as the presence of Pierre Dreyfus (ex-Révolution Constructive) in Pierre Mauroy's shortlived second government reminds us. Duverger writes of this 'third type of Socialism' that: 'only the ownership of the major means of production is to pass from the private to the public sector . . . a vast private sector will continue its activities freely . . . this does not only concern the famous "transition" but also established socialism . . . the exercise of power will make it possible to stem the tendency of developed economies to create a sort of proletariat of small firms reduced to the status of sub-contractors of large ones'.[238] In this context of planism as a reformist attempt to make capitalism work it is interesting that one of the first and most sympathetic accounts of Keynes' *General Theory* in France appeared in the C.G.T.'s

*Atelier pour le plan* in March 1936. While not agreeing with all Keynes' conclusions, it noted that he had destroyed the classical notion of equilibrium; the
Keynesian theory implied the need for state action to reduce the interest rate
or to control investment in order to guarantee a full use of productive
capacity and reduce unemployment.[239] Some of the planists, such as Gaston
Cusin, who acted as advisers to Blum's Popular Front government, had
quickly read and assimilated Keynes;[240] planism predisposed them in such a
direction.

The reference to Keynes should remind us that whatever its future manifestations, planism must be situated in the context of the 1930s. Above all it represented an attempt to find both a political and an economic solution to the
problems thrown up by the Depression. Because it failed politically one is not
able to judge it economically. It is impossible to say if a great chance was
missed; but it is permitted to be at least sceptical. De Man was no economist;
and his planist writings are more concerned with analysing the political and
social effects of the crisis than with exactly how the Plan would be sufficient
to overcome it. There was, we have seen, a tension between his idea of the
plan as economic objective and political instrument. Laurat, on the other
hand, used more strictly economic criteria to delineate the content of the
Plan: the minimum limit of socialization was that sufficient to expand the
domestic market enough to end the crisis; the maximum limit was imposed by
the criterion, necessary in a mixed economy, that the nationalized industries
could be run profitably.[241] It is no coincidence that 1934 and 1935 were the
years in which planism reached its greatest vogue in France: it was in these
years that the economic problem had come to dominate political debate for
the first time. Nor therefore is it surprising that 1934 was also the year in
which Paul Reynaud announced his conversion to devaluation. The planists
offered one way between the strong medicine of present deflation and the
hopes, or fears, of future revolution; the proponents of devaluation, however,
were to offer another.

# 8   Devaluation

C'était pas assez de m'avoir ruiné par la Stabilisation Poincaré . . . c'est toujours sur le petit rentier qu'on s'en prend c'est toujours lui qui paie les pots cassés . . . nous voilà presque ruiner, je dis ruiner Monsieur le Ministre

> (Letter from a 76-year-old rentier to Bonnet, 21 March 1933)

La religion du franc n'est guère autre chose que la religion de la France

> (*Le Matin*, 19 April 1935)

Devaluer, c'est cambrioler la Banque de France. Devaluer, c'est cambrioler les français . . . c'est faire le jeu des requins de la finance et de la Bourse . . . Il n'y a pas de question du franc, il y a une question de France

> (P. Gaxotte, *Je suis partout*, 1 May 1935)

'France has abandoned principle and consistency alike, but she has always refused sacrifices which were avoidable and has obeyed in the end the teachings of experience. We in England have not submitted either to the warnings of theory or to the pressures of facts, obstinately obedient to convention.'[1] This remark, written by Keynes in 1928, describing the respective monetary policies of France and England in the 1920s, could also be applied to the 1930s – with the roles reversed. The attempt of French governments to hang on to the parity of the franc at all costs has become a classic example of wrongheadedness in the conduct of economic policy. But at the time devaluation was denounced with the most extraordinary passion. Paul Reynaud, its most prominent advocate, has given a sample in his memoirs of the many letters of abuse – from 'a small old rentier from Paris', *un Français moyen* and so on – which he received during this period. Some merely vilified him as a 'bandit', a 'Judas', a 'swindler'; others threatened him with 'a dagger in the heart'; others even threatened the life of his daughter.[2] This, then, was more than an abstruse economic controversy: it takes us to the very heart of the nightmares which haunted bourgeois France in the 1930s.

## Government policy: 1932 to 1936

Soon after the war the aged Germain-Martin attempted to justify the economic policies of the governments of France between February 1934 and

167

May 1935, whose Finance Minister he had been. Most importantly he attempted to defend the decision not to devalue the franc: government policy, he argued, had in reality been preparing the conditions for a successful devaluation at the end of 1935 or the beginning of 1936; a devaluation in 1934 or early 1935 would have involved an 'alignment on floating currencies'. A general stabilization of currencies was not yet possible: devaluation had to wait until the dollar and sterling parities were once again fixed. Any attempt to devalue before this would only have initiated either a damaging and endless round of retaliatory devaluations or invited reprisals in the form of tariffs.[3] Whether or not this retrospective rationale was true, it does remind us that in such matters as devaluation, where secrecy is vital, the public pronouncements of governments are not always revealing. Germain-Martin's account prompts at least two questions about the real nature of government policy: first, was the eventual possibility of devaluation envisaged; secondly, did French governments have good reason to believe that devaluation would be met by reprisals abroad?

The official position of all French governments on monetary policy dates back to the World Economic Conference of 1933; but the origins of the disagreements which doomed that conference to failure go back to the beginning of the world crisis and the debate about its causes. The view of many British economists, publicists and Treasury officials was that the crisis had been started and was being prolonged by a disproportion between the quantity of money and the quantity of goods, which had led to a precipitous decline in wholesale prices; this disproportion resulted, however, not from an absolute shortage of gold but from its maldistribution, caused primarily by its accumulation by France and America. Instead of pursuing expansionary monetary policies which would cause a rise in prices and a reversal of gold movements, France and America – especially France – had sterilized their gold, thereby exercising general deflationary pressure on the rest of the world. The British view was therefore that the French should take measures to prevent this 'artificial' flow of gold into France: French capital should be encouraged to invest abroad; the Bank of France should expand credit by means of open market operations; the minimum ratio of reserves to paper currency should be lowered;[4] and after September 1931 such measures became a precondition of sterling's return to gold.

French leaders were, we have seen, sensitive to such criticism; and, worried by the consequences of the gold influx, in 1931 the government and the Bank of France had taken measures to discourage it.[5] But at the same time the Bank produced a whole series of justificatory notes on 'the supposed sterilization of gold in France': defending itself against British allegations, the Bank argued that although not having the right to pursue open market policies, it had in no way attempted to neutralize the effects of the gold imports on the French credit system; if these effects had been insignificant so far the reason lay in the depressed state of economic activity in France: there was no demand for credit and the newly created notes were hoarded. The fundamental reasons for the drain of gold into France lay in France's international creditor position, in the repatriation of French capital which had been exported during the 1920s, and in the fact that France offered a haven of security to foreign capital: the necessary redistribution of gold would therefore take place only when Britain was able to offer similar security, once, that is, the pound had rejoined the gold standard.[6] It was this *dialogue de sourds* between the British, for whom an economic revival and concomitant price rise stimulated by a redistribution of gold was a precondition of a return to gold, and the French, from whom a return to international monetary stability was a precondition of a redistribution of gold and economic revival, which formed the background to the World Economic Conference.

The possibility of such a gathering had been mooted since 1930; but the idea moved closer to reality in May 1932 as a result of conversations between British and American officials: for the first time America declared itself willing to participate providing that the question of war debts was left off the agenda.[7] And the Lausanne Conference on reparations in June 1932 formally agreed that the League of Nations should convene a World Economic Conference after a preparatory Commission of Experts from the main participating countries had drafted an agenda. The precise aims of the Conference – beyond a search for international solutions to the world crisis – were vague; it was to be the task of the Preparatory Commission to work them out.

The first meeting of the Preparatory Commission, which took place in November 1932, ended in deadlock between British and French views.[8] The only comfort for France was that the British delegates had been isolated in their stand against gold: the American experts had sided with the French.[9] Nevertheless the French did not draw much comfort from this impasse: the relatively stable situation of the French economy and the large stock of gold at the Bank of France 'will expose our delegates to all sorts of offensives unless they themselves take the initiative'.[10] At the second meeting of the Commission, at the beginning of 1933, Leith-Ross, the British representative, again stated the British conditions for a return to gold: a rise in world prices; a redistribution of gold stimulated by a modification of central bank structures to allow open market operations; a liberalization of tariffs and quotas (this was linked to the previous condition: if the French and Americans would agree to take more imports they would lose gold); and a settlement of war debts (one cause of the gold drain to America). Rist put the French case: he opposed any artificial attempt to raise world prices; he agreed on the need to settle war debts; he argued that a British return to gold was the main condition for a revival of world trade; and, finally, he stated a preference for bilateral trade negotiations over any general agreement on tariffs and quotas.

Once again the Americans sided largely with France.[11] In spite of this renewed statement of differences the atmosphere at the second meeting of the Commission was much more relaxed than at the first and the experts succeeded in drawing up a draft Agenda for the Conference, advocating the restoration of a fully functioning gold standard, and a greater freedom of international trade by means of the progressive relaxation of tariffs, quotas and other emergency measures of trade restriction. At the same time a series of Annotations to the Agenda enshrined British conditions for the restoration of the gold standard: the lowering of cover ratios; the extension of the credit base of countries abundantly supplied with gold, by means, if possible, of open market operations.[12] In the words of one historian: 'an eclectic list of possibilities, the Agenda was acceptable to every nation but resolved nothing'.[13]

Because the American experts had so forcefully argued the case for a British return to gold, the French delegates, although entirely sharing these views, had to some extent seen themselves as offering a 'nuance of moderation' in a 'sort of duel between the United States and Great Britain'.[14] But this situation might not last. If the British should make concessions about sterling and the Americans about debts, France would obviously come under pressure to make concessions either on internal financial policy or on trade restrictions or both: 'given the Anglo-Saxon mentality there is reason to believe that the measures proposed will be simplistic and rigid'. French policy-makers, therefore, turned to the question of what France would be able to offer in the way of trade liberalization, especially in the area of quotas where the French government was the major offender.[15] But Louis Serre, Minister of Commerce, was against any breach in the wall of protection: the French market would at once be inundated by imports from countries which had devalued their currencies.[16] Even more importantly the fairly anodyne remarks of the Agenda about the relaxation of tariffs and quotas had raised a storm of protest from Chambers of Agriculture; they warned also that the value of the franc should not be considered 'independent of the life of the country'.[17] No French government could afford to ignore such warnings.

The Preparatory Commission had at least allowed respective governments to air their positions. But even this achievement was now threatened by Roosevelt's coming to power in March 1933. Faced with an internal banking crisis, immediately after his inauguration Roosevelt took the dollar off gold, and suggested the idea of further preparatory bilateral discussions in Washington between the American government and all the other countries participating in the Conference. Against this background, Bonnet, French Minister of Finance, had a meeting in London in mid-March with Chamberlain, the Chancellor of the Exchequer. About several issues – hostility to Keynes' recently published plan for public works, a platonic disapproval of quotas, etc. – there was considerable agreement. But when Bonnet, worried by the possibility of a depreciation of the dollar, asked how the British viewed a return to gold, Chamberlain pressed him on whether the French accepted the conditions outlined in the Annotations to the Agenda: on the possibility of lower cover ratios and open market operations, Bonnet was evasive, but eventually agreed that the French government would neither stand in the way of discussions on this question between the Banks of England and France, nor would it oppose a possible change in the Statutes of the Bank of France.[18] But if the British believed that the Bank of France was likely to prove more pliable than the French government, they could hardly have been more wrong: the Bank was in fact highly critical of the experts' Agenda.[19] Although the Bonnet–Chamberlain meeting was inconclusive, both sides were satisfied at the outcome: the French even seem to have believed that the British had moved slightly nearer to exchange stabilization.[20] Bonnet's fears about the dollar were however soon to be realized: in mid-April, while Herriot, chosen to represent France in the Washington talks, was half-way across the Atlantic, Roosevelt announced a gold embargo; the rate of the dollar began to slip, and Herriot's original brief was now redundant. The dollar now moved to the centre of the stage.

Three issues were discussed at the talks between Roosevelt and Herriot: debts, which do not concern us here; currency stabilization; and tariffs.[21] When the French delegation urged the necessity for a stabilization of the dollar, it was confronted with a proposal for a stabilization plan in which the dollar would be depreciated by 15 per cent and then held at this level, at least during the Conference, by a tripartite stabilization fund. The idea took Herriot and his advisers by surprise: one obvious danger, pointed out by Rist, was that, if francs were used to buy dollars, the French Treasury would run the risk, if these subsequently depreciated, of incurring a loss. Instructions were slow to arrive from Paris; and Herriot eventually reserved the French position while not rejecting the idea outright.[22] Before Herriot's arrival in Washington it had been known that Roosevelt intended to propose a tariff truce for the period of the Conference, and the French had been willing to accept the idea with a lot of restrictions.[23] But the depreciation of the dollar changed the situation completely: the French delegation used acceptance of a tariff truce as a bargaining counter for currency stabilization,[24] and the government eventually wired that the delegation could adhere to a truce with important reservations, one of which was the need for a preliminary stabiliz-ation.[25] Agreement was eventually reached in this issue in May, but France accompanied acceptance in principle with reservations about contingency action which could be taken if any currency was to undergo a devaluation.[26] This was, we have seen, an extremely sensitive issue in France.

Although Herriot had made a favourable impression in America, the American Assistant Secretary of State, William Bullitt, told the new French Ambassador, A. de Laboulaye, that the United States was very pessimistic about the prospects for the Conference owing to the French government's lack of enthusiasm for the tripartite stabilization fund.[27] This report was received with alarm in Paris: any further depreciation of the dollar threatened to put the remaining gold standard currencies under pressure and therefore any proposals for stabilization had to be welcomed. Bonnet informed the Quai d'Orsay that Bullitt's accusation was unjustified; France had been very willing to examine the measure but the problem lay rather in agreeing on a dollar–sterling parity: it was known that the British considered a depreciation of 15 per cent to be excessive.[28] France, then, while basically hostile to the idea, was able to hide behind the British, whose reluctance was, for different reasons no less great.[29] The French position was that as long as monetary instability continued 'the French government could in practice, to its great regret, provide no more than nominal participation at the London Conference': immediate conversations should take place between the three central banks and governments.[30] These new urgent instructions were immediately passed on to French representatives in London and Washington;[31] but Rueff, financial attaché in London, reported back that the British were unenthusiastic, believing that it was too early for the United States to have serious views about the parity of the dollar: the Conference would therefore be useless; since on the other hand it was by now inevitable, French opinion should be warned against expecting too much from it.[32] With Leith-Ross, Rueff believed that the best outcome would be for the Conference to adjourn immediately after meeting, and then not to reconvene until ministers of finance had worked out a stabilization agreement.[33]

The uncertainties about American monetary intentions – Congress had authorized Roosevelt to reduce the dollar by up to 50 per cent as a means of raising commodity prices – had pushed the French government into slightly modifying its original position: although it still intended to use the Conference to argue the need for the restoration of a fully functioning gold standard while resisting British preconditions for this, it was willing now to settle for an immediate *de facto* stabilization of the dollar and sterling, and then in return to discuss concrete measures for trade liberalization.[34] But without stabilization it considered the Conference to be without purpose. Thus, when the Conference opened on 12 June its fate depended on secret negotiations over *de facto* stabilization which had started in mid-May and formed no part of its official proceedings. What followed soon developed into pure farce.[35] On 15 June a provisional agreement on stabilization had been reached, and it was wired by Secretary of State Hull to Roosevelt on 16 June. When rumours of the content of this agreement leaked out, American commodity prices plummeted, and on 22 June Roosevelt, disavowing his London delegates, rejected the plan. While Roosevelt's special adviser Moley was carrying the president's latest thoughts across the Atlantic to London, increasing pressure against the Dutch florin made some action increasingly urgent, and negotiations between French, English, Swiss and Dutch officials took place for some kind of declaration on stabilization which would at least halt the speculation. On 30 June Moley, who had arrived two days before, was able to accept this extremely innocuous statement which committed no one to anything, and did not even contain any figures; but Roosevelt, who had left on a sailing trip, could not be contacted, and Bonnet, Chamberlain and others waited in vain on the evening of 30 June for Moley to bring definitive American acceptance. The next day Roosevelt's answer arrived: disavowing his representatives once again, the President had refused the stabilization proposed.[36]

On 3 July followed Roosevelt's resounding declaration denouncing 'the old fetishes of so-called international bankers': this action effectively torpedoed the Conference which 'adjourned' a few weeks later. On the same day, having failed to secure British support, the governments of France, Holland, Switzerland, Belgium and Italy declared that they would remain faithful to the gold standard and to the 'maintenance of the gold standard by their respective countries on the basis of the existing parities'.[37] The gold block was formed: this declaration, made by the government of Daladier on 3 July 1933, was to remain the official basis of French policy until Léon Blum's government.

The immediate impact of this dramatic outcome to the Conference was, we have seen, to strengthen conservative demands for financial retrenchment in France in order to consolidate the position of the franc. Such demands were underlined by the first of many flights of gold which occurred at the end of 1933 as a result of international monetary developments: Roosevelt had embarked on a policy of buying gold at increasingly high prices in order to drive down the rate of the dollar; during this time the Exchange Equalization Account which managed sterling had prevented it from falling in line with the dollar in order to relieve the pressure on the franc;[38] in January 1934 Roosevelt stabilized the dollar – though it was not clear for how long – at the low rate of $35 to the ounce: the pound–dollar rate settled at around $5.10, and the pound–franc rate at 77 F. Between October 1933 and March 1934 the Bank of France lost, as a result of these events, over 5m F. of gold: the franc was in no serious danger, but the warning signs were enough to add piquancy to the already dramatic situation in February 1934; and Doumergue could be presented not only as the restorer of political order but also as the saviour of the franc. The influential American journalist Walter Lippmann wrote a much publicized article in February 1934 predicting the devaluation of the franc; and French officials in London reported periodically that British opinion did not believe the franc would hold.[39]

But although since June 1934 the monetary question had become a question of public debate with the beginning of Reynaud's campaign for devaluation, the resolve of French governments was unaffected. During the course of 1934 measures were taken to strengthen the French balance of payments position by embarking on a policy which the *Revue d'économie politique* described as 'more frankly protectionist than ever': 38 trade agreements were signed, including one in June which finally abolished the exchange compensation tax which had so soured Franco-British relations since 1931.[40] The policy was successful in almost halving the French trade deficit in 1934.

At the end of 1934 and beginning of 1935, three developments potentially threatened to modify this situation: first, the beginning of the Flandin 'experiment'; secondly, the fall in the value of sterling; and, thirdly, American overtures for international currency stabilization at the beginning of 1935. The Flandin experiment was premised on a supposed levelling of French and world price levels and an end to deflation in France: it would obviously be undermined by any further fall in sterling. But towards the end of 1934 the pound started to slide, a situation which, besides worrying the French, put the Belga under pressure and made a Belgian devaluation seem conceivable: at the end of the year the pound stood at 75 F.; the Exchange Equalization Account had tried to prevent this fall, but it was not prepared to use up its reserves in holding an untenable position.[41] Meanwhile, at the end of 1934 French officials picked up the first tentative suggestions that America, which had so spectacularly rejected general currency stabilization in 1933, might be changing its views: on 19 January 1935 the Quai d'Orsay informed the Finance Ministry that it had received information that although the Americans would not take any initiative over an international stabilization agreement, they would put no preconditions – whether on the level of future parities or the issue of debts – on participation in discussions over such an agreement.[42]

It was against this background that preparations took place for Flandin's visit to London at the end of January 1935. The general British position as reported by Emmanuel Monick, French financial attaché in Britain, from a conversation with Leith-Ross in November 1934 was hardly encouraging. First, the pound was considered to be overvalued in relation to the dollar, a rate of $4.50 being considered a more accurate reflection of the two countries' price levels than the prevailing rate of $4.86: stabilization at a figure much higher than this would impose on the British a policy of deflation which, after the experience of the period 1925 to 1931, they were unwilling to accept. Secondly, sterling was undervalued in relation to the franc, but a more realistic rate, such as 85 F., would raise the sterling parity to the unacceptable level of $5.60: recognizing this situation the British government would not inflict commercial reprisals in the event of a Belgian devaluation provided that it took account of the deflation which had already been achieved (thus it would not accept a devaluation back to the 1931 parity). Thirdly, memories of American unreliability in 1933 died hard: in the last analysis Monick ascribed British reluctance to stabilize to 'a profound mistrust in the worth of any commitments that the United States might be brought to make on the subject of currency stabilization'.[43] Although this was a somewhat pessimistic picture, the information about British reactions to Belgian devaluation was potentially important; and Roger Cambon, at the London Embassy, drew special attention to it when reporting to the Quai d'Orsay.[44] In spite of his appraisal of the British attitude Monick suggested that it might be possible to talk the British into at least provisional stabilization subject to modification in the event of price fluctuations; but even if this was not possible, now was certainly the moment to try, since from July 1935 Britain would probably be entering into a pre-electoral period.[45]

In short, at the beginning of 1935 talk of stabilization was very much in the air in France. But what would the position of the franc be in all this? One British fear was that if sterling were stabilized first, France could then devalue at a rate which undervalued the franc relative to sterling.[46] In preparation for Flandin's London visit Leith-Ross talked to Flandin in Paris and Monick in London. To their demands for at least a *de facto* stabilization of the pound or at least some assurances about its future course, he was not forthcoming: the Americans would almost certainly not agree to any sterling–dollar rate acceptable to the British, and although the British did not want any further fall in sterling there was little they could do to stop it; but to the extent that this fall was due to commercial demand for francs and dollars, the French could help by relaxing trade restrictions and accepting a larger import surplus. The French view, of course, was that trade liberalization could only follow exchange stabilization: this was the dilemma which had already surfaced many times before. Monick in return applied some gentle blackmail: without British co-operation the French might be forced to devalue; Flandin was 'by no means complacent as to the position of the franc' and the devaluers were becoming a more significant force in France. Flandin, whose prestige in the countryside was badly in need of a boost, told Leith-Ross that support for devaluation was gaining ground in agricultural circles as a means of raising prices. Monick's own personal view was that there should be a provisional stabilization of the sterling–franc parities on the basis of a 16–20 per cent devaluation of the franc, combined with a relaxation of trade restrictions.[47] But Rowe-Dutton, British financial attaché in Paris, was inclined not to take seriously the threats of devaluation: Tannery had strongly impressed on him the complete impossibility of devaluation in a country like France,[48] and given the state of public opinion an isolated devaluation of the franc seemed out of the question; but, he went on, 'I have suddenly sensed a stream of opinion suggesting that as part of a general agreement for stabilization, the franc should be fixed at say 100. This has reached me from one or two sources and it looks as though a kite were being flown about this'.[49] As if to confirm this analysis Leith-Ross heard from a close friend of Flandin that while Flandin remained opposed to devaluation, he understood that his policies would eventually lead to it but hoped they could be postponed until dollar–sterling stabilization, and then presented as part of an international agreement.[50] But all this was very unofficial. And when Flandin came to England stabilization was not discussed:[51] the British view was only too well known.

As a public affirmation of his resistance to devaluation, Flandin announced that, in accordance with the Stabilization Law of 1928, the government would begin to mint gold coins for circulation within France, a step guaranteed also to win the wavering support of the Fédération Républicaine which had been advocating such a measure for years. But the slide in the pound continued: in March it stood as low as 71; the gold block looked increasingly vulnerable, especially after the collapse of the Belgian government in March. The French therefore resumed their attempts to obtain stabilization. At the beginning of March, Lacour-Gayet of the Bank of France, after consulting Germain-Martin and Tannery, approached Morgenthau, the American Treasury Secretary, to propose that the Federal Reserve Bank and the Bank of France should offer a joint credit to bolster the pound; but this idea was rejected by Morgenthau.[52] Publicly Flandin expressed his disquiet about the fall of the pound, and even threatened the possibility of taking anti-dumping measures, which presumably implied a reimposition of the exchange compensation tax.[53] But this statement was probably largely intended to pacify opinion in France.[54] The government's real thoughts were, on the contrary, moving towards trade liberalization. There was increasing pessimism about the consequences of the fall in the pound: it would force France either into an ever-more contractionary cycle of deflation or into ever-increasing economic isolation. A note by Coulondre of the Quai d'Orsay put the problem dramatically:

perhaps, thanks to a system of managed economy, we might succeed for a while in avoiding a worsening of our trade deficit. We cannot avoid the steady reduction in the volume of trade . . . France will gradually turn herself into a closed economy, as is already the case in agriculture. Is it conceivable that our industrial areas will be able to adapt to this situation . . . What will be the fate of the capitalist regime if it locks itself into this vice?[55]

The alternative was to exploit continuing unofficial American feelers in favour of stabilization.[56] Franco-British views seemed incompatible: the former wanted trade liberalization before stabilization, for the latter stabilization was the precondition of a resumption of international trade. France could break the circle by proposing the progressive abolition of all quotas – though not at first agricultural quotas – *simultaneously* with international currency stabilization; as a protection against the consequences of such a policy, tariffs would need to be increased, but these were less unpopular abroad than quotas which froze international trade and thereby made impossible the adjustments necessary for a proper working of the gold standard. This was the project which France would propose to the American

government in the hope that the two countries could then force the less receptive British to comply; it was hoped also that the Belgians would hold out
until the American answer had been received.[57]

The plan was communicated to Washington in the middle of March.[58] But
the reactions of the United States were, as so often under the Roosevelt
administration, too contradictory to be very helpful: Morgenthau, meeting
de Laboulaye on 10 April, agreed that France and America should act
together for stabilization at current rates and that with 70 per cent of the
world's gold they would be able to put pressure on the British;[59] but Jean
Appert, the French financial attaché in New York, was told unofficially by a
Treasury official that initiatives for stabilization should come from France,
and involve a 15 to 20 per cent devaluation of the franc:[60] to this suggestion
the French could only give a very non-committal agreement to a confidential,
and purely informational exchange of views between the two countries.[61]
And a few days later the Quai d'Orsay reported that Morgenthau was being
much more cautious than he had been earlier to Laboulaye.[62] In short,
American policy was far from fixed.

Although the French government had decided, without achieving great
success, that 'the road to London passes via Washington',[63] this did not rule
out trying out the new policy on the British. Rueff and Monick saw Leith-
Ross in March: they told him that Flandin was anxious to relax quotas – and
to eliminate them within five years – but only if moves were made towards
stabilization. The British answer had not changed: this was illogical precisely
because it was trade restrictions which made stabilization impossible. Rueff
then proposed simultaneous action on quotas and stabilization, but Leith-
Ross was doubtful if the Americans would agree: without a relaxation of
both American and French trade restrictions, stabilization, unless American
prices rose, would suck gold out of Britain or impose deflation on British
governments.[64] Two weeks later, after the devaluation of the Belga, Flandin
confirmed to Leith-Ross the French government's desire to relax quotas; but
added that he had already so alienated agricultural interests that he could not
possibly act without some prior agreement on stabilization.[65] Rueff, on the
other hand, was now pressing for talks on stabilization and trade without any
preconditions: he and Flandin gave the impression that 'they regarded
devaluation as necessary for all other countries of Europe, though not
France'.[66] As usual the British could give no encouragement.[67]

On 13 May Morgenthau announced in a radio broadcast that the
American government would not stand in the way of international exchange
stabilization. The British greeted this unfavourably: Morgenthau had not
proposed to take any of the steps – on commercial policy – which would
make stabilization possible.[68] But he received a gloss on it from an American
Treasury official on a visit to London, who claimed that the British had
seriously underestimated its importance: the American government was, he

said, ready to abandon its authority to devalue up to 50 per cent; it did not put the prevailing sterling–dollar parity of $4.86 as a precondition of stabilization, and was ready to consider $4.60; and it believed stabilization implied a 20 per cent gold block devaluation: a devaluation of this order of magnitude would not be considered by the United States as a hostile action but, on the contrary, as 'conducive to a business recovery in the countries concerned'.[69] And as the speculative pressure on the franc built up during May, the opinion of French financial officials moved in favour of devaluation. Monick, by now a long-time convert, warned that under pressure from agricultural circles and as a means of solving the budget problem, there was a danger of it being too high (30 per cent), though this was, of course, partly a way of pushing the British into compliance.[70] Rueff was 'very interested' by Morgenthau's speech and believed it was an opportunity France could not afford to miss: he was 'not afraid to discuss the eventuality of a French devaluation having to take place if stabilization of the pound and dollar were to take place'.[71] The French Finance Ministry was indeed reported to be coming round to the idea,[72] and Paul Devinat, an economic adviser to Flandin, believed that devaluation was inevitable, but that, owing to pressure from agricultural circles, it would probably be as high as 40 per cent.[73] The Bank of France however was as hostile as ever: Robert Lacour-Gayet told Rowe-Dutton at the end of May that there was even less reason for devaluation than a year ago owing to the 'improved' economic situation (this at the deepest point of the recession!); the only danger to the franc came from the budgetary situation.[74]

But devaluation did not take place; and the explicit task of the Laval government was to save the franc. Talk of stabilization receded. Morgenthau was reported to believe that the British attitude, and the imminence of British elections, ruled out the possibility of even provisional stabilization for the moment.[75] A visiting American banker was told by two Quai d'Orsay officials that a relaxation of trade business depended on stabilization: France was firmly attached to the present value of the franc although a slight devaluation might be envisaged in the context of a general stabilization agreement.[76] Leith-Ross met Laval at an official lunch soon after the formation of his government, and was attacked by him in an 'aggressive manner' over British failure to stabilize. He tried to explain the British position, commenting later: 'M. Laval took this fairly well but I do not imagine that he followed my argument. His knowledge of finance is somewhat limited . . . he appeared to believe that the gold reserves of the Bank of England were as large as those of the Bank of France – a point on which even Monsieur Régnier was able to correct him'.[77] And that, for the moment, was that.

In the autumn Bonnet, Minister of Commerce, made a speech at the League of Nations appealing for trade liberalization and exchange stabilization; but in fact he offered very little new and only irritated the British who would have preferred any concrete proposals to be made in public.[78]

Morgenthau stopped over in Paris in October, but nothing conclusive resulted from the visit.[79] Monick reported from London that not only were the British farther from stabilization than ever but that the pound would be bound to fall further: its relative recovery (it had risen to 75 F. in the spring) was only a reflection of the weakness of the gold block; thus, paradoxically if Laval were to be successful in strengthening the franc, this would only further weaken the pound and thereby further undermine the international position of the franc. The key to the situation lay in the relations between the British and the Americans: 'between these two adversaries we play no more than a walk-on part'. His solution was for a moderate devaluation of the franc – a complement to deflation not a measure of monetary dumping – which, far from inviting reprisals from Britain and the United States, would be seen as a reasonable step towards restoring international exchange stability.[80] But in too many countries too many elections were too imminent to make any immediate action probable.

What then are we to make of Germain-Martin's defence of the position of French governments during 1934 and 1935? Certainly there were officials in the Ministry of Finance and the Quai d'Orsay[81] who by May 1935, if not before, conceived of the possibility of devaluation as part of a general agreement; but the Bank of France remained hostile. This is how a British Treasury official read the situation in May 1935: 'In aptitude for regarding devaluation in a not too unfavourable light Monick is well ahead of Rueff, Rueff is well ahead of Baumgartner, and Baumgartner well ahead of Tannery. Tannery is in fact still rigidly opposed'.[82] And despite his public rhetoric Flandin also eventually conceived of devaluation, and so no doubt many other ministers. But on the other hand no feelers were put out by the government towards this end, and all efforts in the short term were aimed at obtaining *de facto* stabilization of the pound in order to preserve the parity of the franc: isolated remarks by Monick, who was known to favour devaluation, were hardly sufficient to persuade the British that France was serious about devaluation. The Bank of England tried to be as helpful on the exchange rate as domestic constraints would allow,[83] but the British were never seriously sounded out, as Monick would have liked, and as occurred in June 1936, about their reactions to a possible French devaluation. On the other hand, even if the question was not put, there was no reason to believe that such action would have invited reprisals. On the contrary it was known at the end of 1934 that the British considered the franc to be overvalued, and that they did not intend to retaliate against Belgian devaluation; and, as for America, it was clear, especially after May 1935, that a moderate French devaluation was expected, indeed desired as a prelude to international stabilization. If then the French government chose not to devalue in 1934 or 1935 the decision was its own, and the reasons for it must be sought in France, not in the possible reactions of the world outside.

**Paul Reynaud: 'My long struggle'**

On 28 June 1934 in a speech considered revolutionary in the corridors of the Palais Bourbon,[84] Paul Reynaud announced his conversion to devaluation.[85] The event was indeed dramatic: one of the leading figures of the right, with Flandin and Tardieu, during the 1932 elections, it was Reynaud who had brandished the spectre of the 'two sou franc' if the cartel should triumph. But the surprise soon wore off: by January 1935 *Le Temps* could refer to one of Reynaud's 'ritual' speeches in favour of devaluation.[86] From being a partisan of the most rigorous financial orthodoxy Reynaud had become the most prominent and articulate spokesman of a solution considered little less than criminal by the French political establishment. Indeed Action française, with characteristic verve, referring habitually to him as 'vermin' with the 'mug and morals of a termite', went so far as to demand his imprisonment.[87]

Reynaud has given his own account of these events in his memoirs, which depict him as a solitary fighter of lost causes with chapters entitled 'My long struggle for devaluation', 'My long struggle for de Gaulle's armoured corps', 'My struggle against the armistice'. The second volume is called *Envers et contre tous*. He describes how from the first months of 1933 he had come to think of devaluation as necessary to save the French economy; how at the beginning of 1934 he for the first time explicitly and publicly posed the alternative of deflation and devaluation; how during the spring of 1934 he privately explained his fears to Germain-Martin and Tardieu without convincing either; and how, having crossed the Rubicon on 28 June he found himself a political and social outcast ('Paul Reynaud is not someone one invites') reviled by the right-wing press; and, finally, how in spite of the fact that an anti-devaluation candidate of the right refused to stand down in his favour at the second round of the 1936 elections, he was re-elected to his Paris constituency by the narrow margin of 27 votes.[88]

In spite of this heroic narrative it has been alleged that Reynaud was in fact quite a late convert to devaluation, or at any rate that if he really had, as his memoirs claim, been moving in favour since the beginning of 1933, his public utterances did little to show this;[89] and indeed gave quite the contrary impression. Thus, immediately after the speech of 28 June, Georges Boris commented that Reynaud 'is now trying to reverse a trend which he helped to create'.[90] But this is a little unfair. From the beginning Reynaud's attitude to monetary problems had been different from that of the rest of the right. While Roosevelt's actions at the London Conference were almost universally condemned by conservative opinion in France, Reynaud had shown a unique spirit of comprehension, and he criticized the French experts in London for failing to see why it was unrealistic to expect a stabilization of the dollar: Roosevelt's aim, he wrote, was 'to push up prices and relieve the burden on debtors'.[91] Reynaud did not, of course, at this time propose a similar solution for France, but as early as April 1933 he starkly outlined the alternatives: a gold embargo or a thorough programme of financial recovery.[92] Throughout 1933 Reynaud was one of the fiercest advocates of deflation. But his position had always been a completely logical one, going beyond the purely budgetary considerations of most conservative commentators: deflation, he argued, had to spread throughout the economy in order to make France competitive again;[93] without such a policy the franc would not be saved.[94] Thus, when at the beginning of 1934, during the budget debate, Reynaud called on Doumergue's government to choose between deflation and devaluation he was not saying anything new; but, although preferring deflation, he also dismissed various specious arguments against devaluation, such as the fact that France had already devalued once before: the devaluation of 1926 had no bearing on France's present situation.[95] Three months later, in May, he wrote to Doumergue advising a dissolution while the government was still popular, warned of the dangers of pushing deflation too far and proposed that it should be complemented by devaluation.[96] And in June he publicly made the plunge.

Reynaud's position had, then, been a consistently logical one, and after June 1934 he defended devaluation, which he had never presented in apocalyptic terms, with the same lucidity as he had defended deflation in the previous two years. Why Reynaud should have shown so much greater clairvoyance than almost the whole of the rest of the political class – especially the right – is somewhat obscure. Certainly he was a highly gifted individual, but so, for instance, was his former colleague André Tardieu, the Tardieu who wrote to him in January 1935 that he would 'rather die' than devalue.[97] Partly the fact that Reynaud was not included in Doumergue's government in February 1934 allowed him the freedom to speak his mind; and once he had done so, he excluded himself from any immediate return to power: freedom was all that was left to him. Perhaps, seeing that devaluation was inevitable, he had hoped to use it as a means of returning to power in a 'ministry of devaluation'.[98] But the enterprise was risky, and, perhaps underestimating the tenacity of opposition to devaluation, Reynaud had in the short term destroyed his chance of office. His great friend Henri de Kérillis, editor of the *Echo de Paris* and an opponent of devaluation, wrote to him in February 1936: 'You could have been a minister in all the last governments. You have preferred to be a tenacious opponent'.[99] And he blamed Reynaud for letting himself become 'fixated, hypnotized, dominated by a problem. You have neglected everything else . . . you have lost your position as a leader, lost contact with opinion'.[100] At the time Reynaud was nonetheless accused of acting merely as the representative in parliament of the Rue de Rivoli and the Rue de la Paix – of the Parisian luxury export industry.[101] But although he was narrowly re-elected in the 2nd *arrondissement* of Paris, his much reduced majority shows the unpopularity of his cause even in the circles of Parisian commerce; and from the numerous letters of congratulation which he received after his re-election it is clear that many of his constituents who did vote for him had done so in spite of his views on devaluation, such, for example, as the proprietor of a small café who modestly described himself as 'perhaps badly informed' on financial questions. If then Reynaud was re-elected the reason was that expressed in a letter of congratulation from Baron Robert de Rothschild: 'you have not perhaps yet converted me to certain of your ideas . . . But we are nonetheless both on the same side of the barricade – the great barricade'.[102]

The truth would simply seem to be that Reynaud's comprehension of economic and financial problems was far above the average of his contemporaries. He also had the capacity to attract able young advisers, and the gift of listening to them without any political *parti pris*, a characteristic which had obviously encouraged Colonel de Gaulle to submit his ideas to him. Alfred Sauvy, at that time a young statistician, recounts how he was first asked by Reynaud for information on price indices in May 1934, and how after their first meeting Reynaud did not make an important economic speech without consulting him.[103] On international monetary affairs, and especially those relating to the United States, Reynaud was advised by the banker André Istel, who may have had some influence on his views on devaluation. On financial matters he took the advice of the finance inspectors, Yves Bouthillier and Dominique Leca, who was to become his *chef de cabinet* in 1938. A little later he was also to be advised by the very young Michel Debré.[104]

Whether Reynaud was always an entirely effective advocate of devaluation is another question. He had none of the popular and persuasive charm of a Roosevelt nor for that matter a Herriot. Although his parliamentary oratory could at times be devastating in its irony and intellectual rigour – as in his attack on Germain-Martin in May 1935 – his evident ambition and intolerance of fools did not inspire affection. His diminutive figure and nervously energetic personality – he was an enthusiastic gymnast – were far removed from the orotundities and backslapping camaraderie of the Palais Bourbon. His somewhat raffish lifestyle and the irreverent cleverness of his friends and advisers – including many Jews such as Istel, Debré, Mannheimer, Gaston Palewski – inspired in many *bien pensant* conservatives a distrust which did not entirely exclude a degree of anti-Semitism.[105] And as he became increasingly frustrated by the unreasoning opposition to devaluation he became increasingly arrogant: 'I had invited the Chamber to discuss the government's policy; the government invites it to discuss mine'.[106] De Kérillis warned him about this: 'You have given the impression of being obstinate and, what is more serious, a little arrogant . . . "I am right . . . Fifty other countries say it . . . I am right . . . my compatriots are boors." A bad stance to adopt, I assure you'.[107] The advice had little effect: Reynaud wrote back complaining of the prevailing 'dictatorship of stupidity'.[108] Self-satisfaction is the only reward of the unheard prophet.

There is one sense, however, in which Reynaud's account in his memoirs of the devaluation is somewhat misleading: he may have become the most notorious advocate of devaluation; but he was never the only one, nor, more importantly, the earliest one. Among the first public supporters of devaluation was Georges Boris, editor of *La Lumière*, whose heterodox opinions we have had occasion to notice many times. Although not a trained economist, Boris had both practical experience of business and contacts in England which made him more open to unorthodox views on monetary matters.[109] From the beginning of the crisis he had argued the necessity for a reflation of the world economy by a redistribution of gold and the setting up of an international fund to buy up surplus raw materials.[110] In March 1933 he went further down the path of heterodoxy: predicting that Roosevelt would – indeed should – be pushed into a devaluation of the dollar, he proposed (15 months before Reynaud) a voluntary devaluation of the franc as the only alternative to a socially and politically divisive policy of deflation.[111] His commentaries on Roosevelt were enthusiastic, criticizing him only at times for acting too timidly and uncertainly;[112] and when America left the gold standard he wrote of 'this gesture by which posterity will date the end of the great world crisis'.[113] Thus when Reynaud announced his conversion, Boris was quick to seize the implications for the left: 'since his 28 June speech one no longer runs the same risks in declaring oneself a partisan of devaluation'.[114]

Boris was not isolated on the left wing of the Radical Party in holding such views. Bertrand de Jouvenel explained and justified Roosevelt's policies to the readers of *La République*, and proposed an agreement between France, America and Britain for a general devaluation as part of an international plan to raise prices.[115] At the end of 1933, having unsuccessfully denounced deflation to the Radical Congress, he noted that other countries besides France had prepared the conditions of their recovery by throwing off the 'millstone of the gold standard'.[116] Albert Bayet warned in April 1933 against hanging on to the 'illusory wealth' and 'futile glory' of the gold franc.[117] In January 1933, almost one year before Reynaud posed the same dilemma with equal explicitness, Henri Clerc invited the Chamber to choose between deflation and devaluation; at this period Clerc, like Reynaud, preferred the former alternative, not 'for the vain satisfaction of conforming to some mystique of deflation but to allow a revival of our exports'.[118] Clerc, loosely associated with the Young Radicals, had been elected to parliament for the first time in 1932. His was not a very influential voice – but it was a sane and lucid one: while continuing throughout 1933 to advocate deflation, he also attacked 'the sort of fetishism attached to the gold held by the Bank of France' and proposed that France should accept a redistribution of gold.[119] At the beginning of 1934 he no longer believed further deflation to be possible and although his thoughts now turned to planism as a solution to the problems of the French economy – he left the Radicals and became associated with the Neo-Socialists – he warned against depicting devaluation as a catastrophe.[120] And by May 1935 he was publicly in favour of it, though without great enthusiasm.[121]

It is not surprising that Clerc should have moved toward the Neo-Socialists, for there was perhaps no party more ready to accept the idea of devaluation: as early as May 1933, in a debate on the forthcoming World Economic Conference, Montagnon, still a Socialist, advised the government to consider a devaluation without inflation (in his view a possible option) as the only alternative to a deflation which, he prophesied with prescience, would eventually affect even rentes; and warned about the consequences of this for the *classes moyennes*.[122] Although, for interesting reasons which we will examine below, Montagnon announced at the beginning of 1934 that he was in fact against devaluation,[123] before the end of the year he had come out in favour of it.[124] Déat wrote infrequently on monetary affairs although he mocked sentimental panegyrics on 'our dear-little-four-sou-gold-franc',[125] but by early 1935 he too had rallied to devaluation, and his speech in the debate on the grant to decree powers to Flandin, in which he publicly advocated it, was as effective as Reynaud's.[126]

If, however, Reynaud was far from alone in his campaign for devaluation, it was certainly true that none of the previously mentioned figures – except perhaps Boris – proposed it with quite the same singlemindedness. This was not the case with Raymond Patenôtre.[127] Son of a former French ambassador to Washington, and heir, through his American mother, to a considerable fortune, Patenôtre's influence was exercised neither in parliament – he never spoke – nor through any political party – too independent a spirit to join the Radicals, he was the member of a small group of left independents – but rather through his ownership of various newspapers, most importantly *Le Petit Journal*.[128] In a book published in 1932, *La Crise et le drame monétaire*, he had attributed the crisis to an insufficient quantity of money and proposed bimetallism as the only solution. From this position it was but a short step to devaluation to which he became converted in 1933: prevented at first from publicly expressing his views because he held a minor post in Daladier's government – he did, however, write privately to Daladier[129] – after its fall he argued the case for devaluation day after day in the columns of *Le Petit Journal*, republishing his articles as books.[130] *Le Petit Journal*'s powerful campaign reached its culmination on 28 May 1935, two days before Flandin's fall: besides publishing articles by Patenôtre and Reynaud, this issue contained declarations in favour of, or fairly sympathetic to, devaluation by 19 deputies and senators of right and left including Clerc, Déat,

Mendès France, Jammy-Schmidt and Henri de Jouvenel (Bertrand's father).[131]

The fact that Reynaud was not isolated in his advocacy of devaluation does not however diminish the importance of his campaign. Clerc, Déat, Montagnon, de Jouvenel, Nogaro, however persuasive as individuals, were ultimately marginal political figures: all were driven out – whether voluntarily or not – of their political parties; and like so many others they were to be victims of the belief that 1934 would see a recasting of French politics (to some extent it did, but at the expense of such as themselves). And the views of Boris and Patenôtre were already too tainted by unorthodoxy, too Anglo-Saxon, for their conversion to carry much weight. Reynaud was on the other hand a pillar of the political establishment. In short: Patenôtre's advocacy of devaluation made him into a more prominent figure than he had been before; and Reynaud's advocacy made it a more prominent issue than it had been before.

Although the proponents of devaluation had often started from different political positions, their arguments tended, naturally enough, to be similar. We can therefore most easily study the case for devaluation by examining the arguments of its most famous exponent; divergences can be considered later.[132] Reynaud's bombshell was introduced by an empirical observation to be many times repeated: in the 49 countries (later 50) which had devalued there were signs of economic recovery; in the countries of the gold block there was economic stagnation. Nowhere had devaluation led to monetary inflation: the rate of increase in retail prices had everywhere been inferior to the percentage of devaluation. How had devaluation helped the rest of the world? At first Reynaud was inclined to stress its influence in stimulating exports, but soon, like most of its other advocates, he came to lay greater stress on its internal effects:[133] the catastrophic position of the French economy was caused less by the decline in exports – this was a general phenomenon – than by the divergence between wholesale prices (which had slumped and would fall still further) and retail prices (which had to some extent resisted the fall), between prices and costs. The result was a disastrous profit squeeze. Reynaud summarized the problem in a vivid image: 'the French people are undergoing the terrible torture . . . of quartering. Their left wrist is attached to an iron bar deeply embedded in the ground, that of retail prices or the cost of living; and their right is attached to a moving bar, that of wholesale prices, which is magnetically and irresistibly attracted by falling world prices'.[134]

Devaluation, then, by allowing wholesale prices to rise in paper and fall in gold would restore profits; retail prices (costs) would rise, but not in proportion to the rise in wholesale prices.[135] Of course the same process could theoretically be achieved by deflation. But for many reasons Reynaud considered this to be an unsatisfactory solution: the British naval mutiny in

August 1931 had shown that, pushed beyond a certain point, deflation became socially dangerous; the economic policies of Doumergue, Flandin and Laval were anyway doing a lot to prevent it, especially by holding up agricultural prices; and, finally, deflation encouraged hoarding. But it was not true that devaluation would ruin the rentier class: to the extent that it would be accompanied, as it had been everywhere, by a fall in interest rates and rise in the value of government securities, rentiers would reap advantage through the appreciation of their capital; the rise in prices would certainly affect their real incomes but deflation on the other hand worked unfairly to their benefit. As for the form that devaluation would take, Reynaud's ideal solution was for it to form part of an international stabilization agreement: 'do you believe that England will return to gold with the machine gun of the gold block at her back?'[136] But even without a stabilization agreement Reynaud was prepared to envisage either devaluation followed by an immediate return to gold or to let the franc float and find its level; the decision would depend on the circumstances.[137]

In hoping for an early, if not immediate, return to gold after devaluation, Reynaud differed from Patenôtre and Boris for whom this was the least desirable solution: for them the enemy was the gold standard itself.[138] More important than such tactical divergences between Reynaud and the other advocates of devaluation were their different conceptions of the ultimate purpose of devaluation. Although he denied that he was a 'monomaniac' who believed devaluation to be a universal panacea,[139] Reynaud did not intend it to form part of any general plan of reform. His admiration for Roosevelt's policies did not extend beyond his monetary experiments: the rest of the New Deal legislation had, he believed, hindered the process of recovery which devaluation had set in motion. But it was possible to take another view. For Georges Boris, who admired many aspects of the New Deal, devaluation, to have its full effect, needed to be accompanied by a whole series of other measures: a modification of the Bank of France's Statutes to allow open market operations, a large programme of public works, collective bargaining;[140] for Montagnon and Déat, devaluation was a necessary complement to the institution of a plan: in itself it would achieve little;[141] this was also more or less the view of Clerc;[142] and Patenôtre envisaged devaluation combined with a reform of the French credit structure, especially of the Bank of France.[143] In short, devaluation was seen as only the first step towards a reformed, more rationally organized capitalism, if not indeed a step towards socialism. But for Reynaud devaluation was the only guarantee of a return to economic and political liberalism: it was the attempt to prevent it which was pushing governments further down the road of *dirigisme*. In short, he proposed devaluation as the salvation of liberal capitalism, and himself, the rational conservative, as the saviour of a blinkered bourgeoisie.

## 'This sort of monetary Dreyfus Affair' (Reynaud)[144]

The differences which separated Reynaud from the other proponents of devaluation were insignificant compared to the similarities which united him with them against the rest of opinion in France. This was no party issue: devaluation was condemned by all political parties from the Action française to the Communist Party; by economists;[145] by publicists as different as Lucien Romier,[146] Joseph Barthélemy,[147] Henri Michel,[148] and Jacques Duboin;[149] by governments; by Chambers of Commerce;[150] and by all leading representatives of the employers: René Duchemin, President of the C.G.P.F.,[151] Ernest Billiet, President of the Union des Intérêts Economiques,[152] C.-J. Gignoux,[153] Henri Donon, President of the Union of Textile Employers,[154] Edmond Mercier of Redressment Français,[155] Edouard Duhen, President of the Confédération des Groupements Commerciaux et Industriels de France,[156] and so on. The only exception to this unanimity came, we have seen,[157] from agricultural circles; but, as long as there was no threat of reducing tariff barriers – thus, of course, making effective deflation impossible – such pressure was containable and intermittent.

The list could be extended almost endlessly. It demonstrates the weight of opinion opposed to devaluation, but it does not convey the apocalyptic terms in which the debate was conducted. Jean Lescure described the consequences in this way: 'in a country like ours . . . any monetary amputation would prepare the way for catastrophes . . . farms, factories, and shops would have to close their doors'.[158] Doumergue, in his radio homilies to the people of France, used no less lurid language: 'the complete ruin of France: the ruin of all rentiers . . . pensions falling to zero . . . workers' wages reduced to zero'.[159] These were not the pronouncements of marginal figures: Lescure was a leading professional economist; Doumergue, a respected ex-President and saviour in 1934. The argument was conducted in moral terms: 'facility', 'monetary manipulation', 'bankruptcy', 'fraud', 'despoilment' against 'monetary probity', 'healthy currency'.[160] Flandin compared 'the battle of the franc' to Verdun.[161] Reynaud described a 'press campaign, orchestrated with such synchronization that on the same day one would find almost the same expression in different papers',[162] and behind this campaign he saw the hand of the Bank of France.[163] How true this was we cannot know; but certainly the arguments of the many opponents of devaluation were broadly similar enough to enable us to consider them all together, ignoring certain differences. Only one distinction needs to be made. There were a small number of anti-devaluers who were prepared to envisage devaluation, ultimately, as part of a general stabilization agreement: this was the case, for example, of Peyerimhoff among industrialists,[165] Wolff among economists,[165] Lucien Romier,[166] and Emile Roche.[167] But this was for the future; until such a stabilization agreement seemed possible the position of such individuals was indistinguishable from the vast majority who argued – at least publicly – that devaluation was unacceptable under any circumstances. Theirs was rather the extraordinary view expressed by Régnier, 24 hours before becoming Laval's finance minister: 'it is on the franc that England and America must align their currency'.[168]

Although Reynaud had first brought devaluation to the centre of politics, the government initially felt the need to put the intellectual case against it at the beginning of 1934 during the first serious gold flight, and as a rebuttal of Lippmann's article; but the case was further developed by Germain-Martin in June to combat Reynaud's arguments, and a major part of the preface of the 1935 budget was devoted to the problem. After this point very little new was added to the debate.[169] The argument turned on a comparative analysis of the situation of the countries which had devalued and the gold block, and more specifically a comparison between France and Britain – Britain because the British example was made much of by Reynaud and because the anti-devaluers were able to turn it to their advantage. England's recovery was, it was pointed out, extremely relative: unemployment remained much higher than in France,[170] and Duchemin, in a highly influential pamphlet, showed, by choosing highly tendentious dates and methods of calculation, that the foreign trade of the gold block had fallen less than that of the rest of the world.[171] Devaluation, then, would in no sense help foreign trade – though we have seen that this was not the main argument of the devaluers – and this was not surprising: the obstacles to international trade no longer lay primarily in relative price levels but rather in growing protectionism.[172] And the reason for protectionism was precisely the continuation of monetary instability, which a French devaluation would only aggravate by further destabilizing the international economic system: 'it is as if one said a house was badly built because one undermined the ground around it'.[173]

But it could not be completely denied that economic recovery was taking place in Britain. To the extent that this was due to increased international competitiveness it was argued that the situation would not last: devaluation, if any solution at all, was only a temporary one, and sooner or later gold price levels of the countries which had devalued would meet those of France.[174] If this had not happened so far it was because the conditions in which Britain had devalued were quite different from those which would apply to France: the pound had been devalued against a background of falling prices in the rest of the world,[175] and sterling was an important currency which had taken numerous other currencies down with it – two factors which prevented devaluation from resulting in an inflationary increase in import prices; and the existence of the Empire allowed Britain a certain self-sufficiency not available to France.[176] British recovery was based therefore not on devaluation but on the setting up of a system of Imperial Preference at Ottawa, and, more importantly, on cheap money.[177] And why was money cheap? Because Britain had carried out a massive budgetary deflation.[178] Thus, Britain did indeed provide a lesson for France; but the lesson was that of the need for deflation not devaluation: British recovery had taken place *in spite* of devaluation![179]. It was this curious process of selective reasoning which could lead Régnier to tell a surprised Leith-Ross in June 1935 that he enormously admired the work of the national government – on which Laval's economy decrees were to be based.[180]

This brief survey is hardly sufficient to explain the passion with which devaluation was opposed. At a more fundamental level the resistance to devaluation derived not from comparatively complex arguments about relative price levels or comparative analyses of the economies of different countries but rather from a mixture of collective social reflexes – psychological, patriotic or moral. Perhaps four such factors can be suggested. First, there was a simple question of prestige: in the words of Germain-Martin, whatever the temporary difficulties of the French economy, if the franc could only hold, 'the day will come when, thanks to her policy France will be able to play a great role, as much in the monetary as the economic sphere'.[181] France, as the guardian of money orthodoxy, of *sagesse*, could be a beacon in a disordered world.[182] Since 1928 the strength of the franc had made her not only respected but envied throughout the world: was all this to be lost? When Reynaud pointed out to the Chamber's Finance Commission that, by comparison with the dollar and sterling, the franc was an unimportant currency, Laval protested: 'the franc unimportant? I could evoke the memory of a government to which M. Paul Reynaud belonged . . . [of] a night when England appealed for help from the franc [i.e. August 1931]; it was important then . . . we opened all the coffers of our country to put at the disposal of the Bank of England the sums necessary to save the pound'.[183] Reynaud might protest rightly that this was irrelevant demagogy – but its sentimental force was considerable.

Secondly, devaluation was assimilated by its opponents to an attack on economic liberalism. There were, said Germain-Martin, two economic systems in the world: liberty or control.[184] Devaluation would inevitably be followed by government intervention to prevent a rise in prices: 'bread prices will be controlled as in the Revolution or as in Russia'.[185] And the immediate consequences of the Belgian devaluation only seemed to bear out such fears: the 'monetary adventure' of Belgium was leading, said Jenny, to encroaching *étatisme*.[186] Devaluation, like Roosevelt's 'controlled currency' could lead only to 'monetary bankruptcy or Bolshevism'.[187]

The example of Roosevelt brought to mind a third argument: the defence of the rentier: Roosevelt, wrote Romier, had devalued to raise prices and reduce the burden on indebted farmers; but in France it was not the case that most people were debtors, living on credit.[188] The defence of an 'ancestral tradition of morality' was therefore also the defence of a social class.[189] And not of any social class: devaluation implied 'the crushing, even the elimination of those *classes moyennes* who are the backbone of the social structure of France'.[190] To ruin the class of small savers was to destroy the social order.[191] These savers had already suffered from the devaluation of 1926, and from the conversion of 1932: they could not be hit again without fear of the consequences. That this propaganda touched receptive chords in the population can be seen easily enough from the correspondence received by Reynaud. The following is typical of many: 'it was enough to be swindled once in 1927 which four-fifths ruined me. After a new devaluation I would no longer have enough to live'.[192]

But why should devaluation have such disastrous consequences as to entail the destruction of the rentier class, if not all the *classes moyennes*. At this point the argument became a psychological one: what differentiated the situation from both Britain and America was that France had already devalued; as a result it would be impossible to devalue *à froid* as Reynaud wanted: 'it is necessary to take account of the extreme sensitivity of public opinion which, enlightened by a painful experience whose memory has not been effaced, is ignorant of none of the consequences of devaluation'.[193] Over and over again politicians and commentators stressed the likely effects of the collective memory of the 1920s in the event of a devaluation.[194] Even if, then, it was an objectively desirable solution in France it threatened to have highly inflationary consequences owing to the likely reactions of public opinion. As Nogaro pointed out, the fact that the recent devaluation in France had coincided with an important inflation had led the two to be indissolubly associated in peoples' minds: the fact that the devaluation of 1928 had been a consequence and not a cause of inflation was not so often noted.[195] The problem was exacerbated by the existence of some 25 to 30m francs of hoarded banknotes with which a panic-stricken population would flood the market.[196]

Here the opponents of devaluation had an unanswerable argument – unanswerable because only experience could test it. All observers noted the *sang froid* of the British population: the British did not, Nogaro pointed out, talk about the 13 shilling pound as the French talked about the two sou franc.[197] Jenny attributed this phenomenon less to virtues of the British public than to its 'total lack of comprehension of monetary matters'.[198] Montagnon's explanation was different: 'there has in England been a whole literature of articles, books and lectures by well-known economists, Keynes, McKenna, Lord d'Abernon, etc., preparing public opinion for devaluation'.[199] It was precisely this lack of 'moral preparation' which had made Montagnon reluctant to propose a course of action which he would otherwise have favoured.[200] The psychological argument was, then, dangerous because in pointing to the existence of the problem it could simultaneously create it. Henri Clerc testified to the importance of this phenomenon as early as October 1933 when he told the Radical Congress that he was not personally against devaluation for technical reasons; but he considered it psychologically impossible because, 'for the last 16 months, a campaign has been conducted presenting devaluation as something so disastrous that public opinion is persuaded of this fact as a truth against which we can do nothing'. So deflation had to follow its course.[201] Even those theoretically in favour of devaluation were made wary of advocating it.

The case of Léon Blum is instructive in this context. Blum followed international monetary developments closely in *Le Populaire de Paris*, thinking aloud to clarify his own thoughts, and also attempting to explain complicated phenomena to Socialist Party members.[202] In the first instance Blum's articles attempted less to present a firm case for or against devaluation than to demystify the whole issue. From the moment that Roosevelt had devalued the dollar, Blum wondered if it would be possible to 'maintain the franc alone like an isolated rock at its present parity'.[203] And 18 months later, although he refused to formulate any personal preference, he was convinced that the franc could not hold indefinitely.[204] Right up until the elections he attempted to explain why devaluation was probably inevitable and how a government of the left that was actually forced to implement it would be in no sense to blame.[205] The corollary of this prognosis was that it was necessary to 'prepare public opinion which still lacks a sense of reality' on the issue.[206] Rather than expressing a view himself about the desirability or otherwise of devaluation Blum seemed to want to present his party as objectively as possible with the information necessary to allow it to formulate a rational response. The anarchy in the world monetary system was a symptom of the disintegration of capitalism, and therefore the monetary problem was not a fundamental one for Socialists; it was not the main cause of the crisis.[207] It was not up to Socialists to make a 'doctrinal choice among the contrary forms of capitalism'.[208] Their role was merely to take the measures necessary to minimize the damage caused by whatever action was decided upon: in the case of devaluation this meant protecting the workers against any resulting inflation.[209]

But if Blum did not consider it his role to make a decision, he at first tentatively suggested in April 1934 that devaluation was desirable: he brushed aside a number of irrelevant arguments against it – national honour, the fact that France had already devalued in 1928[210] – and warned against the danger of 'monetary fetishism becoming as much as budgetary fetishism, an obstacle to economic recovery'.[211] The example of Britain seemed to him proof that devaluation need not cause a dangerous inflation: indeed he saw it as the starting point of Britain's recovery.[212] But these comments are the most definite that Blum ever made in favour of devaluation. In the immediate aftermath of the Belgian devaluation a year later he reached the provisional conclusion that devaluation was psychologically difficult in countries where the experience of inflation had lodged a whole series of reflex reactions in people's minds.[213] In November 1935 he replied to Reynaud that the Socialist policy was 'neither deflation nor devaluation'.[214] And it was on this platform that the Socialists fought the elections of 1936.

What had pushed Blum into this unrealistic position after his courageous articles of April 1934? He had failed to persuade his Party seriously to consider the issue. At the Congress of Mulhouse (1935) he expressed his despair after having three times attempted to discuss devaluation in *Le Populaire*: 'on each occasion I felt ill at ease, embarrassed... because I could not commit the party on such a serious issue, which the party had not discussed, where it had not formulated its view'.[215] And although Moch proposed that the forthcoming Conseil National be instructed to examine the issue, nothing much was done:[216] Blum's appeal for the Party to formulate a policy went unheeded.

The truth is that the Party felt a profound unease on the whole question; and it was this which more or less forced Blum into silence. A delegate at the Congress of 1934, although refusing to take a position himself, was scandalized that Blum should have used the front page of *Le Populaire* seemingly to advocate devaluation, when the Party had not made up its mind.[217] *Combat marxiste* attacked Blum for giving free propaganda to the enemy – *Le Temps* had attacked Blum for advocating inflation[218] – and alienating that class of small savers which the Party so needed to rally to its cause.[219] And also, the Socialist position, always very vulnerable to attack from the right on financial questions, was not helped by the fact that their new Communist allies attacked devaluation with the same fervour as the right – 'the adulteration of the currency and fraudulent bankruptcy'[220] – and, no doubt for much the same reason: to win over the much courted *classes moyennes*. The Communist argument was that deflation and devaluation were 'Siamese twins', two different ways by which the bourgeoisie shifted the burden of the crisis on to the masses; once deflation could, for social reasons, be pushed no further, the bourgeoisie would simply change its tactics – and devalue the franc. And the Communists triumphantly seized upon any Socialist concessions to devaluation.[221]

The Communists were certainly right to view the Socialist leaders as somewhat lukewarm in their opposition to devaluation: although officially against, they did not attack it with the same fervour as other political groups. Auriol, whom we have seen to be privately in favour of devaluation at this time, condemned both deflation and devaluation in the Chamber in November 1935: but his mention of devaluation was for pure form, and the brunt of his attack was on deflation;[222] Moch and Weill-Raynal's propaganda pamphlets, written for the elections, both officially and briefly declared Socialist opposition to devaluation, but then also both – and both in footnotes – admitted that it was nevertheless very likely to occur.[223] The

C.G.T. was even more ready to admit this possibility, and openly discussed how it would affect the implementation of the measures contained in the Plan.[224] The official position was that the Plan provided the best defence of the franc,[225] but that if, as seemed likely, devaluation was unavoidable, it had to take place as part of a general stabilization agreement,[226] and would anyway be ineffective without the plan: 'no to devaluation – or, after it, the C.G.T. Plan'.[227] Within this official policy there were considerable nuances of opinion: Delaisi and Belin being very much in favour of devaluation, Duret being more hostile, and Laurat lying in between.[228] The C.G.T. had however moved much further towards devaluation than the Socialists were willing to do. And, although among the Socialists there was an altogether different emphasis from that of all other political groups (except the Neo-Socialists), the Party's solution had been in effect to ignore the monetary problem. This 'monetary Dreyfus Affair' had forced one brave and intelligent man into the political wilderness, and another into embarrassed silence.

### Alternatives: 'Let us try to cultivate our garden' (Germain-Martin)[229]

What was the future of France isolated on her rock of gold? What, that is, were the alternatives to devaluation? To this question there were two possible answers: either a *repliement*, a turning in of France on herself, or an attempt to recapture world markets by a policy of strenuous deflation. The premise of the theory that France should cultivate her garden was that the export trade, compared to Britain and Germany, only accounted for a relatively small proportion of French wealth. This made talk of autarky less inconceivable than it might have been elsewhere. And whether desirable or not, it was increasingly the case that the French economy was being squeezed into a straitjacket of quotas and tariffs. It was a fact which even as theoretically internationalist a party as the Radicals felt bound to accept: 'this is a closed economy, a system that we regret and which is not in line with the views of our party, but which we must accept as an unavoidable necessity'.[230] But if there was to be a *repliement* what was it to be on? There were two possibilities: the gold block and the Empire.

The idea of strengthening the commercial ties of the gold block countries with each other had first been mooted by the French government in 1933; but nothing came of it owing to the opposition of Italy.[231] In 1934 demands for such a policy intensified, and could not but be encouraged by the further slump in French foreign trade which took place during the course of the year.[232] In April 1934 the Comité du Rapprochement du Bloc-Or appealed to the French government for support: this organization, founded at Lausanne in February, grouped together a number of Chambers of Commerce from gold-block countries – mainly Switzerland – with the aim of encouraging, by propaganda and other means, an increase in trade between the gold-block countries. The Quai d'Orsay was favourable to the enterprise, although warning that the agricultural policies of some of the member states would make the objective difficult to attain.[233] A few weeks before the Comité first contacted the French government, Germain-Martin and various other cabinet ministers and industrialists, were sounded out by Stoppani, Director of the European Relations Section of the League of Nations, about the possibility of taking steps to promote the economic consolidation of the gold block; after holding conversations in the other gold-block countries Stoppani wrote again in May to Doumergue and Germain-Martin, enclosing a report which summarized the conclusions of these conversations. The report noted that each country's exports to the rest of the gold block held a proportionally greater place in their total trade in 1933 than in 1929 – though only marginally in the case of Italy – and that in theory each country was keen to develop this trend; the most serious obstacle was generally believed to lie in French agricultural policy: 'the doubts which subsist in the other gold-block countries about the possibility of a modification of France's restrictive policy, *constitute perhaps the strongest barrier* to an agreement'.[234]

In spite of these inauspicious omens, a meeting was held in Geneva in September 1934 between representatives of governments of gold-block countries at which it was decided to hold a conference to examine ways of increasing intra-gold-block trade; this conference would meet in Brussels at the end of October.[235] An inter-ministerial committee of the French government which met to formulate a policy for this forthcoming Brussels conference unanimously rejected the idea of proposing an increase in quota allocations to the level of 1931;[236] instead it discussed, among other ideas, the possibility of a six-month truce on agricultural quotas,[237] a proposal opposed by the Ministry of Agriculture.[238] But there were dangers in too restrictive an attitude. Maxime Robert, a Finance Ministry official, pointed out that failure to achieve tangible results might be used as a pretext for devaluation by the Belgian government; he warned of 'the dangers from the monetary point of view, of the very limited nature of the proposals which the French delegation is taking to the gold block conference'.[239] Besides this distrust of Belgium there was also worry about the unenthusiastic attitudes of Holland (very suspicious of Belgium)[240] and Italy, which at one point even wanted to postpone the conference.[241] It was eventually agreed that the French delegation would propose that the conference should propose as a target an increase of 10 per cent in the trade of each country with all the others put together; this would be achieved by bilateral negotiations in which French negotiators would offer a six-month truce on agricultural quotas, a preferential distribution among the gold-block countries of the unused balance of industrial quotas and possibly even preferential tariffs, if the agreement of third parties could be obtained.[242]

The French proposals were easily accepted by the conference: having reaffirmed its faith in monetary stability, it agreed to increase intra-gold-block trade by 10 per cent during the next year; and a permanent commission set up by the conference would hold periodic meetings to monitor the progress of the bilateral negotiations which were to give substance to this aim.[243] There was considerable French satisfaction, even enthusiasm, at this outcome: by dint of having been the only country to have properly prepared its position, France had successfully steered the conference between the negativity of Italy and the impatience of Belgium;[244] and the provision for regular meetings of the Commission was seen as an unprecedented step, as the embryo of a future economic framework for Europe. Even if there was pessimism about the real chances of increasing intra-gold-block trade, psychologically the conference was felt to have strengthened the faltering resistance of the Dutch, Belgian and Swiss governments until France could bring the British round to stabilization (a subject about which, we have seen, there was much discussion at the end of 1934); and a reinforced gold block would make it difficult for the British government, attempting to prevent any sudden and excessive devaluations, to isolate France by encouraging the other gold-block countries to align their currencies on sterling.[245]

All these calculations however depended on the success of the bilateral negotiations which were to follow the conference. And here the results were disappointing: inconclusive negotiations took place with Belgium in November and January with renewed warnings from Claudel, the ambassador in Belgium, that failure would strengthen the hand of the Belgian devaluers.[246] With Holland the results were equally unsatisfactory; the only positive outcome was a very limited agreement with Italy on quotas.[247] The reasons for this relative failure were outlined by the trade minister, Marchandeau: France had offered Belgium 70mi of extra quota allocations but the Belgians had offered nothing substantive in return; an increase in trade with Holland and Italy seemed impossible owing to the further tightening of agricultural quotas; and any system of preferential tariffs threatened, by breaking most-favoured-nation clauses, to jeopardize French trade outside the gold block.[248] In March 1935, Robert Coulondre of the Quai d'Orsay had concluded: 'it would be best to recognize that the gold block does not dispose of the economic potential, and above all of sufficiently complementary markets, to become self-sufficient'.[249] And with the devaluation of the Belga imminent, the efforts of the French government turned again, as we have already seen, to the outside world: to the phasing out of quotas as part of a general agreement to stabilize currencies.

Somewhat surprisingly these abortive attempts to strengthen the gold block do not seem to have aroused much general interest among even the most ardent defenders of the franc. There were scattered complaints that 'the gold block has not been cemented by any economic mortar'.[250] The meeting of the Brussels conference in October was generally noticed, but with little enthusiasm.[251] And in March 1935 when the Belga seemed on the verge of collapse and the Belgian Prime-Minister Theunis was due to arrive for talks in Paris, there was renewed discussion of a gold-block commercial policy, even if it meant giving up most-favoured-nation agreements:[252] but these were the tactics of desperation. In truth no political party or politician or economic commentator seems to have had any real interest in the gold block.

There was at least greater sentimental attachment towards the Empire; and where there had not been sentiment before, the possibility of economic advantage could create it. The Radicals, who had previously been little concerned by colonial questions, now developed an interest in them: the Congress of 1935 proclaimed that as other markets were closing the Empire provided a 'naturally faithful market'.[253] Germain-Martin pointed out that France might be forced to choose between the 'international policy of the pre-war period and an autarchic policy: France and her colonies'.[254] And some Neo-Socialists, although open-minded about devaluation, proposed a more active colonial policy.[255] But undoubtedly the greatest enthusiasm came from the traditionalist right of the Fédération Républicaine: 'the development of the colonial market', declared *La Nation*, 'is the *sine qua non* of a revival of our economy';[256] and for these economic nationalists, for whom French commercial policy ought to have been renegotiated by the revision of most-favoured-nation agreements, this was a theme which was constantly repeated.[257] But the governments had not been inactive: in 1933 Doumergue's government, taking up an idea of Daladier's government,[258] organized an Imperial conference which met in December 1934.

The problems of colonial policy were considerable. In anticipation of the conference, the C.N.E. submitted a report showing that if France's trade with her colonies had declined since 1929, it had done so less than her trade with the rest of the world: the proportion of imports from the colonies had risen from 11.4 per cent (1927) to 23.6 per cent (1933) and exports to the colonies from 12.7 per cent to 27 per cent. Algeria, from having been France's fifth best client (both as buyer and seller) in 1927, had by 1932 become the best; Tunisia had moved from 13th to 7th place. Thus the colonies had to some extent helped France to weather the crisis, and if a revival of world trade was not possible it might be possible through the Empire to fall back on a reorganized imperial system. But the C.N.E. issued two warnings: first, that the economies of Algeria and Morocco were increasing their production of wheat and wine, and that far from the Empire being on the road to developing a 'complementary policy' France's agricultural producers were threatened by the growth of competitive economies in North Africa; secondly, that most of France's industrial raw materials came from outside the Empire, and that it would not be possible to change this situation quickly or completely. The conclusion was that although France, like Britain at Ottawa, might further develop economic links with the Empire, she must not be deluded by the 'mirage of an autonomous France in a splendid isolation'.[259] In spite of such reservations the opening of the conference raised some hopes for the future, if not enthusiasm;[260] but very little information was revealed about its deliberations – 'the conference seems to be taking place in the castle of the Sleeping Beauty' commented *Le Temps*[261] – and when it closed in April 1935 its passing was hardly noticed, and its substantive results were minimal.

The failure of any policy of imperial or gold-block autarky made deflation all the more necessary. Deflation implied, of course, a break in the system of protection which insulated French prices from those of world markets; and the case for such a policy was made many times. But political constraints made such a course of action almost impossible. Deflation also meant cuts in government expenditure, especially the salaries of government servants: this was intended to reduce the burden on producers by allowing a fall in interest rates, a reduction in taxation and further falls in private-sector wage rates. Deflation, it was hoped, would also prepare the conditions of economic revival by restoring business confidence; and the restriction of the activity of the state would remove a whole set of controls which stultified initiative and enterprise. The policy was, then, seen as entirely positive. To the Socialist argument that deflation would only deepen the Depression by reducing consumer demand, it was replied that the state could not create demand: 'what it distributes in certain areas, it has first had to take from others'[262] and no less an authority than Rist dismissed as absurd the claim that new beneficiaries of state money might be more prone to spend it than those from whom it had been taken, their marginal propensity to consume being higher.[263]

It could not, however, be denied that, at least in the short term, deflation had depressed the economy; but in the eyes of conservatives this outcome was not necessarily worse than the 'factitious' and precarious prosperity which might have been generated by devaluation and the much-dreaded inflation. Stagnation, that is, could be chosen up to a point. In the late 1920s, Tardieu and the modernizing business men of Redressement Français had promised the vision of a bright American industrial future; and those sections of the right – small businesses, the traditionalists of the Fédération Républicaine – who were mistrustful of this vision, had nevertheless followed. But in the 1930s the situation was reversed: the possibility and, more importantly, the desirability of a too-rapid pursuit of prosperity and social change was less certain. The confidence of Tardieu and his followers was subsumed in the pessimism of Marin and his followers. Edmond Giscard d'Estaing, one of the leading figures of the Redressement Français, wrote in 1931: 'foreigners shrug their shoulders in seeing in France the sign "gas on every floor", while they have a bathroom in every apartment. We shake our heads. There is just one thing that timidly we dare to point out: at the end of this there is an inevitable collapse'.[264] For Victor Perret of the Fédération Républicaine the 'startling and factitious prosperity' of the 1920s had 'thrown the most balanced characters into confusion ... people go out a lot, they dance every day, they travel ... they have no inclination for restful and happy home life ... we must return to a normal life'.[265] 'A normal life': France was to turn her back on 'the nonsense of Americanization'.[266] There would be no return to the prosperity of the 1920s.[267] In short, as Caillaux had been proclaiming for years, the moment for *grande pénitence* had struck.

Of course, as important as the fact that economic stagnation was accepted – even welcomed – up to a point, is the fact that the invulnerability of the franc and the relative lack of severity of the crisis in France made such a choice possible: the former because the franc could not be forced off gold; the latter because the social and political consequences of allowing stagnation to continue were tolerable, indeed preferable to the upheavals to which the alternative was believed to lead. France could renounce an uncertain future and return to 'the tranquil course of her existence, her misers, her fishermen, the dreams of her small rentiers'.[268] France could cultivate her garden.

## Conclusion

The campaign for devaluation reached its peak in May 1935. But there were signs that by the end of 1935 even many of its most ardent opponents were coming to see it as necessary, or at least inevitable. Caillaux[269] and Germain-Martin[270] both cagily and quietly came round to the need for an 'alignment' of currencies; Rist wrote in May 1935 that only a 'more thorough deflation than any we have known so far' could avoid devaluation, and although he did not draw any conclusion himself the tone of the article was pessimistic;[271] observers took this as a lukewarm conversion.[272] *Le Figaro*[273] and *Le Bulletin quotidien*[274] had also lost some of their anti-devaluation fervour; Peyerimhoff was converted by the spring of 1936.[275] But there were no triumphant conversions, only a subtle change of mood. In the last important financial debate of 1935, in November, speeches by Reynaud and Déat in favour of devaluation were applauded on all benches: there was, said Déat, an enormous majority in the Chamber secretly in favour of devaluation.[276] And at the beginning of 1936 Régnier, who remained Finance Minister in the Sarraut government which followed Laval, virtually admitted to the first cabinet meeting of the new government that since future economies were politically impossible, the franc might not even hold until the elections – unless, as he suggested as a possibility, their date were brought forward![277]

The reasons for this slow conversion are clear enough. Devaluation had been seen as a progenitor of the *économie dirigée*: but Laval's decrees in defence of the franc had led to unprecedented state intervention in economic life. Devaluation had been seen as the destruction of the social order: but the increasing popularity of the Popular Front had shown that stagnation could not necessarily contain social change. After five years the balance between the risks of continuing a policy which resulted in stagnation and embarking on a policy which threatened to result in inflation was shifting in favour of the latter. And the possibility that only exchange controls would be able to preserve the franc threatened to make yet another breach in the crumbling wall of economic liberalism.

But if, then, at the end of 1935, in the hearts and minds of many who had hitherto strongly opposed it, devaluation now seemed unavoidable, most of them did not dare to say it publicly. 'The game is to avoid extracting the chestnut of devaluation from the fire of demagogy' wrote Boris.[278] The three-year campaign against devaluation had done its destructive work. Elections were only three months ahead: there could be no turning back.

# Epilogue: The politics of rearmament 1936–1939

### The elections of 1936

The government of Albert Sarraut which replaced Laval was on the left in spite of itself. It was a government of left concentration – stretching from the U.S.R. on the left to the Républicains de Gauche on the right – with a Popular Front majority: the Socialists voted for it, the Communists abstained for the first time and the Centre Républicain voted against, in spite of the continued presence in the Cabinet of such figures as Régnier and Laval. The government's main role was to effect a transition between Laval and the elections. And like most governments of this kind it would no doubt have been forgotten by history had it not suffered the cruel fate of presiding helplessly over the re-occupation of the Rhineland in March 1936.

In the field of economic policy it performed the necessary holding operation.[1] Régnier, who remained Minister of Finance and arch opponent of devaluation, found himself in the same Cabinet as Déat, himself in favour of devaluation. The beginning of the new financial year was difficult for any government, and the financial problems that Baumgartner had predicted[2] quickly materialized. At the end of February the government borrowed 3m on the London market. The Rhineland crisis increased nervousness, and a number of Treasury Bills were traded in. But the last act of the Chamber was to accept, at the end of March, what it had previously refused in December, that the *Fonds d'outillage* of the 1936 budget could be funded by short-term loans. This was equivalent to raising the ceiling on Treasury Bills by 7.8m to 22.8m.[3] Given that gold exports had resumed at the end of March it was no secret that the Bank would continue to take most of this paper.[4] And Baumgartner admitted that, since any consolidation of this debt in the near future was extremely unlikely, the government was agreeing to 'a more or less definitive inflation'.[5] Only fear of the political consequences, just before an election, had prevented the government reviving the practice of direct advances.[6]

The economic recovery which had begun in the summer of 1935 was reflected by all economic indicators in the early months of 1936: unemployment had undergone its usual seasonal increase, but the peak figure of

489,000 was lower than the corresponding level for 1935; industrial output continued to rise: the general index of industrial production rose from 86 in January to 88 in April; and, finally, the price of wheat continued its upward trend. The slight improvement in the economic situation – and the same had after all occurred at the end of 1932 – was not sufficient to prevent the elections of 1936 from taking place in very different conditions from those four years earlier. The only similarity was that in both years France's economic situation set her apart from most other western countries: but in 1932 this was the isolation of an *île heureuse* relatively unaffected by the world crisis; in 1936 it was the isolation of an unhappy island of economic stagnation in a world on the road to recovery.[7] And no less menacing than the economic situation was the recent occupation of the Rhineland.

A brief examination of the election manifestos of 1936 allows us to estimate the popular resonance of certain of the themes discussed in the preceding pages. Certain negative conclusions can be drawn. First, whatever the interest it aroused for a time in political circles on the left, planism did not have – or was not believed by politicians to have – any great appeal in the country: the C.G.T. Plan was mentioned by two candidates – one U.S.R. and one Radical – and the Belgian Plan by one candidate (U.S.R.).[8] Secondly, the Empire seems to have caused as little interest as in previous years: references, especially on the right, to a policy of imperial development (*mise en valeur*) were not new, and nowhere was it suggested that such a policy might be a way of protecting the franc. Thirdly, devaluation did not dominate the campaign: if mentioned it was condemned by all except four candidates – Jean Médécin (conservative), Pierre Cot, Guy La Chambre (Radical) and André Philip – who intimated obliquely that it might be unavoidable. But other issues occupied a more central position. The left – from the Radicals to the P.C.F. – found its unity in attaching the Leagues and the Bank of France. The new slogan of the election was that the *Banque de France* should become the *Banque de la France*. The formula was vague enough to include the possibility of nationalization, advocated by the Socialists, or merely a reform of its statutes, preferred by the Radicals. On the decrees there was less unanimity: the Socialists and Communists proposed their abolition and condemned the policy of deflation which was their rationale; most Radicals, on the other hand, demanded only 'humanization' or 'rectification', and tended to avoid outright condemnation of deflation.

This position was not dissimilar from that of the right: a typical conservative manifesto declared 'Humanization of the decree-laws. No devaluation. No inflation'.[9] The most striking feature of the right's campaign was the absence of any attempt to defend the record of the Union Nationale governments by reference to the signs of economic revival: 'France,' wrote a Fédération Républicaine candidate, 'still has her ruined rentiers, her discontented *fonctionnaires* and her 500,000 unemployed'.[10] Instead of mounting a

defence of their past, conservatives preferred to argue that all the policies of the previous four years had been implemented by a left-wing Chamber: 'the balance sheet of the Cartel – the decree laws'.[11] Indeed, as much as by the right, the economic recovery – especially the increase in agricultural prices – was mentioned by the left, which attributed it to Laval's replacement by Sarraut.[12] The conservative prescription for the future consisted of more or less a continuation of previous policies. There were two reasons to explain why these had not worked so far: first, the absence of constitutional reform which in some form or other was almost universally advocated; secondly, the activities of the Popular Front: 'it is the conduct of the Popular Front which destroys confidence and prevents recovery of business confidence'.[13] This was the theme on which all conservatives could unite: the Popular Front was characterized as a 'three-headed monster', as a repetition of the cartels of 1924 and 1932 with the sinister addition of the Communists.[14] The following manifesto of a Fédération Républicaine candidate from Paris contains most of the themes which were scattered throughout the propaganda of the right:
'If the Popular Front is victorious:
There will be a flight of capital;
There will be a devaluation leading to total bankruptcy;
There will be anarchy;
There will be war;
For behind the Popular Front lurks the shadow of Moscow.'[15]
Against *La Grande Espérance* of the Popular Front, then, the right could only reply with the politics of fear.

### The Blum experiment

The Popular Front emerged victorious from the election with 70,000 more votes than the left had obtained in 1932.[16] The most significant feature of this result was the shift of influence away from the Radicals towards the Socialists and Communists: for the first time the S.F.I.O. became the largest group in the Chamber. As in 1924 and 1932 the Radicals held the balance of power between left and right: two majorities were possible. But for the moment at least the Radicals were anchored on the left, and on 4 June Léon Blum became France's first Socialist premier of a Socialist and Radical government. His first task was to end a massive wave of strikes and factory occupations which had begun in May: between one and two million workers were on strike. This extraordinary popular movement gradually subsided for a while after an historic meeting between representatives of the employers and the C.G.T. at the Hôtel Matignon (residence of the premier): wages were raised by between 7 and 15 per cent and collective contracts introduced; and the government promised legislation to bring in paid holidays and the 40-hour week. These measures were quickly ratified by parliament, which also approved the reform of the Statutes of the Bank of France, the setting up of a wheat market-ing board and the nationalization of the arms industries.

The flight of gold had continued throughout the election campaign and the Sarraut government had, as predicted, only survived by having most of the extra 8m Treasury Bills rediscounted by the Bank. On taking office Blum publicly reaffirmed his opposition to devaluation. But although the Matignon agreements temporarily restored confidence, by raising French production costs they also made an eventual devaluation all the more unavoidable. On 26 September, therefore, after a renewed flight of gold, the government signed the Tripartite Agreement with Britain and America, devaluing the franc by between 25 per cent and 35 per cent: the pound now stood at between 100 and 115 F. During the first four months of the Blum government there was a severe downturn in economic activity – a result not only of the strikes but also of increasing labour costs by some 20 per cent in an economy already suffering from an over-valued currency. Devaluation provided a much needed stimulus: between September and December indus-trial production rose by 12 per cent; by March 1937 it was at the highest point since June 1931.

Like its predecessors, however, the Blum government was increasingly submerged under a Treasury crisis. A convention between the government and the Bank had put an end to the practice – employed by all governments since Flandin – of disguised advances to the Treasury: the 13.8m surrep-titiously lent since June 1935 was in effect written off and the Treasury was given the possibility of borrowing a further 10m; in future such advances were to be direct and open. And although devaluation provided temporary relief by inducing an inflow of capital in October, by the end of the year the government was surviving only thanks to this arrangement with the Bank: 1.5m was advanced to the Treasury in November; 5–6m in December. But this was no permanent solution since it further undermined confidence in public finance and put the franc under intensified pressure. By the end of January 1937 the Exchange Stabilization Fund set up after the devaluation had used up its entire gold allotment of 10m F.[17] in maintaining the franc at its September 1936 level.

To restore 'confidence', therefore, Blum announced in February 1937 a 'pause' in the further implementation of the Popular Front programme. This involved cuts in civil spending programmes and the appointment of three 'experts' – Rueff, Rist and the banker Paul Baudouin – to manage the stabiliz-ation fund. But the pause did no more than win the government a respite. A renewed run on the franc, combined with – indeed contributing to – a Treasury crisis, forced Blum to appeal for financial decree powers. The Senate refused to grant these and Blum resigned in June 1937. Meanwhile the economic recovery of the early spring had come to an end, and economic activity had started to decline rapidly again from March: by July 1937 the index of industrial production had fallen back to 85, more or less the same level as the beginning of 1936.

As a psychological experience of collective liberation the Popular Front's economic experiment was to become a powerful mobilizing myth; as an attempt to revive the economy it had proved a dismal failure. Four major criticisms have been made of Blum's economic management. But although each of them has a certain technical validity, the government's economic record must be put in the context both of the financial and political situation inherited and, even more importantly, of the way in which that situation had been transformed by the events of 1936. First of all, Blum has been criticized for unnecessarily handicapping himself for four months by delaying devaluation. But in spite of their public pronouncements against devaluation – and of course to announce such a measure in advance would be to jeopardize its chances of success[18] – it is now known that Blum and Auriol, his finance minister, had come round to devaluation soon after the government came to power: on 6 June, Auriol had expressed his willingness for secret negotiations to the American financial attaché; and Blum despatched Monick, who had been instrumental in winning him over to devaluation, to sound out Morgenthau at the end of June.[19] But the discussions dragged on and then petered out until the run on the franc precipitated events in September. Why the delay? Partly because of differences between Britain and the United States; partly no doubt because, consistent with his earlier attitude, Blum did not see devaluation as fundamental and wrongly believed that there was no urgency.

But the most important factor slowing down the monetary negotiations was French insistence on presenting the devaluation as part of an international agreement with Britain and America: the importance of the Tripartite Agreement was not therefore so much in ensuring that devaluation would not invite reprisals, as in making it acceptable – 'alignment' and 'adjustment' were preferred terms – to domestic opinion: Bullitt, the American Ambassador in Paris, remarked ironically that the French wanted to present the devaluation as an appreciation of the dollar and sterling, 'to make it look as if America and England had finally realized that their currencies were wrongly valued'.[20] After three years of hysterical anti-devaluation propaganda the government was understandably nervous about the possible public reaction. In fact, in spite of some ritual opposition from the right, from some anti-Popular Front Radicals and from the P.C.F., the much trumpeted panic did not occur; but the caution was only too reasonable.

A second criticism of Blum is that to be successful in the face of a suspicious and unco-operative capitalist class he needed to take greater controls over the economy, that, to use planist terminology, the 'distributional' reforms carried out in the summer of 1936 were ineffective without 'structural' reforms.[21] But

Blum made clear innumerable times that he was bound by the constraints of the Popular Front alliance: 'our aim is not to transform the social system, it is not even to carry out the Socialist Party's own programme, it is to carry out the programme of the Popular Front'.[22] Although some have criticized this position as timidly legalistic, it was largely unavoidable given a parliamentary majority dependent on Radical support. And, of course, it was precisely in the area of economic policy that the base of the Popular Front alliance was narrowest and most fragile. But it is anyway hard to see what immediate effects 'structural' reforms could have had; and, in the circumstances of 1936, speed was vital given the government's extremely precarious financial situation. Blum did not have time on his side.

This has led to a third criticism: that the government needed to protect its expansionary economic policy by imposing exchange controls.[23] A left-wing government, it is argued, was once again being betrayed by the 'wall of money'. The charge has some truth in it. The wall of money no longer meant the Bank of France, which was not in a position to resist the government as it had under Moret and Tannery. But Blum received no help from the banks: although bank deposits did rise after devaluation this was not reflected in any increase of subscriptions to Treasury Bills. As for the flight of capital which subjected the government to continuous financial pressure, although it could no doubt often be explained by simple prudence – prices were rising fast – it is often difficult to separate 'technical' from 'political' motives. The governor of the Bank could see no 'objective' reasons for the speculative attack which, beginning in April 1937, finally brought Blum down.[24] The myth of the 'wall of money' was, however, hardly new in French politics, and if it was more than a myth, it is surprising that the Socialists had not paid greater attention to the question of how to finance their policy. Blum, we have seen, had been reproached on this score even by many left-wing Radicals in the autumn of 1935.[25] In the summer of 1936 he had placed great hopes in the small saver: the Auriol 'Baby' Bonds, aimed directly at this source, raised some 4.4m between July and September. Blum declared that this would allow the government to dispense with the help of the *mauvais citoyen* who sent his capital abroad.[26]

But once it was seen that the *mauvais citoyen* was necessary and that it was not enough to rely on goodwill, the question of exchange control came to the fore. It had hardly been discussed before 1936 even if the possibility of introducing it had in fact been included in the Popular Front programme. And when Blum assumed office he was quick to reject the idea. There were various reasons for this. First, such a measure was likely to alienate the Radicals: the coalition had to be maintained. Secondly, the government, in the words of Auriol, could not carry out 'at one and the same time a policy of confidence and a policy of constraint'.[27] The problem, of course, was that in 1936 it carried out neither, and when it did choose a policy of confidence – in the form of the pause – it was too late: but the pause was implicit in the choice from the beginning. Thirdly, exchange controls were seen as likely to bring France closer to the restrictive currency policies of Germany and Italy; exchange controls, that is, were a 'fascist' policy. And by bringing France's monetary policy into line with the democratic nations – with Britain and America – Blum hoped to cement the unity of the free world in the face of the fascist menace. He was well aware of a potential conflict between the logic of his domestic economic policy, tending towards greater controls, towards autarky, and the internationalist posture of his foreign policy; but he decided in favour of the latter: 'logically our domestic policy would have taken us in the direction of measures of coercion against capital exports and speculation ... But there is a contradiction between such measures and our foreign policy which seeks common action with the Anglo-Saxon powers'.[28] The Tripartite Agreement was a political and diplomatic as much as a monetary policy. And such a policy, which flowed naturally enough from the anti-fascism which was the cement of the Popular Front, was seen as all the more urgent since the Rhineland invasion which had weakened France *vis à vis* Germany and increased the importance of the British connection.

Fourthly, the 40-hour week, or at least the inflexible way it was introduced, is the feature of Blum's economic policy which has been most criticized.[29] J.-P. Asselain, whose study is the most detailed, has observed how, although both Blum's devaluation and the one carried out, as we shall see, in June 1937, did stimulate the economy, the recovery in both cases seemed to hit the same invisible 'ceiling': rather than to eliminate unemployment, the effect of the shorter working week, given a shortage of skilled labour, was to create bottlenecks in production – to reduce productive capacity.[30] But, as Asselain also remarks, it is difficult to see what choice Blum had in June 1936. The Socialists and some members of the C.G.T. had, we have seen, moved to a more flexible position on the 40-hour week, but in June 1936 such caution was swept aside by the exigencies of the semi-Revolutionary situation. None of the measures contained in the Matignon agreements had after all been in the Popular Front programme.

If Blum's failure can then be explained partly by reference to the past – to the psychosis created about devaluation, to the nature of the Popular Front coalition, to the disastrous financial situation inherited, to his somewhat superficial treatment of the financial problem – it is more important to understand how, by the time the Popular Front programme came to be applied, the world for which it had been drawn up had largely disappeared. This was true for two reasons. First, the Popular Front, conceived in a context of right-wing violence, was born into a world of labour conflict. The Matignon agreements were the prelude to, not the end of, a prolonged period of industrial unrest. The spectacular strikes of 1936 should not obscure the endemic social conflict of the next two years. There were many reasons for what one historian has called this 'social guerilla warfare' whose bitter mood contrasted strikingly with the festive spirit of June 1936:[31] the workers were striving to protect their living standards as prices rose; employers were attempting to restore the old patterns of authority in the workplace. In this conflict, the 40-hour week became the symbol of the victory of labour. Employers neither forgot nor forgave the humiliation of 1936: they were reluctant to invest, or indeed to place any confidence in the government, until labour discipline, as they saw it, had been reimposed and the symbol of their defeat had disappeared. Thus Blum's search for 'confidence', his attempt, as he later put it, to be the 'loyal manager' of the capitalist system, was vitiated from the outset.

The second major transformation in the situation facing Blum resulted from the Rhineland invasion. The increased importance of the relationship with Britain, and America, fundamentally affected, we have seen, Blum's attitude to exchange controls. But even more importantly, the Rhineland occupation made it impossible to avoid the necessity for rearmament. Of course we have seen that arms expenditure had begun to rise in 1935 in spite of Laval's spending cuts; conversely in the second half of 1937 Bonnet, Finance Minister in the government which succeeded Blum's, did attempt to put a brake on arms spending, and Rueff, at the *Mouvement général des fonds*, advised repeatedly in favour of sacrificing rearmament to orthodox finance. But, broadly speaking, whereas between 1932 and 1936 arms spending had been largely subject to financial and economic policy, between 1936 and 1939 the relationship was reversed. And arms spending became an increasingly destabilizing, if unavoidable, factor in government finances: it was the announcement by the Blum government of a 14m F. programme of rearmament in September 1936 which precipitated the financial crisis that preceded devaluation.

The impact of rearmament could have startling consequences: although the Blum government announced a four-year 20m F. programme of public works in August 1936, in fact the civil expenditure of the first Popular Front government declined by comparison with 1935 while its military expenditure increased; in the words of Frankenstein, the Blum government, at least in its public spending, did 'more for guns than for butter'. At first the government had hoped to avoid a choice between them but the financial pressures became too great: as Blum put it, 'it is difficult to carry out simultaneously a bold policy of social reforms and an intensive policy of rearmament'. The spending cuts included in the pause, therefore, affected civil expenditure; arms spending was largely untouched. Rearmament had more than just a destabilizing effect on government finance: by undermining Blum's social and economic programme it also narrowed the base of popular support – already eroded by controversy over non-intervention in Spain – which might have ensured political survival. In 1936 the Senate had not dared oppose the government for fear of the public reaction; in 1937 it had no such qualms.[32]

Blum's government, then, operated in a context for which little had prepared it. The debates which had preoccupied politicians between 1932 and 1936 – devaluation or deflation, balanced budget or deficit, integral Socialism or planism – were now largely irrelevant. First, the exigencies of rearmament had made a deficit inevitable. The existence of a deficit was therefore no longer at issue. The problem was how to fund it, how, if controls over banks were to be avoided, 'confidence' was to be created: in the debate on the budget for 1937 the opposition attacked not so much the government's planned deficit – 21.5m including arms spending – as the continued labour unrest.[33] Secondly, although planism was not completely forgotten, the C.G.T. became less concerned about the Plan than about how to consolidate the labour victory of 1936 in the face of growing resistance from employers. The most visible stake in the conflict – the last line of defence – came to be the 40-hour week. But the real issue was wider than this: was it possible to set up structures within which class conflict could be resolved by conciliation? In December 1936 Blum's government had introduced a compulsory labour arbitration law; but this had only limited success. In June 1936 the workers had erupted into French politics; the next two years were to determine if they could be integrated structurally into the French polity or once again consigned to the ghetto of oblivion. Thirdly, devaluation could no longer be an issue after September 1936. Indeed, during 1937, Bonnet, the apostle of gold-block orthodoxy in 1933, was to let the franc float downwards rather than dissipate the Bank's gold reserves in protecting it: a reserve of 50m was considered a minimum possible 'war chest'. But although *in extremis* the franc was allowed to slip, the main problem of policy became how to prevent it sliding further: the choice was between exchange control and liberalism – and, therefore, once again, 'confidence'. But what was the price of confidence to be?

## Liberalism or exchange control?

These issues were interrelated: for the employers and holders of capital, one price of confidence was the ending of the 40-hour week; for the unions exchange control was the most obvious means of defending their victory in 1936. It could also serve, however, as a guarantee of the government's left-wing posture: when, therefore, even the left came to recognize that effective rearmament depended on extending the 40-hour week – on dismantling part of the achievement of 1936 – exchange control could paradoxically make such a policy more acceptable to labour. Rearmament was at the intersection of all these problems. The course of economic policy depended, then, on the resolution of two questions: how rearmament was to be financed and what labour policy it implied.

The Popular Front government of Chautemps which succeeded Blum in

June 1937 tried to avoid the problem. It was no more successful in dealing with the financial difficulties than its predecessor, in spite of carrying out an even more conciliatory policy towards holders of capital, including the already mentioned attempt to restrict defence spending for 1928. The franc was allowed to float without even the maximum and minimum limits of the Auriol franc. Although the resulting depreciation provided another temporary stimulus to the economy, this was brought to an end at the beginning of 1938 both by the effects of the 40-hour week and the new world economic depression: in April 1938 the index of industrial production was at its lowest point since the end of 1935; unemployment was rising again. A commission to investigate the effects on production of the 40-hour week reported in December but proved to be rather less of a Trojan horse than the law's opponents had hoped. Meanwhile, as inflation ate away the wage rises of 1936, a series of strikes undermined the government's attempt to win confidence. A renewed speculative attack on the franc in September was checked by the so-called Rambouillet Declaration in which the government affirmed its commitment to 'social discipline' and rejected recourse to exchange control. But by the spring of 1938 the Treasury was once again in trouble and the franc under pressure: the government was living on advances from the Bank on which the ceiling now stood at 20m. And Chautemps, who had formed a second entirely Radical government in January, resigned over the Socialists' refusal to support a further grant of decree powers. In effect the Popular Front majority no longer existed.

Between the resignation of Chautemps and the formation of Blum's second government in March 1938, the situation had been simplified by the *Anschluss*: far from further retrenchment being possible, arms spending would have to rise yet again. Blum now proposed explicitly to use rearmament as a means of economic stimulation: a policy of credit expansion would be combined with exchange controls;[34] the 40-hour week would be relaxed in factories working for national defence and this sacrifice by labour would be matched by a financial one by capital in the form of a capital levy.

There were several reasons for Blum's conversion to a more *dirigiste* policy. First the programme had of course no chance of being accepted by the Senate: it allowed Blum to fall *en beauté*.[35] Indeed the political purpose of Blum's government was precisely to prove that the Popular Front formula was no longer workable and to make way for the government of Union Nationale that Blum had in fact himself tried to form. Secondly, by 1938 Blum had drawn the moral of the failure of the liberal experiment conducted until June 1937: 'having taken financial orthodoxy and monetary liberalism as far as they could go, we had realized our mistake'.[36] Thirdly, the Americans had moved to the view that exchange controls were necessary in France and therefore the policy, although still unpopular in London, no longer seemed to drive France automatically outside the camp of democratic nations.[37] Finally, in drawing up his programme Blum was advised by Boris and Mendès France both of whom had read Keynes' *General Theory* during 1937: the economic policy of Blum's second government was therefore perhaps the first in the world to be directly inspired by the *General Theory*, although in fact Blum himself was probably more influenced by the model of German rearmament.[38] Once again Blum was defeated in the Senate; his government had lasted a month.

The uncertainty as to the policy that would be followed by the Radical government of Blum's successor, Daladier, was reflected in the government's initial majority in the Chamber: 576 for and five against. The pragmatic Daladier at first seemed to hope that he would be able to avoid a clear choice between the policy proposed by Blum in May – although he retained Blum's rearmament plans – and that demanded by the right. He took as his finance minister the conservative Radical Paul Marchandeau. Almost immediately the government announced a third devaluation by fixing the minimum exchange rate of the franc at 179 per pound sterling; Bonnet's floating franc was replaced by the 'sterling franc'. The purpose was to attract capital back to France by offering speculators a sizeable profit. In this it was successful: some 18m were repatriated in the following months. The Treasury was the main beneficiary of this phenomenon: between May and June 1938 the government was able to raise 16m F.

As for Daladier's labour policy, his initial strategy was to settle the problem of extending the working week by negotiation in individual key industries. This policy failed as much because of the intransigence of the employers as of the workers: in the aeronautical industry the unions had already agreed to accept a 45-hour week providing the extra five hours were paid at overtime rates; the employers, playing for higher stakes, refused. But it was the refusal of the metallurgical unions to accept any modification of the 40 hours which pushed Daladier into taking a tougher line, outlined in a speech in August 1938. And the Munich crisis in September finally convinced him that a confrontation with the C.G.T. was both necessary and possible: necessary because rearmament had become even more urgent; possible because he had become more popular.[39]

Munich had had a different effect on Marchandeau. The crisis had triggered off yet another financial panic and Marchandeau moved in favour of exchange control as the only way of protecting the rearmament programme given the fragility of any policy based on confidence. In spite of the new American attitude this was nonetheless a considerable conversion. And the policy seems to have had the support of Daladier.[40] But at the end of October the Radical Congress formally ended the Popular Front. The Marchandeau plan was hardly compatible with this political decision nor with the move towards a less conciliatory labour policy. On 30 October, therefore, the Cabinet rejected exchange control; and two days later Paul Reynaud became finance minister. The liberals had won the day.

Reynaud issued a host of decrees designed to promote a durable revival of business confidence: the budget deficit was reduced by an increase in taxation and a reduction in civil expenditure, including the abandonment of what remained of the public works programmes; most importantly, the 40-hour week was considerably relaxed, if not in fact formally ended. The C.G.T. called a general protest strike on 30 November. This was a political failure and was followed by severe repression on the part of the government and employers. The financial results of Reynaud's policy were immediate: in December 7.5m F. of gold was repatriated, and this movement continued, at a slower pace, in 1939. By the time war broke out the reserves of the Bank had again reached 48m Poincaré francs – just below the level considered to be a necessary minimum 'war chest'.

In the autumn of 1938, after eight years of stagnation, the economy at last began to recover: between October 1938 and June 1939 industrial production increased by 20 per cent; the commercial deficit was reduced by 26 per cent; and unemployment fell by 10 per cent in the year to August 1939. By June 1939 the index of industrial production had once more reached the level of 1928. This recovery was no doubt due partly to the revival of business confidence engineered by Reynaud's policies, especially by the crumbling of the resistance of the unions. But the direct stimulus came from arms spending: the output of the metallurgical industries rose from 48m F. in 1938 to 58m F. in the first six months of 1939; this was accounted for entirely by arms production. Arms spending had, we have seen, stimulated certain industries before 1939; only in 1939 can it be said to have had a macro-economic effect.[41] Reynaud's was not, then, simply an experiment in liberalism: the role of the state was important. As such it looks forward, as various historians have pointed out, to the capitalism of of the 1950s rather than the supposedly golden age of pre-1914 liberalism.[42]

By 1939 the French economy was at last able to meet the demands which fighting a war would impose on it. But whatever the causes of this recovery it was achieved at the cost of considerable social conflict. The nation which faced the approaching war was not a deeply demoralized one; but nor was it a deeply united one. Reynaud's success had been achieved against a large section of the nation; just as Blum's failure had occurred largely because he had alienated an important section of the nation. The game of asking what might have been is hazardous, and perhaps futile. But it is impossible not to feel that equally impressive results could have been achieved earlier and at less social cost – to feel, in short, that between 1932 and 1936 an opportunity had been lost.

# Conclusion

The history of the four years from 1932 to 1936 falls into two periods. The 21 months from May 1932 to February 1934 were characterized by the dominance of a financial problem posing as a political problem: how to find a majority to cut government expenditure and prevent financial collapse, without, however, dislocating the majority which had won the elections. Between 1934 and 1936, the political problem having been solved by the very dislocation of that majority, the economic problem was now predominant: government expenditure must be cut in order to stimulate general deflation and avoid devaluation.

There is of course a danger of anachronism in discussing economic policy: not only that of judging policy in the light of theories developed since, but, more generally, that of expecting government intervention in the economy at all. It is only comparatively recently that such a notion has come to be considered normal: the evolution of the economic crisis, said the Radical deputy P. Jacquier, 'only depends indirectly on our actions'.[1] But we have seen enough demands for a more active government policy (and not only from among the Socialists) for it to be valid to wonder why so little was attempted or achieved. First it is necessary to be clear what governments between 1932 and 1934 – with perhaps the exception of the interlude of Paul-Boncour and Chéron – were *not* doing. They had not adopted the conservative response to the crisis which saw it as a pretext for the reversal of a trend which had been deplored but hardly resisted: 'it has become indispensable to modify ... the social system of the providential state ... it is *étatisme* which must be hit'.[2] Such arguments were not always explicitly linked to an argument about the best way to fight the Depression, but they usually implied that only massive budgetary deflation of this kind could restore business confidence, without which revival was impossible.[3] At a more sophisticated level budgetary deflation was seen as preliminary to a general deflation necessary to make French exports competitive again: in the autumn of 1933 Reynaud became the principal exponent of this view.

But none of these positions were held by the governments between 1932 and 1934: it was argued that fighting the Depression and the financial crisis were separate activities, and that alleviating the latter could accentuate the

212

former. Such claims were obviously partly in deference to Socialist (and left-wing Radical) propaganda against deflation: when Paul-Boncour declared that this financial bill 'does not have as its aim . . . the deflation of public sector pay to carry out a deflation of private sector wages'[4] he may have been (and probably was) saying something true, but he was certainly saying something politically expedient if he wanted to retain a cartel majority. Support for this view that the Radical governments' implicit acceptance of the Socialist case was purely tactical emerges from the report on financial policy accepted by the Radical Congress of 1933, which explicitly rejected the *politique de pouvoir d'achat*. But almost as many opinions existed among Radicals as there were Radicals. And the attitude of most Radical ministers or Party members to the budget cuts was different from that of conservatives – for whom they were only a beginning. Gardey, Sarraut's budget minister, warned against the danger of an 'excessively massive deflation which would involve the state giving up its normal role and its social mission'.[5] The problem was that the Radicals did not have the economics of their social humanitarianism. In December 1933 Marchandeau, who succeeded Gardey, set out what seems to have been the policy of governments from 1932 to February 1934: 'we have in the past months perhaps committed an error in not worrying sufficiently about the influence that the economic situation can have on the financial situation. There is a lot to do for our foreign trade and our economic infrastructure . . . But it is only by taking measures liable to give tangible results that we can deal with our immediate difficulties'.[6]

What were these difficulties? The fundamental problem was the fear of a return to the events of 1924–6: Bonnet had kept 'engraved for ever in my mind . . . the memory of this dramatic period and have kept at the bottom of my heart the desire to avoid a repetition of the days we lived through in those years'.[7] Even if the Socialists and others pointed out the differences between 1926 and 1933, there were enough superficial parallels to unleash the same fears and the same responses. If, then, a public spending policy was to be implemented without inflation, it was first necessary to reassure the confidence of potential lenders: hence the almost eternal postponement of such a policy. These fears were not totally exaggerated. At the beginning and end of 1933 the main preoccupation of governments was the immediate problem of funding the floating debt. Commentators as different as Boris and Jenny recognized that if the level of the floating debt did not objectively justify alarm, psychological factors could easily transform the situation: potential lenders, that is, also remembered 1926. And when the Socialists denounced attempts to exaggerate the plight of the Treasury, they were probably underestimating the importance of such psychological factors. But there is also evidence that financial and government circles did at times – whether intentionally or not – exaggerate the gravity of the situation: in January 1933 the government had claimed that the Treasury had no chance in coming months of raising long-term loans, and was dependent on its ability to issue the remaining balance of 5m Treasury Bills; but, we have seen, after the reluctance of the banks to take more than 1m of these Bills (and of the Bank of France to rediscount them), Bonnet was forced into the capital markets and, in spite of the earlier gloomy predictions, the issue of 5.1m in April was quickly subscribed. This suggests that the Socialist claim that it would have been possible to raise funds for a well-conceived programme of public spending was not groundless.

But governments were too preoccupied by the immediate financial difficulties to be able to take this view. Daladier's *cri de coeur* to Blum in October 1933 put this clearly: 'academic debates about systems and doctrines . . . have great interest but we, the government, each week we have to face the problem of bills falling due, we have to pay the employees of the nation'.[8] It is for this reason that the financial situation has been followed in some detail: to show that Radical governments were passively reacting to events, that their freedom of manoeuvre was often, as a result of expectations previously aroused, highly circumscribed (the case with Herriot in June 1932, Daladier in February 1933, Sarraut and Chautemps in the autumn of 1933), or that, even when this was not the case, the weakness of the Treasury pushed them into financial conservation whether, as in the case of Daladier, with perhaps a certain reluctance or, as in the case of Herriot, with the conviction born of the misleading precedent of previous experience.

We have seen that this policy did meet with opposition from Radicals: from some of the *radicalisant* Press (Bayet and de Jouvenel in *La République*. Georges Boris in *La Lumière*), from Party members at the Congresses, from left Radical deputies in the Chamber. But there were severe limitations to the effectiveness of this Radical opposition: besides not being very important quantitatively, it was often not prepared to follow the Socialists beyond opposition to deflation. The Socialist proposals in the autumn of 1933 obtained only a few Radical abstentions; and the Socialist bill of January 1933 was considerably modified. There remained nevertheless a considerable measure of common ground with the Socialists – on the belief that during a depression a deficit was not necessarily disastrous, on the need for a public spending programme, on action against tax fraud. But the left-wing Radicals lacked the ideological coherence which might have made them more effective. It was clearer what they were against than what they were for. As Bayet remarked in January 1933, there was a ' "Chéron plan", a "Socialist plan" . . . but no Radical plan'.[9] More to the point, there was at this stage no 'Young Radical Plan' either; there was no collaborative attempt by the left-wing Radical opposition to work out a response to the problems thrown up by the crisis. Besides restating many of the traditional demands of the Republican left, their response to the crisis was individual rather than collective: Boris and de Jouvenel attacked deflation and laid stress on international monetary action; Clerc (and to a lesser extent Mendès France), accepting reluctantly the need for deflation, stressed that to be coherent it must be general; Kayser was never specific as to the content of policy except that the government should show 'proof of authority and fidelity to Radical doctrines'.[10] The impression is one of disarray. As for the 40-hour week, one of the centre-pieces of Socialist policy, it is rare to find the left-wing Radicals alluding to it at all.

The Socialists could not so easily afford this detachment. Part of the Socialist difficulty came from the need to avoid alienating the C.G.T. and more generally its own electorate: this made it possible to compromise to some extent on the general issue of deflation but not on the particular issue of the *fonctionnaires* except at the risk of alienating the C.G.T. or, possibly, losing electoral support to the Communists. Those who have retrospectively attacked the Socialists for their intransigence are in a sense criticizing them for avoiding the trap which the Radicals are criticized (often by the same people) for having fallen into: that is, for desperately hanging on to a *mystique de gauche* which had almost no substantive policy content. Of course there was the argument, which was that of the future Neo-Socialists, that a Radical government carrying out undesirable policies was preferable to a conservative one carrying out even more undesirable ones. But, besides the fact that this was a dangerously negative stance which gave plausibility to Communist assertions that the Socialists and Radicals were 'accomplices', if it was believed that, as Blum said, one bill to balance the budget would be followed by another and another because the whole policy was self-defeating (and in theory the Neo-Socialists did agree with this view), then wary support inevitably became an ineluctable process and a less undesirable deflationary policy shaded imperceptibly into a more undesirable one. At some point a line would have to be drawn, as indeed the Neo-Socialists were to find – some of them being drawn further into collaboration, some returning to the party they had left, others going elsewhere. The problem of where to draw the line was the chronic Socialist dilemma of a supposedly revolutionary organization operating within the political system as a reformist party – a dilemma complicated by the crisis. It was not complicated but on the contrary simplified for those for whom the crisis was certainly the final crisis of capitalism, a prelude to revolution. But this was not Blum's position – or Auriol's.

This situation was further complicated by the threat of 'fascism'. But, again, the responses to this threat could be very various: collaboration with Radical governments to avoid bringing the parliamentary regime into discredit and limiting the dangers of making France receptive to fascist ideas could also mean, if the economy did not recover, that Socialism would be too associated with the regime to offer any alternative. The tightrope was precarious. Some action seems in retrospect to have been foolish: for instance, to have brought down the government of Daladier in October 1933 (which offered a programme of spending unmatched by any other government of the period) over the issue of the *fonctionnaires*, and then, a second ministerial crisis later, to have abstained on Chautemps' bill (why not Sarraut's?); though of course it could not have been certain in October that a way would not be found of excluding the *fonctionnaires* from any economies. The gains seem to have been non-existent: except, that is, the gain of having remained detached enough to be able to offer a viable alternative in the next two years. And after February 1934 the Socialists were at least released from an agonizing parliamentary dilemma.

February 1934 was a turning point for many other reasons: after it the economic problem could no longer be ignored. The financial problem remained important, and periodic flights of gold – in February 1934, in May 1935, in November 1935 – provided a new element of financial uncertainty and made it increasingly difficult to fund the floating debt. The freedom of manoeuvre of governments remained, therefore, highly circumscribed; and the need to protect the franc and fund government borrowing directly undermined an objective of economic policy: to reduce the rate of interest. But when governments cut expenditure after 1934 they no longer claimed that financial policy was at odds with economic policy. On the contrary, they claimed to be pursuing a coherent policy. The Flandin government, which abandoned budgetary deflation, was an exception to this, but, besides the fact that Flandin's wheat bill was a disguised deflation, his government was an interlude and his policy was forced on him by political circumstances and carried the support of neither his majority, his civil servants, nor indeed his own finance minister. The case of Laval was more complicated than his opponents claimed: but still the objective of his financial decrees was to permit a fall in interest rates and stimulate an economic recovery.

But in spite of differences of rhetoric there were many continuities of policy between the two periods: governments after 1934 might describe their policy as deflationary, but they did not abandon agricultural protection; even Flandin made no attempt to modify the apparatus of quotas and tariffs which insulated the French market from international competition. And this was a great barrier to constructing any policy of gold-block economic solidarity. In September 1933 the government of Daladier had decided to introduce the principle of reciprocity into French commercial policy: 75 per cent of each country's quota allocations were revoked, and had to be negotiated in exchange for the granting of trading advantages to France; this policy became official under the Chautemps government in December and it fell to Doumergue's minister of commerce, Lamoureux, to renegotiate the quota allocations with France's trading partners.[11] This extremely important modification of policy which plunged France into a period of economic warfare with Britain and other countries was barely noticed:[12] there were areas of policy which political debate ignored.

Some continuities of policy were very embarrassing for certain Radicals. To quote *L'Oeuvre*: 'we will be told that the first Radical governments of this parliament also wanted to carry out deflation. But with what precautions! How much less brutally and cruelly'[13] – and, one might add, logically. Daladier, on the other hand, seemed to have forgotten his earlier financial orthodoxy and preferred instead to remember only his abortive public works programme.[14]

He embarked on a rewriting of history by displacing the end of the economic revival which had occurred during 1932, from mid-1933, when he was still in power, to 1934 when the effects of Doumergue's 'deflation' could be blamed.[15] But this selective memory was too convenient: between July 1932 and February 1934 government expenditure had been cut by 6.7m F., although, taking account of various provisions of these bills which over-lapped, the real amount was nearer 5.5m F.[16] This figure, however, by not taking account of cuts in capital expenditure plans made before the budget was even presented, underestimated the real level of deflation: in preparing the budget of 1934 Lamoureux had kept projected expenditure at the level of 1933; but because the effect of the social legislation voted in the 1920s would have been to increase expenditure automatically by 3m he had only kept the figure for 1934 down by cutting capital expenditure, which could be more easily reduced than debt charges or the payment of individuals. It has been calculated that between the budget of 1930–1 and that of 1933–4 the nominal reduction in government expenditure on the construction of schools was 65 per cent, and the real reduction – taking account of the fall in prices – was still 56 per cent.[17] And none of the public works programmes which would have partially made up for this reduction in capital expenditure were voted. Between 1934 and 1936 the governments of Doumergue and Laval cut expenditure by 9.5m,[18] and once again this figure does not take account of reductions in capital expenditure – even taking account of the decree-laws, expenditure projections for 1935 would automatically have been 1m more than for 1934, without further cuts in capital expenditure – which were far from compensated for by the Marquet Plan. Certainly this figure was almost double that of the previous two years; but the contribution of the Radical governments had been nonetheless important, and the nature of the policy was similar.

The governments of the period 1934 to 1936 were no more successful than their predecessors in eliminating budget deficits, and Laval could present a balanced budget for 1936 only by an artifice of book-keeping. At the beginning of 1936 the financial situation was more precarious than ever: the government was surviving only thanks to the Bank of France. Between 1932 and 1936 the budget had been reduced from 50m to 40m F.; but the public debt had grown by 64m F.: approximately 29m between 1932 and 1934 and approximately 36m F. in the next four years. The number of Treasury Bills issued had risen from 4m to almost 21m. Why, despite their heroic efforts, had governments between 1934 and 1936 been so unsuccessful in balancing the budget? The cause lay partly in the depressive effects of the deflation policy itself – government revenues continued to fall – partly in expenditure on attempts to mitigate the social effects of deflation – expenditure on unemployment relief and, in 1935, on the wheat and wine markets – and partly in the increase in military spending. But when Régnier said that 'the state has attempted to sustain activity in spending more than it received'[19] he was merely putting a brave face on a policy that had in no sense been voluntarily carried out. Ministry of Finance officials deplored all proposed public works programmes, and the increase in the floating debt in the second half of 1935 – made possible by the new attitude of the Bank – was seen as unavoidable but regrettable.

Apart from rhetoric, then, the greatest difference between the period 1932 to 1934 and 1934 to 1936 was the way in which expenditure cuts were carried out: in the first two years the brunt of deflation had been carried out by cutting capital expenditure, by cutting military expenditure, and by the conversion of part of the debt (1m F.); after 1934 two of these options were no longer available and part of the burden of deflation could be shifted on to those in receipt of payments from the government – *fonctionnaires* (who had been only slightly hit by the governments of Daladier and Chautemps), pensioners, war veterans and eventually rentiers (some of whom had already suffered by the conversion).

This was, of course, possibly only because for nine months of this period governments were authorized to act by decree law. Although the principle of the decrees did cause some protest on the left, they were on the whole surprisingly easily accepted; there were even those, such as Paul-Boncour, who gave a 'eulogy of the decree laws' arguing that the left should not refuse to accept the principle of a mode of action which it perhaps ought to have used itself.[20] It is slightly paradoxical that it was after February 1934, when, after all, the government seemed to have all the means at its disposal to carry out the policy of its choice, that the campaign for constitutional reform should have attained its greatest intensity. But the decrees were, as *La Revue des deux mondes* pointed out, only a temporary expedient: constitutional reform, that is, would in effect give the government the means to carry out over a long period the policies which the decree powers permitted it to pursue only intermittently.[21] There was no contradiction between the conservative desire both for constitutional reform to strengthen the power of the state and for the state to intervene less in the economy: only a strong state could be a minimal state.[22] But although constitutional revision continued to be an issue until the election of 1936, the agitation for it had died down by the autumn of 1935. Perhaps this was partly because the scope of the Laval decrees had shown how much use a determined government could make of its power. Indeed conservatives had begun to wonder whether Laval did not threaten to subvert the values for which he was held to stand.

The decrees not only allowed the government to transfer the burden of deflation on to the classes which had so far suffered relatively little from the crisis, they also entirely changed the conditions of politics: whereas between 1932 and 1934 the determining factor had been the interplay of forces between the government and its majority in the Chamber (and its Finance Commission), and between these two forces and the Senate (and its Finance Commission), after February 1934 the role of parliament was somewhat minimized. The centre of political interest shifted – to the Bank of France and to the street: the crisis of June 1935 showed the Chamber's weakness more than its strength. The Bank's attitude was partly influenced by the fact of being in competition with the deposit banks. It had already played a role in March 1933, and even if its role after 1934 was less important than the left claimed, a desire to modify the legends of the left should not lead us to go to the opposite extreme of underplaying the Bank's role: in failing to help Germain-Martin at the beginning of 1934, in sabotaging Flandin's credit policy at the beginning of 1935, in influencing the outcome of the ministerial crisis of June 1935 and in ensuring Laval's financial survival after June. Perhaps however the truth was more complicated than the myth of an all powerful Bank holding governments to ransom: politicians could use the threat of the Bank as much as the Bank used them. When, on 6 June 1935, Laval, after seeing officials from the Bank and Finance Ministry, told Herriot that he required more extensive decree powers than he had at first believed, he may have been telling the truth; but it was also true that this information gave him a useful weapon to use in his negotiations with the Radicals. This tactic did not always work: on 16 January 1936 Herriot told Laval that he intended to resign from the government; Laval asked him only to postpone the date of his decision, and the next day Herriot was visited by Tannery who pointed out the gravity of the financial situation; but this time Herriot stood firm.[23]

More important potentially than the influence of the Bank were the reactions of the street: the decree powers might have freed the government temporarily from the obligation to find a majority for deflation in the Chamber, but this did not imply that it could ignore the effects that its policies might have on the social classes most directly hit by them. Was there a point at which deflation would become politically dangerous? The class that could be most easily ignored was the unemployed, partly because it is always easy to ignore the unemployed, partly because unemployment never reached the proportions attained in many other countries: Communist attempts to galvanize the unemployed were, as we have seen, largely unsuccessful. Of course the figure could partly be kept so low in France owing to a considerable emigration of foreign workers and because the agricultural sector was doubt-less able to absorb some unemployed industrial workers. But this does not seem to have been a very important factor although the rural exodus slowed down almost to a halt: a detailed study of unemployment carried out just before the war found that industrial workers were reluctant to take up even seasonal agricultural employment, and this was an area in which foreign labour remained important;[24] in the Seine only 39 workers took up facilities provided by a decree of May 1935 encouraging workers to return to their rural commune of origin.[25]

The *fonctionnaires*, the most directly affected victims of government deflation, provided only a slightly greater threat to public order than the unemployed. In 1933 they had seemed ready to resist cuts with considerable violence; but once a conservative government was in power, armed with decree laws, they accepted their fate relatively easily: in 1935 the protests were more violent than in 1934, and this was a measure of the fact that, until the Laval decrees, the real living standards of all *fonctionnaires* had con-tinued to rise in spite of the cuts carried out in April 1934.[26] But even in July 1935 the *fonctionnaires* were never able to attract broad enough popular support to make their opposition to the government more effective: the dis-turbances at Toulon and Brest were spectacular, but the agitation died down fairly quickly. Laval was helped by the skilful presentation of his decrees, but even more by the fact that they coincided with a rise in agricultural prices. It was from the reactions of the peasantry that governments had most to fear: during 1933, 1934 and the first half of 1935 the situation in the countryside was perceived as extremely explosive both by the Prefects and by politicians. The result was that governments were forced to try and keep up agricultural prices: although this policy failed it was probably successful enough to ensure that deflation would not work. The only government which attempted to ignore the peasantry – that of Flandin – suffered the consequences: disaffec-tion in the countryside probably reached its peak in April 1935. The Radicals therefore had little sympathy left for Flandin by May: his government was defeated both by the Bank of France and the peasantry. Laval, on the other hand, owed his longevity both to the Bank and to the peasantry (or the weather).

It was the attempt both to conciliate the rentiers, by deflation, and the peasantry, by holding up agricultural prices, which resulted in stagnation.[27] It has been suggested here that up to a point stagnation was consciously pre-ferred to other policy options. To understand how this could have been possible it is instructive to compare France with Britain and America. The political response to the crisis in France was importantly conditioned by the peculiar nature of its impact, and particularly by the interaction of three factors: a chronic financial problem; a virtually impregnable monetary position; and a *relatively* mild economic depression, which never threatened the situation of social and economic collapse which it did in Germany and America: it was a slow paralysis rather than a cataclysmic decline. The first factor for at least two years deflected attention from the underlying economic situation and encouraged misleading parallels with the past; the second made it impossible for any government to be forced to devalue through lack of sufficient gold reserves; and the third made it politically possible to continue with current policies.

In Britain the pound was forced off gold and only after devaluation were its benefits appreciated: 'they never told us we could do that' as Sidney Webb is said to have remarked. But once the pound had gone off gold, fear of the consequences of currency stabilization became as important a feature of British policy as the fear of devaluation in France: the British were as obsessed by the memory of the deflation of the 1920s as the French by the memory of the inflation of the 1920s. Roosevelt, while not forced off the dollar, chose to devalue as a means of raising domestic prices and relieving the plight of debt-ridden farmers: but the situation of social collapse with which he was faced made such a decision almost unavoidable. In France, however it was possible to argue plausibly that the presumed consequences of devaluation – given the nervousness of a population haunted by memories of 1926 – would be more socially disruptive than an at least temporary continuation of the prevailing situation.

The relative lack of severity of the Depression in France is reflected also in the comparatively small part that it plays in collective historical memory. The Hunger March of 1933 does not have the same historical resonance as the Jarrow march. Trade unions in the England of the late 1970s denounced a return to the 'policies of the 1930s'; in 1979 M. Gaston Defferre could certainly liken M. Barre's deflation to Laval's, but the comparison stands out for its rarity. The literature of the 1930s in France is most notable for the heroics of a Malraux or the misanthropy of a Céline. France does not have its *Grapes of Wrath*, its *Love on the Dole*, its *Road to Wigan Pier*; Simone Weil's *La Condition ouvrière* was about the conditions of work, not about the lack of it. In June 1936 one of the workers' main demands was for *congés payes*, for less work not more.

The conclusion that stagnation was to an extent chosen – or accepted as a lesser evil – is contrary to much recent writing on the subject of French economic history, which has tended to rehabilitate the entrepreneurs and businessman who in an earlier generation had, we have seen, been stigmatized for their resistance to change, their 'malthusianism'.[28] But this conclusion is not intended as a contribution to this wider argument: that during a period of unprecedented world economic depression, there should have been limited optimism about the future possibilities for economic growth is hardly surprising, and was not a phenomenon unique to France. Rare were individuals like Keynes who could write with enthusiasm and hope in the 1930s about the economic possibilities for their grandchildren. But what is probably true is that the stylized image of a tranquil, rural France of the *petits rentiers*, the *petits paysans*, turning their backs on the horrors of the future, had a greater resonance in France than elsewhere, and that the Depression gave it new force.

Standing against the official consensus of government and opposition were the planists and the devaluers. Obviously the Socialists did not approve of the policies which governments had followed between 1932 and 1936. But by resisting planism they showed that they implicitly shared the government assumption that stagnation could continue without obliging them to over-throw whatever orthodoxy was being defended. Both conservative and Radical governments and the Socialist opposition shared similar lack of con-fidence in the regenerative possibilities of capitalism. Certainly the Socialists' *politique du pouvoir d'achat* was an attempt to make the capitalism work again, to alleviate the effects of the crisis. But the system was seen as doomed. As Faure had said: the cause of the crisis was capitalism; the remedy was Socialism.[29] Everything else was a palliative. The irony is that in 1936 it was Blum who was called upon to become the 'loyal manager' of capitalism.

At first sight it is perhaps surprising that one should assimilate the planists with the advocates of devaluation since on various points they stood in almost perfect symmetrical opposition to each other, although they were both concerned about the best means of protecting and winning over the *classes moyennes*. The argument over planism was conducted exclusively on the left, just as the argument over devaluation was conducted almost exclus-ively on the right (for the Socialists it was not a fundamental issue); planists proposed a solution to the crisis oriented towards the national economy, the domestic market, while advocates of devaluation looked for international solutions. But what did link the two positions was their resolute modernity. Both Boris and Patenôtre shared ultimately a robust optimism in the future of capitalism;[30] Laurat, de Man and Déat shared a similar faith, if not in capitalism, at least in the immediate possibilities of restoring prosperity and material well-being.

It is interesting in this context to consider their attitude to developments taking place in America. Throughout twentieth-century French history (and before) reflection on American experience has acted as a means of reflecting about the possible future of France. In the 1920s reflection on America was a reflection on prosperity, materialism and modernization: the enthusiasm of Dubreuil or Mercier was balanced by the revulsion of Duhamel, Dandieu and Aron.[31] But in the 1930s reflection on America was reflection upon what was seen as a desperate and vigorous attempt to salvage the most powerful capitalist regime by means which at the same time subverted the orthodox liberal economics which were both the emanation and support of that regime. On the right, therefore, Roosevelt was denounced with a fervour verging on hysteria: after Reynaud had announced his conversion to devaluation the *Journal des débats* could find nothing more devastating to say than 'It is fundamentally the American policy that M. Paul Reynaud is proposing'.[32] The attitude of the Socialists was obviously entirely different, but still their attitude to the New Deal remained ambivalent: this is after all what lay at the heart of the argument about 'intermediary regimes'. Altogether different was the attitude of many planists and devaluers: Georges Boris's *La Révolution Roosevelt* (1934), Bertrand de Jouvenel's *La Crise du capitalisme américain* (1933) and André Philip's *La Crise et l'économie dirigée* (1935) were all enthusiastic about various aspects of the New Deal;[33] Patenôtre, himself half-American, followed developments there with enthusiasm; Déat's enthusiasm was no less great even if he was less clear exactly what he was enthusiastic about. This did not matter: America was as much a symbol for an attitude as the exemplar of a policy. The argument, then, was not only about how to overcome the problems of the Depression, it was also about the present and future of French society and civilization.

# Appendix

**Circulation of Treasury Bills (bons de trésor) on the last day of each month: May 1932–May 1936**

**1932**        (thousands of millions of francs)
May:            4.2
June:           4.4
July:           4.4
August:         4.4
September:      5.1
October:        5.0
November:       8.5
December:       9.7

**1933**
January:        10.0
February:       10.8
March:          10.4
April:          10.1
May:            11.9        (including an English loan of 1.9)
June:           13.4        (English loan 2.5)
July:           14.8        (English loan 1.5)
August:         14.0        (English loan 1.3)
September:      14.7        (English loan 1.3)
October:        14.1        (English loan 1.3)
November:       11.5
December:       10.1

**1934**
January:        9.0
February:       8.7
March:          9.0         (including a Dutch loan of 0.8)
April:          10.0        (Dutch loan 1.3)
May:            12.0        (Dutch loan 1.3)
June:           12.0        (Dutch loan 0.9)
July:           11.5        (Dutch loan 0.5)
August:         11.0        (Dutch loan 0.5)
September:      10.0        (Dutch loan 0.1)
October:        9.9
November:       9.8
December:       9.7

**1935**         (thousands of millions of francs)
January:        9.9
February:      11.0
March:         11.6
April:         10.9
May:           11.0
June:          12.7
July:          12.9
August:        14.6
September:     14.3
October:       14.3
November:      14.0
December:      14.0

**1936**
January:       13.5
February:      13.7
March:         15.3
April:         17.5
May:           20.8

**Laws governing the ceiling on Treasury Bills**

| Date of law | New Level of ceiling (thousands of millions of francs) |
|---|---|
| 7 August 1926 | 5.0 |
| 20 July 1932 | 7.0 |
| 22 July 1932 | 10.6 |
| 17 September 1932 (to cover cost of conversion operation) | 8.6 |
| 30 December 1932 | 15.6 |
| 23 December 1933 | (ceiling to be reduced to 12 by 31 March 1934 and to 10 by 30 September 1934) |
| 30 January 1935 | 15.0 |
| 23 March 1936 (allows *Fonds d'outillage et d'armement* of the 1936 budget to be covered by Treasury Bills) | 22.8 |

# Notes

## Introduction

1 The phrase is used by, among others, J.-C. Asselain, *Histoire économique de la France*, Vol. 2 (1984), p. 99.

2 These figures come from D. Landes, *The Unbound Prometheus* (1969), p. 391.

3 This is the attitude that informs for example, many of the contributions to E. M. Earle (ed.), *Modern France* (1951) or A. Sauvy, *Histoire économique de la France entre les deux guerres* (1965–75). There is a voluminous literature on the question of French growth – or lack of it – in the nineteenth century: Asselain, *Histoire economique de la France*, Vol. 1, provides a brief introduction; J. Bouvier *et al.*, *Histoire économique et sociale de la France*, edited by E. Labrousse and F. Braudel, Vol. 4 (1979–80) is the most recent major synthesis and has an extensive bibliography.

4 Thus J. J. Carré, P. Dubois and E. Malinvaud write in their study of French post-war economic growth that the 'historian wanting to locate the beginning of the long acceleration of the French growth rate could probably just as well start around 1900 as around 1950'; quoted by F. Caron, *Histoire économique de la France. XIX–XX siècles*, 1981, p. 157.

5 Caron, *Histoire économique*, p. 159; J. J. Carré, P. Dubois and E. Malinvaud, *La Croissance française* (1972), p. 618.

6 J. T. Emmerson, *The Rhineland Crisis* (1977), pp. 111–12.

7 F. Bédarida, 'La Gouvernante anglaise', in R. Rémond and J. Bourdin, eds., *Edouard Daladier, chef de gouvernement avril 1938–septembre 1939* (1977), pp. 228–40. A. Adamthwaite, 'France and the Coming of War', in W. Mommsen and L. Kettenacker, eds., *The Fascist Challenge and the Policy of Appeasement* (1983), pp. 246–56, argues that French leaders used this supposed dependence on Britain as an alibi for executing an appeasement policy which they anyway intended to pursue. Whichever view is correct, neither denies the reality of French weakness.

8 A. Adamthwaite, *France and the Coming of the Second World War 1936–1939* (1977), p. 105. But the British did not succeed in imposing their preference for Chautemps.

9 R. Young, *In Command of France: French Foreign Policy and Military Planning 1933–1940* (1978), pp. 17–22.

10 Adamthwaite, *France*, pp. 38–9; J.-B. Duroselle, *La Décadence 1932–1939* (1979), pp. 166–8.

11 R. Frankenstein, 'Apropos des aspects financiers du réarmement français 1935–1939', *Revue d'histoire de la deuxième guerre mondiale*, 102 (April 1976), p. 2.

12 R. Frankenstein, *Le Prix du réarmement français 1935–1939* (1982), p. 26.

13 Ibid., pp. 50–63.

14 J.-M. d'Hoop, Le Problème du réarmement français jusqu'à mars 1936', *La France et l'Allemagne 1932–1936*, Franco-German Colloquium, 1975 (1980), pp. 75–89.
15 Duroselle, *La Décadence*, p. 30.
16 Frankenstein, *Le Prix du réarmement*, pp. 124–5, 171.
17 Adamthwaite, *France*, p. 6.
18 Young, *In Command of France*, pp. 1–4, 251.
19 For example, Adamthwaite, *France*, pp. 5–6, 27–8; R. Girault, 'The Impact of the Economic Situation on the Foreign Policy of France 1936–9', in Mommsen and Kettenacker, eds., *The Fascist Challenge*, pp. 209–26; R. Frankenstein, 'The Decline of France and French Appeasement Policies', in Ibid., pp. 236–45; Young, *In Command of France*, pp. 22–3.
20 Bouvier *et al.*, *Histoire économique et sociale*, eds. Labrousse and Braudel.
21 See the works and articles of P. Saly, M. Margairaz, S. Wolikow, M. Wolfe and T. Kemp, all cited in the text and bibliography.
22 See the works and articles of G. Lefranc, R. Frankenstein, J.-C. Asselain, J.-P. Cuvillier, D. Lecomte and D. Pavy, G. Bourdé, and the colloquia on the governments of Léon Blum and Edouard Daladier, all cited in the text and bibliography.
23 Duroselle, *La Décadence*, p. 178; Adamthwaite, *France*, p. 41.
24 See Young, *In Command of France*, pp. 131–2.
25 Asselain, *Histoire économique de la France*, Vol. 2, pp. 92–9, provides a brief discussion of these writers, to whom might be added S. Wolikow, 'La Crise des années trente en France: aspects spécifiques de la crise', C.H.I.M.T. 17–18, 1976, pp. 11–48.
26 J.-N. Jeanneney, *François de Wendel en république: L'argent et le pouvoir 1914–1940*, 3 vols. (1976). Jeanneney's *L'Argent caché* (1984), also contains interesting general reflections on the influence of financial and business interests in these years: see especially pp. 43–70.

## 1 The context

1 Duroselle, *La Décadence*, p. 17. The story comes from Léon Noël's, *Les Illusions de Stresa* (1976).
2 E. Herriot, *Jadis II: d'une guerre à l'autre, 1914–1936* (1952), p. 544.
3 For the financial problems of post-war France see: R. M. Haig, *The Public Finances of Post-War France* (1929), and J. H. Rogers, *The Process of Inflation in France, 1914–1927* (1929); a useful survey of monetary policy in the whole inter-war period is M. Wolfe, *The French Franc between the Wars, 1919–1939* (1951).
4 For the economic history of the inter-war period see, besides the works of Sauvy, Caron, Bouvier, and Asselain, C.-J. Gignoux, *L'Economie française entre les deux guerres, 1919–1939* (1942); T. Kemp, *The French Economy 1913–1939: The History of a Decline* (1972); 'The French Economy under the Franc Poincaré', *Economic History Review*, 24, 1 (Feb. 1971), pp. 82–99.
5 Carré *et al.*, *La Croissance française*, p. 218.
6 For a discussion of the *classes moyennes* see A. Bergounioux *et al.*, *L'Univers politique des classes moyennes* (1983).
7 Sauvy, *Histoire économique*, Vol. 2, p. 137.
8 A. Bouton, *La Fin des rentiers* (1931), p. 279.
9 M. Perrot, *La Monnaie et l'opinion publique en France et en Grande Bretagne* (1955), contains interesting contemporary quotations, pp. 117–90.

10  G. Ziebura, *Léon Blum et le parti socialiste 1872–1934* (1967), pp. 193–221.
11  On the Redressement, see: R. Kuisel, *Ernest Mercier: French Technocrat* (1967), pp. 48–88.
12  M. Fine, 'Towards Corporatism: the Movement for Capital–Labor Collaboration in France 1914–36' (Unpublished Ph.D. thesis, University of Wisconsin, 1971), p. 188. For the attitudes and organization of business in this period, see H. Ehrmann, *Organized Business in France* (1957), pp. 15–30.
13  A favourite theme of Sauvy's: *Histoire économique*, Vol. 1, pp. 431–2; Vol. 2, pp. 20–3, 37–9, 86–7, 194–5.
14  For details on the teaching of economics see a special number of the *Revue d'économie politique* in 1937 devoted to 'L'Enseignement économique en France et à l'étranger'.
15  C.R.C.R., May 1934, pp. 173–4.
16  As his adviser Raymond Moley wrote: 'I doubt if Roosevelt or I could have passed an examination such as is required of first year students in elementary economics'. Quoted by C. Kindleberger, *The World in Depression, 1929–1939* (1973), p. 24, Fn. 9.
17  For example, Sauvy, *Histoire économique*, Vol. 2, pp. 67, 103–4; Kindleberger, *World in Depression*, p. 251. For the reception of the *Economic Consequences* in France see F. Crouzet, 'Réactions françaises devant "Les conséquences économiques de la paix" de Keynes', *Revue d'histoire moderne et contemporaine*, 19 (Jan.–Mar. 1972), pp. 6–26.
18  See pp. 165–6.
19  See, for example, G. Blondot, *Les Théories monétaires de J. M. Keynes* (1933), especially pp. 141–7, which is basically an exposition of the *Treatise* from a fairly critical standpoint; there was a long article on the *Treatise* by J.-M. Jeanneney in R.E.P. (Mar.–Apr. 1936), pp. 358–92; and in the 1948 edition of his *A History of Economic Doctrines from the Time of the Physiocrats to the Present Day*, pp. 738–49, written originally in collaboration with Charles Gide, Charles Rist was highly critical of *The General Theory*.
20  Frédéric Jenny, *Le Temps*, 7 September 1931.
21  Pierre Rossillion, *La Nation*, 16 January 1932.
22  Jeanneney, R.E.P. (Mar.–Apr. 1936), p. 358.
23  A survey is provided by G. Pirou, *Histoire des doctrines économiques en France depuis 1870* (1934).
24  A. Thibaudet, *Les Idées politiques de la France* (1932), p. 55.
25  J. M. Keynes, *Théorie générale de l'emploi, de l'intérêt et de la monnaie* (1969), p. 6. The work first appeared in French in 1942; Keynes' preface was dated 20 February 1939.
26  S. H. Clough, *France: History of National Economics 1789–1939* (1939) is a history of this tradition of intervention.
27  The phrase is from R. Kuisel, *Capitalism and the State in Modern France* (1981), p. 1.
28  Pirou, *Histoire des doctrines économiques*, pp. 122–3.
29  E. Roll, *A History of Economic Thought* (1938), p. 300.
30  Travaux du Congrès des économistes de la langue française, *Economie libérale et économie dirigée. L'étalon-or* (1933), p. 77.
31  J. Rueff, 'L'enseignement de M. Colson', *Revue politique et parlementaire*, Nov. 1933. He describes Colson as 'a liberal, enemy of any interference in the free play of economic forces'.
32  R.E.P. 1909. He later wrote *Les Crises périodiques de surproduction* (1911).

33 See Rist's remarks to the congress of French economists, in Travaux du Congrès, *Economie libérale* (1933), pp. 66–9. He repeated the argument in his report for the Conseil National Economique on the origins of the crisis, reproduced in *Essais sur quelques problèmes économiques et monétaires* (1933), pp. 324–33. But it should be noted that at the Congress both Aftalion and Lescure did not show total hostility to the notion of the *économie dirigée.* Travaux du Congrès, *Economie libérale*, pp. 94, 106.

34 The point is made by C. Kindleberger in S. Hoffmann, *et al., France: Change and Tradition* (1963), pp. 151–2. For the preoccupation with monetary problems see: A. Aftalion, *Monnaie, prix et change* (1937); J. Rueff, *Théorie des phénomènes monétaires* (1927); C. Rist, *La Déflation en pratique* (1924), and *Essais*; B. Nogaro, *La Monnaie et les phénomènes monétaires contemporaines* (1935).

35 Aftalion, in Travaux du Congrès, *Economie libérale* (1933), p. 108.

36 Quoted in M. Dobb, *Theories of Value and Distribution since Adam Smith* (1973), p. 16, Fn.

37 C.R.C.R., October 1934, p. 265.

38 J. Duboin, *La Grande relève des hommes par la machine* (1932), p. 17. Duboin was the author of numerous other works on the same theme: *Nous faisons fausse route* (1932); *Ce qu'on appelle la crise!* (1936); *Kou l'Ahuri ou la misère dans l'abondance* (1935).

39 The following brief introduction to French parties and politics in this period is based on a number of standard and well-known works. I have therefore largely omitted note references in the following paragraphs.

40 A. Kriegel, *Le Pain et les roses* (1968), p. 195.

41 Roche–Caillaux Correspondence, E.R.J.C. 9, Dr I. Roche to Caillaux, 13 September 1935. On Caillaux in this period see: J.-C. Allain, *Joseph Caillaux*, Vol. 2: *L'Oracle, 1914–44* (1981); J. Zay, in his memoirs, *Souvenirs et solitude* (1946), pp. 321–3, has anecdotes on Caillaux's extraordinary imperiousness.

42 L. Lamoureux, 'Mémoires', p. 1083. These memoirs are unpublished: a microfilm of the manuscript is available at the B.D.I.C. at Nanterre. F. Goguel, *Le Rôle financier du Sénat français* (1937), is confined largely to the period up to 1926.

43 P. Delouvrier and R. Nathan, *Politique économique de la France 1929–1939* (1955–6), have a few remarks on the formation of policy, especially Fascicule I, p. 27.

44 Lucien Romier quoted by Gignoux in La Société des Anciens Elèves de L'Ecole Libre des Sciences Politiques, *L'Economie dirigée* (1934), p. 275 (a series of lectures organized by the Ecole Libre).

45 See G. Dubost, *Le Conseil national économique, ses origines, son avenir* (1936).

46 On the Inspectorate, see P. Lalumière, *L'Inspection des finances* (1959).

47 J.-B. Duroselle, 'Notes de lecture: Inspecteurs des Finances et politique étrangère dans les années trente', *Relations internationales* 13 (1978), pp. 117–22.

48 L. Trotabas, *Les Finances publiques et les impôts de la France* (1937), pp. 66ff.

49 On financial institutions see: M. Myers, *Paris as a Financial Centre* (1936); G. Guenser, *Le Marché monétaire français et son contrôle par la Banque de France* (1938); A. Dauphin-Meunier, *La Banque de France* (1936); J. Bouvier, *Un Siècle de banque française* (1973); J. S. G. Wilson, *French Banking Structure and Credit Policy* (1957) – largely about the situation after 1945.

50 M.F.B. 12678 contains an interesting note by Moret, dated 31 March 1933, on the problems of placing Treasury Bills.

51  Bouvier, *Un Siècle*, pp. 157–8.
52  See the study dated March 1936, by Emile Moreau and Quesnay, entitled 'L'adaptation du rôle de la Banque à la situation de 1936'. It is contained in the Roche–Caillaux Papers, E.R.J.C. 6, Dr 2.

## 2  The inheritance

1  J.O. Ch., 7 November 1929, pp. 3000–1.
2  The bill was J.O. Doc. C. 1929, No. 2479. On public works policy in the 1930s see P. Saly, *La Politique des grands travaux en France 1929–1939* (1977).
3  *Devant le pays* (1932), pp. 104–7. See also the long memorandum dated 1 November 1931 on the delays in implementing the bill in Tardieu's papers A.N. 324 A.P. 48. Such claims were also made by many of his supporters: for example, André François-Poncet, J.O. Ch., 17 January 1931, p. 88. These assertions are wrongly followed by R. Binion, *Defeated Leaders: The Political Fate of Caillaux, Jouvenel and Tardieu* (1960), p. 308. M. Clague, 'Vision and Myopia in the New Politics of André Tardieu', *French Historical Studies* 1 (1973), pp. 105–29, is more accurate; see also Saly, *La Politique*, pp. 303–8.
4  J.O. Doc. C. 1929, No. 2479.
5  Quoted in R. Skidelsky, *Politicians and the Slump: the Labour Governments of 1929–31* (1967), p. 141.
6  Wolfe, *The French Franc*, p. 85. But J. Marseille, 'Les origines inopportunes de la crise de 1929 en France', *Revue économique* 31, 4 (July 1980), pp. 648–84, casts doubt on the notion that France was affected by the crisis later than the rest of the world.
7  R.E.P. 1931, p. 696.
8  Ibid., p. 701.
9  Ibid., pp. 690–709.
10  R.E.P. 1932, pp. 778–9.
11  For discussion of French price indices see Wolfe, *The French Franc*, pp. 86–90; and A. Aftalion, *L'Or et sa distribution mondiale* (1932), Pt 2, Chapter 2.
12  R.E.P. 1932, pp. 1110–19.
13  For a criticism of this view, see Wolikow, 'La Crise'.
14  These figures refer to the trade of France *and* her colonies with the rest of the world.
15  R.E.P. 1930, p. 471.
16  R.E.P. 1931, p. 692.
17  R.E.P. 1932, pp. 586, 771–2.
18  Wolfe, *The French Franc*, p. 94.
19  The expenditure of tourists was difficult to estimate. See Meynial in R.E.P. 1933, pp. 669–70.
20  Wolfe, *The French Franc*, p. 90. The two indices of retail prices produced by the Statistique Générale de la France were heavily based on foodstuffs, which is why the retail price index continued to rise in 1930.
21  Ibid., p. 77.
22  See below, chapter 8, p. 168.
23  Details of these measures in Aftalion, *L'Or*, pp. 223–9.
24  R.E.P. 1931, pp. 518–21; 1932, pp. 581–5.
25  Part of the additional credits went to cover an inadequate provision of expenditure for unemployment relief, but tax revenues continued to exceed original predictions, owing largely to increased customs duties.

26 In the words of R.E.P. 1932, p. 597: 'with a light heart and almost with relief'.
27 L. Germain-Martin, *Le Problème financier* (1936), p. 25.
28 Responsibility for the servicing of another 1.9m F. of government debt was passed on to the Caisse d'Amortissement.
29 R.E.P. 1932, p. 595.
30 Over a financial year of only nine months.
31 In covering the two preceding deficits and the colonial deficit, or on expenditure hived off to the Treasury to pay for various recently voted pieces of social legislation.
32 Gardey, J.O. Sen., 24 March 1932, p. 471; Lamoureux, J.O. Ch., 9 February 1932, pp. 529–34.
33 R.E.P. 1932, p. 617.
34 Ibid., p. 744.
35 J.O. Ch., 13 February 1930, p. 706.
36 *Le Temps*, 7 September 1931; 14 September 1931.
37 J.O. Doc. C. 1932 No. 5820.
38 François-Poncet, J.O. Ch., 8 July 1930, p. 2988.
39 R.E.P. 1932, p. 516.
40 R.E.P. 1931, p. 520.
41 R.E.P. 1932, pp. 578, 592. Sauvy, *Histoire économique*, Vol. 2, pp. 19–21, is therefore wrong in saying that the question of prices did not preoccupy opinion at this time.
42 J.O. Ch., 13 February 1930, pp. 689–90. In the same debate César Chabrun, an independent Socialist, devoted his entire speech to the dangers of monetary expansion: Ibid., pp. 704–9.
43 J.O. Ch., 19 January 1931, p. 117; see Auriol, J.O. Ch., 9 February 1932, p. 538.
44 Daladier Papers, I DA 2 Dr. 1 sdrb: 'Schéma sur la situation économique' (dated 19 January 1931). (Probably written by the economist Henri Michel.) Or more pithily: 'it would be a hundred times better to have less gold in the Bank of France and more jobs in factories'. Ibid., 'Note sur quelques points d'un discours de Tardieu'.
45 J.O. Ch., 19 January 1931, p. 121.
46 For example, de Lastyrie, J.O. Ch., 11 February 1932, p. 579: 'I don't remember that a few years ago, when France was going through bad days, the Anglo-Saxon countries, who are today conducting such a strident campaign for a better distribution of gold, took much notice of this theory to let us benefit from their gold reserves'.
47 J.O. Doc. Admin. 1931, p. 152. This was a report of February 1931 by the C.N.E. on ways of combatting unemployment.
48 For example, de Lastyrie, J.O. Ch., 11 February 1932, p. 577; Germain-Martin, *Le Problème financier*, p. 66.
49 de Chappedelaine, J.O. Ch., 8 July 1930, p. 2987.
50 J.O. Doc. Admin. 1931, p. 153. J. Perret, *Le Cancer du chômage* (1936), advocated the same solution.
51 G. Letellier *et al.*, *Enquête sur le chômage*, Vol. 1: *Le Chômage en France de 1930 à 1936* (1938), p. 37. Chapter 2 contains a full discussion of the validity of unemployment statistics. See also the two reports by the C.N.E. in J.O. Doc. Admin., 26 February 1931, pp. 149–58; 13 December 1931, pp. 1425–33.
52 Letellier *et al.*, *Enquête sur le chômage*, Vol. 1, pp. 46–7. Chapter 3 of this work contains a discussion of short-time working.
53 J.O. Ch., 12 February 1932, pp. 620–1. The hiccup which took place in the

number of *chômeurs secourus* in July 1932 was due simply to a decree of 24 June which enabled the unemployed to continue to receive unemployment relief at the end of 180 days instead of having to apply to *bureaux de bienfaisance*.

54  Letellier *et al.*, *Enquête sur le chômage*, Vol. 1, p. 38.
55  Ibid., p. 119.
56  De Tastes, J.O. Ch., 13 November 1931, p. 3853. See also Taittinger, J.O. Ch., 13 November 1931, p. 3850; Taudière, J.O. Ch., 17 November 1931, p. 3884.
57  For a critique of the so-called Rueff law, and a discussion of the controversy it caused, see N. Parsiades, *Essai sur les relations entre le chômage, les prix et le profit: étude critique de la loi de M. Rueff* (1949).
58  For example, the maximum sum which unemployment funds could pay was raised to 7 F. a day (decree of 13 February 1931); the percentage of the state subsidy was raised to reach a possible maximum of 90 per cent (25 February 1931; 31 December 1931). Details of these and other measures in the Report on the 1933 Labour Budget: J.O. Doc. C. 1932 No. 5834.
59  On the subject of French commercial policy see: F. Haight, *French Import Quotas: A New Instrument of Commercial Policy* (1935); J. Perthuis de la Salle, *La Politique française du contingement* (1935). There is a short survey of French inter-war commercial policy by A. Hirsch, 'La Politique commerciale', in Sauvy, *Histoire économique*, Vol. 4, pp. 9–48.
60  Saly, *La Politique*, pp. 315–29.
61  J.O. Doc. C. 1930, No. 3388.
62  J.O. Ch., 8 July 1930, p. 2989.
63  J.O. Ch., 22 January 1931, p. 214.
64  J.O. Ch., 17 January 1931, p. 89.
65  J.O. Doc. C. 1931, No. 5523.
66  J.O. Doc. Admin., 13 December 1931, p. 1431.
67  Lamoureux's report in J.O. Doc. C. 1931, No. 5657; see also J.O. Ch., 24 November 1931, pp. 4014–16.
68  Daladier Papers I DA 2 Dr 1. sdra.
69  And, in its report at the beginning of 1931, the C.N.E. wrote, in envisaging a policy of public works to fight unemployment, that the situation was different from the brief slump of 1926–7 when the dominant problem was the franc; 1931 was different owing to the large reserves of the Treasury. But by the end of 1931 this optimism was quite outdated.
70  For example, Piétri, budget minister, in J.O. Ch., 11 February 1932, p. 592.
71  J.O. Sen., 24 March 1932, p. 481.
72  de Lastyrie in J.O. Ch., 11 February 1932, p. 583.
73  Auriol, J.O. Ch., 9 February 1932, p. 538: there was only 'one way to save oneself from this crisis: carry out a deflation of military expenditure'.
74  For example, De Monzie, J.O. Ch., 11 February 1932, p. 590.
75  J.O. Ch., 11 February 1932, p. 582.
76  Louis Aubert *et al.*, *André Tardieu* (1957), pp. 86–7.
77  Binion, *Defeated Leaders*, p. 299.
78  A. Tardieu, *La Révolution à refaire*, Vol. 1, *Le Souverain captif* (1937), p. 15; A. Prost, *Les Anciens combattants et la société française* (1977), Vol. 1, p. 129 shows how Tardieu was forced to accept a pension for the war veterans that was more generous than he had wanted.
79  H. Dubief, *Le Déclin de la Troisième République* (1976), p. 17.
80  Kuisel, *Capitalism and the State*, pp. 90–2. For an expression of this interventionist philosophy see François-Poncet's address to the C.N.E., 5 November 1930 in Tardieu's paper A.N. 324 A.P. 48.

81 Chautemps pointed to the 'paradox of a cabinet carrying out a social policy with a minister who is insulted by the very newspapers who are the main supporters of the government to which he belongs'. J.O. Ch., 7 February 1930, p. 565.

82 H. Hatzfeld, *Du Paupérisme à la sécurité sociale* (1971), pp. 138–40, 152–7.

83 Ibid., p. 35. See also the similar observation of F. Goguel, in *La Politique des partis sous la Troisième République* (1946), pp. 388–9.

84 J.O. Ch., 9 June 1931, p. 2895.

## 3 Programmes of the left

1 Pierre Rossillion, *La Nation*, 27 February 1932. He was the paper's financial columnist and director; unless otherwise stated all references to *La Nation* will be to his articles.

2 10 August 1932.

3 J. Moch, *Rencontres avec Léon Blum* (1970), p. 65.

4 Quoted in Ziebura, *Léon Blum*, p. 193.

5 M. Marjolin has been kind enough to show me a draft of the memoirs which he is at present writing, and to which I am indebted for this information.

6 The quotations come from the typescript of a lecture by Blum, probably given in early 1933, contained in the Roche–Caillaux Papers, E.R.J.C. Dr 1.

7 *Le Populaire*, 2 April 1935.

8 R. Belin, *Du Secrétariat de la C.G.T. au gouvernement de Vichy* (1978), p. 103. Raymond Bouyer, also of the C.G.T., wrote rather cavalierly that 'adapting to the 40 hours is . . . possible; as for how to do so, the employers will find the means if they are forced', *Le Populaire*, 30 September 1932. Both quotations are from C.G.T. members; but the S.F.I.O. was, if anything, even more casual about the issue.

9 André Philip, *Henri de Man et la crise doctrinale du socialisme* (1928), p. 28; B. Montagnon, *Grandeurs et servitudes socialistes* (1929), p. 171, spoke of a party reformist in practice and revolutionary in talk.

10 Montagnon, *Grandeurs*, p. 171.

11 Ibid., p. 66.

12 Philip, *Henri de Man*, pp. 34–44.

13 *Socialisme et rationalisation* (1927), p. 58. Even if a crisis was possible, he saw it as 'infinitely remote', p. 111.

14 *Grandeurs*, pp. 57–64.

15 *Perspectives socialistes* (1930), pp. 102–3, 107.

16 See his preface to Moch, *Socialisme et rationalisation*, pp. i–viii.

17 Gabriel Lafaye wrote, in *Le Populaire*, 20 January 1931, of the need 'to avoid pessimism . . . to recognize that the French market has an elasticity allowing it to absorb the impact of all kinds of shocks'.

18 L. Blum, *Le Socialisme devant la crise* (1933), p. 17.

19 C. Spinasse, *La Crise économique* (1931), p. 15; J. Moch, *Socialisme, crise, nationalisations* (1932), p. 17; Blum, *Le Socialisme*, p. 13; Lucien Laurat, *La Liquidation socialiste de la crise* (1934), pp. 18–19.

20 Laurat, *La Liquidation*, p. 24. L. Blum, *Le Socialisme à vu clair* (1936), p. 28.

21 Blum, *Le Populaire*, 29 December 1932.

22 Laurat, *La Liquidation*, p. 24; Spinasse, *La Crise économique*, p. 9.

23 Blum, *Le Socialisme à vu clair*, pp. 17–18.

24 On underconsumptionist doctrines in this period see T. Markovitch, *Les Théories modernes de sous-consommation* (1938).

25 *Le Populaire*, 5 October 1933. But Blum's enthusiasm for the New Deal was

considerable: William Bullitt, American ambassador in Paris, described how on hearing of Roosevelt's re-election in 1936, Blum 'seized me and kissed me violently . . . I listened without batting an eye to as genuine an outpouring of enthusiasm as I have ever heard . . . Blum himself said to me that he felt his position had been greatly strengthened because he is attempting in his way to do what you have done in America'. Quoted by J. Colton in 'Politics and Economics in the 1930s: the Balance Sheet of the "Blum New Deal" ', in C. K. Warner, ed., *From the Ancien Régime to the Popular Front* (1969), p. 181.

26  For example, Rosenfeld, *Le Populaire*, 23 July 1932.
27  See the evolution of Marjolin's views, *Le Populaire*, 16 November 1933; 24 February 1935; 15 December 1935; 22 December 1935; 4 January 1936.
28  Blum, *Le Populaire*, 7 October 1933.
29  Blum, *Le Populaire*, 6 July 1935.
30  T. Judt, *La Reconstruction du Parti Socialiste* (1976), pp. 71–8.
31  See L. Lévy, *Comment ils sont devenus Socialistes* (1932).
32  Besides *La Liquidation*, see his *Un Système qui sombre* (1932); *Le Socialisme à l'ordre du jour: problèmes et tâches du marxisme contemporain* (1933); *La Crise mondiale* (1935); *Economie dirigée et socialisation* (1932). He had in fact written a book on Luxemburg: *L'Accumulation du capital d'après Rosa Luxembourg* (1930). Markovitch, *Les Théories*, pp. 74–94, has a section on Laurat. He writes: 'he is the most fertile of the French writers in this group [under-consumptionists]. He is also the only one to have made any really original contributions to the doctrine'.
33  Blum, *Le Socialisme à vu clair*, p. 15. The crisis was, then, linked to the 'fundamental contradictions' of the capitalist system: Blum, *Le Socialisme*, p. 15; also Moch, *Socialisme*, p. 19.
34  C.R.C.S. 1934, pp. 170–2. He thought it was possible that 'we see the crisis as deeper than it really is', *Lettres à Brigitte: le Parti Socialiste, ses principes et ses tâches* (1933), p. 133.
35  Moch, *Socialisme*, p. 18; Blum, *Le Socialisme*, p. 18.
36  C.R.C.S. 1934, p. 270.
37  P. Faure, *Au Seuil d'une révolution* (1934), p. 128.
38  Blum, *Le Populaire*, 18 January 1933. The policy was, then, one of 'palliatives not remedies': Moch, *Socialisme*, p. 50.
39  *Le Populaire*, 31 January 1932.
40  Moch, *Arguments et documents contre le capitalisme, crise, déflation* (1936), p. 89.
41  Marjolin, *Le Populaire*, 3 March 1935.
42  Marjolin, *Le Populaire*, 5 May 1935.
43  Marjolin, *Le Populaire*, 26 June 1935. This is a case where the example of the New Deal modified Socialist views and led them to give public works a more important role: Marjolin, *Le Populaire*, 4 January 1936.
44  Moch, *Socialisme*, p. 50.
45  *Programme du Parti Socialiste* (S.F.I.O.), (1932), p. 6.
46  See below, pp. 114–15.
47  For many this was the most important part of the policy. See Lebas, *Le Populaire*, 27 September 1932.
48  R.E.P. 1932, p. 148.
49  M. Margairaz, 'Les Propositions de politique économique, financière, et monétaire de la S.F.I.O. de 1934 à 1936' (memoir, University of Paris–VIII (1972), p. 130).

50  Blum gave the figure of 40 hours at the conference in January 1932; it was included in the election manifesto; mentioned by Faure, *Au Seuil d'une révolution*, p. 218; and by Lebas, *Le Populaire*, 27 September 1932; 28 February 1933.

51  Blum, *Le Socialisme*, p. 18.

52  Ibid.; Faure, *Au Seuil d'une révolution*, p. 28. But Duboin's views were not approved by the Socialists: Lebas, *Le Populaire*, 2 March 1934; Faure, *Le Populaire*, 16 November 1934. J. Neré, *La Crise de 1929* (1969), has suggested that for the C.G.T. the 40-hour week was primarily a measure of redistribution, and for the Socialists part of the purchasing power policy: the truth seems to be that both attitudes existed in both organizations.

53  Blum, *Le Populaire*, 29 December 1932; 2 January 1933. As J.-M. Jeanneney has pointed out in 'La Politique économique de Léon Blum', R. Rémond and P. Renouvin, eds., *Léon Blum chef de gouvernement 1936–1937* (1967), p. 230, the Socialists in fact had no idea how important labour was as a factor of production, but their estimates were certainly below the truth; see also Sauvy, *Histoire économique*, Vol. 2, pp. 194–6.

54  Blum, *Le Populaire*, 2 April 1934; or 2 March 1934.

55  Blum, *Le Populaire*, 3 July 1935; also 16 November 1934.

56  J.O. Ch., 8 December 1933, p. 4493.

57  *Le Populaire*, 16 December 1930.

58  Serge Wolikow talks discreetly of the 'discrepancy between the Party's writings and its real activity', 'Le P.C.F. devant la crise 1929–1932', C.H.I.M.T., 39 (1975). I have found this article very useful apart from the fact that Wolikow is concerned, albeit in a sophisticated way, to justify the line ultimately pursued under Thorez: thus he tries to portray the *tournant* of 1930–1, carried out under the aegis of Thorez, as a transformation from a crude and mechanistic to a more realistic analysis of the crisis, permitting an effective policy of mass popular appeal. But this *tournant* was in fact a paltry, almost imperceptible, affair (at the level of policy, that is), by comparison with that of 1934.

59  Extracts from the Tenth Plenum of the E.C.C.I., J. Degras, ed., *The Communist International 1919–1943. Documents*, Vol. 3, *1929–43* (1965), p. 42. This prediction of an imminent economic crisis made only a little before the onset of the Depression was less prescient than at first appears: the Comintern had done no more than express some very general ideas about the end of capitalist stabilization which were all part of the Soviet Party's strategy of an attack on the supposedly right-wing tendencies of Bukharin and others.

60  Resolution of the enlarged E.C.C.I. Presidium, February 1930, in Degras, ed., *The Communist International*, p. 107.

61  Manuilski, *Les Partis communistes et la crise du capitalisme*. Report to the Tenth Assembly of the Executive Committee of the Comintern, p. 46. See also his intervention at the Eleventh Plenum, reproduced in *Les Partis communistes et la crise du capitalisme* (1931).

62  See S. Wolikow, 'Economie et société: l'analyse et la pratique du P.C.F.', C.H.I.M.T., 38 (1974), pp. 22–54.

63  *L'Humanité*, 23 July 1930. Reproduced in *Oeuvres du Maurice Thorez*, II, pp. 57–60; also his intervention to the Central Committee, Ibid., pp. 44–56. For an account of these events, P. Robrieux, *Maurice Thorez: vie secrète et vie publique* (1975), pp. 120–33.

64  See *Le Parti communiste devant l'Internationale* (1931).

65  Ibid.; see also M. Thorez, *La Situation en France et l'action communiste*.

*Rapport au Comité central sur les travaux du XI<sup>e</sup> assemblée plenière du Comité exécutif de l'Internationale* (1931). Also reproduced in *Oeuvres*, II, pp. 9–82. (My references are to the original pamphlet.)

66  The best account of this affair is J.-P. Brunet, 'Une Crise au Parti communiste français: l'affaire Barbé–Célor'. *Revue d'histoire moderne et contemporaine*, 16 (July–Sept. 1969), pp. 438–61.

67  See Serret in *Les Cahiers du bolchévisme*, April 1932, 'Sur le caractère et l'issue de la crise'; and Gitton's reply is in Ibid., March 1931.

68  Thorez, ibid., April 1932.

69  For example, to Lachatte's article in ibid., April 1931.

70  Payot, ibid., February 1930, March 1931; Thorez, *En avant pour l'issue révolutionnaire de la crise* (1932), p. 51. This pamphlet was his report to the Seventh Congress of the P.C.F. in March 1932; it is reproduced in *Oeuvres*, II. (My references are to the original.)

71  For example the article on textiles in *Les Cahiers*, March 1931.

72  Wolikow, 'Le P.C.F. devant la crise 1929–1932', p. 65.

73  Bernier, *Les Cahiers*, September 1930.

74  Berlioz, ibid., April 1931.

75  Vassart, ibid., February 1931.

76  Berlioz, ibid., April 1931; Thorez, *Oeuvres* II 1, p. 132.

77  Serret, *Les Cahiers*, February 1931; also Lenoir, ibid., 15 January 1933; Vassart, ibid., March 1931.

78  Payot, ibid., March 1931.

79  Thorez, *Oeuvres* II 1, p. 144.

80  Ibid., p. 145.

81  Vassart, *Les Cahiers*, March 1931.

82  Kuusinen, ibid., July 1933.

83  Thorez, *En Avant*, p. 71.

84  Payot, *Les Cahiers*, March 1931.

85  Lenoir, ibid., 1 February 1932.

86  Thorez, *En Avant*, p. 71.

87  *Les Cahiers*, July 1933.

88  Thorez, *La Situation*, p. 76.

89  Constant, *Les Cahiers*, July 1933.

90  Thorez, *La Situation*, pp. 73–4.

91  R. Bourderon *et al.*, *Le P.C.F. étapes et problèmes* (1981), pp. 65–6. The quotation comes from D. Tartakowsky's contribution, 'Le "Tournant" des années trente'.

92  Tartakowsky can only provide as evidence the fact that the membership of the Party increased 'slightly' before the famous National Congress at Ivry in 1934. Ibid., p. 72. Wolikow, in his contribution in the same volume, 'Le P.C.F. et le Front Populaire', is even less helpful: the P.C.F. and the C.G.T.U. showed 'a certain dynamism . . . a new influence, even if this wasn't immediately reflected in figures', p. 117; also p. 129. Once again one feels that an apologia is being written.

93  See, for example, the differing reactions of the C.G.T. and the C.G.T.U. to the wage cuts at the rubber factory at Halluin in the Nord: A.N. F.<sup>7</sup> 13008, reports of January 1932.

94  Ibid., report of 31 January 1932.

95  J.-P. Brunet, *St Denis: La ville rouge* (1980), p. 291.

96 On the *journée* of 21 February 1931, see A.N. F.[7] 13531–2.
97 O. Piatinski, *Le Chômage et la crise: précisons nos tâches!* (1931), p. 59.
98 A.N. F.[7] 13565, report of 10 August 1931 (on the *journée* planned for 16 September 1931).
99 See the reports on this subject scattered in A.N. F.[7] 13030–9. But Brunet, *St. Denis*, pp. 292–5, claims that in St Denis after 1931 the Communist-inspired protests of the unemployed were slightly more successful. Perhaps Doriot's influence played a part here.
100 In fact the Algerians were, after their protests, allowed to join the committee anyway. For another example of the actual subservience of the committees to the P.C.F. see A.N. F.[7] 13550, report of 29 January 1932, telling how the committee of the 18th *arrondissement* put up a poster attaching the dissident *pupiste* party.
101 For the preceding account of the situation in the Seine see A.N. F.[7] 13550, reports of 9 January, 31 January, 15 March, 18 March, 20 February, 24 February 1933. See also A.N. F.[7] 13131, reports of 19, 26 January 1933, on the continuing weakness of the Communist attempts to organize the unemployed in the Paris region.
102 Brunet, *St Denis*, pp. 348–52.
103 A.N. F.[7] 13565 is devoted to hunger marches.
104 J. Duclos, 'Rapports devant l'Internationale communiste', C.H.I.M.T., 1975, p. 298. This issue of C.H.I.M.T. published two previously unpublished reports by Duclos, with an introduction by S. Wolikow.
105 See the editorial in *Les Cahiers*, 15 September 1931.
106 *En Avant*, p. 113.
107 C.R.C.R. 1934 (May), p. 110; C.R.C.R. (October), pp. 358–63.
108 A. Bayet, *Le Radicalisme* (1932), pp. 49–53.
109 C.R.C.R. 1932, p. 53; see also C.R.C.R. 1934 (May), p. 65.
110 Bayet, *Le Radicalisme*, pp. 11, 21, 35.
111 Daladier, C.R.C.R. 1931, p. 43.
112 Cavalier, C.R.C.R. 1934 (May), p. 95.
113 Mendès-France, C.R.C.R. 1932, p. 192.
114 For example by Gilles, C.R.C.R. 1934 (May), p. 85; Clerc, ibid., p. 83.
115 For example Cornu, C.R.C.R. 1934 (October), p. 34.
116 Bayet, *Le Radicalisme*, pp. 64–9; Brachard, C.R.C.R. 1934 (October), p. 171.
117 On the Young Radicals see M. Schlesinger, 'The Development of the Radical Party in the Third Republic: the New Radical Movement 1926–32', *Journal of Modern History*, 46, 3 (Sept. 1974), pp. 476–501; A. Werth, 'Le Mouvement "Jeunes Turcs": Phenomène radical d'entre les deux guerres', *Les Cahiers de la République* 2 (1956), pp. 100–5, and S. Berstein, *Histoire du Parti radica! II: Crise du radicalisme 1926–1939* (1982), pp. 94–125. This is now the standard work on the Radical Party between the wars.
118 Déat drew on studies by Sauger and de Jouvenel in *Perspectives*, pp. 114–15.
119 Ibid., pp. 84–5; Montagnon, *Grandeur et servitude socialistes*, pp. 162–6.
120 *L'Economie dirigée* (1928), pp. 29–36. He analysed the attempts of American employers to create a solidarity between themselves and their employees.
121 Ibid., p. 108.
122 J. Kayser, 'Le Radicalisme des radicaux', in G. Michaud, ed., *Tendances politiques dans la vie française depuis 1789* (1960), p. 83.
123 C.R.C.R. 1931, p. 255.
124 C.R.C.R. 1934 (May), p. 88.

125  Palmade, C.R.C.R. 1931, p. 144.
126  For example, Clerc, ibid., p. 246; Bonnet, C.R.C.R. 1932, p. 152.
127  Delbos, ibid., p. 34.


4  **From *le 8 Mai* to *le 6 Février***

 1  Du Clain, *La Lumière*, 7 May 1932. (This was the pseudonym of François Albert
    and, later, Georges Gombault.)
 2  Ibid., 2 July 1932.
 3  Report in *Le Populaire*, 31 January 1932.
 4  *L'Oeuvre*, 8 April 1932.
 5  *Barodet*, 1932, Simon (Démocrate Populaire), Finistère; Niel (Action Paysanne),
    Aveyron.
 6  Ibid., Poillot (Gauche Radicale), Côte d'Or.
 7  Ibid., Médécin (Independant de Gauche), Alpes Maritimes.
 8  Ibid., Simon.
 9  Ibid., Le Mire (U.R.D.), Eure.
10  Ibid., Médécin.
11  Ibid., Blaisot (U.R.D.), Calvados.
12  Berstein, *Histoire du Parti Radical* II, p. 201.
13  These four were the two Communists – Midol and Péri – the centre-left deputy,
    Raymond Patenôtre, and the conservative, Patenôtre-Desnoyers.
14  Bonnefous and Reibel.
15  *Barodet*, 1932, Clerc (Radical), Hte Savoie.
16  Ibid., Lissar (U.R.D.), Basses Pyrénées.
17  Ibid., Riche (Gauche Radicale), Ardennes.
18  Ibid., Lissar.
19  *Le Temps*, 15 April 1932. Report of a speech by Reynaud.
20  Blum, *Le Populaire*, 16 April 1932.
21  Blum, *Le Populaire*, 9 April 1932; Boris, *La Lumière*, 9 April 1932 ('Bilan
    budgetaire des Droites'); speech by Caillaux reported in *Le Temps*, 24 April
    1932.
22  Report of speech in *Le Temps*, 15 April 1932; see the strong reaction from Blum,
    *Le Populaire*, 16 April 1932.
23  Speeches reported in *Le Temps*, 18 April 1932.
24  Report of speech at La Tour du Pin in *Le Temps*, 19 April 1932.
25  See his declaration to the newspaper *Le Progrès* in *Le Temps*, 30 April 1932.
26  *L'Oeuvre*, 18 April 1932.
27  Boris, *La Lumière*, 9 April 1932 ('Pour lutter contre la crise').
28  *L'Oeuvre*, 12 April 1932; also *L'Oeuvre*, 4 May 1932: electoral unity 'in no way
    prejudices decisions to be taken in the future'.
29  As with the governments of Steeg (December 1930) and Chautemps (February
    1930).
30  Speech at Narbonne reported in *Le Populaire*, 11 April 1932; also his article in
    *Le Populaire*, 16 May 1932.
31  Auriol, C.R.C.S. 1932, p. 121; also Grignon, ibid., p. 41; Kahn, ibid., p. 62.
32  Hauck, ibid., p. 50; Varenne, ibid., p. 70. Such remarks, coming from known
    participationists, were not disinterested.
33  Ibid., pp. 170–6.
34  Exceptions were Farinet, ibid., pp. 32–7; Pivert, pp. 89–90.

35  For example, Faure, ibid., p. 207, who said of his proposals: 'I think they will be refused'; Lebas, ibid., pp. 105–12.

36  Among the most exigent see Lebas, ibid., pp. 105–12; among the least see Kahn, ibid., pp. 60–6.

37  *Le Populaire*, 4–12 May 1932.

38  C.R.C.S. 1932, p. 216.

39  Ibid., pp. 220–3. Blum had been against this.

40  The text of the communiqué is in Herriot, *Jadis* II, pp. 298–300.

41  C.R.C.S. 1932, pp. 284–6.

42  Kahn, ibid., pp. 77–8; Hauck, ibid., pp. 48–53; Varenne, ibid., p. 204.

43  Herriot, *Jadis* II, pp. 294–5; Du Clain, *La Lumière*, 4 June 1932; L. Germain-Martin, *Le Problème financier* (1936), p. 103.

44  Herriot, *Jadis* II, pp. 292–4.

45  Larmour, *The French Radical Party*, pp. 112–14; Berstein, *Histoire du Parti radical* II, pp. 213–18.

46  P.V.C., 4 July 1932.

47  C.R.C.S. 1932, p. 189; Herriot, *Jadis* II, p. 292.

48  On Herriot's motives see Larmour, *The French Radical Party*, pp. 113–18 and Berstein, *Histoire du Parti radical* II, pp. 218–19.

49  For general biographical details on Germain-Martin, see his unpublished 'Contribution à l'histoire nationale de la France 1890–1945' (3 vols.). For his views on the economic and financial situation see his article in *Capital*, 18 February 1932 (conserved in Herriot's papers) or his *Les Problèmes actuels des finances publiques en France* (1933).

50  Germain-Martin, 'Contribution', Vol. 2, p. 29; Berstein, *Histoire du Parti radical* II, p. 217.

51  Herriot Papers, Dossier 22, letter of 5 June 1932.

52  Boris, *La Lumière*, 18 June 1932; Herriot, *Jadis* II, pp. 314–15.

53  'A first step down the path of a stabilization at the expense of the workers', Berlioz, *L'Humanité*, 3 July 1932; see also *Le Populaire*, 1 April 1932; Boris, *La Lumière*, 2 July 1932.

54  *Le Populaire*, 1 October 1932.

55  J. Lhomme, 'Le Pouvoir d'achat de l'ouvrier français au cours d'un siècle: 1840–1940', *Le Mouvement social* 63 (April–June 1968), pp. 41–69. All such estimates are necessarily approximate because figures of wage levels existed only for certain sectors; see also the estimates of Sauvy, *Histoire économique*, Vol. 2, pp. 403–7; and Letellier *et al.*, *Enquête sur le chômage*, Vol. 1, Chapter 4, which contains a general discussion of the available statistics on wages.

56  Sauvy, *Histoire économique*, Vol. 2, pp. 83, 100–1.

57  A.N. F.´ 13038: report of 10 March 1933; see also A.N. F.´ 13030, Montluçon, 1 February 1933.

58  For example, *Le Temps*, 13 May 1932.

59  The bill is J.O. Doc. C. 1932, No. 336; Lamoureux's report is J.O. Doc. C. 1932, No. 379. The original bill contained economies of 2.6m F. and tax increases of 1.5m F.

60  M.F. B. 33 190, Nos. 91 and 95: notes of 30 May, 24 June 1932 on the state of the Treasury.

61  Palmade, P.V.C., First Sitting, 2 July 1932.

62  J.O. Ch., 11 July 1932, p. 2529.

63  Talking privately to the Senate Commission, Germain-Martin made no mention of such a programme. P.V.S., 12 July 1932.

64  C.R.C.R. 1932, p. 34.
65  *La Lumière*, 16 July 1932; the same argument was put by the Radical, Henri Clerc, *L'Oeuvre*, 22 January 1933.
66  P.V.C., 2 July 1932. The Commission abolished a five per cent reduction in allowances of *fonctionnaires*.
67  P.V.S., 12 July 1932.
68  Bedouce, P.V.C., 4 July 1932; du Clain, *La Lumière*, 9 July 1932.
69  J.O. Ch., 11 July 1932, pp. 2586–8.
70  *Le Temps*, 21 April 1932.
71  Du Clain, *La Lumière*, 11 June 1932; on these divisions of the right, see Piétri, in Aubert *et al.*, *André Tardieu*, pp. 100–1. The tactic was not without success: Gaston Palewski wrote to Reynaud on 29 August that there would be nothing to gain from a ministerial crisis since 'Flandin had persuaded the disciples of the scheme [concentration], that it would be enough to take him, and exclude the Centre Républicain': Reynaud papers, A.N. 74 A.P. 20.
72  P.V.S., 12 and 13 July 1932; Du Clain, *La Lumière*, 23 July 1932.
73  J.O. Ch., 1 July 1932, p. 2588.
74  Du Clain, *La Lumière*, 23 July 1932; *L'Oeuvre*, 17 July 1932.
75  J.O. Doc. C. 1932, No. 575.
76  *Le Populaire*, 20 October 1932.
77  *Le Populaire*, 21 October 1932.
78  Bonnet was an example of the former, Caillaux of the latter: Larmour, *The French Radical Party*, pp. 118; 122; 288–9.
79  For example André, C.R.C.R. 1932, p. 22; Mendès-France, ibid., p. 166.
80  Bergery, ibid., p. 82.
81  Bergery, ibid., pp. 82–5; Mendès-France, ibid., pp. 186–92; Bonnaure, ibid., p. 207.
82  C.R.C.R. 1932, pp. 229–30.
83  The budget is J.O. Doc. C. 1932, No. 575 (it involved a reduction in the pay of *fonctionnaires* earning over 10,000 F.); the public spending bill is J.O. Doc. C. 1932, No. 771 (the 'exceptional' expenditure was spread over two years).
84  M.F. B. 33 190, Nos. 105, 106 bis: notes of 9 October, 8 November 1932.
85  His report is J.O. Doc. C. 1932, No. 926; see also his exposé, P.V.C., 15 November 1932. His criticisms were not exempt from partiality since he was preparing for the future by taking the lead of the orthodox Radicals: Du Clain, *La Lumière*, 17 December 1932; but Saly, *La Politique des grands travaux en France*, p. 334, shows that they were quite accurate.
86  P.V.C., 17 and 18 November 1932. Also criticisms by the Radicals Deyris, Lassalle, Jaubert.
87  P.V.C., 19 November 1932. The government's promise was obviously meaningless.
88  P.V.S., 9 November 1932.
89  Boris, *La Lumière*, 25 May 1932; de Jouvenel, *La République*, 2 February 1933.
90  *Le Populaire*, 27 December 1932.
91  J.O. Doc. C. 1932, No. 744.
92  J.O. Ch., 17 November 1932, p. 3089.
93  R.E.P. 1933, pp. 615–16; 835–50.
94  Ibid., pp. 594–5. All economic indicators for December 1932 nonetheless showed a decline over December 1931 (itself down on December 1930).
95  Blum, *Le Populaire*, 24 December 1932; Du Clain, *La Lumière*, 31 December 1932.

96 J. Paul-Boncour, *Entre deux guerres. Souvenirs sur la IIIᵉ République* (1945), Vol. 2, pp. 274–6.
97 The bill was J.O. Doc. C. 1933, No. 1261.
98 For mention of the recovery see Chéron, J.O. Ch., 26 January 1933, p. 268. Sauvy, *Histoire économique*, Vol. 2, pp. 38–9, is wrong to say that it passed unnoticed.
99 See appendix, pp. 224–5.
100 *Le Temps*, 9 January 1933.
101 J.O. Ch., 26 January 1933, p. 270 (the figure of 48m F. included Bons de la Défense Nationale). Between June 1926 and December 1930 the ratio of the floating debt to the total national debt had been reduced from 33 per cent to 13 per cent.
102 Auriol, *Le Populaire*, 12–14 November 1933. The Socialist bill was J.O. Doc. C. 1933, No. 1258. It also proposed the nationalization of insurance companies and hiving off of expenditure on war pensions to the *Caisse d'Amortissement*.
103 The right, playing the *politique du pire* and opposing the tax increases, also contributed to destroying the bill. Larmour's analysis in *The French Radical Party*, pp. 127–8, is generally good.
104 P.V.C., 23 January 1933; *L'Oeuvre*, 28 January 1933.
105 *Mémoires d'un instituteur syndicaliste* (1979), pp. 178; 186–95.
106 Paul-Boncour, J.O. Ch., 27 January 1933, p. 356; Taittinger, a few weeks later, appealed to everyone to 'make his public *mea culpa*', J.O. Ch., 11 February 1933, p. 572; also Caillaux, J.O. Sen., 18 February 1933, p. 201.
107 *The French Radical Party*, p. 125.
108 Du Clain, *La Lumière*, 14 January 1933.
109 See Déat's account, *Le Populaire*, 4 February 1933.
110 Ibid., 1 February 1933.
111 Larmour, *The French Radical Party*, pp. 127–30; Berstein, *Histoire du Parti Radical II*, pp. 256–7. The post of Finance Minister had been offered to the conservative Bonnet while negotiations were still supposedly going on with the Socialists.
112 *La République*, 2 February 1933; Bayet, *La République*, 31 January 1933.
113 On the Fédération Nationale des Contribuables see W. A. Hoisington, 'Toward the Sixth of February: Taxpayer Protest in France, 1928–1934', *Historical Reflections* 3, 1 (1976), pp. 49–67. Information about the Comité is more scarce: see P. Nicolle in *Comité de salut économique. Rapport de la commission permanente* (1934); P. Nicolle, *Pour nettoyer les écuries* (1934). Accounts of the activities of these organizations can be found scattered throughout A.N. F.[7] 13030–40.
114 Bonnet, P.V.C., 9 March 1933; Note on the 'Politique financière et économique du gouvernement au cours de l'année 1933' in Daladier Papers I D.A. 3 Dr 3 sdrb; and G. Bonnet, *Vingt ans de vie politique 1918–1938: De Clemenceau à Daladier* (1969), pp. 156–7; details on the Dutch loan: M.F. B. 33 191, No. 31: note of 15 February 1933.
115 P.V.C., 1 July 1933. On the state and estimated needs of the Treasury: M.F. B. 33 191, Nos. 23, 46 bis, 47.
116 M.F. B. 33 191, No. 6: note of 25 January 1933. There were also small exports of gold.
117 Bonnet gave details of these negotiations with Moret, J.O. Ch., 25 January 1935, pp. 213–15, during the vote on Flandin's credit policy.
118 Auriol, P.V.C., 18 January 1933; 17 May 1933; *La Lumière*, 25 March 1933.

119  Bonnet, P.V.C., 7 March 1933; 1 July 1933.
120  P.V.S., 9 March 1933.
121  Lamoureux, P.V.C., 7 February 1933.
122  See the government's letter in Jacquier's report on the budget: J.O. Doc. C. 1933, No. 1534.
123  Lamoureux, P.V.C., 15 April 1933, said that it was 'politically impossible' to balance the budget in 1933; but he also told the Senate that the moment when it must be balanced could not be long-delayed: J.O. Sen., 13 May 1933, p. 1061.
124  Lamoureux, J.O. Sen., 13 May 1933, p. 1077.
125  Blancho, J.O. Ch., 25 February 1933, p. 1019.
126  *L'Humanité* kept up a constant stream of criticisms denouncing the Socialists' *'politique de trahison'*: for example Ferrat, ibid., 2 May 1933.
127  This was a compromise because the Senate's original draft had hit all *fonctionnaires* earning above 9,000 F.
128  See J.O. Doc. S. 1933, No. 51; P.V.S., 15 and 16 February 1933; J.O. Sen., 22 February 1933, pp. 307–10.
129  Jacquier's report on the budget is J.O. Doc. C. 1933, No. 1545; Roy's report for the Senate, J.O. Doc. S. 1933, No. 560. For a narrative of these events see Bonnefous, *Histoire politique de la Troisième République*, Vol. 5, pp. 151–8.
130  P.V.C., 1 July 1933.
131  Below, pp. 172–3.
132  P.V.C., 17 October 1933.
133  P.V.C., 15 May, 27 June, 1 July 1933.
134  The most important previous bill was J.O. Doc. C. 1932, No. 993.
135  For example Triballet J.O. Ch., 23 June 1933, p. 3077.
136  J.O. Doc. C. 1933, No. 1797. On the complex legislation regulating the wheat market see J. Sirol, *Les Problèmes français du blé* (1934); G. Damougeot-Perron, *La Crise du blé en France et dans le monde* (1935) (hostile to regulation).
137  Provost-Dumarchais, J.O. Sen., 24 May 1933, p. 1421.
138  J.O. Sen., 27 May 1933, p. 1474.
139  J.O. Ch., 23 June 1933, p. 3081.
140  P.V.S., 24 June 1933.
141  *Le Populaire*, 25 June 1933.
142  J.O. Sen., 27 May 1933, p. 1471.
143  26 June 1933; or see *Le Temps*, 25 June 1933.
144  Daladier Papers 1 DA 2 Dr 1 sdrb. In his letter to Reynaud, Reynaud Papers A.N. 74 A.P. 20, Palewski suggested that the idea that Daladier might one day break with the Young Turks was considered possible in political circles.
145  *Le Populaire*, 21 March 1933; Larmour, *The French Radical Party*, p. 132 and Fn. 94, p. 279.
146  Daladier Papers, 1 DA 3 Dr 4 sdra.
147  Report in *Le Populaire*, 17–19 April 1933.
148  Ziebura, *Léon Blum et le Parti Socialiste 1872–1934* (1967), pp. 346–53.
149  Blum attributed it partly to the lack of a sufficiently flexible decision-making body between the C.A.P. and the Conseil National. C.R.C.S. 1933, pp. 359–60.
150  Blum, ibid., pp. 371–2.
151  For example, Reverbori, ibid., p. 261.
152  This was not the only time that such complaints were heard. In the syndicalist review *Homme réel* (February 1935, No. 14), *Le Populaire* was criticized for giving more space to Mme de Noailles (who had died in 1933) than to the pro-

letarian novelist Henri Poulaille. It was not always so easy to have been a friend of Proust and to be a leader of the French section of the Socialist International!

153  For example the Bas-Rhin Federation had moved its support from the Party to the Group since the Congress of Avignon because of the danger of precipitating the country into Union Nationale or fascism and war. C.R.C.S. 1933, pp. 280–5; also ibid., pp. 226–7.

154  Ibid., p. 151 (Renaudel).

155  Ibid., p. 244.

156  See below, p. 142.

157  C.R.C.S. 1933, pp. 193–7.

158  Ibid., pp. 269–74.

159  Ibid., pp. 294–5.

160  Ibid., pp. 303–4.

161  The Congress had been faced with three motions: the *Vie socialiste* motion (Renaudel) defending the Group (752 votes); a Centrist one (Auriol) condemning it in moderate terms (971); and the *Bataille socialiste* motion strongly condemning it (2177).

162  C.R.C.S. 1933, p. 340.

163  But not from as many as hitherto: several deputies, such as Blum and Auriol, had against their better judgement voted with the majority of the Group out of party discipline; if a split had occurred they would have been released from this obligation and thrown into opposition.

164  C.R.C.S. 1933, pp. 182–4.

165  For example, *Le Journal des débats*, 2 June 1933; *Le Temps*, 2 June 1933.

166  Respectively: Alliance Démocratique, *Un Programme d'action pour l'Alliance Démocratique* (1933), pp. 19–22; *La Nation*, 28 May 1933; *Le Temps*, 14 June 1933.

167  A.N. 74 A.P. 14. See also the letter from the Comité National de l'Entente Economique (which included Nicolle's Comité) asking if Reynaud was in favour of further budget cuts – and the accompanying note of warning: '*Mon cher ami*, I'm told you haven't replied to the C.N.E.E. . . . I think it would be advisable for a Paris deputy to answer in the affirmative.' As deputy for the 2nd *arrondissement* – a quarter of *commerçants* and cafés – Reynaud was particularly susceptible to such pressure.

168  P.R.O. T. 188/63: letter of 20 March (to Leith-Ross?).

169  M.F.B. 33 191, No. 66: note of 12 July 1933; also No. 71: note of 22 September (Escalier).

170  *Le Temps*, 31 July 1933 ('Après Londres').

171  17 June 1933; see also *Le Journal des débats*, 12 June 1933.

172  15 July 1933.

173  See 'Enquête sur le Congres Radical', *Le Temps*, 15 September 1933; Kayser and François Albert were also both neutralized, the former as a collaborator of Daladier, the latter as a minister. Larmour, *The French Radical Party*, p. 132.

174  C.R.C.R. 1933, pp. 244–7.

175  For example, Parouteau, ibid., p. 254; Sennac, ibid., p. 260; Willard, ibid., p. 269.

176  Ibid., p. 236. De Jouvenel had no illusions about the mood of the Congress: 'I have not tried to convince you, I have only wanted to warn you.' Ibid., p. 247.

177  Ibid., pp. 227–9.

178  Lamoureux, 'Mémoires', pp. 1305–6. Caillaux's impatience with Daladier's

delay in balancing the budget emerges also from his correspondence with Roche: Roche–Caillaux papers E.R. J.C. 9 Dr 1: Caillaux to Roche, 8 June 1933; Roche to Caillaux, 4 August 1933.

179  Not including the British loan.
180  P.V.C., 17 October 1933.
181  The bill was J.O. Doc. C. 1933, No. 2360.
182  J.O. Doc. C. 1933, No. 2406. See chart in Saly, *La Politique des grand travaux en France*, p. 556.
183  P.V.C., 17 October 1933.
184  But the bill also included various concessions to the left: a special contribution on the profits of petrol importing companies, control over arms manufacture.
185  J.O. Doc. C. 1933, No. 2435. (Jacquier's report on the bill.)
186  For the Commission's amendments see: J.O. Doc. C. 1933, No. 2435. In fact the Socialist position on deflation retained its ambiguity. Auriol declared that compromise might be possible 'if it were a question of an exceptional surtax, for everybody . . . in a spirit of republicanism': J.O. Ch., 23 October 1933, p. 3929.
187  Blum wrote of Daladier's 'calculated attack on the Party, his glacial anger . . . his insults': *Le Populaire*, 25 October 1933. A. Werth, *France in Ferment* (1934), pp. 66–70, describes the atmosphere well.
188  P.V.C., 17 November 1933. This, however, also included paying off the English loan.
189  M.F. B. 33 191, No. 78: note of 7 November 1933 (Baumgartner).
190  Auriol, J.O. Ch., 23 November 1933, p. 4243; Blum, *Le Populaire*, 30 November, 1 December 1933.
191  J.O. Doc. C. 1933, No. 2523.
192  P.V.C., 17 November 1933.
193  See Jacquier's report, J.O. Doc. C. 1933, No. 2555.
194  *Le Populaire*, 24 November 1933; for the Socialist *contre-projet*: J.O. Ch., 23 November 1933, p. 4242.
195  J.O. Ch., 8 December 1933, p. 4494.
196  *Le Populaire*, 13 December 1933.
197  P.V.S., 15 December 1933; J.O. Doc. S. 1933, no. 647.
198  17 December 1933.
199  'They are our brothers and we must defend them against themselves', *Le Temps*, 30 October 1933.
200  R.E.P. 1934, pp. 909–13.
201  See below, Chapter 8.
202  M.F. B. 33 190, No. 83: note of 22 November 1933 (addressed to Germain-Martin). The note, however, was concerned with devaluation as a financial measure – a means of solving the Treasury's problems – not with its economic effects.
203  R.E.P. 1934, p. 698; Régnier, P.V.S., 28 November 1933.
204  At least another 12 people died during the various demonstrations of the next week. See the report on the events of 6 February: J.O. Doc. C. 1934, No. 3383. See also S. Berstein, *Le 6 Février 1934* (1975).

## 5  Varieties of deflation 1934–1936

1  For example Déat, *L'Oeuvre*, 14 February 1934; Roche, C.R.C.R. May 1934, p. 47; J.O. Doc. C. 1934, No. 3383, p. 1348 (the report of the commission set up to examine the causes of the events of 6 February).

2   André Philip, C.R.C.S. 1934, p. 209.
3   *L'Oeuvre*, 12 May 1934, commented on the lack of interest shown by the Radical Congress of May 1934 in economic questions; Herriot, *Jadis II*, p. 427, noted the same.
4   For example Jenny, *Le Temps*, 1 January 1934. *The Economist*, 21 January 1934, commented that the 'necessity for diminishing the import surplus has become almost an obsession with most leading Frenchmen'.
5   C.R.C.R. May 1934, p. 171.
6   For example Herriot in *Jadis II*, pp. 377–8; see Berstein, *Histoire du Parti radical II*, pp. 286–7.
7   *Mes causeries avec le peuple français* (1934), p. 19.
8   See his *Les Problèmes actuels des finances publiques en France* (1933); *Sommes-nous sur bonne route?* (1934).
9   Herriot, *Jadis II*, p. 390.
10  The phrase is Herriot's, *Jadis II*, p. 397.
11  See J.O. Doc. C. 1933, No. 2784.
12  M.F. B. 192, Nos. 11, 14; notes of 6 and 15 February 1934; report by Germain-Martin, dated 18 March 1934, in the Tardieu papers, A.N. 324 A.P. 46.
13  Germain-Martin, *Bonne route?* (1934), pp. 251–2; Jenny, *Le Temps*, 12, 19 February 1934. Although it was tempting for the government to present the financial crisis as a result of the political situation, this was only partially true: on 31 January Roosevelt had announced a stabilization of the dollar at a level slightly lower than the market rate prevailing in Paris, and this permitted operations of arbitrage – speculation on the disparity between the two rates. The raising of the French bank rate from two and a half per cent to three per cent was not enough to prevent this operation remaining profitable.
14  P.V.C., 17 February 1934.
15  M.F. B. 33 192, No. 28: a report of the negotiations between the Bank and the banks at three meetings held at the Rue de Rivoli. For Germain-Martin's account, and the intervention of Mayer, see his 'Contribution', Vol. 2, pp. 98–100.
16  Herriot, *Jadis II*, p. 397.
17  Germain-Martin, *Bonne route?*, pp. 35; 38.
18  Government communiqué in *Le Temps*, 23 April 1934; Germain-Martin, P.V.C., 19 and 21 February 1934.
19  See the report introducing the decrees, *Le Temps*, 6 April 1934.
20  The bill is J.O. Doc. C. 1934, No. 3451; the Finance Commission report is J.O. Doc. C. 1934, No. 3633.
21  *La Nation*, 24 April 1934.
22  R. Pinon, *Revue des deux mondes*, 1 May 1934, p. 230; *La Nation*, 24 April 1934.
23  *L'Oeuvre*, 17 February 1934.
24  Ibid., 5 May 1934 under the signatures of Kayser, Sauger, Alléhaut, etc.
25  Published in *La République*, 14 April 1934, and later as a pamphlet (in modified form): *On a voté . . . et maintenant?* (1936). On the outmanoeuvring of the Young Radicals see: Berstein, *Histoire du Parti radical II*, pp. 300–8.
26  For example the comments of Alléhaut, C.R.C.R. May 1934, p. 61; Cavalier, ibid., p. 94 ('deference towards financial powers'); Secqueville, ibid., p. 89.
27  Also rejected was a third motion for the nationalization of the Bank of France proposed by Sennac, Cudenet and other members of the Seine Federation who left the Party in disgust.

28  C.R.C.R. May 1934, pp. 183–203.
29  *L'Oeuvre*, 9 February 1934.
30  J.O. Ch., 20 February 1934, p. 547; see also below, pp. 183–4, also Jacquier, J.O. Ch., 20 February 1934, p. 541; 27 May 1934, p. 1812.
31  *L'Oeuvre*, 14 May 1934.
32  C.R.C.R. May 1934, pp. 174–5. Only on its attitude to the Leagues did Daladier dare to criticize the government.
33  Blum, *Le Populaire*, 2 March 1934; 2, 5, 6, 8, 12 April 1934; 3, 9, 12, 13, 17, 18, 19 June 1934.
34  On the demonstrations of 12 February see A. Prost, 'Les Manifestations du 12 février 1934 en province', *Le Mouvement social* 54 (1966), pp. 7–27.
35  A.N. F.[7] 13029: Seine, reports of 23, 28 April; Seine-Inférieure, 12, 16 April; Haut-Rhin, 16 April. See also F.[7] 13025, Doubs, 9 April; 13027, Hte Marne, 23 April. (There is no reason to believe this was special pleading: the Prefects were, we will see, far from sanguine about the situation in the countryside.) The only exception to this picture was in the attitude of retired *fonctionnaires*, whose cause attracted more general support, and who, it was noted, were radicalized in a new way by cuts in their pensions: for example A.N. F.[7] 10327, Nièvre, 30 April; A.N. F.[7] 13026, Ile et Vilaine, 16 April. This discontent was slightly appeased by a decree of 10 May modifying the earlier decree affecting *retraités*.
36  *L'Humanité*, 29 April 1934.
37  For example A.N. F.[7] 13028 Seine-Inférieure, 5 May.
38  *Le Populaire*, 2 May 1934; *Les Cahiers du bolchévisme*, 15 May 1934.
39  The strikes of 12 February had been tacitly allowed by the government.
40  *Les Cahiers*, 15 June 1934.
41  *Jadis II*, p. 403.
42  Donon, *Rapporteur* of the Senate Agricultural Commission, J.O. Sen., 29 June 1934, p. 87.
43  J.O. Doc. C. 1934, No. 3196; ibid., No. 3834.
44  Germain-Martin, *Le Problème financier*, p. 276; P.V.C., 23 October 1934.
45  A.N. F.[7] 13026, Haute Loire, 7 May 1934; A.N. F.[7] 13030, Allier, 12 November; A.N. F.[7] 13026, Ile et Vilaine, 23 September, 8 October. Such examples could be almost indefinitely multiplied: for example A.N. F.[7] 13027, Marne, 28 April 1934; A.N. F.[7] 13028, Deux Sèvres, 13 August; A.N. F.[7] 13026, Loiret, 22 April. This was also the year of Daniel Halévy's *Visites aux paysans du centre 1907–1934* (1935): he found a few ever-repeated themes: 'France has always grown her grain, neither too much, nor too little ... if government statistics say the contrary, they are false. It's a question of fraud', p. 196.
46  M.F. B. 33 192, No. 3 bis: 24 January 1934.
47  On this rearmament programme, see Frankenstein, *Le Prix du réarmement français*, pp. 50–7.
48  'Two months ago it needed 4m economies to save France; today it needs 3m of new expenditure': *La Lumière*, 15 May 1934; Brosselette, *Notre temps*, 11 March 1934; Moch, J.O. Ch., 14 June 1934, p. 1492.
49  J.O. Ch., 21 February 1934, p. 626.
50  M.F. B. 33 192, No. 31: note of 4 May 1934.
51  Herriot, *Jadis II*, p. 401; Du Clain, *La Lumière*, 31 May 1934.
52  Herriot, *Jadis II*, pp. 441–2.
53  J.O. Doc. C. 1934, No. 3729 is the bill; the report on it is ibid., No. 3768; Saly, *La Politique des grands travaux en France*, pp. 346–62, has full details.
54  J.O. Ch., 5 July 1934, p. 2034; the debate is in ibid., pp. 2028–74.

55 M.F. B. 33 192, Nos. 32 and 43; notes of 7 May, 14 June 1934 (Boisanger).

56 Figures from Jacquier, Marquet's successor, J.O. Ch., 8 February 1935, p. 427; Saly, *La Politique des grands travaux en France*, p. 365.

57 R.E.P. 1935, pp. 616; 1008–15.

58 Germain-Martin, P.V.C., 23 October 1934; *Le Problème financier*, pp. 251–3. The number of Bills in circulation had started to rise again from May.

59 P.V.C., 23 October 1934.

60 J.O. Doc. C. 1934, No. 3825 (the budget of 1935).

61 P.V.C., 26 September 1934.

62 *Le Temps*, 17 September 1934, quoted this with approval: 'economic prosperity depends on our institutions'.

63 On the general problem of constitutional reform in 1934 see: J. Gicquel and L. Sfez, *Problèmes de la réforme de l'Etat en France depuis 1934* (1949); and M. Margairaz, 'La Droite et l'Etat en France dans les années trente', C.H.I.M.T. 20–1 (1977), pp. 91–136.

64 A. Tardieu, *L'Heure de la décision* (1934); and 'Réformer ou casser', *La Revue des deux mondes*, 1 March 1934, pp. 135–61.

65 On the Commission, see Gicquel and Sfez, *Problèmes de la réforme de l'Etat*, pp. 39–72.

66 *La Nation*, 21 April 1934; Blaisot, ibid., 28 April 1934; Pinon, *La Revue des deux mondes*, 1 April 1934, p. 713.

67 27 June 1934; also *Journal des débats*, 8 July; *Paris-Midi*, 18 June 1934.

68 Doumergue, *Mes causeries avec le peuple français*, pp. 60–80.

69 13 November 1934; also 1 July, 3 September 1934.

70 *La Journée industrielle*, 23 October, 10 November 1934; *La Nation*, 22 December 1934; *Le Figaro*, 9, 13 November 1934. For many other examples of this kind see Margairaz, 'La Droite et l'Etat', pp. 124–7.

71 Constant, *Les Cahiers du bolchévisme*, 15 September 1934; also Duclos, ibid., 15 November 1934: the aim was '*to gag the workers* ... in order to be better able to impose a starvation policy'.

72 *Le Populaire*, 1 October 1934.

73 Ibid., 2 November 1934.

74 For example *La Journée industrielle*, 4–5 November 1934. In fact the Commission's proposal, accepted by the executive committee of the Party in June, was more far-reaching than Doumergue's: it allowed the possibility of a dissolution within three months of an election; Doumergue's proposal prescribed at least a year.

75 'Mémoires', pp. 1501–3.

76 Herriot, *Jadis II*, p. 393; also ibid., p. 401.

77 Ibid., p. 457.

78 In August, however, the Prefect of the Seine could report that although the political activity of left-wing groups was continuing, on the right 'activity is non-existent because of the holidays': A.N. F.[7] 13028, Seine, 4 August 1935. *Congés payés*, if only conservatives had understood, could have been seen as an instrument of social control, not a harbinger of Socialist revolution!

79 See, generally, Berstein, *Histoire du Parti radical II*, pp. 327–36.

80 Ibid., p. 338, notes that few of the congresses of the Federations preparing for the national congress seemed at all interested by the constitutional issue.

81 C.R.C.R. 1934 (October), pp. 250–73.

82 Herriot, *Jadis II*, p. 466; *L'Oeuvre*, 28 October 1934; note by Daladier on the formation of the Popular Front in 1 DA 6 Dr6 sdrb.

83 *L'Oeuvre*, 16 September 1934; see also ibid., 30 October 1934; Roche, *La République*, 27 July 1934.
84 *La Nation*, 3 November 1933; *La Journée industrielle*, 30 November 1934.
85 Daladier Papers 1 D.A. 6 Dr 2 contains this correspondence.
86 *La Lumière*, 11 August, 1 September 1934.
87 C.R.C.R. (October) 1934, p. 262.
88 Berstein, *Histoire du Parti radical* II, pp. 334–5.
89 Roche–Caillaux papers, E.R.J.C. 9 Dr 1, letter of 30 July 1934.
90 Ibid., Roche to Caillaux, 1 September 1934.
91 J.O. Ch., 15 February 1935, p. 517.
92 R. Pinon, *La Revue des deux mondes*, 1 December 1934, p. 713. Rueff told a British official that Flandin was the most intelligent premier for years: P.R.O. T. 160 13427/2; Rowe-Dutton to Leith-Ross, 17 May 1935.
93 P.-E. Flandin, *Discours. Le Ministère Flandin, novembre 1934–mai 1935* (1937), p. 33.
94 Herriot, *Jadis II*, p. 486.
95 Germain-Martin, 'Contribution', Vol. 2, p. 139. See also M.F. B. 33 192, No. 69: a note by de Boisanger commenting on this plan, 17 November 1934.
96 Flandin, *Discours*.
97 Boris, *La Lumière*, 17 November 1934.
98 *L'Oeuvre*, 15, 29 November 1934.
99 Tardieu papers, A.N. 324 A.P. 3: Tardieu to Jacques Bardoux, 4 February 1935; see also the preface to his *Sur la pente* (1935). The Marin papers contain numerous letters of protest from Fédération Républicaine members at his participation in Flandin's government: A.N. 317 A.P. 99.
100 Romier, *Le Figaro*, 9 November 1934; *Le Temps*, 13 November 1934; Gignoux, *La Journée industrielle*, 28 November 1934.
101 P. de Pressac, *La Revue politique et parlementaire*, 10 January 1935.
102 Flandin, *Discours*, pp. 49, 174 (speeches of 27 November 1934; 10 March 1935).
103 For the account of Flandin's economic policy see ibid., *passim*.
104 Flandin wrote in his memoirs: 'my task was to rebuild the coalition by postponing constitutional reform, but without losing the support of conservative elements': *Politique française 1919–1940* (1947), p. 161, Fn. 1.
105 For example Boris, *La Lumière*, 11 December 1935 ('M. Flandin commence à voir clair').
106 M.F. B. 133 192, Nos. 62, 64; notes of 19 October, 5 November 1934.
107 1 December 1934, p. 1028.
108 See below, pp. 185–6.
109 For example Boris, favourable to devaluation, in *La Lumière*, 1 December 1934; A. Fabre-Luce against devaluation, in a special number of *L'Europe nouvelle* of 9 March 1935, devoted to the 'Flandin experiment'.
110 For example *Le Temps*, 16 November 1934: 'the adaptation of our prices has more or less been carried out'.
111 Sauvy, *Histoire économique de la France*, Vol. 2, p. 509.
112 Flandin, *Discours*, p. 26.
113 After the Chamber's amendments: details in J.O. Doc. S. 1934, No. 610.
114 P.V.S., 26 January 1935.
115 Jenny, *La Revue politique et parlementaire*, 10 January 1935; Romier, *Le Figaro*, 5 December 1934; Caillaux, J.O. Sen., 13 December 1934, p. 1233.
116 Dr Pressac, political commentator of *La Revue politique et parlementaire*, 10 January 1935.

117 Full details in J.O. Doc. C. 1934, No. 4215 (the bill itself), No. 4225 (the report on it); J.O. Doc. S. 1934, No. 637. See H. Hitier, 'Le Marché du blé', *La Revue des deux mondes*, 15 June 1934, pp. 866–84, on the situation when Flandin took over.

118 J.O. Ch., 10 December 1934, p. 3013.

119 J.O. Ch., 11 December 1934, p. 3093.

120 For example Deschamps in *La Lumière*, 15 December 1934, whom one might have expected to be against the bill, wanted to give it a chance. The mood was best summed up by Borgeot, the *Rapporteur* of the Senate's Agriculture Commission: 'we accept the return to liberty without enthusiasm', J.O. Sen., 22 December 1934, p. 1505.

121 *Le Populaire*, 13 December 1934 ('Des fléaux S.V.P.').

122 The bill was J.O. Doc. C. 1934, No. 4440; the report on it ibid., No. 4250; the Senate report J.O. Doc. S. 1934, No. 554.

123 See O. de Puiffe de Magondeaux, *Les Ententes industrielles obligatoires et le corporatisme en France* (1937), p. 68; E.-S. Massoubre, *Les Ententes professionnelles dans le cadre national et la doctrine économique* (1935), p. 11.

124 Procès verbaux de la Commission du Commerce de l'Industrie, 16 January 1935.

125 Peissel, Procès verbaux, 10 January 1935; Reynaud and Moch, P.V.C., 6 February 1935.

126 26 January 1935; or *La Journée industrielle*, 16 February 1935; *Le Temps*, 11 January 1935 ('Engrenage').

127 Between, for instance, Duchemin of the C.G.P.F. and Peyerimhoff of the Comité des Houillières: *Bulletin quotidien*, 24 January 1935; the *Bulletin* itself was hostile: 11 January 1935. On Louis Renault's hostility see: P. Fridenson, *Histoire des usines Renault I: Naissance de la grande entreprise* (1972), pp. 252–3.

128 Massoubre, *Les Ententes professionnelles*, pp. 94–6.

129 Details in Barèty's report on the bill, J.O. Doc. C., No. 4531.

130 Frankenstein, *Le Prix du réarmement français*, pp. 57–8.

131 J.O. Ch., 25 January 1935, p. 320. 'Direct' intervention because there might well be borrowing by the Post Office, railways, etc.

132 M.F. B. 33 192, No. 72: note of 21 December 1934.

133 The bill itself was J.O. Doc. C. 1935, No. 4505. See also Germain-Martin's explanations, P.V.C., 23 January 1935; J.O. Ch., 25 January 1935, pp. 220–2; P.V.S., 26 January 1935. The report of the Senate Commission is in J.O. Sen. 1935, pp. 51–4.

134 Germain-Martin, P.V.S., 26 January 1935.

135 J.-N. Jeanneney, *François de Wendel en république: L'argent et le pouvoir 1914–1940* (1976), p. 733.

136 Especially since it was hoped that the *prospect* of rediscount by the Bank might be enough to allow the Bills to be absorbed by the market without any necessity actually to present them to the Bank.

137 To this end special rediscount facilities at the Bank and the Caisse were granted to the Compagnie Parisienne de Reescompte in an attempt to give it a role similar to that of the London discount houses: Myers, *Paris as a Financial Centre*, p. 173. But Boisanger's note, M.F. B. 33 192, No. 69, advised against adopting in France the system of adjudication of Treasury Bills practised on the London market.

138 Blum, *Le Populaire*, 25 January 1935; Boris, *La Lumière*, 12 January 1935.

139 Auriol, J.O. Ch., 25 January 1935, p. 219; J.O. Doc. C., No. 4531.

140 Bonnet, J.O. Ch., 25 January 1935, p. 215; Jenny, *Le Temps*, 21 January 1935.

141  *La Revue politique et parlementaire*, 10 January 1935.

142  Jeanneney, *François de Wendel en république*, pp. 727–8. De Lastyrie, J.O. Ch., 25 January 1935, p. 203; *La Nation*, 12 January 1935.

143  *Le Temps*, 24 January 1935; *La Nation*, 2 February 1935; Lemèry, J.O. Sen., 29 January 1935, pp. 54–6; Caillaux, ibid., pp. 60–2.

144  Jeanneney's account is absolutely authoritative: *François de Wendel en république*, pp. 731–74.

145  J.O. Ch., 15 February 1935, p. 520.

146  The Bank's communiqué was issued on 21 February 1935. *Le Temps*, 22 February 1935; Jenny, *La Revue politique et parlementaire*, 10 March 1935; for the technical aspects of the policy see: Guenser, *Le Marché monétaire français*, pp. 289–306.

147  P.V.C., 21 February 1935. In 'Contribution', Vol. 2, pp. 140–1, he is more critical and talks of only 'limited aid'; for this he blames de Rothschild's influence alone.

148  P.R.O. T. 188/109: Leith-Ross's report of a conversation with Flandin, 24 March 1935.

149  Jeanneney, *François de Wendel en république*, p. 748; see also Boris, *La Lumière*, 16 March 1935.

150  *La Lumière*, 12 January 1935; also Reynaud, J.O. Ch., 25 January 1935, p. 208; *L'Europe nouvelle*, 9 March 1935.

151  See Jeanneney, *François de Wendel en république*, pp. 725–30 for an authoritative account of the myth and the truth. The conspiracy theory was especially developed by *La Lumière* – for example 20 April ('M. de Wendel dévoile le Plan de la Réaction'), 1 June 1935 ('Un coup monté') – but later became absolutely general: Blum, *Le Populaire*, 25 June 1935 ('Les conjurés de la panique'); F. Delaisi, *La Banque de France aux mains des deux cents familles* (1936).

152  *Histoire économique de la France*, Vol. 2, p. 137.

153  P.V.C., 4 April 1935.

154  Boris, *La Lumière*, 6 April 1935.

155  Flandin, *Discours*, p. 181.

156  Du Clain, 16 March 1935.

157  Berstein, *Histoire du Parti radical II*, p. 346.

158  On Dorgèrism see G. Wright, *Rural Revolution in France: the Peasantry in the Twentieth Century* (1964), pp. 50–4; S. Berger, *Peasants Against Politics* (1972), pp. 108–12; P. Ory, 'Le Dorgèrisme: Institution et discours d'une colère paysanne 1929–1939', *Revue d'histoire moderne et contemporaine* 22 (April–June 1975), pp. 168–87.

159  *L'Oeuvre*, 18 January 1935.

160  J.O. Ch., 7 February 1935, p. 385 (11 Radicals abstained).

161  *Le Temps*, 10 February 1935 ('Malaise').

162  For example *La Nation*, 16 March 1935.

163  Corbière, *La Nation*, 26 January 1935.

164  A.N. 324 A.P. 3: letters of 29 January and 25 February 1935.

165  *Le Temps*, 26 January 1935; Caillaux, J.O. Sen., 29 January 1935, pp. 60–2; *La Nation*, 16 February 1935; de Wendel's speech is in *La Nation*, 24 April 1935.

166  Frankenstein, *Le prix du réarmement français*, p. 116. For the first quarter government expenditure on wheat came to 590mi F.; for the year it was 1.8m F. In 1934 the total was 390mi. Extra-budgetary spending on defence came to 2.8m in 1935; 613mi in 1934; see M.F. B. 33 183, 184.

167  M.F. B. 33 193, No. 17: note of 1 April 1935 (Baumgartner).

168  P.V.C., 4 April 1935.

169 The letter is reproduced by him in *Le Problème financier*, pp. 319–20, and is also quoted by Jeanneney, *François de Wendel en république*, pp. 753–4.
170 Flandin, *Discours*, pp. 174–9.
171 P.R.O. T. 188/109: Leith-Ross's report of a conversation with Flandin, 24 March 1935.
172 M.F. B. 33 193, No. 19: note of 9 April 1935 (Baumgartner).
173 M.F. B. 33 193, No. 17: note of 1 April 1935.
174 P.V.C., 30 April 1935.
175 According to Jeanneney, on 3 May, at a meeting attended by Deroy the new Director of the Caisse and by Baumgartner, Germain-Martin declared himself to be in favour of decree powers: *François de Wendel en république*, pp. 760–1; p. 1312, Fn. 20.
176 P.V.S., 26 January 1935.
177 *Le Populaire*, 17–18 May: *L'Oeuvre*, 15, 18 May 1935.
178 Marjolin, *Le Populaire*, 7 March 1935; Blum, *Le Populaire*, 11 March 1935.
179 Germain-Martin, P.V.C., 29 May 1935 (Second Sitting). He described, in graphic terms, this 'speculation of unprecedented violence . . . passengers have been put off boarding French ships for which they had bought tickets, by being told that Paris was given over to Communism'.
180 Details on gold losses: M.F. B. 33 193, Nos. 31, 46, 51.
181 The fact that the largest gold losses occurred after the raising of the discount rate shows that the profit margins on which speculators were gambling were important enough to render this measure ineffective; if the Bank was slow to act, the reason seems to have lain more in Tannery's inexperience than in any political intentions on his part: Jeanneney, *François de Wendel en république*, p. 762.
182 M.F. B. 33 193, No. 32 bis: note of 23 May 1935 (Baumgartner). They reached a low point for the month of 10.3m on 27 May.
183 Herriot, *Jadis II*, p. 537; Jeanneney, *François de Wendel en république*, p. 760; M.F. B. 33 193, No. 38: note of 1 June, referring to letters exchanged between the Bank and the government on 23 May.
184 Herriot, *Jadis II*, p. 537.
185 Details in Barèty's report: J.O. Doc. C. 1935, No. 5338.
186 Flandin, P.V.C., 29 May 1935 (First Sitting).
187 Quoted in Jeanneney, *François de Wendel en république*, p. 1311, Fn. 15.
188 Roche-Caillaux papers, E.R.J.C. Dr 7: Tannery to Caillaux, 3 June 1935.
189 The British Ambassador reported that many Radicals who had originally been favourable to Bouisson turned against him after a weekend visit to their constituencies had shown them the unpopularity of further deflation: P.R.O. F.O. 371 18793, pp. 287–94.
190 The remark is quoted in Herriot, *Jadis II*, p. 551. My account of this crisis comes from ibid., pp. 547–53; A. Werth, *The Destiny of France* (1937), pp. 142–52; Boris and Du Clain, *La Lumière*, 15 June 1935; *Le Temps*; reports in P.R.O. F.O. 371 18793, pp. 287–312. Much of this was rumour and it is difficult to be precise about details. There is one very curious discrepancy: all accounts, except Herriot's, mention how Piétri's abortive ministry was sabotaged by the Bank. But Herriot, whose account is the most detailed – and he was a leading participant – is the only one to mention that Laval had been, before Piétri, forced by the Bank to abandon his attempt to form a government; and he attributes Piétri's failure to lack of co-operation from Auriol and Blum. Did the Bank really intervene twice, or has Herriot – or, more implausibly, have all the other witnesses – displaced the incident?
191 *La Lumière*, 8 July 1935, described him as a 'déflationiste mou'.

192 'I am not a financial specialist. I try to use common sense', P.V.C., 12 November 1935.
193 Quoted in F. Kupferman, *Pierre Laval* (1976), p. 53.
194 Politzer, *Les Cahiers du bolchévisme*, 1 August 1935.
195 *Combats pour un ordre financier* (1972), pp. 45–6; he attempted to persuade both Laval and Cathala, the Minister of Agriculture, of the folly of resisting devaluation – but in vain: *De l'Aube au crépuscule: autobiographie* (1977), pp. 124–5. It is interesting to note in this context de Wendel's comment on Laval's three advisers: Gignoux was 'a good choice, but those of Dautry and Rueff, especially the latter, less reassuring': Jeanneney, *François de Wendel en république*, Fn. 48, p. 1314.
196 See Gardey's criticisms in P.V.S., 22 November 1935.
197 See Barèty's report on the 1936 Budget, J.O. Doc. C. 1935, No. 5584.
198 R.E.P. 1936, p. 1009.
199 The text of the decrees can only be found in the *Journal officiel* for the day of their promulgation; but Barèty gives a full list with dates of issue: J.O. Doc. C. 1935, No. 5584, pp. 1301–7. As for their presentation by government apologists, see *La Revue des deux mondes*, 1 October 1935, 'Le Redressement des finances publiques'; Gignoux, *La Revue politique et parlementaire*, 10 October 1935; G. Damougeot-Perron, *L'Economie française et les décrets-lois* (1936); lots of useful comments in R.E.P. May 1936.
200 The cut was moderated for *fonctionnaires* earning less than 10,000 F. and later (8 August 1935) for small rentiers over 65 years old.
201 In 1935 – when they did not apply for a full year – the decrees saved less than the figures quoted above: 3m F. according to Régnier, J.O. Ch., 29 November 1935, p. 2249.
202 For example a decree of 31 October limited the amount of grain that could be ground, and prohibited the construction of new mills; a decree of 30 October prohibited the construction of new factories for the refining of sugar beet.
203 Details in the report on the 1936 labour budget: J.O. Doc. C. 1935, No. 5599; and Saly, *La Politique des grands travaux en France*, pp. 366–72.
204 For example a decree of 30 October revived Flandin's abortive legislation on cartels – but for the silk industry alone (in fact the necessary majority of producers required to make these cartels enforceable by law was never obtained).
205 *L'Humanité*, 17–31 July 1935, *passim*.
206 J.O. Ch., 30 November 1935; or see *Le Peuple*, 18 July 1935.
207 *L'Oeuvre*, 25 July 1935; Clerc, ibid., 8 August; Déat, ibid., 13 September 1935.
208 Gignoux, *La Revue politique et parlementaire*, 10 October 1935.
209 See the 1936 budget: J.O. Doc. C. 1935, No. 5582.
210 *La Lumière*, 20 July 1935.
211 M.F. B. 33 193, No. 38: note of 1 June 1935.
212 P.V.C., 2 July 1935; Herriot, *Jadis II*, pp. 569–71. Between April and June the gold reserves of the Bank fell by 10m, but the note issue by less than 1m.
213 M.F. B. 33 193: note of 16 September 1935.
214 *Le Temps*, 19 August 1935 (this issue also contained the Bank's communiqué). The Socialist analysis put the situation well: Laval had quietly overcome the Bank's resistance and at the same time as carrying out a 'vast programme of deflation . . . he has made the Bank accept a policy which it has always considered as one of inflation': *Le Populaire*, 27 August 1935.
215 For example, M.F. B. 33 194, No. 1: note of 15 January 1936 (Baumgartner).
216 J.O. Doc. C. 1935, No. 5582; ibid., No. 5584 (the Commission's report); J.O. Doc. S. 1935, No. 640 (the Senate Commission's report).

217 Of which 1.2m F. was saved by the cut in rentes; and 1.1m F. by the reductions in public sector pay.
218 The report on the navy budget noted that 2m of recurrent expenditure had been detached from the budget: J.O. Doc. C. 1935, No. 5593; see also Frankenstein, *Le Prix du réarmement français*, pp. 61–3.
219 Below, pp. 127–8.
220 M.F.B. 33 194, No. 3: note of 26 January 1936.
221 If the number of Bills issued under the terms of the law passed in January – 4.5m – was added to the 3.3m of medium term bonds also issued under the terms of the same law to permit a consolidation of the floating debt, the combined total was above the 5m limit authorized by the law. The ceiling had only been passed by 1m because when the January bill was voted there remained a balance of 1.5m on previous authorizations to issue long and medium term bonds. This was noted by Gardey in his report on the budget.
222 M.F.B. 33 194, No. 1: note of 15 January 1936.
223 J.O. Ch., 29 November 1935, p. 2238; *La Lumière*, 4 January 1936, announced that 'M. Laval has breached the ceiling on Bills'.
224 *Le Temps*, 1–2 November 1935; *La Nation*, 16 November 1935; Pinon, *La Revue des deux mondes*, 15 November 1935, pp. 472–3.
225 *Le Temps*, 9, 12, 15–18 November 1935.
226 J.O. Ch., 29 November 1935, p. 2230.
227 Laval, P.V.C., 22 October 1935; *Le Temps*, 1 October 1935.
228 R.E.P. 1935, pp. 817–36, 1042–66.
229 On the causes of the recovery: Sauvy, *Histoire économique de la France*, Vol. 2, pp. 166–71; J.O. Doc. C. 1935, No. 5844; R.E.P. 1936, pp. 818–19. For the importance of demand from defence expenditure in particular industries: R.E.P. 1936, pp. 733, 833, 905–6.
230 For example Régnier, J.O. Ch., 29 November 1935, p. 2250.
231 The rise was higher than this figure indicated because two-year army service had been introduced in May.
232 Rist commented: 'it was precisely in August, that is to say at the moment when a deliberate policy of budgetary deflation was undertaken, that prices began to rise', R.E.P. 1936, p. 579.
233 J.O. Doc. C. 1935 No. 5584; J.O. Doc. S. 1935, No. 640.
234 J.O. Doc. C. No. 5582; Damougeot-Perron, *L'Economie française*, pp. 3–4, 121, blamed the Depression on excessive state intervention in economic activity.
235 *Le Populaire*, 21 July 1935; Boris, *La Lumière*, 20 July 1935.
236 J.O. Ch., 13 December 1935, p. 2484; *Le Peuple*, 26 July 1935, derided Laval's *economie dirigée*; also d'Harcourt, ibid., p. 2486; Perret, *La Nation*, 27 July 1935.
237 *Le Capital, dernières nouvelles financières et politiques*, 28 October 1935.
238 Damougeot-Perron, *L'Economie française*, p. 171. See also the conclusion of Bouvier *et al.*, *Histoire économique et sociale*, pp. 660–1; 'It is from the policy of Laval and not that of Léon Blum that dates the employers' distrust of State policy'.
239 Henri Garnier, *La France en face d'un redressement financier et en face de son avenir* (1935), pp. 22, 34.
240 Below, pp. 198–9.

## 6 The programme of the Popular Front

1 The best general account is still G. Lefranc, *Histoire du Front populaire 1934–1938* (1974).

2 There is something on this in ibid., Chapter 3; Berstein, *Histoire du Parti radical II*, pp. 381–9; Margairaz, 'Les Propositions de politique économique', pp. 272–300.

3 *La Lumière*, 13 July 1935.

4 For example Moch, *L'Oeuvre*, 7 March 1934; Kayser, ibid., 17 February 1934.

5 Déat, ibid., 30 August 1935; Du Clain, *La Lumière*, 22 June, 26 July 1935.

6 Blum, *Le Populaire*, 19, 21, 23 July 1935.

7 Blum, ibid., 18 July 1935; Marjolin, ibid., 20 September 1935.

8 Marjolin, ibid., 4 January 1936.

9 E. Weill-Raynal, *Contre la déflation budgétaire: pour une politique financière socialiste* (1936), p. 3.

10 Marjolin, *Le Populaire*, 23 July 1935.

11 Marjolin, ibid., 23 May 1935; Weill-Raynal, *Contre la déflation budgétaire*, p. 4.

12 Marjolin, *Le Populaire*, 22 December 1935.

13 This was published in 1936 as *La Toute-puissance bancaire et la nationalisation du crédit*.

14 C.R.C.S. 1935, pp. 104–8.

15 J. Moch, *Rencontres avec Léon Blum* (1970), p. 118; R. Abellio (pseudonym of Georges Soulès), *Ma Dernière mémoire II: Les militants 1927–1939* (1975), pp. 100–13.

16 See *Le Populaire*, 23 March 1935, for a report on the first meeting of the U.T.S. on 20 March 1935.

17 C.R.C.S. 1935, p. 517. This was a motion of the Drôme Fédération of which Moch was a member.

18 *Rencontres*, p. 118; also letter to the author.

19 J. Moch, *Arguments et documents contre capitalisme, la crise et la déflation* (1936), p. 82.,

20 *Le Populaire*, 6 August 1935.

21 Ibid., 3 and 4 August 1935.

22 Ibid., 6 August 1935.

23 Ibid., 7 August 1935.

24 See for example Amédée Dunois, *De la Concentration capitaliste aux nationalisations* (1936).

25 For example Politzer, *Les Cahiers du bolchévisme*, 1 August 1935.

26 Even serious historians sympathetic to the Communists continue to write in this way: for example D. Blumé *et al.*, *Histoire du réformisme en France depuis 1920*, Vol. 1 (1976), p. 123.

27 Dupuy, *Les Cahiers*, 15 November 1935.

28 *Les Cahiers du bolchévisme – Agiateur*, March 1934, No. 3.

29 Politzer, *Les Cahiers*, 15 November 1935.

30 Constant, ibid., 15 September 1935.

31 *Le Bulletin quotidien*, 13 December 1935.

32 ' "Secteurs abrités" et "non abrités" dans le déséquilibre actuel de l'économie française', R.E.P. July–August 1935, pp. 1330–59.

33 See his articles in *L'Oeuvre*, 18 June 1935; 10 November 1935.

34 Ibid., 11 July 1935; see also Gaston Martin in ibid., 17 June 1935; Kayser in ibid., 21 June 1935, and in *La République*, 9 June 1935.

35 C.R.C.R. 1935, p. 356.

36 The P.C.F.'s original proposal is in *L'Humanité*, 24 November 1934; the C.A.P.'s reply in *Le Populaire*, 28 November 1934; the reply of the P.C.F. in

ibid., 11 December 1934; Faure's reply in ibid., 21 December 1934; ibid., 20 January 1935 contains Blum's *post-mortem* and Zyromski's compromise; see also *Les Cahiers*, 1 January 1935.

37  See Constant, *Les Cahiers*, 1 April 1934 ('Les réformistes et la crise'); Duclos in ibid., 15 December 1934; ibid., 1 January 1935 ('Planisme et Marxisme'); Romier, ibid., 15 February 1935.

38  Thorez, ibid., 15 November 1934.

39  Monmousseau, ibid., 1 September 1934.

40  *Le Populaire*, 20 January 1935.

41  Ibid., 4 March 1935.

42  C.R.C.S. 1935, pp. 1–93.

43  Among such *militants* were Minjoz (Jura), ibid., pp. 309–11; Briche (Jura), ibid., pp. 321–8.

44  For example Pivert (Seine), ibid., p. 29; Costedot (Ariège), ibid., pp. 236–48; Vieux (Loire), ibid., p. 267.

45  For example Reynaud (Rhine), ibid., pp. 396–403; Séverac, ibid., pp. 223–5; Vieux, ibid., p. 265.

46  *Le Populaire*, 3 August 1935.

47  Ibid., 23 September 1935.

48  Ibid., 10 July 1935.

49  Ibid., 11 July 1935.

50  Ibid., 12 July 1935.

51  Politzer in *Les Cahiers*, October 1935; see also Blum's note to Zyromski, published by Lefranc, *Histoire du Front populaire*, Appendix 9, pp. 433–5.

52  *Le Populaire*, 23 September 1935.

53  Duclos gives the negotiations over the Platform only half a page in his memoirs, *Mémoires II 1935–1939* (1969), pp. 73–4.

54  See Chapter 7, below.

55  On Walter and the C.V.I.A. see Delmas, *A Gauche de la barricade* (1950), pp. 29–34; Lefranc, *Histoire du Front populaire*, pp. 45–6.

56  See Chapter 7.

57  On the Radical attitude see Berstein, *Histoire du Parti radical II*, p. 372. For the setting up and deliberations of the Committee see two articles by J. Kayser: 'Le Parti radical-socialiste et le Rassemblement populaire 1935–1938', *Bulletin de la Société d'Histoire de la Troisième République*, April–July 1955; 'Souvenirs d'un militant 1934–1939', *Les Cahiers de la République* , 12 (March 1958).

58  Delmas, *A Gauche*, p. 42.

59  Kayser, *L'Oeuvre*, 17 July 1935; also Paz in *Le Populaire*, 9 July 1935; Jouhaux, *Le Peuple*, 15 July 1935.

60  Moch, *L'Oeuvre*, 22 July 1935.

61  For the organizations represented at this meeting see *Le Populaire*, 6 August 1935. The meeting was originally scheduled for 8 August but on 22 July the C.G.T. decided to advance it because of the grave situation caused by the Laval decrees: see *Le Temps*, 24 July 1935. Was this the only reason? Perhaps the fact that the Comité du Rassemblement Populaire had entered into competition made it necessary to act fast – to forestall the adoption of any other programme by the left. Fears of such competition surfaced in September: see A.N.F. 13580, report of 1 September 1935.

62  The Kayser papers contain notes by Lange on the meetings of the first commission and on the September meeting: 2 KA 5 Dr 5.

63  The representatives were in the order of organizations given in the text: Faure,

Séverac, Auriol, Louis Levy, Grumbach; Duclos, Gitton, Bonte, Péri; Kayser, Anxionnaz, Perney, Lange, Aubaud; Ramadier, Etienne, Montagnon; Jouhaux, Belin, Guiraud; Monmousseau, Racamond, Reynaud; Rivet, Gerôme (Walter); Rabaté, Cudenet; Fontenay; Kahn, Basch. This list is given by Kayser in 'Le Parti radical-socialiste', p. 276. On the second economic sub-committee sat, among others, Zyromski, Auriol, Politzer, A. Jaubert (Radical).

64  *L'Oeuvre*, 29 June 1935.
65  *Le Populaire*, 1 July 1935.
66  Ibid., 2 July 1935. It contained no mention of either nationalizations or *offices*.
67  Kayser, 'Le Parti radical-socialiste', p. 276.
68  *La Lumière*, 7 September 1935; also 3 August.
69  Speech reported in *Le Temps*, 2 September 1935.
70  Vaillant-Couturier, *L'Humanité*, 24 July 1935.
71  *A Gauche*, p. 42.
72  *Europe*, 15 September 1935. Bayet considered this too timid: *La Lumière*, 28 September 1935; as for the P.C.F. proposals, he believed they would not raise enough fast enough: ibid., 7 September 1935.
73  *Le Populaire*, 5 September 1935.
74  *Le Populaire*, 24 October 1935.
75  Du Clain, *La Lumière*, 14 September 1935.
76  It is noticeable that the four Radical delegates to the Comité consisted of three left-wingers and only one deputy (Aubaud).
77  My account of this crisis comes from reports in *Le Temps*, *Le Populaire*, *L'Oeuvre*; A. Werth, *The Destiny of France* (1937), pp. 142–52; Herriot, *Jadis II*, pp. 547–53; and a detailed article by Bonte in *Les Cahiers*, 15 September 1935.
78  Ibid.
79  *Le Populaire*, 6 June 1935.
80  Herriot, *Jadis II*, p. 550.
81  *Le Populaire*, 9 June 1935.
82  *Le Temps*, 7 June 1935.
83  Herriot, *Jadis II*, p. 565.
84  *Le Temps*, 2 August 1935.
85  C.R.C.S. 1935, p. 376.
86  Lebas, *Le Populaire*, 24 June 1935; Faure, ibid., 22 June 1935.
87  Ibid., 10 June 1935.
88  Ibid., 2, 4 July 1935.
89  Ibid., 26 July 1935.
90  Ibid., 29 July 1935.
91  C.R.C.S. 1935, pp. 223–4; *Le Populaire*, 7 June 1935.
92  See respectively Herriot, *Jadis II*, pp. 564–5; *Le Temps*, 29 August 1935; ibid., 23 August 1935; *La République*, 16 August 1935.
93  *L'Humanité*, 1 August 1935.
94  *L'Oeuvre*, 7 August 1935.
95  *Le Temps*, 13, 20, 26 September 1935; *L'Oeuvre*, 12, 19 September 1935.
96  *Le Temps*, 3, 4 October 1935.
97  Details of the draft in *La République*, 5 October 1935; and *Le Journal du Commerce*, 30 October 1935. On its status see Belin, *Le Peuple*, 6 October 1935; Millet, *Le Temps*, 9 January 1936.
98  *L'Oeuvre*, 3 October 1935.

 99 Ibid., 10 October 1935.
100 P.V.C., 22 October 1935.
101 Berstein, *Histoire du Parti radical* II, pp. 397–8.
102 C.R.C.R. 1935, p. 373. His political report to the Congress is in *La République*, 13 October 1935 (his italics).
103 A supporter such as Potut spoke of 'rectification and modification': C.R.C.R. 1935, p. 228.
104 Ibid., p. 223.
105 *Le Populaire*, 15 October 1935.
106 16 October 1935.
107 C.R.C.R. 1935, pp. 228–32.
108 *L'Oeuvre*, 22 July 1935; 7 September 1935.
109 Herriot, *Jadis II*, p. 611.
110 *Le Populaire*, 19 November 1935: report of Conseil National meeting on the previous day.
111 See Herriot, *Jadis II*, pp. 607, 610.
112 Du Clain, *La Lumière*, 14 September 1935.
113 Duclos, *L'Humanité*, 2 August 1935.
114 *L'Oeuvre*, 31 October 1935.
115 *Jadis II*, p. 611; see also the change of view of Du Clain in *La Lumière* between 20 July and 19 October 1935.
116 For example Duclos, at the Délégation des Gauches, reported in *Le Temps*, 29 October 1935.
117 *Le Populaire*, 17 November 1935.
118 See Du Clain's analysis in *La Lumière*, 16 November 1935.
119 *Jadis II*, p. 610, p. 614; *Le Temps*, 16 November 1935.
120 Du Clain, *La Lumière*, 16 November 1935.
121 Bayet, *La Lumière*, 30 November 1935.
122 Analyses of Du Clain, *La Lumière*, 16 November 1935; and *L'Oeuvre*, 11 November 1935.
123 *Le Populaire*, 30 November 1935.
124 P.V.C., 12 November 1935 (Second Sitting).
125 Herriot, *Jadis II*, pp. 608–10.
126 *Le Populaire*, 23 November 1935.
127 Herriot, *Jadis II*, p. 610.
128 *L'Oeuvre*, 15 November 1935; and the editorial, ibid., 1 November 1935, did not want 'chaos for the sake of chaos'.
129 *Le Populaire*, 14 November 1935.
130 Reported in *Le Temps*, 17 November 1935.
131 Du Clain, *La Lumière*, 23 November 1935; Guérin, *L'Oeuvre*, 19 November 1935.
132 As Larmour, *The French Radical Party*, p. 186, points out, the real figure of Radical support was probably higher since various reliable Lavalists voted for the government, knowing that it was safe. In the previous day's vote on whether to give priority to the financial *interpellations*, 74 Radicals voted for the government, 19 abstained, 56 voted against. The number of Radical supporters of the government's financial policy was, therefore, higher than in June!
133 Berstein, *Histoire du Parti radical II*, pp. 400–2.
134 Belin, *Du Secrétariat de la C.G.T.*, p. 82; Delmas describes the drawing up of the Programme in *A Gauche*, pp. 42–3 and *Mémoires d'un instituteur syndicaliste*

(1979), pp. 251–2. He was present because the meetings of the Comité were held at the headquarters of his union.

135  Kayser, 'Le Parti radical-socialiste', p. 277.
136  Kayser papers, 2 KA 5 Dr 6: Kayser's report to the Radical Bureau, 21 November 1935.
137  Kayser, 'Le Parti radical-socialiste', p. 278; Delmas, *Mémoires*, p. 252.
138  Kayser, 'Souvenirs d'un militant', p. 76; see also n. 136 above.
139  Politzer, *Les Cahiers du bolchévisme*, 1 December 1935.
140  See Blum's note for Zyromski in Lefranc, *Histoire du Front populaire*, Appendix 9, p. 439; the same point was made by Auriol in a note of 24 August 1935 published by G. Lefranc in *L'Expérience du Front populaire* (1972), pp. 32–44.
141  Lacoste, *L'Atelier du plan*, 15 October 1935.
142  Dupiol, ibid.
143  Duret, ibid.
144  Politzer, *Les Cahiers du bolchévisme*, 1 December 1935; also ibid., 15 December 1935.
145  Belin, *Du Secrétariat de la C.G.T.*, p. 82. See also the testimony of Auriol in Lefranc, *Histoire du Front populaire*, p. 94.
146  See Chapter 7, below.
147  See Blum's note cited in Lefranc, *Histoire du Front populaire*, Appendix 9, p. 439.
148  Kayser, 'Souvenirs d'un militant', p. 78. Roche, *La République*, 15 January 1935, claimed that the Bureau had over-ruled the advice of a technical committee set up to give advice on the programme.
149  Berstein, *Histoire du Parti radical II*, pp. 403–13; Larmour, *The French Radical Party*, pp. 184–6.
150  The programme has been frequently republished: for example in G. Lefranc, *Histoire du Front populaire*, pp. 475–9.
151  Politzer, *Les Cahiers du bolchévisme*, 1 February 1936.
152  *Le Populaire de Nantes*, 22 January 1936 in Kayser papers, 2 KA 5 Dr 6.
153  C.R.C.R. 1935, pp. 212–20.
154  *L'Oeuvre*, 2 December 1935.
155  A.N. F.[7] 13030, report of the *Commissaire spécial* of Digne, 24 September 1935; A.N. F.[7] 13040, Prefect of the Rhône, 27 September 1935; Prefect of the Hautes-Pyrénées, 24 September 1935.
156  A.N. F.[7] 13040, report of 5 August 1935; see also reports by the Prefects of Alpes-Maritimes, A.N. F.[7] 13030, 24 July; Rhone, A.N. F.[7] 13040, 30 July; Haute-Garonne, A.N. F.[7] 13034, 3 August.
157  A.N. F.[7] 13034, Ile et Vilaine, 25 September 1935; see also A.N. F.[7] 13030, Aisne, 25 September; Alpes-Maritimes, 25 September.
158  A. Corbin, 'Prélude au Front populaire: étude de l'opinion publique dans le département de la Haute-Vienne: février 1934–mai 1936' (unpublished *troisième cycle* thesis, University of Poitiers, 1968), pp. 99–107.
159  A.N. F.[7] 13034, Indre, 25 September 1935.
160  A.N. F.[7] 13032, 20 September 1935.
161  A.N. F.[7] 13032, Côtes du Nord, 25 September 1935; Calvados, 28 September; A.N. F.[7] 13033, Finistère, 3 October; A.N. F.[7] 13036, Manche, 23 November.
162  A.N. F.[7] 13032, Côtes du Nord, 1 October 1935.
163  *A Gauche*, p. 43.
164  *Le Peuple*, 14 January 1936.

## 7 Plans and planners

1 L. Laurat, *Un Système qui sombre* (1932), p. 7.
2 For example Faure, *Au Seuil d'une révolution*, p. 45; J. Duret, *Le Marxisme et les crises* (1933), pp. 195–6. A Socialist election poster of 1932 showed photographs of trains in Brazil which were powered by coffee instead of coal.
3 For England see A. Marwick, 'Middle Opinion in the Thirties: Planning, Progress and Political Agreement', *English Historical Review* 79, 111 (April, 1964), pp. 285–98.
4 On *Plans* see J.-L. Loubet del Bayle, *Les Non-conformistes des années trente une tentative de renouvellement de la pensée politique française* (1969), pp. 93–101. The series 'Crises et Plans' included works by de Jouvenel and Moch.
5 On these fringe groups see Loubet del Bayle, *Les Non-conformistes*, and J. Touchard, 'L'Esprit des années trente' in G. Michaud, ed., *Tendances politiques dans la vie française depuis 1789* (1960), pp. 65–87.
6 There are various studies which consider aspects of planism: Claude Harmel, 'Le Troisième anniversaire du Plan de la C.G.T.', *Etudes sociales et syndicales* 120 (Sept. 1965); and 'A propos de Henri de Man et de Léon Blum', *Contrat social* 9, 4 (July–Aug. 1965); J. Amoyal, 'Les Origines socialistes et syndicalistes de la planification en France', *Le Mouvement social* 87 (April–June 1974), pp. 137–69; G. Lefranc, 'Histoire d'un groupe du Parti Socialiste SFIO: Révolution Constructive 1930–8' and 'Le Courant planiste dans le mouvement ouvrier français de 1933 à 1936', both reprinted in *Essais sur les problèmes socialistes et syndicaux* (1970), pp. 169–220; and 'La Diffusion des idées planistes en France', *Cahiers Vilfredo Pareto: Revue européenne des sciences sociales* 12, 31 (1974), pp. 189–96; Z. Sternhell, *Ni droite, ni gauche: l'idéologie fasciste en France* (1983), Chapters 4–6; Kuisel, *Capitalism and the State*, Chapter 4; Margairaz, 'Les Propositions de politique économique', Chapter 5; G. Brun, 'Techniciens et technocratie en France 1918–45', 3 vols. (Unpublished *Doctorat d'Etat*, Paris II, 1977), pp. 83–92, 259–67; J.-F. Biard, 'L'Idée du Plan dans le mouvement syndical et socialiste français entre les deux guerres' (Unpublished *Doctorat d'Etat*, Paris I, 1977).
7 Henri de Man, *Cavalier seul* (1948), p. 159.
8 Biographical material can be found in his autobiographies *Après coup* (1941) and *Cavalier seul*. There is only one biography in English or French: Peter Dodge, *Beyond Marxism: The Faith and Works of Hendrik de Man* (1966). In 1973 a conference to discuss de Man's thought took place in Switzerland: the papers presented are published in *Cahiers Vilfredo Pareto* 12, 31 (1974) (for France, see especially the contributions of A. G. Slama, A. Dauphin-Meunier and G. Lefranc). For a contemporary account of de Man's ideas see: M.-L. Roux, *Le Socialisme de M. Henri de Man* (1937). See also: E. Hansen, 'Depression Decade Crisis: Social-Democracy and *Planisme* in Belgium and the Netherlands, 1929–1939', *Journal of Contemporary History* 16, 2 (April 1981), pp. 293–322 and, 'Hendrik de Man and the Theoretical Foundations of Economic Planning: The Belgian Experience, 1933–40', *European Studies Review* 8, 1 (Jan. 1978), pp. 235–57.
9 Described, for example, by B. Lavergne, in his preface to Philip, *Henri de Man et la crise doctrinale du socialisme*, p. 14, as the most important Socialist text since *Das Capital*.
10 *The Psychology of Socialism* (English translation 1928), p. 22.
11 Ibid., pp. 329–34.

12  That is not to say that he denied that the Socialist movement owed an enormous amount to Marx. See his panegyric on Marx in *Le Socialisme constructif* (1933), pp. 181–3.
13  *Psychology*, p. 116.
14  *Socialisme constructif*, p. 86.
15  *Psychology*, p. 452.
16  The title of one of his books was *Joy in Work* (English translation 1929).
17  *Psychology*, p. 64. Such preoccupations to some extent bring de Man close to the 'Young Marx' of the Economic and Philosophical Manuscripts. These had not been published when he wrote *Psychology*; but after they did appear, in 1932, one finds several references to them in de Man's work: for example *L'Idée socialiste* (French translation 1935; first appeared in German in 1933), pp. 213–14; 226–7. This revelation of a new Marx did not invalidate the attack on Marxism inasmuch as the attack, highly practical in intention, was on Marxist practice: 'vulgar Marxism is a living error; pure Marxism is a dead truth': *Psychology*, p. 417.
18  *Socialisme constructif*, p. 91.
19  *Psychology*, pp. 446–81.
20  Ibid., p. 472.
21  Ibid., p. 451.
22  See the third of the 'Pontigny Theses' in which de Man summarized the principles of planism at a conference held at Pontigny in 1934. They are reproduced in *L'Idée socialiste*, pp. 531–4.
23  Interview with de Man published by the C.G.T.'s Institut Supérieur Ouvrier (I.S.O.) in *Problèmes d'ensemble du fascisme*, p. 22.
24  H. de Man, *Le Socialisme devant la crise* (n.d.), p. 7. This was the eighth *Cahier* published by Révolution Constructive. See below, p. 146.
25  H. de Man, *Pour un Plan d'action* (1933), p. 7. The rest of this paragraph comes from this pamphlet which was the first of the *Cahiers* published by Révolution Constructive.
26  'What characterizes the white-collar proletarian, is that he does not want to be of the proletariat, and that the more he is the less he wants to be so': *Socialisme constructif*, p. 207.
27  *L'Idée socialiste*, p. 490 makes this explicit.
28  Ibid., pp. 501–4.
29  De Man's departure had been planned before the Nazi seizure of power. In 1932 Vandervelde had appealed for his help: 'my education,' he told de Man, 'dates from a period when one placed much less importance on economic and financial problems . . . Help us and see if you can't give us a good programme of action against the crisis', and thus, although de Man at this time hoped his ideas might be adopted at the forthcoming congress of the Social Democratic Party in 1933, he had already decided to leave Germany: *Après coup*, pp. 98–206.
30  The text of the Plan was published separately as *Le Plan du Travail*, and is reproduced in an appendix to *L'Idée socialiste*.
31  Abellio, *Ma dernière mémoire II*, p. 56.
32  See Faure, *Au Seuil d'une révolution*; Jean Lebas, *Le Socialisme: but et moyen, suivi de la réfutation d'un néo-socialisme* (1931); J.-B. Séverac, *Lettres à Brigitte: le Parti socialiste ses principes et ses tâches* (1933). Vallon described the latter as a 'new Manifesto for a girls' boarding school': *La Vie socialiste*, 21 October 1934.
33  Quoted by G. Lefranc, 'Le Plan d'action d'Henri de Man', *L'Homme réel* (Jan. 1934).

34  'Subtle rather than profound' commented Soulès: Abellio, *Ma dernière mémoire II*, p. 94.
35  As in his analyses of the differences between Socialism and Bolshevism or the distinction between the 'conquest' and 'exercise' of power.
36  'We are not Neo-Socialists, we are Jauressians', he declared: *La Vie socialiste*, 2 September 1933.
37  Déat, *Perspectives socialistes* (1930), p. 37.
38  Ibid., p. 128.
39  For example, *Perspectives*, pp. 123–4; B. Montagnon, *Grandeur et servitude socialistes* (1929), pp. 78–87.
40  *Perspectives*, pp. 85, 162–3; *Grandeur*, pp. 161–6.
41  See G. Lefranc, 'La Crise des néo-Socialistes' in *Le Parti socialiste et l'exercice du pouvoir* (a colloquium held at the Centre d'Histoire du Socialisme, October 1976).
42  Bonnafous, Preface to Montagnon *et al.*, *Neo-Socialisme?*, p. 55.
43  Ibid., p. 120; Déat, *La Vie socialiste*, 2 December 1933; Lafont, J.O. Ch., 23 November 1933, p. 4254.
44  The first Manifesto of the new party stressed the importance of action based on a union of all anti-capitalist forces within the boundaries of the nation alone: *La Vie socialiste*, 25 November 1933.
45  *La Vie socialiste*, 6 April 1934; see also Déat, *L'Oeuvre*, 4 January 1934.
46  Vallon, *La Vie socialiste*, 21 October 1933.
47  Déat, *L'Oeuvre*, 4 January 1934; also in *Notre temps*, 7 January 1934; Montagnon, *Notre temps*, 17 January 1934.
48  Vallon, *Notre temps*, 11 January 1934.
49  Lefranc suggests two other reasons why de Man should have chosen Révolution Constructive: he placed great weight on obtaining the support of the unions, and Lefranc's contacts in this connection were good; secondly, the leaders of Révolution Constructive had an intellectual audience which extended beyond exclusively Socialist circles: *Essais*, p. 154.
50  Full list of members and all details in Lefranc, *Essais*, pp. 169–96.
51  G. Lefranc, *Révolution constructive* (1932), p. 80.
52  Lefranc had known de Man since August 1927, and had been among the book's first readers in France: *Essais*, p. 183, Fn. 1.
53  See *Bulletin de révolution constructive*, June 1933 (Trimestrial).
54  Lefranc, *Essais*, p. 182.
55  Text of letter published in ibid., p. 183.
56  *Révolution constructive*, p. 94.
57  L. Laurat, *Le Socialisme à l'ordre du jour: problèmes et tâches du marxisme contemporain* (1933), p. 3.
58  Ibid., p. 60.
59  Ibid., pp. 15–16.
60  Ibid., p. 18..
61  René Michaud, *Combat marxiste*, 15 December 1933. Laurat may indeed have himself influenced de Man, who was no economist: he tells us that in April 1933 he had met de Man and discussed the Russian experience with him, 'Mémoires d'un planiste 1932–1939', *Etudes sociales et syndicales*, September 1965, pp. 19–24. The parallel with N.E.P. was also drawn by others: Lefranc, *Le Populaire*, 20 September 1934, Déat, *La Vie socialiste*, January 1934.
62  The text and signatories of the motion are in *Combat marxiste*, 15 February 1934.
63  Abellio, *Ma dernière mémoire II*, p. 228.

64 Lefranc, *Essais*, pp. 185–6.
65 *Le Populaire*, 12 March 1934.
66 For example Pommera, *Combat marxiste*, 15 December 1933 ('How the de Man plan is distorted and diminished').
67 It is particularly ironic that Blum should have been so hostile to de Man's earlier writings because, although he claimed to be a Marxist, his humanist account of the nature of Socialist belief in his famous pamphlet, *Pour être socialiste*, was really very similar to that of de Man: 'Socialism is born out of the sense of human equality, while the society in which we live is entirely based on privilege . . . Socialism is therefore a morality and almost a religion, as much as a doctrine': *Pour être socialiste* (1919; ninth edition 1933), pp. 3–5.
68 *Le Populaire*, 4 and 5 January 1934; also Faure, ibid., 29, 30 December 1934.
69 Ibid., 6 and 7 January 1934. Thus his reference to 'Henri de Man's *plan de travail* [sic], or rather his plan of campaign'.
70 Ibid., 21 January 1934.
71 Ibid., 22, 23 and 26 January 1934.
72 *Combat marxiste*, 15 May 1934 ('Pour le ralliement des masses').
73 R. Michaud, ibid., 1 April 1934 ('Le Plan et le Pouvoir').
74 Itard and Lefranc, *Le Populaire*, 13 March 1934; *Eléments d'un plan français* (1934), p. 9 (this was the *Cahier* 5/6 of Révolution Constructive).
75 *Eléments*, p. 9.
76 Lefranc and Itard, *Le Populaire*, 7 May 1935.
77 Laurat, *L'Atelier pour le plan*, 1 May 1936; or *Combat marxiste* September 1935 ('Socialisations et nationalisations').
78 Itard, *Le Populaire*, 18 April 1934; or Pommera, *Combat marxiste*, 15 December 1933.
79 Itard, *Le Populaire*, 31 January 1934.
80 Meillat, *Combat marxiste*, 15 December 1933.
81 This confusion very clear in ibid., September 1935.
82 Not all Socialist planists held this view: e.g. Moch, C.R.C.S. 1935, p. 235: the implementation of the Plan 'cannot be subordinated to the conquest of power'; or Delaisi, *Le Plan et les paysans*, in L'Institut Supérieur Ouvrier, *Crise et Plan*, Lecture 4 (1934).
83 A theme of all planist writing: for example Lemaître, *Combat marxiste*, December 1933 ('Socialisations et classes moyennes'); *Eléments*, p. 7; Philip, C.R.C.S., 1934, pp. 210–12.
84 Itard and Lefranc, *Le Populaire*, 26 December 1934; Lefranc, *L'Homme réel* 1, p. 23.
85 Itard and Lefranc, *Le Populaire*, 13 March 1934.
86 P. Boivin, ibid., 16 April 1934 (he was one of the original members of Révolution Constructive).
87 C.R.C.S. 1034, p. 216.
88 Boivin, *Le Populaire*, 16 April 1934. Nor was he worried that this might frighten off the *classes moyennes*; on the contrary '*they have a thirst for violence . . . what they detest most is parliamentarianism*': *L'Homme réel*, No. 14, February 1935.
89 R. Michaud, *Combat marxiste*, 1 April 1934 ('Le Plan et le pouvoir').
90 *Eléments*, p. 10.
91 For example C.R.C.S. 1934, pp. 162–9 (Grumbach); pp. 251–71 (Boivin); pp. 301–6 (Paz). Some discussion of content by Moch, ibid., pp. 177–93; Coeylas, ibid., pp. 283–91; Desphelippon, ibid., pp. 292–7.
92 *Problèmes d'ensemble du fascisme*, p. 24.

93  On this Plan see below, p. 152; for criticisms of it: Itard, *Le Populaire*, 18 April 1934; Michaud, *Combat marxiste*, 13 April 1934; Moch, C.R.C.S. 1934, p. 183.

94  Parti socialiste S.F.I.O. 31ᵉ congrès national, 20–23 mai 1934, rapports de la C.A.P., p. 4.

95  C.R.C.S. 1934, pp. 170–7 (Séverac); p. 22 (Faure); pp. 330–8 (Belos); pp. 231–9 (Lévy).

96  C.R.C.S. 1934, p. 358.

97  Ibid., p. 359.

98  Ibid., pp. 393–402.

99  There were 30 abstentions by planist hardliners: 17 from the Drôme (Soulès) and 12 from the Manche (Le Corre).

100 For example Itard, *Le Populaire*, 27 June 1934; *Combat marxiste*, 1 June 1934 ('Après Toulouse').

101 Lefranc and Itard, *Le Populaire*, 31 January 1934, or Moch, C.R.C.S. 1934, p. 182.

102 C.R.C.S. 1934, pp. 312–13.

103 Ibid., p. 267.

104 Ibid., p. 318.

105 *Le Populaire*, 17 April, 10 May 1934.

106 See Boivin, ibid., 16 May 1934.

107 *Bataille socialiste*, 15 April 1934.

108 Ibid., May–June 1934. The members of Bataille Socialiste were also reserved about the notion of a provisional mixed economy: Zyromski and Modiano in ibid.

109 *L'Oeuvre*, 30 April 1934.

110 C.R.C.S. 1934, p. 200; also Louis-Lévy, ibid., p. 236; or Blum J.O. Ch., 19 February 1934, p. 510.

111 Op. cit., p. 40. Déat himself admitted that some of his earlier analysis needed modification: *Vie socialiste*, 24 November 1934.

112 *Le Populaire*, 20 July 1933.

113 Ibid., 19 July, 1 August 1933.

114 Ibid., 2, 3, 18 August 1933.

115 Ibid., 26 July 1933.

116 Ibid., 14 August 1933.

117 Duret, *L'Atelier pour le plan*, 1 May 1936.

118 C.R.C.S. 1934, p. 358; *Le Populaire*, 26 January 1934.

119 Déat remarked that planism 'abolishes the essential distinction between the eve and the aftermath of the revolution . . . it implies a continuity of action': *L'Homme nouveau*, June 1934.

120 *Le Populaire*, 3 February 1934.

121 Quoted by Henri Noyelle in 'Les Plans de reconstruction économique et sociale á l'étranger et en France', R.E.P., 1934, p. 1638.

122 Numerous lists were made in various publications: for example Noyelle, 'Plans'; C. Pomaret, 'Catalogue des Plans', *Etat moderne*, April 1935; R. Branger in *X Crise*, April 1935; *La Vie socialiste*, 28 April 1934.

123 Published as the first three *Cahiers* of Révolution Constructive.

124 See above, p. 83.

125 *Notre temps*, 9 May 1934.

126 *La Vie socialiste*, 14 April 1934.

127 G. Valois, 'Pour le Plan syndical et coopératif', *Nouvel age*, 1 June 1934.

128  Published by Groupe du 9 juillet, *Plan du 9 juillet* (1934).
129  On these last four, see below, pp. 152–3; 156–60.
130  Le Comité du Plan, *Le Plan français* (1936).
131  *L'Oeuvre*, 15 March 1934.
132  Quoted by Harmel, 'A propos de Henri de Man'.
133  A. Delmas, *A Gauche de la barricade* (1950), p. 22, tells how it was said of a unionist that he had 'gone to the bad' if he went into politics; see also Belin, *Du Secrétariat de la C.G.T. au gouvernement de Vichy* (1978), p. 30.
134  Harmel, 'Le Troisième anniversaire du Plan'; Lefranc, *Essais*, p. 189, Fn. 2.
135  Lefranc, *Essais*, p. 189, Fn. 2. Lacoste had first announced the Plan in the *Tribune des fonctionnaires* on 4 November 1933; and he published a resumé of it on 2 December.
136  Already in January Belin had drawn up the skeleton of a Plan published in *La Voix du peuple*, January 1934; see also Belin, *Du Secrétariat de la C.G.T.*, p. 46.
137  *La Voix du peuple*, March 1934.
138  Lefranc and Itard, *Le Populaire*, 13 March 1934; *Combat marxiste*, 15 March 1934, which nevertheless had reservations.
139  Itard, *Le Populaire*, 7 May 1934. This 'Plan' was published separately by La Confédération Générale du Travail as *La Réorganisation économique dans la liberté*; and in *La Voix du peuple*, April 1934.
140  For this reason, Lefranc didn't even bother to attend the Toulouse Congress, *Essais*, p. 187, Fn. 3.
141  A full list of members is given by Lefranc, *Essais*, p. 210; some details also given by Laurat, 'Mémoires', p. 22.
142  Published separately as *Le Programme d'action civique des anciens combattants* (1934); see also Robert Bobin, *La Vie socialiste*, 7 April 1934.
143  On its prehistory, see Prost, *Les Anciens combattants*, Vol. 1, pp. 153–70; Vol. 3, pp. 188–216. He shows the Programme had been in the air since 1933. The influence of de Man was of course therefore not a factor; but it was important in affecting the way the action of the veterans was interpreted at large.
144  This is not to say that the authentic planists would have considered the nebulous ideas of the veterans to be 'structural reforms' as they understood them.
145  *Le Temps*, 14 April 1934; Prost, *Les Anciens combattants*, Vol. 1, pp. 167–8.
146  *Notre temps*, 18 March 1934.
147  *Le Peuple*, 26 March 1934; see also Desphelippon, *Combat marxiste*, 1 June 1934.
148  Respectively *Notre temps*, 28 March; *L'Oeuvre*, 31 March 1934.
149  *La Vie socialiste*, 26 May 1934.
150  *L'Oeuvre*, 29 March, 13 April 1934.
151  Ibid., 11 August 1935.
152  *L'Oeuvre*, 22 March 1934.
153  *La Vie socialiste*, 21 April 1934.
154  Ibid., 12 May, 9 June 1934. The latter article had an escape clause, envisaging the possibility of a postponement of the great day until October.
155  Ibid., 14 July 1934; *L'Oeuvre*, 14 September 1934.
156  *Notre temps*, 18 March 1934.
157  R. Bobin, *La Vie socialiste*, 1 December 1934.
158  For information on this plan – especially its reception – see the monthly *L'Homme nouveau* edited by Georges Roditi. This journal, slightly *fascisant* in tone (though it published articles by figures such as Lacoste and Marjolin),

became the plan's main organ of support. The Coutrot papers have various drafts of its economic section: J.C. 11 Dr 2.

159 For Caillaux see: the Roche–Caillaux papers, E.R.J.C. 9 Dr 1: Roche to Caillaux, 10 August 1934; for the participation of Leca and Devaux see: the Coutrot papers, J.C. 11 Dr 3 sdrb; for Montagnon: ibid., Coutrot to Romains, 25 August 1934; for the meeting of the Group see *L'Oeuvre*, 30 October 1934; article by Varages, *L'Homme nouveau*, November 1934.

160 See the account of the Congress of the *fonctionnaires'* union in *Information sociale*, 21 December 1934.

161 *Révolution constructive: Organe mensuel du groupe de Révolution constructive* No. 4, December 1934. I owe the information about Marjolin's early participation to my interview with M. Marjolin. For some information on further meetings of the 9 July Group see: J.C. 11 Dr 3 sdrb.

162 *Problèmes d'ensemble du fascisme*, p. 23; see also the fifth Pontigny thesis; and J. Duret, *Sens et portée du Plan* (n.d.), p. 20.

163 *X Crise*, March–April 1935. Révolution Constructive had itself wondered whether the nationalization of credit would have the same psychological impact – as a slogan – in France as in Belgium, and whether therefore it would not be preferable to emphasize 'a demand which does not make the same logical sense, but which responds more directly to the profound aspirations of the masses' – such as the nationalization of the arms industries: Preface to *Cahier* 2, p. 2.

164 *X Crise*, March–April 1935.

165 There was a third version, in 1939, which does not concern us here: see Amoyal, 'Les Origines socialistes', pp. 167–9. The text of the first version was published by La Confédération Générale du Travail as *Contre la crise pour une économie dirigée, exposé sur le Plan de rénovation économique de la C.G.T.*; the second as *Le Plan de rénovation économique et sociale*. Lefranc tells us that it was he who, at the last moment, drew up this second version: *Essais*, p. 217; preface to Belin, *Du Secrétariat de la C.G.T.*, p. 13, Fn. 13.

166 *Sens et portée*, p. 6.

167 Ibid., p. 16.

168 Lacoste, *L'Atelier pour le plan*, 15 May 1935; Jouhaux, ibid., 15 August 1935.

169 R. Bouyer, *Plan et metallurgie*, in L'Institut Supérieur Ouvrier, *Crise et Plan*, Lecture 2 (1934), p. 11. As a result of the more serious analysis of this issue prompted by the Plan, the 40-hour week was treated with a new flexibility: the possibility of longer hours in some sectors was envisaged: Belin, *L'Homme réel*, June 1935.

170 On the financing of the works, see Delaisi and Duret, *L'Atelier pour le plan*, 15 May 1936.

171 Duret, *L'Atelier pour le plan*, 15 February 1936.

172 L. Jouhaux, J. Duret and M. Harmel, *La C.G.T., ce qu'elle est, ce qu'elle veut* (1937), p. 166.

173 J. Dupiol, *Les Banques, l'épargne et la distribution des crédits* (1935); Ganivet (pseudonym of Dauphin-Meunier), *Etude du système bancaire* in L'Institut Supérieur Ouvrier, *Crise et Plan*, Lecture 9 (1934), and in *L'Homme réel*, October 1934.

174 Delaisi, *L'Atelier pour le plan*, 15 September 1935.

175 Zoretti, ibid., 1 May 1936.

176 The same was true of the nationalization of the insurance companies which was included for social reasons but was, said Zoretti, one of the 'rare detachable

parts of the Plan': ibid.; see also J. Dupiol, L. Zoretti, G. Lefranc, *La National-isation des industries clés* (n.d.).

177  L. Jouhaux, *Conditions de la lutte contre le fascisme*, in L'Institut Supérieur Ouvrier, *Crise et Plan*, Lecture 1 (1934); see also Duret, *L'Atelier pour le plan*, 1 May 1936: it was necessary 'to win the active support' of the majority who had 'a very strong instinctive attachment to property'.

178  'Les Origines socialistes', p. 166.

179  *L'Atelier pour le plan*, 1 May 1936.

180  For example Itard, *Le Populaire*, 19 January 1935.

181  *Combat marxiste*, 1 January 1935.

182  Zyromski, *Le Populaire*, 30 November 1934; H. and R. Modiano, *Bataille socialiste*, 15 November 19340; very reserved, however.

183  C.R.C.S. 1935, p. 316.

184  R. Bobin, *La Vie socialiste*, 1 December 1934; also Déat, *La Vie socialiste*, 24 November 1934 ('Pour l'élaboration d'un plan . . . d'un plan unique').

185  *La Vie socialiste*, 1 December 1934. The veterans' Plan was published as *La République des combattants*; comparisons of the three plans were made by Bobin, *La Vie socialiste*, 24 November, 1 December, 8 December 1934.

186  Ibid., 9 February 1935.

187  *Combat marxiste*, 1 March 1935.

188  Itard and Lefranc, *Le Populaire*, 26 December 1934.

189  *Le Peuple*, 29 January 1935.

190  *L'Homme nouveau*, June 1934.

191  Laurat, *L'Atelier pour le plan*, 15 July 1935; also Jouhaux in *L'Atelier pour le plan*, 1 January 1936 ('L'expérience américaine').

192  *Combat marxiste*, 1 December 1934 ('Le Plan de rénovation économique de la C.G.T.'); *Révolution constructive: Organe mensuel*, 4, December 1934.

193  It is also noted by Amoyal, 'Les Origines socialistes', p. 150; and B. Georges and D. Tintant, *Léon Jouhaux dans le mouvement syndical français*, Vol. 2 (1979), p. 104.

194  Biard, 'L'Idée du Plan', pp. 215–18, claims however – unconvincingly in my view – that the Belgian Plan was not a model for the French one.

195  See F. Delaisi, 'Plan et paysans'.

196  *Combat marxiste*, 1 December 1934; *Révolution constructive: Organe mensuel*, 4, December 1934; Modiano, *Bataille socialiste*, 15 November 1934.

197  *Combat marxiste*, 1 June 1935.

198  Jouhaux quoted by Michaud, *Combat marxiste*, 1 April 1935.

199  *Le Peuple*, 1 January 1935.

200  See comments of Delmas and Lacoste at the Congress of the Fédération des Fonctionnaires reported in *Information sociale*, 20 December 1934.

201  L. Zoretti, 'Analyse de la crise', L'Institut Supérieur Ouvrier, *Crise et Plan*, p. 42.

202  *La Vie socialiste*, 28 April 1934.

203  Epstein, *Combat marxiste*, 15 November 1934.

204  Albertini and Itard, *Le Populaire*, 19 January 1935. The approval was highly reserved.

205  C.R.C.S. 1935, pp. 569–71.

206  Ibid., p. 558; *Le Populaire*, 24 June 1935.

207  *Le Populaire*, 27 July 1935.

208  *Combat marxiste* ('Le planisme à Mulhouse: Idées qui font leur chemin'), June 1935.

209 On the Pontigny Congress see *L'Homme réel*, December 1934; *Information sociale*, 13 December 1934. The French delegation, including Belin, Laurat, Lacoste, Dulot (editor of *Information sociale*), de Jouvenel and Dauphin-Meunier, was the second largest after that of Belgium.
210 Lefranc, *Essais*, p. 213.
211 G. Lefranc, *Le Mouvement ouvrier devant le corporatisme*, in L'Institut Supérieur Ouvrier, *Crise et Plan*, Lecture 15 (1934).
212 *Le Populaire*, 14 January 1935.
213 Dumoulin, ibid., 2 September 1935.
214 Lebas, ibid., 24 June 1935.
215 Of the French participants in the second congress of plans in April 1936, the only S.F.I.O. members to attend – Laurat, Lefranc, Philip, Zoretti – did so in a purely personal capacity.
216 *L'Humanité*, 8, 9, 10 January 1934; see also Chapter 6, Note 37, above.
217 *La Vie socialiste*, 21 April 1934.
218 Ibid., 18 December 1934; 10 February 1935; 2 March 1935.
219 Ibid., 30 March 1935 has a declaration of the Comité's aims. The Comité went on meeting, somewhat futilely, in 1936 and 1937; there is a little about this in the Coutrot papers J.C. 4 Dr 1 sdrc.
220 *La Vie socialiste*, 26 January 1935.
221 The issue was an embarrassment until Marquet resigned from the Party in October preempting a likely decision of the Party to enforce his resignation from the government, ibid., 27 October 1934.
222 See criticisms S. Collette at the Party's third Congress: *La Vie socialiste*, 9 February 1935.
223 *Le Temps*, 2 November 1935.
224 Itard and Lefranc, *Le Populaire*, 26 December 1934.
225 *L'Homme réel*, October 1934; Duret, *Sens et portée*, p. 21.
226 Quoted in *Information sociale*, 13 December 1934; see also the critical comments of delegates at the 1935 Congress of the C.G.T., *Compte rendu*, 29th Congress, pp. 149, 169. The point is also noted by Georges and Tintant, *Léon Jouhaux*, Vol. 2, p. 93.
227 Thus Amoyal's comment, 'Les Origines socialistes', pp. 149–50, that planists took up 'the old struggle between *les petits et les gros*' seems to me unhelpful. For them the slogan 'que les riches paient' was pure demagogy. Capitalism was a system which, once understood, could be manipulated. To quote Delaisi: 'increasingly capitalism appears no longer as a system . . . in which an active minority exploits a majority but a series of mechanisms in which those who know how to work them can impose their will on the most democratic people in the world', *L'Atelier pour le plan*, 15 September 1935.
228 *La Vie socialiste*, 7 July 1934.
229 *L'Homme réel*, February 1935.
230 *Le Populaire*, 6 August 1935.
231 J.O. Doc. C. 1933, No. 1313; J.O. Doc. C. 1934, No. 3537 (Ramadier's report); a good summary given in the Senate Commission's report J.O. Doc. S. 1936, No. 114, which slightly modified the bill in a conservative direction. The debate was short: J.O. Ch., 11 February 1936, pp. 329–40.
232 *Entre deux guerres*, p. 279.
233 Margairaz, 'Les Propositions', p. 252.
234 Sternhell, *Ni droite, ni gauche*, especially pp. 136–233.
235 See especially Amoyal, 'Les Origines socialistes'. The two interpretations are not

necessarily entirely antithetical: fascism in France, and not only in France, has been viewed by some as a political form of the impulse towards modernization. See K.-J. Müller, 'French Fascism and Modernization', *Journal of Contemporary History* 11, 4 (October 1976), pp. 75–107; Sternhell, *Ni droite, ni gauche*, p. 221.

236 *Réflexions sur l'économie dirigée* (1932), p. 18. Dodge, *Beyond Marxism*, p. 47, writes that de Man's first visit to America was a revelation: 'he transferred to America the function of providing a means of realising those values that had led him to Socialism'. But he was also aware of the dangers of technocratic bureaucracy: *L'Idée socialiste*, p. 569.

237 *Socialisme à l'ordre*, pp. 26–9.

238 Duverger, *Le Monde*, 19–20 July 1981.

239 *L'Atelier pour le plan*, 15 May 1936 ('Sur l'économie dirigée de J. M. Keynes').

240 See Cusin's testimony in R. Rémond and P. Renouvin, eds., *Léon Blum chef de gouvernement*, p. 292.

241 Laurat's remarks to the First Congress of Plans, *Information sociale*, 13 December 1934.


## 8 Devaluation

1 J. M. Keynes, *Essays in Persuasion* (1931), p. 117.

2 P. Reynaud, *Mémoires I: Venu de ma montagne* (1960), pp. 404–15. Many more such letters can be found in Reynaud's papers: A.N. 74 A.P. 20.

3 L. Germain-Martin, *Le Problème de la dévaluation du franc en 1934* (1948), pp. 6, 28–9.

4 The British view is summarized by I. Drummond, *The Floating Pound and the Sterling Area 1931–1939* (1981), pp. 121–33.

5 See above, p. 26.

6 M.F. B. 32 318: the Bank's notes of 25 October 1932 and 13 February 1933.

7 On the background to the Conference see Drummond, *The Floating Pound*, pp. 120–5; also J. R. Moore, 'A History of the World Economic Conference, London 1933' (Ph.D. thesis, State University of New York at Stony Brook, 1971); M.A.E. Y. Internationale 73: Note of 3 June 1932.

8 M.A.E. Y. Internationale 73: Massigli to Paris, 2, 3, 7 November 1932.

9 D.D.F., ser. 1, Vol. II, No. 143: a note on the second meeting of the Preparatory Commission, 29 December 1932.

10 M.F. B. 32 319: note of 15 November 1932 on a meeting of experts from the Quai, the M.F. and the Ministry of Commerce.

11 D.D.F., ser. 1, Vol. II, Nos. 180 (Boisanger to Paul-Boncour, 9 January 1933), 397 (note by Rist and Parmentier on the second meeting of the Commission, 11 March 1933).

12 The Annotations were published, in slightly abbreviated form, as a supplement to *The Economist*, 28 January 1933.

13 Moore, 'A History of the World Economic Conference', p. 71.

14 D.D.F., ser. 1, Vol. II, No. 397.

15 M.F. B. 32 319: note of 15 November 1932 on France's position at the Economic Conference.

16 M.F. B. 32 317: report on the second meeting of the inter-ministerial committee preparing France's position at the conference, 8 April 1933.

17 M.F. B. 32 321 contains a whole dossier of reactions of Chambers of Agriculture. Most of the resolutions were cast in identical form: they demanded

'absolute and immediate protection of the agricultural productivity of the country'.

18  D.D.F., ser. 1, Vol. III, No. 1: report on the Franco-British meeting, 17 March 1933.
19  M.F. B. 32 320: note of 8 April 1933.
20  Drummond, *The Floating Pound*, pp. 141–3.
21  D.D.F., ser. 1, Vol. III, No. 258: a note of 9 May 1933 summarizing these talks.
22  D.D.F., ser. 1, Vol. III, Nos. 187, 190, 194, 258; M.A.E. Y. Internationale 74, 1 May 1933: Herriot to Paris. Details of the tripartite plan in R. Sayers, *The Bank of England 1891–1944* (1976), Vol. 3, pp. 276–9.
23  D.D.F., ser. 1, Vol. III, No. 163: Paul-Boncour to Herriot, 21 April 1933.
24  Ibid., No. 188: Herriot to Paul-Boncour, 26 April 1933.
25  Ibid., No. 193: Paul-Boncour to de Laboulaye, 27 April 1933.
26  Ibid., No. 227: The French government had slightly relaxed its original position (ibid., Nos. 214, 224) after extremely urgent prior warnings from de Fleutiau Ambassador in London, about the dangers of seeming intransigent and isolated (ibid., Nos. 221, 225).
27  Ibid., No. 262: de Laboulaye to Paul-Boncour, 10 May 1933.
28  Leith-Ross had told the French experts in Washington that the British would not accept any devaluation of the dollar without a parallel depreciation of sterling: ibid., No. 190. See also what he told Rueff in London: M.F. B. 12617: Rueff to Paris, 24 May 1933.
29  Sayers, *The Bank of England*, Vol. 2, p. 277.
30  M.F. B. 32 318: Bonnet to M.A.E., 13 May 1933.
31  D.D.F., ser. 1, Vol. III, Nos. 274, 275: Paul-Boncour to de Laboulaye and Cambon, 14 May 1933.
32  Ibid., No. 288: Cambon to Paul-Boncour, 17 May 1933.
33  M.F. B. 12617: Rueff to Paris, 24 May 1933.
34  M.F. B. 32 319: note of 8 June 1933 on the French position at the London Conference.
35  There are various accounts of the collapse of the Conference: Moore, 'A History of the World Economic Conference', is the most detailed, but also very anti-French and pro-Roosevelt; C. Kindleberger, *The World in Depression*, pp. 216–18, is more balanced; see also F. Friedel, *Franklin D. Roosevelt: Launching the New Deal* (1973), pp. 454–89; Drummond, *The Floating Pound*, pp. 162–73; H. Feis, 1933: *Characters in Crisis* (1966); Bonnet, *Vingt ans de vie politique*, pp. 171–78; M.F. B. 32 323: note of 30 September 1933.
36  Roosevelt's attitude was hardened by a new French default on debts on 15 June.
37  D.D.F., ser. 1, Vol. III, p. 567, Fn. 2.
38  Sayers, *The Bank of England*, Vol. 2, pp. 467–8.
39  M.F. B. 31 730: Le Norcy to Paris, 2 February 1934; M.F. B. 12617: Le Norcy to Paris, 5 February 1934; D.D.F., ser. 1, Vol. VIII, No. 121: Corbin to Laval, 22 November 1934.
40  R.E.P. 1935, pp. 1039–48, gives details.
41  Sayers, *The Bank of England*, Vol. 2, pp. 467–8. Phillips, principal assistant secretary of the Treasury, regretted the fall in the pound but argued that little could be done about it, P.R.O. T. 188/109: note of 11 January 1935.
42  M.F. B. 32 324: M.A.E. to M.F., 19 January 1935. The information came from the American economic attaché in London via Monick now financial attaché in London. This was not the only indication: on 2 January de Laboulaye in Washington had been tentatively sounded out about France's attitude to a

stabilized sterling–dollar parity of $4.86: M.F. B. 32 323: M.A.E. to Ministry of Finance, 9 January 1935. But Appert, financial attaché in New York, reported that there was still little interest in stabilization in government circles: M.F. B. 32 324: Appert to Paris, 28 December 1934; 28 January 1935.

43  D.D.F., ser. 1, Vol. VIII, No. 116: Monick to Germain-Martin, 22 November 1934. This analysis was confirmed in a speech by Chamberlain on 21 December 1934. Monick did not however take the figure of $4.50 as any more than a bargaining position: he noted that *The Economist* had talked of $4.65 and the City of $4.86.

44  M.F. B. 12678: Cambon to Paris, 29 December 1934.

45  D.D.F., ser. 1, Vol. VIII, No. 453: Monick to Corbin, 11 January 1935.

46  Drummond, *The Floating Pound*, p. 185. The French were aware of this: see M.F. B. 12678; Le Norcy to Paris, 14 November 1933; 6 February 1934.

47  P.R.O. T. 188/109: notes of an interview with Flandin, 1 February 1935; P.R.O. F.O. 371 18795 Leith-Ross to Vansittart, note of an interview with Monick, 23 January 1935.

48  P.R.O. F.O. 371 18795: Rowe-Dutton's report of a conversation with Tannery, 24 January 1935.

49  P.R.O. T. 188/109: Rowe-Dutton to Leith-Ross, 25 January 1935. But he added that even a devaluation of this kind was a long way off. Leith-Ross was inclined to take Monick's remarks about devaluation more seriously: his information was that French opinion on devaluation was changing fast; even Moreau, former governor of the Bank, was said to have changed his mind on 'pure gold doctrine': P.R.O. T. 188/109: Leith-Ross to Rowe-Dutton, 28 January 1935.

50  P.R.O. T. 188/109: note of a visit from Strakosch. It was Strakosch who had spoken to a 'personal friend of Flandin'.

51  Drummond, *The Floating Pound*, pp. 186–7.

52  S. V. O. Clarke, *Exchange-Rate Stabilization in the mid-1930s: Negotiating the Tripartite Agreement* (1977), p. 69. A note of 8 March 1935, in M.F. B. 32 324, reports that, after meeting Germain-Martin and Tannery on 6 March, Lacour-Gayet saw the Secretary of the American Embassy on 7 March 1935.

53  J.O. Ch., 5 March 1935, pp. 638–9.

54  So Rowe-Dutton believed (P.R.O. F.O. 371 19600, 9 March 1935) and Monick hoped (see his conversation of 6 March 1935 with Leith-Ross: P.R.O. F.O. 371 19600).

55  M.F. B. 32 324: note of 11 March 1935; for an equally pessimistic assessment of the prospects of deflation see also his note of 26 January 1935, in M.A.E. Série B. Commerciale 57 7.

56  Coulondre reported that de Laboulaye had reported further unofficial démarches on 6 March 1935: Morgenthau had suggested, not a conference but talks between France, America and Britain. Coulondre to M.F.B. 32 324, 9 March 1935.

57  This policy was outlined in two notes: Coulondre's of 11 March 1935, M.F. B. 32 324; and a note on gold block policy by the *Mouvement général des fonds*: M.F. B. 32 323, 12 March 1935.

58  M.F. B. 32 323: Paris to Washington, 14 March 1935. It asked the French embassy to propose to Roosevelt Franco-American conversations (on the basis of the plan outlined above) to which the British should be invited.

59  J. M. Blum, *From the Morgenthau Diaries: Years of Crisis 1928–1938* (1959), p. 132.

60  M.F. B. 21848: Appert to Paris, 12 April 1935.

61  M.F. B. 21848: Paris to Washington, 25 April 1935.
62  M.F. B. 32 324: de la Baume (M.A.E.) to M.F., 2 May 1935.
63  Coulondre's note of 11 March 1935, M.F. B. 32 324.
64  P.R.O. F.O. 371 19600: a note by Leith-Ross on a conversation with Rueff and Monick on 6 March 1935. As Corbin was to write later about the mistrust exist-ing between London and Washington: 'we could ask ourselves if we haven't overall more lost than gained from the incomprehension which is developing between the two countries': M.F. B. 33 201: Corbin to M.A.E., 6 June 1934.
65  P.R.O. T. 188/109: Leith-Ross to Hopkins: report of a meeting with Flandin on 2 March 1935.
66  P.R.O. T. 160 13427/2: Leith-Ross to Phillips, 26 March 1935.
67  Ibid., a note by Phillips, 30 March 1935, in reply to the note by Leith-Ross, 26 March 1935: 'reluctantly against' conversations. See also the marginal com-ments of Chamberlain: 'I very much doubt the value of our giving advice which could hardly be represented as disinterested. I have an idea the gold block are quite alive to the possible consequences if they "overdo" it'.
68  Drummond, *The Floating Pound*, p. 191.
69  M.F.B. 12618: Monick to Paris, 17 May 1935; P.R.O. F.O. 371 19600: note by Leith-Ross on an interview with Monick on 16 May 1935.
70  P.R.O. F.O. 371 18795: note by Leith-Ross, 16 May 1935, on an interview with Monick.
71  P.R.O. T. 160 13427/2: Rowe-Dutton to Leith-Ross, 17 May 1935.
72  P.R.O. F.O. 371 19600: Leith-Ross to Gwatkin, 20 May 1935.
73  P.R.O. T. 188/109: note by Leith-Ross, 29 May 1935, on a 'long talk with Devinat'.
74  P.R.O. F.O. 371 18795: note by Rowe-Dutton of an interview with Lacour-Gayet, 28 May 1935. For a possible source of this optimism see above, p, 104.
75  M.F. B. 21848: Appert to Paris, 13 June 1935.
76  *Foreign Relations of the United States* (1952), Vol. 2, p. 223. Memorandum of 28 June 1935 by Williamson, 2nd Secretary of the Embassy.
77  P.R.O. F.O. 371 19601: note by Leith-Ross of a meeting with Laval, 9 July 1935.
78  M.F. B. 12619: Monick to Paris, 5 October 1935.
79  *From the Morgenthau Diaries*, p. 138; P.R.O. F.O. 371 19601, pp. 496–7: Rowe-Dutton to Waley, 17 October 1935.
80  M.F. B. 33 201: Monick to Paris, 1 September 1935.
81  Cambon, at the London embassy, had always drawn special attention to Monick's pro-devaluation despatches: see M.F. B. 12678: Cambon to Paris, 29 December 1934; also M.F. B. 12678: Cambon to Paris, 9 September 1935.
82  Drummond, *The Floating Pound*, p. 191. On Rueff see also above, p. 105. But in April 1936 Rowe-Dutton reported that Rueff was reluctant to be associated with the propaganda against devaluation, owing perhaps to the influence of the Bank: P.R.O. T. 160 13427/3: Rowe-Dutton to Waley, 6 April 1936.
83  Sayers, *The Bank of England*, Vol. 2, pp. 467, 471.
84  *L'Oeuvre*, 29 June 1934.
85  In fact in this speech he did not explicitly choose between deflation and devalu-ation; he confined himself to pointing out the contradictions between the government's economic and monetary policies, and appealed to it to choose between them. But any doubt as to his personal choice was quickly dispelled: see his letter to *Le Temps*, 29 August 1934.
86  *Le Temps*, 27 January 1935.

 87  H. de la Tour du Pin, 'La Presse de droite contre la dévaluation: sa campagne
      contre Paul Renyaud' (memoir, University of Paris I, 1972), pp. 99, 112. To this
      thesis I also owe the second epigraph to this chapter.
 88  Reynaud, *Mémoires I*, pp. 350–419; *Mémoires II: Envers et contre tous* (1963),
      pp. 19–38.
 89  La Tour du Pin, 'La Presse de droite', pp. 28–39; Dubief, *Le Déclin de la
      Troisième République*, p. 30, talks of Reynaud's 'belated' lucidity; Duroselle, *La
      Décadence*, p. 214.
 90  *La Lumière*, 14 July 1934.
 91  *La Liberté*, 20 June 1933; also *La Liberté*, 8 July 1933 ('Nous avons été
      manoeuvrés').
 92  *La Liberté*, 30 April 1933. Reynaud tells us, *Mémoires I*, p. 363, that Tardieu,
      who was director of *La Liberté*, was himself alarmed by these articles: 'talk
      about anything you want but, for the love of God, don't talk of the monetary
      problem'.
 93  J.O. Ch., 26 January 1933, pp. 311–20; J.O. Ch., 12 February 1933, pp. 702–4;
      J.O. Ch., 22 October 1933, pp. 3886–90.
 94  J.O. Ch., 7 December 1933, pp. 4425–31.
 95  J.O. Ch., 20 February 1934, pp. 541–4.
 96  Reynaud papers, A.N. 74 A.P. 20: letter of 19 May 1934.
 97  Tardieu papers, A.N. 324 A.P. 14: letter of 4 January 1935.
 98  As was alleged by Du Clain, *La Lumière*, 23 March 1935; and E. Monick, *Pour
      mémoire* (1970), p. 30. Although such calculations can hardly have been absent
      from his mind, the return to power would not have been so simple: after the fall
      of Flandin, he writes in his *Mémoires I*, p. 391, Lebrun ought to have formed a
      government which would secretly prepare a devaluation; but given the import-
      ance of secrecy he could hardly have been a member.
 99  Letter of 13 February 1936, quoted in Reynaud, *Mémoires II*, p. 33.
100  A.N. 74 A.P. 20: letter of 12 July 1935.
101  For example *Le Populaire*, 30 November 1935; *Le Peuple*, 23 October 1934. He
      was also accused of having business interests in Mexico which would have
      benefitted from devaluation.
102  A.N. 74 A.P. 8: contains these and several hundred more letters of congratu-
      lation.
103  A. Sauvy, *De Paul Reynaud à Charles de Gaulle: un économiste face aux
      hommes politiques 1934–1967* (1972), pp. 9, 13.
104  I owe this information to a letter from M. Sauvy. Monick, *Pour mémoire*, p. 30,
      portrays Reynaud almost as Istel's uncomprehending puppet over devaluation,
      but this doesn't tally with other accounts.
105  D. Leca, *La Rupture de 1940* (1978), p. 28.
106  J.O. Ch., 3 December 1934, p. 2943.
107  A.N. 74 A.P. 20: letter of 12 July 1935.
108  Ibid., letter of 3 August 1935.
109  For biographical details on Boris, see M.-F. Toinet, 'Georges Boris 1888–1960:
      un Socialiste humaniste' (*Troisième cycle* thesis, University of Paris X, 1969).
110  For example *La Lumière*, 14 January 1933.
111  Ibid., 11 March 1933.
112  Ibid., 18 April 1933.
113  Ibid., 28 April 1933.
114  Ibid., 14 July 1933.
115  *La République*, 21 April 1933; see also ibid., 25 April 1933, 3 May 1933, 12
      June 1933.

116 *La Lumière*, 11 November 1933.
117 *La République*, 25 April 1933.
118 J.O. Ch., 26 January 1933, pp. 275–6; also *La République*, 21 January 1933.
119 J.O. Ch., 26 January 1933, p. 276; see also his speech in J.O. Ch., 11 February 1933, p. 708, which pointed out that England had benefitted from devaluation; and his intervention in C.R.C.R. 1933, p. 247.
120 J.O. Ch., 20 February 1934, pp. 546–9; J.O. Ch., 25 January 1935, pp. 203–6.
121 See *X Crise*, May–June 1935; *La République*, 15 September 1935.
122 J.O. Ch., 30 May 1933, p. 2681; also *L'Oeuvre*, 20 October 1933.
123 *La Vie socialiste*, 7 April 1934; *L'Oeuvre*, 20 January 1934.
124 *L'Oeuvre*, 15 September 1934.
125 *La Vie socialiste*, 28 April 1934.
126 J.O. Ch., 31 May 1935, pp. 1724–5. Among economists Bertrand Nogaro, until 1934 a Radical deputy, was by 1935 ready to envisage devaluation: *X Crise*, May–June 1935.
127 Patenôtre's assistance is mentioned by Reynaud, *Mémoires I*, p. 390, but he omits to say that Patenôtre's campaign predated his own: thus Duroselle, *La Décadence*, p. 218, describes him as Reynaud's 'disciple'.
128 Biographical details in J.-C. Broustra, *Le Combat de Raymond Patenôtre* (1969). On the *Petit Journal* in the 1930s, see F. Kupferman and P. Machefer, 'Presse et politique dans les années trente: le cas du *Petit Journal*', *Revue d'histoire moderne et contemporaine* 22 (Jan.–Mar. 1975), pp. 7–51.
129 Letter published as Appendix 6 to *Voulons-nous sortir de la crise* (1934), pp. 159–65.
130 Besides ibid., see also *Pour la dévaluation. Contre la dictature d'or* (1934); *Vers le bien-être* (1936).
131 *Le Petit Journal*, 28 May 1935. The full list is as follows: Frossard, Scapini, Laniel, Polimann, Deudon, Bardon, Cornu, Torres, Renaitour, Charabot, Mendès France, Boulay, Goujon, Lillaz, Outrey, and those mentioned in the text.
132 Except where notes give precise references, what follows can be considered a summary of Reynaud's speeches in J.O. Ch., 28 June 1934, pp. 1841–61; 3 December 1934, pp. 2938–46; 25 January 1935, pp. 206–12; 30 May 1935, pp. 1719–24; 29 November 1935, pp. 2242–8; his pamphlet *Jeunesse, quelle France veux-tu?* (1936); his letters to *Le Temps*, 29 August 1934; to *Le Matin*, 16 August 1934; to *Le Figaro*, 28 January 1934; 4 and 5 February 1935; his article in *Information sociale*, 12 September 1934; his lecture in *X Crise*, 23 November 1935.
133 See also Patenôtre, *Voulons-nous*, p. 235: '[Duchemin] examines the question from the external angle . . . but neglects the domestic angle which is even more important'.
134 Letter to *Le Temps*, 29 August 1934.
135 See also Patenôtre, *Vers le bien-être*, p. 22.
136 J.O. Ch., 3 December 1934, p. 2943. Germain-Martin sent Reynaud a copy of a confidential report from Monick in London – probably that cited in Note 43 – intending to prove that Britain was not yet ready to stabilize, but Reynaud drew the different moral that she would not take any trade reprisals in the event of French devaluation: A.N. 74 A.P. 20: Reynaud to Germain-Martin, 31 January 1935.
137 J.O. Ch., 25 January 1935, pp. 210–11. To de Kérillis he wrote that a floating franc would be a *pis aller*: A.N. 74 A.P. 20: Reynaud to de Kérillis, 21 February 1935.

138  Boris, *La Lumière*, 15 December 1934; Patenôtre, *Vers le bien-être*, pp. 104–6, ideally wanted the franc to be linked to the pound.
139  J.O. Ch., 28 May 1935, p. 1721.
140  *La Lumière*, 14 April 1934.
141  Déat, *La République*, 1 January 1936; Montagnon, *L'Oeuvre*, 15 September 1934.
142  *X Crise*, July–August 1935.
143  *Voulons-nous*, pp. 72ff; *Vers le bien-être*, Pt 2.
144  *Mémoires I*, p. 419.
145  Rist, *Information sociale*, 9 September 1934.
146  *Le Figaro*, 26, 28 January 1935; 4 February 1935.
147  *Capital*, 5 August 1934; 13 December 1935.
148  *Interpellations*, October 1934.
149  *L'Oeuvre*, 1, 19 September 1934.
150  *L'Heure de choisir*: speech by Henri Garnier to a meeting of Chambers of Commerce, 7 May 1935.
151  *Y'aurait-il intérêt à dévaluer le franc?* (October 1934).
152  *La Journée industrielle*, 21 November 1935.
153  Ibid., 18–19 November 1934.
154  *Capital*, 27 March 1934.
155  Kuisel, *Ernest Mercier*, p. 93.
156  *La Dévaluation? Expédient facile mais redoutable illusion* (June 1935). M. Perrot, who produces an impressive litany of anti-devaluation propaganda, mentions a manifesto of 32 industrial groups in May 1935, signed by, among others, Peyerimhoff, Citröen and Fougère, *La Monnaie*, pp. 214–15, 227.
157  Above, pp. 170; 175; 177.
158  *Capital*, 9 November 1934.
159  *Mes causeries*, pp. 61–2 (speech of 24 September 1934).
160  J.O. Doc. C. 1934, No. 3825 talked of 'an ancestral tradition of morality'.
161  J.O. Ch., 31 May 1935, p. 1728.
162  P.V.C., 12 November 1935.
163  *Mémoires II*, p. 26.
164  *Capital*, 27 March 1935.
165  R.E.P. Nov.–Dec. 1934, p. 1745–6.
166  *Le Figaro*, 17 August 1934.
167  *La République*, 2 September 1934; 20 August 1935.
168  *L'Oeuvre*, 13 June 1935.
169  What follows is a summary of the case against devaluation. The arguments used can be found throughout the press, and in speeches and pamphlets. There are two frequent arguments which I have not mentioned here because they have already come up in this chapter: the threat of retaliation, and the impossibility of aligning the franc on floating currencies.
170  J.O. Doc. C. 1934, No. 3825; Duchemin, *Y'aurait-il intérêt*, p. 40; Jenny, *Le Temps*, 19 August 1935; Romier, *Le Figaro*, 26 January 1935.
171  Duchemin, *Y'aurait-il intérêt*, pp. 49–52. See Nogaro's criticism of the figures in *Le Problème de la 'dévaluation' en France* (1935), pp. 25–33.
172  Romier, *Le Figaro*, 13 August 1935; *Le Temps*, 29 June 1934; Jenny, *Le Temps*, 3 December 1934; Duchemin, *Y'aurait-il intérêt*, pp. 55–6; Duhen, *La Dévaluation?*, p. 4.
173  Romier, *Le Figaro*, 5 July 1934. Germain-Martin said that France would be doing a disservice to the world by adding to monetary instability: J.O. Ch., 28

June 1934, p. 1751; *Le Temps*, 5 December 1934, said that England was secretly grateful to France for preserving a last haven of monetary orthodoxy.
174 Duchemin, *Y'aurait-il intérêt*, p. 40: 'the glorious days of the English experiment are perhaps over'.
175 Jenny, *Le Temps*, 30 April 1934; *Le Temps*, 12 July 1934; Garnier, *L'Heure de choisir*, p. 11; Fabre-Luce, *Europe nouvelle*, 9 March 1935.
176 J.O. Doc. C. 1934, No. 3825: France 'depends on the outside world for the acquisition of many of her raw materials'; *Le Temps*, 12 July 1935.
177 Romier, *Le Figaro*, 29 June 1934; Jenny, *Le Temps*, 19 August 1935; Duchemin, *Y'aurait-il intérêt*, p. 38.
178 J.O. Doc. C. 1934, No. 3825; Duchemin, *Y-aurait-il intérêt*, p. 38; Romier, *Le Figaro*, 9 February 1935; *Le Temps*, 12 July 1934; *La Nation*, 19 June 1934. See also Perrot, *La Monnaie*, p. 212.
179 Jenny, *Le Temps*, 19 August 1935.
180 P.R.O. F.O. 371 19601: note on a meeting with Laval, 9 July 1935.
181 J.O. Ch., 28 June 1934, p. 1851.
182 'The world will not emerge from the crisis which ravages it unless France shows it the way': *La Nation*, 25 May 1935. See also *Le Journal des débats*, 29 July 1934: as monetary disorder increased the day would come when France would 'play a role worthy of her destiny'.
183 P.V.C., 12 November 1935.
184 *Problèmes actuels*, p. 64.
185 Albert-Petit, *Le Journal des débats*, 13 August 1934.
186 *Le Temps*, 1 April 1935; see also Romier, *Le Figaro*, 20 March 1935.
187 *Le Temps*, 5 July 1933 ('La monnaie dirigée').
188 *Le Figaro*, 14 August 1934.
189 This is the argument followed in an interesting article by M. Margairaz, 'La Droite française face à la crise: incompétence ou choix politique?', C.H.I.M.T. 20–1 (1977), pp. 69–88. But he perhaps underestimates the irrational element in the anti-devaluation campaign. He sees the right as having cynically exploited the fears of the rentiers; on the contrary, it shared them.
190 Jenny, *Le Temps*, 15 April 1934.
191 Régnier, J.O. Ch., 29 November 1935, p. 2249; *Le Journal des débats*, 24 June 1933: devaluation would hit the 'solidity of the social order'.
192 A.N. 74 A.P. 20: letter of 16 May 1935. See also M.F. B. 33204 which contains a large dossier of poignant letters from rentiers who had taken up the 4.5 per cent conversion loan in September 1932, complaining about the issue of the 5.25 per cent loan of March 1933; it is from these that the first epigraph to this chapter comes.
193 Jenny, *Le Temps*, 30 April 1934.
194 J.O. Doc. C. 1934 No. 3825: 'The French people can still remember the years 1924, 1925 and 1926'; Duchemin, *Y'aurait-il intérêt*, p. 22; Germain-Martin, *Les Problèmes actuels des finances publiques en France* (1933), p. 24.
195 *La Crise économique dans le monde et en France* (1936), p. 161, Fn. 1.
196 Jenny, *Le Temps*, 14 August 1935; J.O. Doc. C. 1934, No. 3825; Duchemin, *Y'aurait-il intérêt*, p. 19. The hoarding of notes was an obsession during the period. Usually the figure was estimated to be around 25m to 40m.
197 P.V.C., 17 May 1933.
198 *Le Temps*, 3 September 1935.
199 J.O. Ch., 20 May 1933, p. 2682. See also his article in *L'Oeuvre*, 15 September 1934.

200  *L'Oeuvre*, 20 February 1934.
201  C.R.C.R. 1933, p. 249; see also his article in *L'Oeuvre*, 11 November 1935.
202  *Le Populaire*, 21 November 1933; 15 September 1934.
203  Ibid., 28 March 1933.
204  Ibid., 29 September 1934.
205  Ibid., 2 November 1935.
206  Ibid., 25 March 1933.
207  Ibid., 24 September 1934.
208  Ibid., 28 September 1934.
209  Ibid., 29 September 1934.
210  Ibid., 16 July 1934; 20 July 1934.
211  Ibid., 17 March 1934.
212  Ibid., 14 April 1934.
213  Ibid., 7 April 1935.
214  J.O. Ch., 29 November 1935, p. 2247.
215  C.R.C.S. 1935, pp. 211–12.
216  Moch, ibid., p. 296; the proposal was adopted without dissent, ibid., p. 516.
     Naville, from the extreme left, was the only other delegate to discuss the issue:
     ibid., pp. 388–97. Marjolin had also discussed devaluation in his economic
     column in *Le Populaire*, moving from hostility in 1934 to resignation in 1935,
     mixed with warnings about its psychological dangers in France: *Le Populaire*, 6
     July 1934; 10, 24, 31 March 1935; 7 July 1935. As a result of these articles he
     received a postbag of angry letters from party members (I owe this information
     to the draft of his memoirs).
217  C.R.C.S. 1934, p. 61.
218  *Le Temps*, 20 March 1934.
219  Coffinet, *Combat marxiste*, 15 April 1934; also 15 May 1934 ('Encore la
     dévaluation', 'Défense des épargnants'). But by 1935 *Combat marxiste* had
     shifted closer to devaluation: see Pommera, ibid., 1 June 1935.
220  Constant, *Les Cahiers du bolchévisme*, 15 September 1935.
221  Politzer, *Les Cahiers du bolchévisme* 1, 15 December 1935.
222  J.O. Ch., 28 November 1935, pp. 2235–9.
223  Weill-Reynal, *Contre la déflation budgétaire*, p. 40, Fn. 2; J. Moch, *Arguments
     et documents contre capitalisme, la crise, et la déflation* (1936), p. 98, Fn. 1. See
     also the cases of Spinasse, J.O. Ch., 28 June 1934, p. 1824; and André Philip, *La
     Crise et l'économie dirigée* (1935), pp. 192–7.
224  For example Delaisi, *L'Atelier pour le plan*, 15 May 1936.
225  Jouhaux, ibid., 15 June 1936.
226  Delaisi, ibid., 15 October 1935.
227  *Le Peuple*, 1 June 1935.
228  On Delaisi see Note 224, above; on Belin, p. 129, above; on Duret, *L'Atelier
     pour le plan*, 1 January 1936; on Laurat, ibid., 15 May 1935.
229  L. Germain-Martin, *Sommes-nous sur bonne route?* (1934), p. 32.
230  Quoted by S. Berstein, 'Les Conceptions du Parti radical en matière de politique
     économique extérieure', *Relations internationales* 13 (1978), p. 82. The remark
     was made at the Congress of 1933.
231  D.D.F., ser. 1, Vol. VII, No. 377: note by Coulondre, 16 October 1934.
232  Above, p. 88.
233  M.A.E. Série B Commerciale 57 7 contains correspondence with the Comité.
     The affair is discussed by Duroselle, *La Décadence*, pp. 215–16 to which I am
     indebted for drawing my attention to this source.

234 M.F. B. 32 323 contains an account of Stoppani's soundings and his report. These are his figures on the proportion of each gold block country's exports to the rest of the gold block:

| | 1929 | 1933 |
|---|---|---|
| Belgium | 31% | 39.7% |
| France | 34.7% | 37% |
| Italy | 18.9% | 20.3% |
| Holland | 21.4% | 29.7% |
| Switzerland | 22% | 32.8% |

235 D.D.F., ser. 1, Vol. VII, No. 365: communiqué of gold block conference, 25 September 1934.
236 The idea had been mooted by some other countries at Geneva, but decisively rejected by Lamoureux, Commerce Minister: M.F. B. 32 323: Massigli to Paris, 25 September 1934.
237 M.F. B. 32 323: account of the interministerial committee meeting of 29 September 1934. The problem with this idea was that since Holland, Belgium and Italy did not have agricultural quotas, it was not clear what they could give in return.
238 M.A.E. Série B. Commerciale 57 7: Minister of Agriculture to Minister of Commerce, 9 October 1934.
239 M.F. B. 32 323: note of 12 October 1934.
240 M.A.E. Série B. Commerciale 57 7: French legation in Holland to Paris, 16 October 1934.
241 Ibid., contains telegrams between France's ambassador in Rome, Chabrun, and Paris during October 1934.
242 Ibid.: note on a meeting of the French delegation, 15 October 1934; see also note cited in Fn. 231, above.
243 D.D.F., ser. 1, Vol. VII, No. 508.
244 M.A.E. Série B. Commerciale 57 7: note of *Directeur adjoint* (*Relations commerciales*), 20 October 1934.
245 Ibid.: note of the *Directeur adjoint* (*Relations commerciales*), 26 January 1935; see also Duroselle, *La Décadence*, pp. 216–17.
246 M.A.E. Série B. Commerciale 57 7: Claudel to M.A.E., 3 November 1934.
247 Details of all these negotiations are given in an undated note in ibid. The agreement signed with Italy on 15 January was very limited: Italy agreed to maintain the level of quotas accorded to France in the previous year; France agreed to maintain her level of agricultural quota allocations for Italy – in spite of having reduced them for other countries – and to try and increase industrial quota allocations.
248 Ibid.: letter of Marchandeau to Laval, 29 January 1934.
249 M.F. B. 32 324: note of 11 March 1935.
250 Legueu, *Le Figaro*, 7 July 1934; Romier, ibid., 11 August 1934; *La Journée industrielle*, 18–19 November 1934.
251 *Le Journal des débats*, 22 October 1934; Romier, *le Figaro*, 20 October 1934; *Le Temps*, 19 October 1934 said that the conference might turn out to be more important than the Conference of London; *La Nation*, 27 October 1934.
252 *Le Temps*, 9 March 1935; Jenny, ibid., 18 March 1935.
253 Berstein, 'Les Conceptions du Parti radical', pp. 83–4.
254 J.O. Ch., 3 December 1934, p. 2942.
255 For example Montagnon, *La Vie socialiste*, 7 April 1934; Marion, *Notre temps*, 1 March 1934.

256  *La Nation*, 16 June 1934.
257  For example *La Nation*, 3 January 1931; 3 March 1934.
258  A.N. F.[10] 2164: report of meeting of inter-ministerial committee, 9 March 1933.
259  J.O. Doc. Admin., 3 March 1935, pp. 175–94.
260  *Le Temps*, 4 December 1934; Romier, *Le Figaro*, 4 December 1934; *Le Journal des débats*, 5 December 1934: *La Nation*, 15 December 1934.
261  *Le Temps*, 18 February 1935.
262  *Le Temps*, 20 July 1935.
263  R.E.P. May 1935, p. 549.
264  *Journal des débats*, 27 July 1931, quoted by R. Schor, 'Une étude d'opinion: la droite française face à la crise mondiale de 1929', *L'Information historique* 2 (1974), pp. 64–70.
265  *La Nation*, 13 June 1931.
266  Ibid., 31 January 1931.
267  Romier, *Le Figaro* 5, 14 December 1934.
268  Julia, *Le Temps*, 9 October 1931. Quoted by Schor in 'Une étude d'opinion'.
269  J.O. Sen., 26 December 1935, p. 956. He talked of a currency 'alignment' involving some 'sacrifices'.
270  Boris announced this in *La Lumière*, 11 May 1935. It is hinted at in Germain-Martin's intervention to the Interparliamentary Committee on Commerce: *La Journée industrielle*, 1 October 1935. A copy of his full report to the Committee is contained in M.F. B. 32 324.
271  R.E.P. 1935, p. 549.
272  Vallier, *La Nation*, 31 August 1935; Boris, *La Lumière*, 11 May 1935.
273  For example the article by Habbé in the financial section, 3 November 1935; by Romier on 15, 16 November 1935.
274  11 December 1935. But a devaluation was only envisaged if foreign currencies should depreciate any further; a continuation of the status quo was seen as quite possible.
275  See D. Lecomte and D. Pavy, 'Le Front populaire face au mur d'argent: le problème du contrôle des changes dans les années 1936–1938' (memoir, University of Paris VIII, 1971), p. 96.
276  J.O. Ch., 29 November 1935, p. 2240; see also Boris, *La Lumière*, 9 November 1935.
277  M.F. B. 33 189, No. 3: 26 January 1936.
278  *La Lumière*, 21 December 1935.

## Epilogue

 1  Various minor measures were passed: the government accepted the principle of a national unemployment fund proposed by left-wing deputies, and sent the matter back to the Finance Commission for discussion: J.O. Ch., 6 February 1936, pp. 234–57; small shopkeepers were protected by a bill banning *magasins à prix unique*: J.O. Ch., 20 February 1936, pp. 478–84; the shoe industry was protected by a bill prohibiting the construction of new factories for two years, a measure aimed against the Bata company which planned to build a large plant in France: J.O. Ch., 27 February 1936, pp. 605ff; 28 February 1936, pp. 654–64. Finally on the last day of the session further measures of 'humanization' of the decree laws were taken: the sum involved – some 200mi – was insignificant, but for electoral reasons the psychological impact was considered to be important: J.O. Ch., 19 March 1936, pp. 989ff.

2  Above, p. 108.
3  To understand how this figure was reached, see M.F. B. 194, No. 27: note of 22 May 1936.
4  Jenny, *Le Temps*, 23 March 1936.
5  M.F. B. 33 194, No. 15: note of 18 March 1936.
6  M.F. B. 33 194, No. 36: note of 11 June 1936.
7  But the recovery was noticed by contemporaries up to a point: Régnier, P.V.S., 6 March 1936; Jenny, *La Revue politique et parlementaire*, 10 January 1936.
8  *Barodet* 1936. The deputies were respectively Bernard-Ferron (Loire et Cher), Pecherot (Drôme), Barthe (Hérault).
9  Ibid., Ponsard (Bouches du Rhône).
10  Ibid., Dupont (Seine).
11  Ibid., Dignac (Gironde).
12  For example ibid., Ramadier (Aveyron); but some on the right did attribute it to Laval: for example de la Groudière (Manche).
13  Ibid., De Lastyrie (Seine).
14  Ibid., De la Myre-Mory (Lot et Garonne).
15  Ibid., D'Aromon (Seine). J. Legendre, *Pour lutter contre le front populaire* (1936) contained every permutation of anti-Popular Front propaganda. It is published by the Centre de Propagande des Républicains Nationaux. On the elections of 1936, see G. Dupeux, *Le Front populaire et les elections de 1936* (1959).
16  The rest of this chapter is intended to be a synthesis of the available literature on the economic and financial policies of the years 1936 to 1939. Although I have at times given precise page references to particular works, I have relied most fundamentally on the following: R. Frankenstein, *Le Prix du réarmement français 1935–1939* (1982), – of very much wider significance than its title implies; D. Lecomte and D. Pavy, 'Le Front populaire face au mur d'argent: le problème du contrôle des changes dans les années 1936–1938' (memoir, University of Paris – VIII, 1975); R. Rémond and P. Renouvin, eds., *Léon Blum, chef de gouvernement, 1936–1937* (1967); the colloquia of the Fondation Nationale des Sciences Politiques, edited by R. Rémond and J. Bourdin, eds., *Edouard Daladier, chef de gouvernement, avril 1938–septembre 1939* (1977), and *La France et les français en 1938–1939* (1978); G. Bourdé, *La Défaite du Front populaire* (1977).
17  This 10m came out of the 17m increase in the Bank of France's holdings after the revaluation of its reserves resulting from the devaluation.
18  In fact, both Blum and Auriol had publicly hinted in June that they were not uncompromising in their opposition to devaluation: Wolfe, *The French Franc*, pp. 145–6.
19  For the negotiations over devaluation see Monick, *Pour mémoire*; R. Girault, 'Léon Blum, la dévaluation de 1936 et la conduite de la politique extérieure de la France', *Relations internationales* 13 (1978), pp. 91–109; J.-P. Cuvillier, *Vincent Auriol et les finances publiques du Front populaire*, pp. 11–25; Clarke, *Exchange-Rate Stabilization*.
20  Clarke, *Exchange-Rate Stabilization*, p. 39.
21  This is one of Lefranc's major criticisms: he was of course an ex-planist; Kuisel, *Capitalism and the State*, p. 124, seems partially to share this view.
22  Quoted in Rémond and Renouvin, eds., *Léon Blum, chef de gouvernement*, p. 253.
23  See M. Kalecki, 'The Lessons of the Blum Experiment', *The Economic Journal*

48 (March 1938), pp. 26–41. J. Bouvier, 'Un Débat toujours ouvert: la politique économique du Front populaire', *Le Mouvement social* 54 (Jan.–Mar. 1966), reviews the debate.

24  Frankenstein, *Le Prix du réarmement*, p. 155.
25  Above, p. 121.
26  Lecomte and Pavy, 'Le Front populaire', p. 102.
27  Frankenstein, *Le Prix du réarmement*, p. 128.
28  Lecomte and Pavy, 'Le Front populaire', p. 127.
29  Sauvy, *Histoire économique*, Vol. 2, pp. 297–307; J. M. Jeanneney in Rémond and Renouvin, eds., *Léon Blum, chef de gouvernement*, pp. 226–7; R. Marjolin, 'Reflections on the Blum Experiment', *Economica* 5, 18 (May 1938), pp. 177–91.
30  J.-C. Asselain, 'Une Erreur de politique économique: la loi des quarante heures de 1936', *Revue économique* 25, 4 (July, 1974), pp. 672–705. This article is the best review of the debate on the 40-hour week.
31  A. Prost in Rémond and Bourdin, eds., *Edouard Daladier*, p. 100.
32  The preceding two paragraphs rely heavily on Frankenstein, *Le Prix du réarmement*, Chapter 7.
33  *The Economist*, 17 November 1936.
34  These were not explicitly mentioned but the plan implied them and its authors intended them.
35  Berstein, *Histoire du Parti radical II*, pp. 528–35.
36  Quoted in Frankenstein, *Le Prix du réarmement*, p. 185.
37  On the new American attitude see I. Drummond, *London, Washington and the Management of the Franc 1936–39* (1979), pp. 30, 42–4; and Frankensetin, *Le Prix du réarmement*, pp. 186–7, 198.
38  See the testimony of Georges Boris, *Servir la République* (1963), pp. 191–9.
39  See Rémond and Bourdin, eds., *Edouard Daladier*, especially the contributions of A. Prost, 'Le Climat social', pp. 99–110; E. du Réau, 'L'Aménagement de la loi instituant la semaine de quarante heures', pp. 129–49.
40  Berstein, *Histoire du Parti radical II*, p. 561.
41  Frankenstein, *Le Prix du réarmement*, p. 223.
42  Kuisel, *Capitalism*, pp. 126–7; Frankenstein, *Le Prix du réarmement*, pp. 298–9.


## Conclusion

1   J.O. Doc. C. 1933, No. 1535.
2   *Le Temps*, 12 September 1933.
3   Ibid., 3 July 1933.
4   J.O. Ch., 27 January 1933, p. 355.
5   P.V.C., 16 November 1933.
6   J.O. Ch., 7 December 1933, p. 4435.
7   J.O. Ch., 7 December 1933, p. 4437.
8   J.O. Ch., 23 October 1933, p. 3934.
9   *La République*, 29 January 1933.
10  *L'Oeuvre*, 7 November 1933.
11  On the negotiations see Lamoureux, 'Mémoires', pp. 1363ff.
12  There were exceptions: for example, Mendès-France, *Notre Temps*, 9 March 1934.
13  11 August 1935.

14 C.R.C.R. October 1934, p. 264.

15 *L'Oeuvre*, 18 June 1935.

16 J.O. Doc. C. 1934, No. 3825 gives full details.

17 P. Saly, 'La Politique française des grands travaux 1929-1939 fut-elle keynésienne?', *Revue économique* 31, 4 (July 1980), p. 721.

18 This is taking the effects of the decrees for a full year.

19 P.V.C., 22 October 1935.

20 *L'Oeuvre*, 11 August 1935; Varenne, ibid., 29 August 1935.

21 R. Pinon, *La Revue des deux mondes*, 1 August 1935, p. 718.

22 Albert-Petit, *Le Journal des débats*, 22 September 1934: 'disons nous bien qu'il faut un Etat fort, mais que l'étatisme est tout contraire'.

23 Herriot, *Jadis II*, pp. 635–6.

24 Letellier *et al.*, *Enquête sur le chômage*, Vol. 1, p. 182.

25 Ibid., p. 317.

26 Sauvy, *Histoire économique*, Vol. 2, pp. 409–11.

27 I have concentrated mainly on the attempt to keep up wheat prices; but this was only the most conspicuous example of a tendency for which many other cases could be cited. The most obvious is wine but there were others: in February 1934 the Chamber, in spite of the protests of the Senate Finance Commission, passed a law extending subsidies to pine resin farmers: J.O. Doc. C., 22 February 1934, pp. 650–1; P.V.S., 7 March 1934. At other times the Senate could be more successful in encouraging prices to fall at all cost: the Finance Commission successfully detached an article of the 1934 budget regulating the growth of large scale retail stores ('magasins à prix unique'): P.V.S., 23 February 1934; but this measure designed to protect small shopkeepers was eventually passed in 1936: see above, Epilogue, Note 1. This was a case incidentally when the Senate was not, as it has usually been judged – D. Salem, 'Le Sénat "conservateur" de la Troisième République', *Revue d'histoire économique et sociale* 50, 4 (1972), pp. 535–42 – on the side of traditionalism; to quote one senator: 'let the laws of economics play and eliminate useless organisms': P.V.S., 23 February 1934.

28 Above, p. 1. To the works of Carré, Dubois, and Malinvaud, and Caron, already cited as representative of this tendency, can be added M. Lévy-Leboyer, 'Le Patronat français a-t-il été malthusien?', *Le Mouvement social* 88 (July–Sept. 1974), pp. 3–49.

29 Above, p. 39.

30 Boris, *La Lumière*, 31 August 1935; R. Patenôtre, *Vers le bien-être* (1936), pp. 121–32.

31 H. Dubreuil, *Standards: le travail américain vu par un ouvrier français* (1929); G. Duhamel, *Scènes de la vie future* (1930); R. Aron and A. Dandieu, *Le Cancer américain* (1931) and *Décadence de la nation française* (1931). For surveys of this meditation upon American experience see: P. Gagnon, 'French Views of the Second American Revolution', *French Historical Studies* 2, 4 (Fall 1962), pp. 430–49; D. Strauss, *Menace in the West: The Rise of French Anti-Americanism in Modern Times* (1978); for reactions to Roosevelt's monetary experiments see: M. Vaïsse, 'Le Mythe de l'or en France: les aspects monétaires du New Deal vus par les français', *Revue d'histoire moderne et contemporaine* 16 (July–Sept. 1969), pp. 462–79.

32 29 June 1934.

33 To this list could be added Marjolin's, *Les Expériences Roosevelt* (1934). But it adopted a much more critical stance.

# Bibliography

(For ease of reference I have divided the bibliography into sections. Some of the divisions – between, for example, socialist works and planist works – cannot help being at times somewhat arbitrary. The section of secondary printed works contains various books written during the 1930s. This is because I have made the distinction according to whether the work in question was intended to influence the debate it discussed, or merely to offer a comment upon it. Again, the distinction is sometimes arbitrary.)

## I UNPUBLISHED SOURCES

### France

*Ministère de l'Economie – Ministère du Budget (Archives Economiques et Financières)*

B. 32 315–25 (Largely on the preparation and aftermath of the World Economic Conference)

B. 33 201 (Mainly on gold block policy)

B. 33 182–5 (Tables on the state of the Treasury communicated to the Presidents of the Finance Commissions)

B. 33 189–94 (Information on the state of the Treasury)

B. 31 730 ⎫
B. 12617–19 ⎬ (Reports from financial attaché, and others, in London)
B. 12678 ⎭

B. 21848 (Reports from financial attaché in New York)

B. 33 204–5 (on various loan issues)

## Archives Nationales

(a) *Archives de la direction des renseignements généraux du Ministère de l'Intérieur*
F.⁷ 13008 (Reports of Prefects and *Commissaires spéciaux* of the Nord)
F.⁷ 13024–9 (Weekly reports of Prefects for the period 26 March 1934 to 1 December 1934)
F.⁷ 13030–42 (Reports of Prefects and *Commissaires spéciaux*: these usually monthly reports, which cover the period 1919–36, are very incomplete: they are all missing for the entire period of Flandin's ministry; others are missing much more).
F.⁷ 13131 (On the activity of the Communist Party)
F.⁷ 13529–65 (On unemployment 1931–6. Mainly local statistics but also report of marches, demonstrations, etc.)
F.⁷ 13580 (On the C.G.T. 1935)
(b) *Ministère des Colonies*
F.¹⁰ 2164 (On the preparation of the Imperial Conference)

## Ministère des Affaires Etrangères

B. Commerciale 57 7 (On gold block policy)
Y. Internationale 73–4 (On the World Economic Conference)

## Chambre des Deputés

Procès-verbaux de la Commission des Finances, 1932–6
Procès-verbaux de la Commission du Commerce et de l'Industrie, 1935

## Sénat

Procès-verbaux de la Commission des Finances, 1932–6

## Private papers

Léon Blum (Fondation Nationale des Sciences Politiques)
Jean Coutrot (Fondation Nationale des Sciences Politiques)
Edouard Daladier (Fondation Nationale des Sciences Politiques)
Edouard Herriot (Ministère des Affaires Etrangères)
Jacques Kayser (Fondation National des Sciences Politiques)
Louis Marin (Archives Nationales)
Paul Reynaud (Archives Nationales)
Emile Roche–Joseph Caillaux (Fondation Nationale des Sciences Politiques: the most interesting section of these papers for the 1930s – the Roche–Caillaux correspondence – has been published by Roche in the work by him listed below).
André Tardieu (Archives Nationales)

## Unpublished memoirs

Louis Germain-Martin, *Contribution à l'histoire nationale de la France* (In the possession of M. Henri Germain-Martin)
Lucien Lamoureux, 'Mémoires' (Microfilm in the Bibliothèque de Documentation Internationale Contemporaine, Université de Paris X)

**Great Britain**

*Public Record Office*
F.O. 371 (Foreign Office: general correspondence)
T. 160 840 13427 (Treasury: on currency stabilization)
T. 188 (Treasury: Leith-Ross papers)


## II PUBLISHED DOCUMENTS

France. *Barodet*. Chambre des Députés. Programmes, professions de foi et engage-
    ments électoraux, 1932.
France. *Barodet*. Chambre des Députés. Recueil des textes authentiques des pro-
    grammes et engagements électoraux des députés proclamés élus, 1936.
France. Journal officiel de la République française. Annexe. Documents adminis-
    tratifs, 1932–6. (Includes all the reports of the C.N.E.)
France. Journal officiel de la République française, annales de la Chambre des
    Députés: Débats parlementaires, 1932–6.
    Documents parlementaires, 1932–6.
France. Journal officiel de la République française, annales du Sénat: Débats
    parlementaires, 1932–6.
    Documents parlementaires, 1932–6.
France. Ministère des Affaires étrangères. Documents diplomatiques français, 1932–
    1939, 1ère série (1932–5), Tomes I–VIII. Paris, 1964–79.
Great Britain. Department of Overseas Trade. *Economic Conditions in France* (dated
    June 1934). Report by Sir Robert Cahill. London, 1934.
United States. *Foreign Relations of the United States*, 1935. Vol. 2, Washington,
    1952.


## III NEWSPAPERS AND PERIODICALS

(The dates which immediately follow the name of the paper or periodical indicate the
period for which it has been consulted; the absence of any date signifies that it has been
consulted for the whole period 1932–6).


### Conservative and business opinion

*Le Bulletin quotidien*, 1934–5 (organ of the Société d'Etudes et d'Information
    Economiques)
*Le Capital, dernières nouvelles financières et politiques*, 1934–5
*Le Figaro*, 1933–5
*Le Journal des débats*, 1933–5
*La Journée industrielle, quotidien de l'industrie, du commerce et de l'agriculture*,
    1935–5
*La Liberté* (occasional issues consulted)
*La Nation* (weekly organ of the Fédération Républicaine)
*La Revue des deux mondes* (bi-monthly)
*La Revue politique et parlementaire* (monthly: consulted sporadically)
*Le Temps* (also invaluable as a daily record of events)

## Radical and radicalisant

*La Lumière* (weekly)
*L'Oeuvre*
*La République*, 1933–6

## Communist

*Les Cahiers du bolchévisme* (bi-monthly)
*L'Humanité* (consulted sporadically)

## Socialist and Planist

*L'Atelier pour le plan* (monthly; first issue May 1935)
*Bataille socialiste*, 1934–5 (monthly journal of Zyromski's *tendance*)
*Bulletin de révolution constructive: Organe d'information et d'études socialistes*, June 1933
*Combat marxiste* (monthly; first issue December 1933)
*L'Homme nouveau* (eclectic monthly journal which took up the cause of the Plan du 9 juillet. Articles by Déat, Vallon, Marjolin, etc.)
*L'Homme réel* (Syndicalist monthly sympathetic to planism; first issue January 1934)
*Information sociale*, 1934
*Notre temps, Journal des générations du feu et de l'après-guerre*, 1934. (At this time a daily paper with contributions from Déat, de Jouvenel, Clerc, etc.)
*Le Peuple*, 1933–6 (official C.G.T. daily)
*Le Populaire de Paris*
*Révolution constructive: Organe mensuel du groupe de révolution constructive*, December 1934
*La Vie socialiste*, 1933–5 (formerly the weekly journal of the *tendance* Renaudel in the S.F.I.O., it became the official journal of the Neo-Socialists. It folded in July 1935.)
*La Voix du peuple*, 1933–6 (official C.G.T. monthly journal)

## Other

*The Economist*
*Europe* (consulted sporadically)
*L'Europe nouvelle* (consulted sporadically)
*Le Journal du commerce*, 30 October 1935
*La Revue d'économie politique*
*X Crise. Bulletin du Centre polytechnicien d'études économiques*

## IV MEMOIRS AND DIARIES

Abellio, R. (pseudonym of G. Soulès). *Ma dernière mémoire II: les militants 1927–1939*, Paris, 1975
Auriol, V. *Hier demain*, 2 Vols. Paris, 1945
Belin, R. *Du Secrétariat de la C.G.T. au gouvernement de Vichy*, Paris, 1978
Blum, J. M., ed. *From the Morgenthau Diaries, Years of Crisis, 1928–38*, Boston, 1959

Bonnet, G. *Vingt ans de vie politique 1918–1938: De Clemenceau à Daladier*, Paris, 1969
Delmas, A. *A gauche de la barricade*, Paris, 1950
  *Mémoires d'un instituteur syndicaliste*, Paris, 1979
Duclos, J. *Mémoires I 1896–1934*, Paris, 1968
  *Mémoires II 1935–1939*, Paris, 1969
Flandin, P.-E. *Politique française 1919–1940*, Paris, 1947
Herriot, E. *Jadis II: d'une guerre à l'autre, 1914–1936*, Paris, 1952
Jouvenel, B. de *Un Voyageur dans le siècle, 1903–1945*, Paris, 1980
Kayser, J. 'Souvenirs d'un militant 1934–1939', *Les Cahiers de la République* 12 (March 1958), pp. 69–82
Laniel, J. *Jours de gloire et jours cruels, 1908–1958*, Paris, 1971
Laurat, L. 'Mémoires d'un planiste 1932–1939', *Etudes sociales et syndicales*, September 1965, pp. 19–24
Leca, D. *La Rupture de 1940*, Paris, 1978
Leith-Ross, F. *Money Talks: Fifty Years of International Finance*, London, 1968
Man, H. de *Après coup*, Brussels–Paris, 1941
  *Cavalier seul*, Geneva, 1948
Moch, J. *Rencontres avec Léon Blum*, Paris, 1970
Monick, E. *Pour mémoire*, n.p., 1970
Noël, L. *Les Illusions de Stresa*, Paris, 1976
Paul-Boncour, J. *Entre deux guerres. Souvenirs sur la III^e République. II: 1919–1934*, Paris, 1945
Reynaud, P. *Au coeur de la mêlée*, Paris, 1951
  *La France a sauvé l'Europe*, 2 Vols. Paris, 1947
  *Mémoires*, 2 Vols. Paris, 1960–3
Roche, E. *Avec Joseph Caillaux*, Paris, 1972
Rueff, J. *Combats pour un ordre financier*, Paris, 1972
  *De l'Aube au crépuscule: autobiographie*, Paris, 1977
Sauvy, A. *De Paul Reynaud à Charles de Gaulle: un économiste face aux hommes politiques 1934–1967*, Tournai, 1972
Zay, J. *Souvenirs et solitude*, Paris, 1946

## V PUBLISHED PRIMARY SOURCES
### Socialist party

Office de documentation et de propagande du Parti socialiste (S.F.I.O.) *Les partis politiques devant le Socialisme.* Paris, 1932
Parti socialiste S.F.I.O. XXIX^e congrès national, Paris, 29 mai–1^er juin 1932, Compte rendu sténographique, Paris, 1932; rapports de la C.A.P., Paris, 1932
  XXX^e congrès national, Paris, 14–17 juillet, 1933, Compte rendu sténographique, Paris, 1933; rapports de la C.A.P., Paris, 1933
  XXXI^e congrès national, Toulouse, 20-3 mai 1934, Compte rendu sténographique, Paris, 1934; rapports de la C.A.P., Paris, 1934
  XXXII^e congrès national, Mulhouse, 9–12 juin 1935, Compte rendu sténographique, Paris, 1935; rapports de la C.A.P., Paris, 1935
*Programme du Parti socialiste* (S.F.I.O.), Paris, 1932
*Programme du Parti socialiste: élections législatives de 1936.* Paris, 1936

Blum, L. *Discours de Romans* (24 July 1932), Edition de la Fédération socialiste de la Drôme, Valence, 1932

*Pour être socialiste*, Paris, 1919
*Le Socialisme devant la crise*, Paris, 1933
*Le Socialisme a vu clair*, Paris, 1936
Brissaud, A. *La Nationalisation des assurances*, Paris, 1933
Déat, M. *Perspectives socialistes*, Paris, 1930
Dunois, A. *De la Concentration capitaliste aux nationalisations*, Paris, 1936
Faure, P. *Au Seuil d'une révolution*, Limoges, 1934
*Le Socialisme dans la bataille électorale*, Paris, 1936.
Laurat, L. *La Crise mondiale*, Paris, 1935
*La Crise mondiale et ses perspectives*, Paris, 1931
*Economie dirigée et socialisation*, Paris, 1932
*La Liquidation socialiste de la crise*, Paris, 1934
*Le Socialisme à l'ordre du jour: problèmes et tâches du marxisme contemporain*, Paris, 1933
*Un système qui sombre*, Paris-Brussels, 1932
Lebas, J. *Le Socialisme: but et moyen, suivi de la réfutation d'un néo-socialisme*, Lille, 1931
Levy, L. *Comment ils sont devenus socialistes*, Paris, 1932
Marjolin, R. *Les Expériences Roosevelt*, Paris, 1934
Moch, J. *Arguments et documents contre capitalisme, crise, déflation*, Paris, 1936
*Le Rail et la nation*, Paris, 1931
*Socialisme, crise, nationalisations*, Paris, 1932
*Socialisme et rationalisation*, Brussels, 1927
Montagnon, B. *Grandeur et servitude socialistes*, Paris, 1929
Philip, A. *La Crise et l'économie dirigée*, Paris, 1935
*Henri de Man et la crise doctrinale du socialisme*, Paris, 1928
and Monceau, A. *La Toute-puissance bancaire et la nationalisation du crédit*, Paris, 1936
Séverac, J.-B. *Lettres à Brigitte: le Parti socialiste, ses principes et ses tâches*, Paris, 1933
Spinasse, C. *La Crise économique* (speech delivered on 27 February 1931). N.p., n.d.
Weill-Raynal, E. *Contre la déflation budgétaire: pour une politique financière socialiste*, Paris, 1936

## Communist Party

Parti Communiste. *Le Parti communiste devant l'Internationale*, Paris, 1931
*50 millions de chômeurs:150 millions d'hommes ont faim*, Paris, 1931
VIII$^e$ congrès du Parti communiste français, Villeurbanne, 22–5 janvier 1936, Paris, 1936

Degras, J. ed. *The Communist International 1919–1943. Documents. Volume 3 1929–43*, London, 1965
Duclos, J. *La Dévaluation: qui est responsable? qui doit payer?* Paris, 1936
*En avant pour le Front unique d'action anti-fasciste*, Paris, 1934
'Rapports devant l'Internationale communiste', C.H.I.M.T., 1975, pp. 289–318
Manuilski, D. *Les Partis communistes et la crise du capitalisme* (1931)
Piatinski, O. *Le Chômage et la crise: précisons nos tâches!* Paris, 1931
Thorez, M. *En avant pour l'issue révolutionnaire de la crise*, Paris, 1932
*Oeuvres de Maurice Thorez*, 23 Vols. Paris, 1950–65
*La Situation en France et l'action communiste*, Paris, 1931

**Radical Party**

Parti républicain-radical et radical-socialiste. 28$^e$ congrès du Parti républicain-radical et radical-socialiste tenu à Paris, 5–8 novembre 1931. Paris, 1931
    29$^e$ Congrès . . . Toulouse, 3–6 novembre 1932. Paris, 1932
    30$^e$ Congrès . . . Vichy, 5–8 octobre 1933. Paris, 1933
    Congrès extraordinaire . . . Clermont-Ferrand, 11–13 mai 1934. Paris, 1934
    31$^e$ Congrès . . . Nantes, 25–8 octobre 1934. Paris, 1934
    32$^e$ Congrès . . . Paris, 24–9 octobre 1935. Paris, 1935

Bayet, A. *Le Radicalisme*, Paris, 1932
Bonnet, G. *Le Parti radical devant les problèmes du temps présent*, Paris, 1936
    *Le Redressement financier réalisé par les gouvernements radicaux-socialistes, juin 1932–février 1934*, Paris, 1934
Caillaux, J. *The World Crisis. The lessons which it teaches and the adjustments of Economic Science which it necessitates* (The Cobden Lecture for 1932). London, 1932
Jaubert, A. *L'Action parlementaire du Parti radical: le programme des grands travaux et les collectivités locales*, Paris, 1936
Jouvenel, B. de *L'Economie dirigée*, Paris, 1928
Roche, E. *On a voté . . . et maintenant?* Paris, 1936

**Conservative and business opinion**

Alliance Démocratique. *Un Programme d'action pour l'Alliance Démocratique*, Paris, 1933
    *Ce qu'il faut savoir de la dévaluation*, Paris, 1935

Damougeot-Perron, G. *L'Economie française et les décrets-lois* (preface by L. Germain-Martin), Paris, 1936
Damougeot-Perron, G. and Lacout, G. *Le Franc devant la crise*, Paris, 1934
Doumergue, G. *Mes causeries avec le peuple français*, Paris, 1934
Duchemin, R.-P. *La Crise actuelle, ses causes et ses conséquences du point de vue financier.* Neuilly (Seine), 1932
    *Y'aurait-il intérêt à dévaluer le franc?* Paris, October 1934
Duhen, E. *La Dévaluation? Expédient facile mais redoutable illusion*, Paris, 1935
Flandin, P.-E. *Discours. Le ministère Flandin, novembre 1934–mai 1935.* Paris, 1937
Garnier, H. *La France en face d'un nouveau redressement financier et en face de son avenir* (Speech to the Meeting of presidents of the Chambers of Commerce, 5 November 1935). Paris, 1935
    *Le Bilan d'une année.* (Speech of 5 February 1935). Paris, 1935
    *L'Evolution de la politique économique et financière française.* (Speech of 6 November 1934). Paris, 1934
    *L'Heure de choisir.* (Speech of 7 May 1935). Paris, 1935
Germain-Martin, L. *La Politique économique et financière en France de 1930 à juin 1935*, Paris, 1947
    *Le Problème de la dévaluation en 1934*, Paris, 1948
    *Le Problème financier*, Paris, 1936
    *Les Problèmes actuels des finances publiques en France*, Paris, 1933
    *Sommes-nous sur bonne route?* (*Problèmes financiers du temps présent*). Paris, 1934

Giscard d'Estaing, E. *La Maladie du monde. Essai de pathologie monétaire*, Paris, 1933

Henriot, P. *La Mort de la trêve*, Paris, 1934

Legendre, J. *Pour lutter contre le Front populaire*, Paris, 1936

Marin, L. *La Crise économique*. (Lecture given at the University of Liège, 24 April 1931)

Michel, H. *La Dévaluation belge: une opération aussi délicate que décevante*, Paris, 1936

Nicolle, P. *Comité de salut économique. Rapport de la commission permanente*, Paris, 1934

    *Pour nettoyer les écuries*, Paris, 1934

Pinot, M. *La Semaine de quarante heures, le chômage et les prix*, Paris, 1933

Reynaud, P. *Jeunesse quelle France veux-tu?* Paris, 1936

Romier, L. *Problèmes économiques de l'heure présente*, Montreal, 1933

    *Si le capitalisme disparaissait*, Paris, 1933

Tardieu, A. *Devant le pays*, Paris, 1932

    *L'Heure de la décision*, Paris, 1934

    *La Réforme de l'Etat, les idées mâitresses de 'L'heure de la décision'*, Paris, 1935

    *La Révolution à refaire*. Vol. I, *Le souverain captif*, Paris, 1936

    'Réformer ou casser', *La Revue des deux mondes*, 1 March 1934, pp. 135–61

    *Sur la pente*, Paris, 1935


**C.G.T. and planist**

Le Comité du Plan, *Le Plan français* (preface by Déat), Paris, 1935

La Confédération Générale du Travail. 28ᵉ Congrès, Paris, 26–9 septembre 1933, Compte rendu sténographique, Paris, 1933

    29ᵉ Congrès, Paris, 24–7 septembre 1935. Paris, 1935

    *Actualité du plan*, Paris, 1936

    *Contre la crise, pour une économie dirigée, exposé sur le plan de rénovation économique de la C.G.T.* Paris, Sept. 1934

    *La Nationalisation du crédit*, Paris, n.d.

    *La Réorganisation économique dans la liberté*, n.p., 1934.

    *Le Plan de rénovation économique et sociale* (Preface by L. Jouhaux consisting of his speech to the 1935 Congress of the C.G.T.)

    *Pourquoi une politique de grands travaux*, Paris, 1936


Dupiol, J. *Les Banques, l'épargne et la distribution des crédits*, Paris, 1935

Dupiol, J., Zoretti, L. and Lefranc, G. *La Nationalisation des industries clés*. (Publications de l'Institut Supérieur Ouvrier, XXI). Paris, n.d.

Duret, J. *Sens et portée du Plan* (Publications de l'Institut Supérieur Ouvrier, XII), Paris, n.d.

Groupe du 9 juillet. *Plan du 9 juillet*, Paris, 1934

L'Institut Supérieur Ouvrier. *Crise et Plan*, Quinze conférences sur le Plan de la C.G.T. (Lectures by Jouhaux, R. Bouyer, Laurat, Duret, L. Zoretti, Dauphin-Meunier (Ganivet), Lefranc, Lévy-Bruhl, Lacoste, Delaisi). Publications de l'I.S.O., IV. Paris, 1934

Jouhaux, L., Duret, J. and Harmel, M. *La C.G.T., ce qu'elle est, ce qu'elle veut*, Paris, 1937

Laurat, L. *Le Plan du Travail vu de Moscou*, Paris, 1935

Lefranc, G., Boivin, P. and Deixonne, M. *Révolution constructive*, Paris, 1932

Man, H. de 'Une heure avec Henri de Man au Bureau d'Etudes Sociales (12 July 1934)', *Problèmes d'ensemble du fascisme*, Publications de l'Institut Supérieur Ouvrier, IX, Paris, 1935
    *L'idée socialiste*, Paris, 1935
    *Joy in Work*, London, 1929
    *The Psychology of Socialism*, London, 1928
    *Réflexions sur l'économie dirigée*, Paris-Brussels, 1932
    *Le Socialisme constructif*, Paris, 1933
Montagnon, B. *Troisième gerbe d'idées économiques et sociales: Essai de synthèse Neo-Socialiste*, Paris, Jan. 1935
Montagnon, B., Marquet, A. and Déat, M. *Néo-Socialisme? Ordre, autorité, nation.* (Preface by M. Bonnafous). Paris, 1933
Noyelle, H. 'Les Plans de reconstruction économique et sociale à l'étranger et en France', *Revue d'économie politique* 5 (Sept.–Oct. 1934), pp. 1595–668
Pomaret, C., 'Catalogue des Plans', *Etat moderne*, April 1935
Révolution Constructive: *Cahier 1*: Man, H. de *Pour un Plan d'action*. Paris, 1933
    *Cahier 2*: Alter, V. *Esquisse d'un programme économique socialiste*, Asnières, n.d.
    *Cahier 3*: *Vers un Plan britannique: les études de la Ligue socialiste*. (Preface by A. Philip), Asnières, n.d.
    *Cahier 4*: Le Bail, J. *Pour l'unité*, Asnières, n.d.
    *Cahiers 5/6*: *Eléments d'un Plan français*, Asnières, 1934
    *Cahier 7*: Moulin, L. *Etudes sur la révolution*, Asnières, n.d.
    *Cahier 8*: Man, H. de *Le Socialisme devant la crise*, Paris, n.d.
Union fédérale des associations françaises d'anciens combattants. *La République des combattants*, Paris, 1934
Union nationale des combattants. *Le Programme d'action civique des anciens combattants*, Paris, 1934
Valois, G. 'Pour le Plan syndical et coopératif', *Nouvel age*, 1 June 1934

### Other contemporary French works on the crisis and economic policy

Aron, R. and Dandieu, A. *Le Cancer américain*, Paris, 1931
    *Décadence de la nation française*, Paris, 1931
Boris, G. *La Révolution Roosevelt*, Paris, 1934
    *Problème de l'or et crise mondiale*, Paris, 1931
Bouniatan, M. *Dépression, progrès technique et dévaluation*, Paris, 1935
Chabrun, C. *Déflation et dévaluation: Rapports, travaux et comptes-rendus, voeux et résolutions de la 3ᵉᵐᵉ semaine de la monnaie*, Paris, 1933
Delaisi, F. *La Banque de France aux mains des deux cents familles*, Paris, 1936
    *La Bataille d'or*, Paris, 1933
Delmas, A. *Contre l'absurde déflation*, Paris, Dec. 1933
Duboin, J. *Ce qu'on appelle la crise!* Paris, 1936
    *La Grande relève des hommes par la machine*, Paris, 1932
    *Kou l'Ahuri ou la misère dans l'abondance*, Paris, 1935
    *Nous faisons fausse route*, Paris, 1932
Duhamel, G. *Scénes de la vie future*, Paris, 1930
Duret, J. *Le Marxisme et les crises*, Paris, 1933
Jouvenel, B. de *La Crise du capitalisme américain*, Paris, 1933
Lachapelle, G. *Le Désordre financier*, Paris, 1934
Navachine, D. *La Crise et l'Europe économique*, 2 Vols., Paris, 1932
Nogaro, B. *La Crise économique dans le monde et en France*, Paris, 1936
    *Le Problème de la 'dévaluation' en France*, Paris, 1935

Noyelle, H. *Utopie libérale, chimère socialiste, économie dirigée*, Paris, 1934
Patenôtre, R. *La Crise et le drame monétaire*, Paris, 1932
  *Pour la dévaluation. Contre la dictature d'or*, Paris, 1934
  *Vers le bien-être*, Paris, 1936
  *Voulons-nous sortir de la crise?* Paris, 1934
Pirou, G. *La Crise du capitalisme*, Paris, 1936
  *La Monnaie française depuis la guerre: Inflation, stabilisation dévaluation*, Paris, 1936
  *Néo-libéralisme, néo-corporatisme, néo-socialisme*, Paris, 1939
Rist, C. *Essais sur quelques problèmes économiques et monétaires*, Paris, 1933
  *La Déflation en pratique*, Paris, 1924
Sapiens (pseudonym of A. Fabre-Luce) *Une hypothèse: la dévaluation française de 1936*, Paris, 1936
  *Une hypothèse: le controle des changes français de 1938*, Paris, 1938
La Société des Anciens Elèves de l'Ecole Libre des Sciences Politiques, *L'Economie dirigée*, Paris, 1934 (lectures by A. Siegfried, E. Monick, C.-J. Gignoux *et al.*)
Thiers, A. *Ni inflation, ni déflation. Une solution au problème financier*, Paris, 1934
Travaux du Congrès des économistes de la langue française, 1933: *Economie libérale et économie dirigée. L'êtalon-or.*
  1935: *Evolution du crédit et contrôle des banques. La Réforme économique aux Etats-Unis*, Paris, 1935

## VI SECONDARY WORKS

### Books

Adamthwaite, A. *France and the Coming of the Second World War 1936–1939*, London, 1977
Aftalion, A. *Les Crises périodiques de surproduction*, Paris, 1911
  *Monnaie, prix et change*, Paris, 1937
  *L'Or et sa distribution mondiale*, Paris, 1932
Allain, J.-C. *Joseph Caillaux, Vol. II; l'oracle, 1914–1944*, Paris, 1981
Arndt, H. *The Economic Lessons of the Nineteen-Thirties; a report*, London, 1944
Asselain, J.-C. *Histoire économique de la France*, 2 Vols, Paris, 1984
Aubert, L. *et al. André Tardieu*, Paris, 1957
Augé-Laribé, M. *La Politique agricole de la France de 1880 à 1940*, Paris, 1950
Barral, P. *Les Agrariens français de Méline à Pisani*, Paris, 1968
Bergounioux, A. *et al. L'Univers politique des classes moyennes*, Paris, 1983
Berger, S. *Peasants against Politics*, Cambridge, Mass., 1972
Berl, E. *La Politique et les partis*, Paris, 1932
Berstein, S. *Le 6 février 1934*, Paris, 1975
  *Histoire du Parti radical I: La recherche de l'âge d'or 1919–1926*, Paris, 1980
  *Histoire du Parti radical II: Crise du radicalisme, 1926–1939*, Paris, 1982
Bettelheim, C. *Bilan de l'économie française 1919–46*, Paris, 1947
Binion, R. *Defeated Leaders: the Political Fate of Caillaux, Jouvenel, and Tardieu*, New York, 1960
Blondot, G. *Les Théories monétaires de J. M. Keynes*, Paris, 1933
Blumé, D. *et al. Histoire du réformisme en France depuis 1920*, Vol. 1, Paris, 1976
Bonnefous, E. *Histoire politique de la Troisième République*, Vols. 4 and 5, Paris, 1960–2
Boris, G. *Servir la République*, Paris, 1963
Bourdé, G. *La Défaite du Front populaire*, Paris, 1977

Bourderon, R., Burles, J., Girault, J. *et al. Le P.C.F. étapes et problèmes*, Paris, 1981
Bouton, A. *La Fin des rentiers*, Paris, 1931
Bouvier, J. *Un siècle de banque française*, Paris, 1973
Bouvier, J. *et al. Histoire économique et sociale de la France*, edited by E. Labrousse
    and F. Braudel, Tome 4, Vol. 2, Paris, 1979–80
Broustra, J.-C. *Le Combat de Raymond Patenôtre*, Paris, 1969
Brower, D. *The New Jacobins: the French Communist Party and the Popular Front*,
    New York, 1968
Brunet, J.-P. *St. Denis: La ville rouge*, Paris, 1980
Caron, F. *Histoire économique de la France. XIX–XX siècles*, Paris, 1981
Carré, J.-J., Dubois, P. and Malinvaud, E. *La Croissance française*, Paris, 1972
Clarke, S. *The Reconstruction of the International Monetary System: the Attempts of
    1932 and 1933*, Princeton, N.J., 1973
    *Exchange-Rate Stabilization in the mid-1930s: Negotiating the Tripartite Agree-
    ment*, Princeton, N.J., 1977
Clough, S. H. *France: History of National Economics 1789–1939*, New York, 1939
Colton, J. *Léon Blum: Humanist in Politics*, Cambridge, Mass., 1974
Cuvillier, J.-P. *Vincent Auriol et les finances publiques du Front populaire ou
    l'alternative du contrôle et de la liberté*, Paris, 1978
Damougeot-Perron, G. *La Crise du blé en France et dans le monde*, Paris, 1935
Dauphin-Meunier, A. *La Banque de France*, Paris, 1937
Delouvrier, P. and Nathan, R. *Politique économique de la France 1929–1939*, Paris,
    1955–6
Dobb, M. *Theories of Value and Distribution since Adam Smith*, Cambridge, 1973
Dodge, P. *Beyond Marxism: The Faith and Works of Hendrik de Man*, The Hague,
    1966
Drummond, I. *The Floating Pound and the Sterling Area 1931–1939*, Cambridge,
    1981
    *London, Washington and the Management of the Franc 1936–39*, London, 1979
Dubief, H. *Le Déclin de la Troisième République*, Paris, 1976
Dubost, G. *Le Conseil national économique*, Paris, 1936
Dubreuil, H. *Standards: le travail américain vu par un ouvrier français*, Paris, 1929
Dupeux, G. *Le Front populaire et les élections de 1936*, Paris, 1959
Duroselle, J.-B. *La Décadence 1932–1939*, Paris, 1979
Earle, E. ed. *Modern France*, 1951
Ehrmann, H. *Organized Business in France*, Princeton, N.J., 1957
Einzig, P. *France's Crisis*, London, 1934
    *The World Economic Crisis, 1929–1931*, London, 1931
Elbow, M. *French Corporatist Theory 1789–1948*, New York, 1953
Emmerson, J. T. *The Rhineland Crisis*, London, 1977
Feis, H. *1933: Characters in Crisis*, Boston, Mass., 1966
Frankenstein, R. *Le Prix du réarmement français (1935–1939)*, Paris, 1982
Frédérix, P. *L'Etat des forces en France*, Paris, 1935
Freidel, F. *Franklin D. Roosevelt: Launching the New Deal*, Boston, Mass., 1973
Fridenson, P. *Histoire des usines Renault I: Naissance de la grande entreprise*, Paris,
    1972
Gaucher, F. *Contribution à l'histoire du socialisme français (1905–1933)*, Paris, 1934
Georges, B. and Tintant, D. *Léon Jouhaux dans le mouvement syndical français*, Vol.
    2, Paris, 1979
Gicquel, J. and Sfez, L. *Problèmes de la réforme de l'Etat en France depuis 1934*, Paris,
    1949

Gignoux, C.-J. *L'Economie française entre les deux guerres, 1919–1939*, Paris, 1942

Girault, J. *Sur l'implantation du Parti communiste français dans l'entre-deux-guerres*, Paris, 1977

Goguel, F. *La Politique des partis sous la Troisième République*, Paris, 1946
   *Le Rôle financier du Sénat français*, Paris, 1937

Guenser, G. *Le Marché monétaire français et son contrôle par la Banque de France*, Paris, 1938

Guitard, P. *Chômage*, Paris, 1933

Haig, R. M. *The Public Finances of Post-War France*, New York, 1919

Haight, F. *French Import Quotas: A New Instrument of Commercial Policy*, London, 1935

Halévy, D. *Visites aux paysans du centre 1907–1934*, Paris, 1935

Harris, S. E. *Exchange Depreciation: Its Theory and History with Some Consideration of Related Domestic Policies*, Cambridge, Mass., 1936

Hatzfeld, H. *Du Paupérisme à la sécurité sociale*, Paris, 1971

Hodson, H. V. *Slump and Recovery 1929–1937*, London, 1938

Hoffmann, S. *et al. France: Change and Tradition*, London, 1963

Irvine, W. D. *French Conservatism in Crisis: the Republican Federation of France in the 1930s*, Baton Rouge and London, 1979

Jeanneney, J.-N. *François de Wendel en république: L'argent et le pouvoir 1914–1940*, 3 vols., Lille, 1976
   *L'Argent caché*, Paris, 1984

Judt, T. *La Réconstruction du Parti socialiste*, Paris, 1976

Kemp, T. *The French Economy 1913–1939: the History of a Decline*, London, 1972

Keynes, J. M. *Essays in Persuasion*, London, 1931
   *Réflexions sur le franc*, Paris,
   *The General Theory of Employment Interest and Money*, London, 1936

Kindleberger, C. *The World in Depression, 1929–1939*, London, 1973

Kriegel, A. *Le Pain et les roses*, Paris, 1968

Kuisel, R. *Capitalism and the State in Modern France*, Cambridge, 1981
   *Ernest Mercier: French Technocrat*, Berkeley, Cal., 1967

Kupferman, F. *Pierre Laval*, Paris, 1976

Lachapelle, G. *Les Finances de la Troisième République*, Paris, 1937

Lacouture, J. *Léon Blum*, Paris, 1977

Lalumière, P. *L'Inspection des finances*, Paris, 1959

Landes, D. *The Unbound Prometheus*, Cambridge, 1969

Larmour, P. *The French Radical Party in the 1930s*, Stanford, Cal., 1964

Lefranc, G. *Essais sur les problèmes socialistes et syndicaux*, Paris, 1970
   *L'Expérience du Front populaire*, Paris, 1972
   *Histoire du Front populaire 1934–1938*, Paris, 1974
   *Le Mouvement socialiste sous la Troisième République*, 2 vols., Paris, 1963

Letellier, G., Perret, J., Zuber, H. E. and Dauphin-Meunier, A. *Enquête sur le chômage*, Vol. 1: *Le chômage en France de 1930 à 1936*, Paris, 1938

Letellier, G., Marjolin, R. *et al. Enquête sur le chômage*, Vol. 2: *Les chômeurs à Paris, Lyon, Mulhouse d'après les fiches des fonds de chômage*, Paris, 1941
   Vol. 3: *Dépenses des chômeurs et valeur énergétique de leur alimentation*, Paris, 1949

Loubet del Bayle, J.-L. *Les Non-conformistes des années trente: une tentative de renouvellement de la pensée politique française*, Paris, 1969

Malivoire de Camas, J. *La France et le chômage: étude de la législation*, Paris, 1933

Marcus, J. T. *French Socialism in the Crisis Years 1933–36*, New York, 1958

Markovitch, T. *Les Théories modernes de sous-consommation*, Paris, 1938

Massoubre, E.-S. *Les Ententes professionnelles dans le cadre national et la doctrine économique*, Paris, 1935

Moch, J. *Le Front populaire, grande éspérance*, Paris, 1971

Mommsen, W. and Kettenacker, L. eds. *The Fascist Challenge and the Policy of Appeasement*, London, 1983

Myers, M. *Paris as a Financial Centre*, London, 1936

Neré, J. *La Crise de 1929*, Paris, 1969

Nogaro, B. *La Monnaie et les phenomènes monétaires contemporaines*, Paris, 1935

Parsiades, N. *Essai sur les relations entre le chômage, les prix et le profit: étude critique de la loi de M. Rueff*, Paris, 1949

Peel, G. *The Economic Policy of France*, London, 1937
    *The Financial Crisis of France*, London, 1925

Perret, J. *Le Cancer du chômage*, Paris, 1936

Perrot, M. *La monnaie et l'opinion publique en France et en Grande Bretagne*, Paris, 1955

Perthuis de la Salle, J. *La Politique française du contingement*, Paris, 1935

Piettre, A. *L'Evolution des ententes industrielles en France depuis la crise*, Paris, 1936
    *La Politique du pouvoir d'achat devant les faits*, Paris, 1938

Pirou, G. *Histoire des doctrines économiques en France depuis 1870*, Paris, 1934

Prost, A. *La C.G.T. à l'époque du Front populaire*, Paris, 1964
    *Les Anciens combattants et la société française*, 3 vols., Paris, 1977

Puiffe de Magondeaux, O. de *Les Ententes industrielles obligatoires et le corporatisme en France*, Paris, 1937

Rain, P. and Chapsal, J. *L'Ecole Libre des Sciences Politiques, 1871–1945*, Paris, 1964

Rémond, R. and Bourdin, J., eds. *Edouard Daladier, Chef de gouvernement, avril 1938–septembre 1939*, Paris, 1977
    *La France et les français en 1938–1939*, Paris, 1978

Rémond, R. and Renouvin, P., eds. *Léon Blum, chef de gouvernement (1936–1937)*, Paris, 1967 (The proceedings of a *colloque* held at the Fondation Nationale des Sciences Politiques in 1965)

Rist, C. and Gide, C. *A History of Economic Doctrines from the time of the Physiocrats to the Present Day*, London, 1948

Robbins, L. *The Great Depression*, London, 1934

Robrieux, P. *Maurice Thorez: vie secrète et vie publique*, Paris, 1975

Rogers, J. H. *The Process of Inflation in France, 1914–1927*, New York, 1929

Roll, E. *A History of Economic Thought*, London, 1938

Romains, J. *Correspondance André Gide – Jules Romains; l'individu et l'unanime* (Cahiers Jules Romains I), Paris, 1976

Roussel, C. *Lucien Romier*, Paris, 1979

Roux, M. L. *Le Socialisme de M. Henri de Man*, Paris, 1937

Rueff, J. *Théorie des phenomènes monétaires*, Paris, 1927

Saly, P. *La Politique des grands travaux en France 1929–1939*, New York, 1977

Sauvy, A. *Histoire économique de la France entre les deux guerres*, 4 Vols., Paris, 1965–75

Sayers, R. S. *The Bank of England 1891–1944*, 3 Vols., Cambridge, 1976

Schuker, S. *The End of French Predominance in Europe*, Chapel Hill, N.C., 1976

Sherwood, J. *Georges Mandel and the Third Republic*, Stanford, Cal., 1970

Sirol, J. *Les Problèmes français du blé*, Paris, 1934

Skidelsky, R. *Politicians and the Slump: the Labour Government of 1929–31*, London, 1967
Sternhell, Z. *Ni droite ni gauche: l'idéologie fasciste en France*, Paris, 1983
Strauss, D. *Menace in the West: The Rise of French Anti-Americanism in Modern Times*, Westport, Conn., 1978
Svennilson, I. *Growth and Stagnation in the European Economy*, Geneva, 1954
Thibaudet, A. *Les Idées politiques de la France*, Paris, 1932
Trotabas, L. *Les Finances publiques et les impôts de la France*, Paris, 1937
Van de Wee, H., ed. *The Great Depression Revisited: Essays on the Economics of the Thirties*, The Hague, 1972
Varga, E. *The Great Crisis and its Political Consequences, 1928–34*, London, 1934
Weill, S. *La Condition ouvrière*, Paris, 1951
Werth, A. *The Destiny of France*, London, 1937
    *France in Ferment*, London, 1934
Wilson, J. S. G. *French Banking Structure and Credit Policy*, London, 1957
Winch, D. *Economics and policy: A historical study*, London, 1969
Wolfe, M. *The French Franc Between the Wars, 1919–1939*, New York, 1951
Wright, G. *Rural Revolution in France: the Peasantry in the Twentieth Century*, Stanford, Cal., 1964
Young, R. *In Command of France: French Foreign Policy and Military Planning 1933–1940*, Cambridge, Mass., and London, 1978
Ziebura, G. *Léon Blum et le Parti socialiste, 1872–1934*, Paris, 1967

*Articles*

Aldcroft, D. H. 'The Development of the Managed Economy Before 1939', *Journal of Contemporary History* 4, 4 (Oct. 1969), pp. 117–37
Amoyal, J. 'Les Origines socialistes et syndicalistes de la planification en France', *Le Mouvement social* 87 (Apr.–June 1974), pp. 137–69
Asselain, J.-C. 'Une Erreur de politique économique: la loi des quarante heures de 1936', *Revue économique* 25, 4 (July 1974), pp. 672–705
Berstein, S. 'Les Conceptions du Parti radical en matière de politique économique extérieure', *Relations internationales* 13 (1978), pp. 781–89
Boudot, F. 'Sur des problèmes de financement de la défense nationale (1936–1940)', *Revue d'histoire de la deuxième guerre mondiale* 81 (January 1971), pp. 49–72
Bouvier, J. 'Contrôle des changes et politique économique extérieure de la S.F.I.O. en 1936', *Relations internationales* 13 (1978), pp. 111–15
    'Un Débat toujours ouvert: la politique économique du Front populaire', *Le Mouvement social* 54 (Jan.–Mar. 1966), pp. 175–81
Brunet, J.-P. 'Une Crise au Parti communiste français: l'affaire Barbé-Célor', *Revue d'histoire moderne et contemporaine* 16 (July–Sept. 1969), pp. 436–61.
Clague, M. 'Vision and Myopia in the New Politics of André Tardieu', *French Historical Studies* 8, 1 (1972), pp. 105–29
Colton, J. 'Politics and Economics in the 1930s: the Balance Sheet of the "Blum New Deal" ', in C. K. Warner (ed.), *From the Ancien Régime to the Popular Front*, New York and London, 1969, pp. 181–208
Crouzet, F. 'Réactions françaises devant "Les Conséquences économiques de la paix" de Keynes', *Revue d'histoire moderne et contemporaine* 19 (Jan.–Mar. 1972), pp. 6–26

Duroselle, J.-B. 'Notes de lecture: Inspecteurs des Finances et politique étrangère dans les années trente', *Relations internationales* 13 (1978), pp. 117–22

Frankenstein, R. 'Apropos des aspects financiers du réarmement français 1935–1939', *Revue d'histoire de la deuxième guerre mondiale* 102 (April 1976), pp. 1–20

Fridenson, P. 'L'Idéologie des grands constructeurs dans l'entre-deux guerres', *Le Mouvement social* 81 (Oct.–Dec. 1972), pp. 51–68

Gagnon, P. 'French Views of the Second American Revolution', *French Historical Studies* 2, 4 (Fall 1962), pp. 430–49

Girault, R. 'Léon Blum, la dévaluation de 1936 et la conduite de la politique extérieure de la France', *Relations internationales* 13 (1978), pp. 91–109

Hansen, E. 'Depression Decade Crisis: Social Democracy and *Planisme* in Belgium and the Netherlands 1929–1939', *Journal of Contemporary History* 16, 2 (April 1981), pp. 293–322

    'Hendrik de Man and the Theoretical Foundations of Economic Planning: The Belgian Experience, 1933–40', *European Studies Review* 8, 1 (Jan. 1978), pp. 235–57

Harmel, C. 'A propos de Henri de Man et de Léon Blum', *Contrat social* 9, 4 (July–Aug. 1965), pp. 261–3

    'Le Trentième anniversaire du Plan de la C.G.T., *Etudes sociales et syndicales* 120 (Sept. 1965), pp. 2–19

Hoffmann, S. 'Paradoxes of the French Political Community' in S. Hoffmann *et al.*, *France: Change and Tradition*, London, 1963, pp. 1–117

Hoisington, W. A. 'Toward the Sixth of February: Taxpayer Protest in France, 1928–1934', *Historical Reflections* 3, 1 (1976), pp. 49–67

d'Hoop, J.-M. 'Le Problème du réarmement français jusqu'à mars 1936', in *La France et l'Allemagne 1932–1936, Communications presentées au Colloque franco-allemand tenu à Paris du 10 au 12 mars 1977*, Editions du Centre National de la Recherche Scientifique, Paris, 1980, pp. 75–89

Kalecki, M. 'The Lesson of the Blum Experiment', *The Economic Journal* 48 (March 1938), pp. 26–41

Kayser, J. 'Le Parti radical-socialiste et le Rassemblement populaire 1935–1938', *Bulletin de la Société d'Histoire de la III<sup>e</sup> République*, April–July, 1955, pp. 271–84

    'Le Radicalisme des radicaux, in G. Michaud, Ed., *Tendances politiques dans la vie française depuis 1789*, Paris, 1960, pp. 65–88

Kemp, T. 'The French Economy under the Franc Poincaré', *Economic History Review* 24, 1 (Feb. 1971), pp. 82–99

Kindleberger, C. 'The Post-war Resurgence of the French Economy', in S. Hoffmann *et al.*, *France: Change and Tradition*, London, 1963, pp. 118–58

Kuisel, R. 'Auguste Detoeuf, Conscience of French Industry, 1926–47', *International Review of Social History* 20, pt. 2 (1975), pp. 149–74

Kupferman, F. and Machefer, P. 'Presse et politique dans les années trente: le cas du "Petit Journal" ', *Revue d'histoire moderne et contemporaine* 22 (Jan.–Mar. 1975), pp. 7–51

Lefranc, G. 'La Crise des Néo-Socialistes', *Le Parti socialiste et l'exercice du pouvoir* (a colloquium held at the Centre d'histoire du Socialisme, October 1976)

    'La Diffusion des idées planistes en France', *Cahiers Vilfredo Pareto: Revue européenne des sciences sociales* 12, 31 (1974), pp. 189–96

Lévy-Leboyer, M. 'Le Patronat français a-t-il été malthusien?', *Le Mouvement social*, No. 88 (July–Sept. 1974), pp. 3–49

Lhomme, J. 'Le pouvoir d'achat de l'ouvrier français au cours d'un siècle: 1840–1940', *Le Mouvement social* 63 (April–June 1968), pp. 41–69

Margairaz, M. 'A propos du réformisme: le Parti Socialiste S.F.I.O. face à l'économie et à la société (1930–39)', *Cahiers d'histoire de l'institut Maurice Thorez* 39 (1975), pp. 8–31

'La Droite et l'Etat en France dans les années trente', *Cahiers d'histoire de l'institut Maurice Thorez* 20–1 (1977), pp. 91–136

'La Droite française face à la crise: incompétence ou choix politique?', *Cahiers d'histoire de l'institut Maurice Thorez* 20–1 (1977), pp. 69–88

'Les Socialistes face à l'économie et à la société en juin 1936', *Le Mouvement social* 93 (Oct.–Dec. 1975), pp. 87–108

'Capitalisme et Etat. A propos des politiques économiques en France: de la crise à la seconde guerre mondiale', *Cahiers d'histoire de l'institut Maurice Thorez* 31 (1979), pp. 91–114

Marjolin, R. 'Reflections on the Blum Experiment', *Economica* 5, 18 (May 1938), pp. 177–91

Marseille, J. 'Les Aspects spécifiques de la crise en France', *Cahiers d'histoire de l'institut Maurice Thorez* 16 (1976), pp. 83–8

'Les Origines "inopportunes" de la crise du 1929 en France', *Revue économique* 31, 4 (July 1980), pp. 648–84

Marwick, A. 'Middle Opinion in the Thirties: Planning, Progress and Political Agreement', *English Historical Review* 79, 111 (April, 1964), pp. 285–98

Müller, K.-J. 'French Fascism and Modernization', *Journal of Contemporary History* 11, 4 (October 1976), pp. 75–107

Ory, P. 'Le Dorgérisme: Institution et discours d'une colère paysanne 1929–1939', *Revue d'histoire moderne et contemporaine* 22 (April–June 1975), pp. 168–87

Prost, A. 'Les Manifestations du 12 février 1934 en province', *Le Mouvement social* 54 (Jan.–March 1966), pp. 7–27

Salem, D. 'Le Sénat "conservateur" de la Troisième République', *Revue d'histoire économique et sociale* 50, 4 (1972), pp. 535–42

Saly, P. 'Les Grands travaux des années trente ou l'art de faire semblant de lutter contre la crise', *Cahiers d'histoire de l'institut Maurice Thorez* 16 (1976), pp. 89–93

'La Politique française des grands travaux 1929–1939 fut-elle keynésienne?', *Revue économique* 31, 4 (July 1980), pp. 706–42

Schlesinger, M. 'The Development of the Radical Party in the Third Republic: the New Radical Movement, 1926–32', *Journal of Modern History* 46, 3 (Sept. 1974), pp. 476–501

Schor, R. 'Une étude d'opinion: la droite française face à la crise mondiale de 1929', *L'Information historique* 1 (1974), pp. 23–8; 2 (1974), pp. 64–70

Touchard, J. 'L'Esprit des années trente' in G. Michaud, ed., *Tendances politiques dans la vie française depuis 1789*, Paris, 1960, pp. 90–120

Vaisse, M. 'Le Mythe de l'or en France: les aspects monétaires du New Deal vu par les Français', *Revue d'histoire moderne et contemporaine* 16 (July–Sept. 1969), pp. 462–79

Weill-Raynal, E. 'Les Obstacles économiques à l'expérience Léon Blum', *La Revue Socialiste*, June 1956, pp. 49–56

Werth, A. 'Le Mouvement "Jeunes Turcs": Phenomène radical d'entre les deux guerres', *Les Cahiers de la République* 2 (1956), pp. 100–5

Wolfe, M. 'French Inter-war Stagnation Revisited' in C. K. Warner, ed., *From the Ancien Régime to the Popular Front*, New York and London, 1969, pp. 159–80

Wolikow, S. 'La Crise des années trente en France: Aspects spécifiques de la crise', *Cahiers d'histoire de l'institut Maurice Thorez* 17–18 (1976), pp. 11–48

'Economie et société: l'analyse et la pratique du P.C.F.', *Cahiers d'histoire de l'institut Maurice Thorez* 38 (1974), pp. 22–54

'Le P.C.F. devant la crise 1929–1932', *Cahiers d'histoire de l'institut Maurice Thorez* 39 (1975), pp. 32–91

### Unpublished theses

Biard, J.-F. 'L'Idée du Plan dans le mouvement syndical et socialiste français entre les deux guerres' (*Doctorat d'Etat*, University of Paris – I, 1977)

Brun, G. 'Techniciens et technocratie en France 1918–45', 3 Vols. (*Doctorat d'Etat*, University of Paris – II, 1977)

Corbin, A. 'Prélude au Front populaire: étude de l'opinion publique dans le département de la Haute-Vienne, février 1934–mai 1936', (*3ᵉ cycle* thesis, University of Poitiers, 1968)

Fine, M. 'Towards Corporatism: The Movement for Capital–Labor Collaboration in France, 1914–1936 (Ph.D. thesis, University of Wisconsin, 1971)

De La Tour du Pin, H. 'La Presse de droite contre la dévaluation: sa campagne contre Paul Reynaud' (memoir, University of Paris – I, 1972)

Lecomte, D and Pavy, D. 'Le Front populaire face au mur d'argent: le problème du contrôle des changes dans les années 1936–1938' (memoir, University of Paris – VIII, 1975)

Margairaz, M. 'Les Propositions de politique économique, financière et monétaire de la S.F.I.O. de 1934 à 1936' (memoir, University of Paris – VIII, 1972. Now available in the AUDIR microfiche series)

Moore, J. 'A History of the World Economic Conference, London 1933' (Ph.D. thesis, State University of New York at Stony Brook, 1971)

Toinet, M.-F. 'Georges Boris (1888–1960), un Socialiste humaniste' (*3ᵉ cycle* thesis, University of Paris – X, 1969. Now available on microfiches)

# Index

Aftalion, Albert, 15, 229 n. 33
Agricole, Fleurent, 66
Agriculture, 220; in 1920s, 11; price levels, 25, 63, 85–6, 109; peasant protest, 69, 89, 101; minimum price legislation, 69–70, 86; Flandin policy to, 95, 220; and deflation, 86; reduction in peasant protest, 132; and C.G.T. Plan, 156, 159; and devaluation, 170, 175, 178, 187
Alain, 119
Albertini, Georges, 164
Alliance Démocratique, 16–17, 19, 73, 92, 109
Appert, Jean, 177
Aron, Robert, 222
Asselain, Jean-Charles, 206
Auriol, Vincent, 13, 36, 38, 41, 72, 73, 78, 109, 118, 129, 160, 204, 215, 243 n. 161, n. 163, 244 n. 186, 256 n. 63

Bank of France, 119, 187, 201, 219, 251 n. 190, 254; in 1920s, 5, 25–6; and gold influx, 168–9; and commercial banks, 21–2, 66–7, 81–2; gold losses from, 77, 80, 102–3, 108; and Flandin government, 94, 97–9, 100, 101; and Laval government, 104, 107, 252 n. 214; and the left, 119, 122, 125, 131, 157; and Popular Front governments, 203, 209
Barbusse, Henri, 112
Bardoux, Jacques, 101
Baréty, Léon, 92
Barre, Raymond, 13, 221
Barthélemy, Joseph, 110, 187
Basch, Victor, 120, 127, 133
Baudouin, Paul, 203
Baumgartner, Wilfrid, 21, 74, 101, 102, 104, 108, 200; and devaluation, 79, 179
Bayet, Alfred, 47, 48, 49, 92, 121, 183, 214, 256 n. 72
Bedouce, Albert, 36, 62
Belin, René, 36, 128, 129, 133, 152, 153, 156, 158, 159, 164, 193, 256 n. 63, 267 n. 209

Bergery, Gaston, 61, 74, 116
Billiet, Ernest, 187
Blaisot, Camille, 83
Blum, Léon, 4, 17, 18, 20, 35, 37, 38, 41, 60, 73, 90, 106, 110, 120, 126, 127, 128, 141, 143, 152, 214, 215, 243 n. 163, 262 n. 67; and 1932 election, 54, 55; and economics, 13, 36; and Roosevelt, 38, 234 n. 25; and Radicals in 1932, 56–7, 123, 127; and Daladier, 70, 76; and nationalizations, 114–15, 118–19, 130, 163; and Popular Front programme, 121, 122, 123–4, 129; and Neo-Socialists, 143, 149–50; and planism, 145–6, 148; and devaluation, 191–2, 204; first government of 202–8; second government of, 209–10
Blumel, André, 113
Bonnefous, Georges, 142
Bonnet, Georges, 13, 20, 49, 66, 68, 74, 76, 81, 86, 170–1, 172, 173, 178, 207, 208, 213, 214, 241 n. 111
Bonnevay, Laurent, 122
Boris, Georges, 47, 59, 74, 99, 107, 116, 180, 182, 185, 186, 199, 210, 214, 222, 223
Bouisson, Fernand, 104, 105, 122, 162, 251 n. 190
Bouthillier, Yves, 182
Bracke, Alexandre, 118
Branger, Jacques, 156
Brüning, Heinrich, 113
Budget, of 1932, 61; of 1933, 68; of 1934, 76, 82; of 1935, 89, 94–5; of 1936, 107–8; of 1937, 208; deficits in, 26–7, 58–9, 60–1, 63, 67, 76, 82, 94, 103, 208, 217–18
Bullitt, William, 171, 172, 204, 234 n. 25

Caillaux, Joseph, 13, 19, 48, 49, 56, 57, 60, 75, 78, 92, 104, 155, 198, 243 n. 178
Cambon, Roger, 175, 271 n. 81
Campinchi, César, 126
Chamberlain, Neville, 170–1, 173, 271 n. 67
Chappedelaine, Louis de, 28, 31
Chassaigne-Goyon, Paul, 33

299